GENERAL MAXWELL TAYLOR

BOOKS BY JOHN M. TAYLOR

KOREA'S SYNGMAN RHEE

FROM THE WHITE HOUSE INKWELL

GARFIELD OF OHIO

GENERAL MAXWELL TAYLOR

The Sword and the Pen

JOHN M. TAYLOR

Foreword by
Justice Lewis F. Powell, Jr.

DOUBLEDAY

NEW YORK LONDON TORONTO SYDNEY AUCKLAND

PUBLISHED BY DOUBLEDAY
a division of Bantam Doubleday Dell Publishing Group, Inc.
666 Fifth Avenue, New York, New York 10103

DOUBLEDAY and the portrayal of an anchor with a dolphin
are trademarks of Doubleday, a division of Bantam Doubleday
Dell Publishing Group, Inc.

Library of Congress Cataloging in Publication Data
Taylor, John M., 1930–
    General Maxwell Taylor : the sword and the pen.
    Includes index.
    1. Taylor, Maxwell D. (Maxwell Davenport), 1901–1987.
2. United States. Army—Biography.   3. Generals—
United States—Biography.   I. Title.
U53.T38T38   1989   355'.0092'4   [B]   88-31055

ISBN 0-385-24381-2
Copyright © 1989 by John M. Taylor
ALL RIGHTS RESERVED
PRINTED IN THE UNITED STATES OF AMERICA
JUNE 1989
FIRST EDITION
BG

To
L. H. T.

Contents

PART ONE

THE STUDENT

PART TWO

THE WARRIOR

PART THREE

THE STRATEGIST

PART FOUR

THE MANDARIN

Foreword

A good portion of this biography has been written in the relatively short time since the death of General Maxwell D. Taylor on April 19, 1987. Normally the writing of a serious biography is postponed until there is time to gain perspective on the career and contributions of the subject. In this instance, however, the author is the elder son of General Taylor and a scholar who already enjoys a fine reputation as the author of three books in the fields of history and biography. He has also been a frequent contributor to historical magazines. Perhaps no son can write with total detachment about an admired father, but it will be evident that this book reflects primarily the scholarship of the author and only tangentially a son's affection for his father. Jack Taylor has also had the competent assistance of his wife, Priscilla, a recognized scholar and editor.

As so often happens in history, a major war affords opportunities for leadership and prominence that infrequently occur on a comparable scale in peacetime. If one thinks of Maxwell D. Taylor only as a soldier, he certainly ranks—at least in my view—among the top dozen American military leaders in World War II. There were seven "five star" officers: Marshall, Eisenhower, King, MacArthur, Arnold, Bradley, and Nimitz. These men, each of whom was ten years or more older than Taylor, are remembered as the "great captains" who led our country to victory. Of the seven, three also earned larger places in our history. In the long reach, Marshall may be admired even more for the reconstruction plan that bears his name than as the senior Army officer of World War II. Eisenhower, commander of the Allied forces in the war against Germany, served as President during what may be viewed as the "golden era" of the United States, when its leadership of the free world was not questioned. And MacArthur is remembered in part for his postwar role as the father of the Japanese constitution.

Maxwell Taylor similarly occupies a larger place in our history.

When his full career is viewed, it is clear that his service to our country, in war and peace, was the most diverse of World War II's famous generals. Following Taylor's death, Secretary of Defense Caspar W. Weinberger issued a statement in which he said that the general would be remembered as "one of the great military men in America" and that he "epitomized what it means to be a soldier, a diplomat and a scholar." President Reagan called him "a soldier's soldier and a statesman's statesman."

Taylor was only forty-four years old when World War II ended. At that time he was a major general, one of the youngest. I served as an Air Force intelligence officer in the war against Germany and was in the African, Sicilian, and Western European campaigns. Although I did not know Taylor personally during those years, I was familiar at the time with his important roles, first in Sicily and Italy. Later he became famous as the commander of the 101st Airborne Division who jumped behind enemy lines in Normandy in the early morning hours of D-day. He was the first American general to fight on German-held territory in Western Europe, and he shared with his soldiers the grave risks of that hazardous but highly successful operation. In September 1944 he led his division in the unhappy Arnhem operation memorialized in Cornelius Ryan's *A Bridge Too Far*. The failure there was not on the part of either the 82d or Taylor's 101st Division. Rather, the catastrophe suffered by the British was due to faulty intelligence and the delayed arrival of Montgomery's ground forces.

The 101st Airborne occupied the Berchtesgaden area early in May 1945 as the war was ending. It was there that Hitler and his leaders had their chalets, and there was talk that this would be the "last redoubt" of the German armed forces. In fact, by early May there were thousands of German soldiers in the area, not preparing to fight but fleeing to avoid capture by the Russians. Of particular importance there was the discovery—and safeguarding—of Goering's stolen art collection, some of which was found buried in an air raid shelter. General Taylor's troops also were careful to guard a famous Mozart Museum in Salzburg. Scholar that he was, Taylor took special precautions to protect these treasures of

Western civilization that otherwise could have been scattered irre-
trievably by looters.

Japan surrendered before the 101st could be moved to the
Pacific. Following the war's end, Taylor was appointed superintendent of West Point, the second youngest (after MacArthur) ever to
hold this post. Probably no other superintendent possessed schol-
arly qualifications comparable to those of Maxwell Taylor. He was
a gifted linguist, fluent in French, Spanish, Japanese, and German,
and with a smattering of Chinese and Italian. As he had served
prewar tours in Japan and China, he knew the Orient as well as
Europe. Taylor was a voracious reader, familiar with the classics
and able to quote extensively from many of them. He "human-
ized" the curriculum at West Point, adding courses not previously
taught in literature and the arts.

As an indication of the scope and variety of Taylor's career, I
will merely mention some other roles in which he served his country. He was the American commander in West Berlin, commander
of the Eighth Army in Korea, and Army chief of staff under Eisenhower. Following disagreements with the Eisenhower administration with respect to our security policies, Taylor retired from the
Army—as he thought, for good. Following the Bay of Pigs, however, President Kennedy, who had read some of Taylor's writings,
persuaded him to become the personal military adviser to the
President and later to serve as chairman of the Joint Chiefs of
Staff. For as long as Kennedy lived, Taylor was among the small
group of able Americans who were his closest advisers.

Taylor initially shared the view, expressed so eloquently by Kennedy in his inaugural address, that America would defend freedom wherever it was threatened. This was a noble but unrealistic
perception of America's role, and particularly of its capability, as
the leader of the free world. It was a view also that did not anticipate subsequent political decisions that led to the ultimate disaster
of Vietnam. At first a "gradualist" with regard to the employment
of American military resources in Southeast Asia, Taylor later
concluded that "no one, not even the President, has the moral
right to put a man on the battlefield or in hostile air space and

restrict him from taking all the measures needed for his survival and the execution of his mission."

I served on the Blue Ribbon Defense Panel appointed by President Nixon in 1969 to study certain aspects of the Defense Department. As a member of a small subcommittee, I visited South Vietnam in 1970. Much of the Western press was continuing to report the Communist Tet offensive as a serious defeat for the United States and its ally. In fact the Communists had suffered severe losses and were able to hold few of their short-term gains. We visited senior commands from the DMZ to the delta. Although our mission did not include the subject, senior officers with whom we talked emphasized their handicaps in fighting an undeclared war in which our forces were not allowed to invade North Vietnam. Also, in the absence of a declared war, there was no censorship. Television cameras indiscriminately portrayed, night after night, the horrors of a war in which it was difficult to distinguish friend from foe. Taylor would write about the effect of biased media coverage and the extent to which this eroded support by the American people. Indeed, prominent Americans broadcast from Hanoi criticizing their *own* country even as American soldiers were being killed by the North Vietnamese.

I know of no other nation in history that deliberately fought a major war with no intention or effort to use its full available forces to carry the war to the enemy's heartland: in Vietnam the capability to do so clearly existed. The effect of this strategy on the attitudes of our own people, and on foreign attitudes toward America, are well known. Less well known are its consequences in Southeast Asia, which include the exodus of the boat people from Vietnam and Communist genocide in Cambodia.

To this point I have tried to give an overview of the career and some of the views of Maxwell Taylor. I turn now to the friendship I shared with Max, a friendship that I shall always remember. Because of my admiration for what he had done and written, I was eager to meet him. We met some years ago, when I had the privilege of introducing him when he spoke at Stratford, the historic home of the Lee family in Virginia. Later, not long after I became a justice of the Supreme Court in 1972, I was admitted to membership in the Alibi Club. This club, consisting of only fifty members, is now in its 104th year. Over this period it has occupied the same quaint little house at 1806 I Street, N.W., in Washington. For the most part, the membership is composed of congenial men who have served our country in responsible military or civilian capacity. General Marshall was a member. Through this club, and through other shared interests, Max and I became close friends. Our wives also were congenial, and my wife and I looked forward to the Taylors' frequent dinner parties, at which Max and Diddy charmed their guests. We have never known a more devoted couple than the Taylors, who shared the identical birthday of August 26, 1901.

Although Max and I saw each other at the Alibi and elsewhere, we also corresponded with some frequency on substantive issues. I was impressed by the breadth of his interests, cultural as well as historical, extending even to decisions of the Supreme Court. For the most part we shared a concern about the dangerous world in which we live. We were in accord as to the seriousness of the continuing Soviet threat and as to the difficulty that citizens of a democracy have in understanding the techniques and objectives of the cold war. Although Max and I had some divergent views about the proper composition of the armed services, I agreed with him as to the need for major changes in the command structure of the Pentagon. In the light of his vast military and diplomatic experience, I often thought that he was both generous and tolerant to consider my own views, given my status as a layman with no remotely comparable experience.

During the last four or five years of his life, Taylor's ability to walk and even to speak was gradually destroyed by a type of sclerosis known as Lou Gehrig's disease. His mind remained clear to the end, as did his delightful sense of humor. Although he was hospitalized for the last few months of his life, I have a letter dated November 30, 1986, in which he commented on an article in the London *Economist* that I had sent him. He agreed with me that "sending arms to Iran [was] incredible." Then, referring to his failing health, he quoted an unknown poet as saying:

> I walk not badly with my cane,
> With specs I'm only half blind.
> My dentures hold and cause no pain
> But I surely miss my mind.

It was abundantly clear from his letters that, virtually to the end, he remained deeply interested in national and world events. Yet he never ceased to engage in self-deprecating humor.

I have a file containing more than a decade of correspondence with my dear friend. It is a file that I will keep. Max's death on April 19 was not unexpected and I am sure he would have viewed it as merciful. At the moving funeral service at Fort Myer, Ambassador Philip Bonsal, a respected diplomat and longtime friend of the Taylors', spoke eloquently of General Taylor's "example," and correctly said that his friendship would remain a constant treasure in the lives of all of us who knew him. His younger son Tom's superb tribute brought tears to the eyes of most of us. He emphasized the closeness of the Taylor family—a closeness not often found in the lives of the world's great leaders. It typifies the mind and spirit that I was privileged to know. Maxwell Taylor's place in history will be a large one.

—JUSTICE LEWIS F. POWELL, JR.
Washington, D.C.
November 1987

Preface

Some years ago, when my biography of President James A. Garfield appeared, my mother examined a copy and commented to the effect, "This is a very handsome book, Jack—but when are you going to write one about your father?" "Never," I replied.

It was not that the thought had never crossed my mind. For many years I had combined a career in government with a certain amount of historical writing. And I had no particular hang-up about writing about the paterfamilias. My government experience, however, most of it in intelligence and international affairs, had given me a healthy respect for the complexities of decision making, particularly in arcane areas such as weapons technology. Things were a good deal less complicated in the time of James A. Garfield.

In about 1986, however, I became eligible to retire from the government, and the prospect of a Maxwell Taylor biography held considerable appeal. Indeed, I would have done well to have acted slightly earlier, for by the time I mentioned my intention to my father he had lost the ability to speak other than short sentences, and there could be no extended discussion of issues as they arose in my research.

Fortunately, I had my own knowledge acquired over fifty-seven years, plus some notes and letters and some splendid collateral sources. My father had cooperated in a number of oral histories, and these were extremely valuable, having taken place at widely separated times. The best of these, incidentally, is that done with Mrs. Elspeth Rostow for the John F. Kennedy Library. The Taylor Papers at the National Defense University are also valuable, although their coverage of the various periods in his life is very uneven. They include perhaps every speech he delivered as Army chief of staff, but they are very lean for the years before 1945.

Space does not permit me to list here the scores of my father's colleagues who assisted with detailed letters or interviews; most of these are cited in the end notes. Several persons, however, were good enough to read selected chapters and give me their comments. These include General Julian Ewell, General Jerry Higgins, Ambassador U. Alexis Johnson, General Harry Kinnard, General Ned Moore, Colonel Thomas A. Rehm, General Bernard W. Rogers, and, within the family, my brother Tom and my daughter Katharine Maxwell Taylor.

Various institutions whose holdings were pertinent to my project were uniformly accommodating. The John F. Kennedy Library and the Alfred P. Sloan Foundation made available important primary sources concerning the Cuban missile crisis. Archivists at the LBJ Library were most helpful in directing me to the most pertinent portions of President Johnson's papers. The staff of the U.S. Military Academy Library and the Army War College were similarly accommodating, although it is regrettable that the Army War College imposes restrictions on the use of its fine collection of oral histories. Special thanks are due to Susan Lemke, chief of special collections and history at the National Defense University, and her assistant, Tina Lavato, both of whom not only facilitated my use of the Taylor Papers but accommodated many miscellaneous requests as well.

Two of my father's close friends, Justice Lewis F. Powell, Jr., and General Bernard W. Rogers, were kind enough to make available to me relevant portions of their correspondence with General Taylor over the years.

One major obstacle, ironically, was General Taylor's old service, the Army. Incumbent Chief of Staff John Wickham denied my request for access to classified portions of the Taylor Papers on the remarkable grounds that I had no "need to know." Because the LBJ Library had declassified a significant amount of Vietnam-related material from the Johnson years, this was not a serious impediment, beyond demonstrating the Army's continuing penchant for shooting itself in the foot in matters touching on public relations.

Assistance in one area fell in a very special category. My wife, Priscilla, a professional editor, had previously assisted in the editing of General Taylor's own publications. As a result, she brought to this project not only extraordinary professional skills but a knowledge of the subject to supplement my own. It was she, for instance, who suggested that the final chapter would be incomplete without some discussion of my father's small library. But perhaps her greatest contribution was a cheerful willingness to drop whatever project she had on her own desk to cope with disruptive behavior on the part of my word processor.

I have been asked whether an author learns anything about someone as close as a parent in the course of writing his biography. In my own case, the answer is an emphatic yes. Before undertaking this project I had only a vague knowledge that General Taylor had been criticized for recommending, after his secret trip to Rome in 1943, that the proposed airborne drop near Rome be scrubbed; I was not aware that his critics included "Beetle" Smith and the redoubtable Samuel Eliot Morison. Similarly, while I knew of the enjoyment that my father had gained from his pursuit of languages, I did not fully appreciate how useful they had been to him professionally. Finally, I was unaware—as he himself had been unaware—that there had been a high-level attempt to remove him as ambassador to South Vietnam.

Taylor's role in three wars, to say nothing of his participation in the Bay of Pigs investigation and the Cuban missile crisis, made him a key player in U.S. foreign affairs during the middle decades of this century. As a result, it is safe to say that this will not be the last study of Maxwell Taylor. I have, however, attempted to provide a full and objective biography and to strike a balance between portraying the "personal" Taylor I knew and the soldier-statesman whose actions and recommendations merit close examination.

—JOHN M. TAYLOR
McLean, Virginia
February 1989

Prologue

THE WHITE HOUSE CALLING

The night of the debacle, America's new President, John F. Kennedy, had already put in a long day. It was nearly ten o'clock when, prodded by his staff, he put on formal dress in preparation for the annual reception for members of Congress. There was a fairy-tale quality to the sight of the young President and his radiant first lady descending the main staircase to the music of the Marine Band. For more than an hour he mingled easily with the guests, a study in grace and confidence.

Shortly before midnight, however, Kennedy slipped away to the Cabinet Room. There he met with his senior security advisers: Secretary of State Dean Rusk, Secretary of Defense Robert McNamara, Chairman of the Joint Chiefs General Lyman Lemnitzer, and Chief of Naval Operations Admiral Arleigh Burke. A deputy director of the Central Intelligence Agency, Richard Bissell, spoke briefly and to the point. In Cuba, he said, the CIA-sponsored invasion faced disaster. Only American air power could save it.

The meeting went on until nearly two o'clock. Kennedy had said from the outset that he would not permit the overt commitment of U.S. military forces in support of the attempt by Cuban exiles to overthrow Fidel Castro. But now the President hedged, and he agreed to provide short-term air cover for the insurgents' B-26 bombers that had heretofore proved so vulnerable to Castro's tiny air force.

Kennedy was stunned at the evening's revelations. Only days before, these same advisers had assured him that every conceivable contingency had been taken into account. Now virtually every assumption on which the expedition had been based had been proved false. There was no general uprising in Cuba, Castro's air force had not been destroyed, and the 1,400-man invasion force was in danger of annihilation. Kennedy determined to find out what had gone wrong.

At the time of the Bay of Pigs operation, the soldier who had once been chief of staff of the U.S. Army had just embarked on a second postretirement career. Following a year in Mexico, where he had headed Mexico City's principal power company, Maxwell Davenport Taylor had accepted a rather unlikely job tender: the presidency of Lincoln Center for the Performing Arts, then under construction in Manhattan. Even Taylor was surprised at this turn of events. He had never had more than casual contact with the performing arts, and his taste in music hardly went beyond early Beethoven. But Lincoln Center was not looking for an artistic director; it was Taylor's managerial expertise that was needed during the construction period.

In part because he had written a book critical of President Eisenhower's security policies, Taylor had been viewed with favor by the incoming Kennedy administration. But when the President-elect had offered him a prestigious ambassadorship, Taylor had declined. The general had his hands full studying the science of acoustics and had no desire to return to government. Even more than most military professionals, Max Taylor had spent his life on the move, and he was ready to put down some roots. He and his wife, Diddy, had purchased a spacious condominium in a venerable Park Avenue apartment building, the first home they had ever owned. They had brought with them a Mexican couple as cook and houseman and were almost as well equipped to entertain as they had been in Mexico City. At the age of fifty-nine, Taylor was still vigorous, and he was looking forward to making more of an impact at Lincoln Center than he had been able to do in Mexico, where his company had been bought out by the government.

On April 21, 1961, two days after the collapse of Brigade 2506, Taylor was told at a luncheon in New York that the White House was trying to reach him. Such a message could mean anything, and he finished his meal before returning the call. Within seconds he was talking with the President, whom he had met only once before in his life. Would he be willing, Kennedy asked, to come down to Washington and chair an investigation into what had gone wrong at the Bay of Pigs? Taylor was noncommittal, but he agreed to go down to Washington and talk about it.

Planning for the Bay of Pigs operation had begun in March 1960, as evidence accumulated that Castro's revolution in Cuba had been co-opted by the Communists. There appeared to be a consensus in Washington that Castro had to go. How could the United States expect to lead the fight against communism world-wide while Castro flaunted his defiance just ninety miles offshore? Kennedy first learned of the proposed U.S. counterstroke as President-elect, when CIA Director Allen Dulles briefed him and key members of the incoming administration. Initially, he had doubts about the proposed invasion. He continued wary at the first White House meeting, held on January 28, to discuss its feasibility.

Security for the operation was proving deplorable. The Cuban exile community in Florida was notably porous, and the press was aware that something was up. On March 31 Kennedy was passed a memo concerning a conversation between one of his staff members and a reporter from *U.S. News and World Report.* The reporter's sources in Miami had told him that an invasion of Cuba was imminent and that the insurgents expected it to trigger a mass uprising. Executives of the New York *Times,* too, knew of the invasion, and Kennedy asked that they suppress their story. In a compromise worthy of the federal government, the *Times* printed the story but limited the headline to a single column.

Nevertheless, pressures for the operation were mounting. Kennedy himself had made the presence of a Communist power just offshore an issue in the presidential campaign. The Guatemalans were uneasy about the insurgent force training on their soil and had made it clear that their hospitality had limits. Castro was believed to be on the verge of receiving MIG fighter aircraft from the Soviet Union—he had none yet. And if such deliveries were to materialize, the United States would have to provide its own air cover for the expedition or scrub the project.

Allen Dulles put the matter bluntly to the President. If Kennedy did not give the green light, he would deny a group of patriotic exiles a once-in-a-lifetime opportunity to deliver their homeland from Communist rule. Failure to act would encourage the export of Cuban communism throughout Latin America. Domestically, the political repercussions would be considerable if a disbanded, disillusioned Cuban Brigade were to be set loose to complain of how Kennedy had betrayed the anti-Communist cause. Dulles asked the President whether he was ready to tell this "group of fine young men" who had asked "nothing other than the opportunity to restore a free government in their country" that they would "get no sympathy, no support, no aid" from the United States?[1]

Such pressure was not easy to resist, and the activist young President was not the one to do so. In February, however, after the proposed landing site had been moved west to the Bay of Pigs, Kennedy asked the Joint Chiefs to examine the plan a final time. After sending an inspection team to the brigade's base in Guatemala, General Lemnitzer again put the Chiefs' imprimatur on the plan.

On Monday, April 10, the insurgents were trucked from their base in Guatemala to Puerto Cabezas in Nicaragua. On Friday, CIA "advisers" spelled out the tactical plan. First, strikes from Nicaragua by insurgent B-26s would incapacitate Castro's air force. Then the insurgents would seize three beaches around the Bay of Pigs, while the defenders were kept off balance by a parachute drop inland and a diversionary landing some three hundred miles to the east. The plan as approved by Kennedy was an all-Cuban operation. CIA operatives on the ground, however, assured the insurgents that if problems arose the Americans would move in. And if worst came to worst, the Cubans could "melt away" into the countryside of the land that they called home.

In the end, Kennedy gave his assent and the operation went forward. He emphasized, however, that it must appear to be a Cuban, not an American, undertaking. To assure control of the air, CIA planners had called for B-26 strikes against Castro's two main airfields. These were flown on Saturday, April 15, and five Cuban aircraft were destroyed. Although the officers of Brigade 2506 were told at the time that the entire Cuban air force had been destroyed, this was far from the case. Castro still had six B-26s of his own, plus miscellaneous other aircraft. The most important of the latter were several T-33 jet trainers that, suitably armed, were capable of flying rings around anything the insurgents could put in the air.

After the raid, two of the insurgent aircraft flew on to Miami, where the pilots claimed to be defectors from the Cuban air force. This deception was a failure on all counts. There had been enough invasion rumors in the Cuban community in Florida to cast immediate doubt on the pilots' story, while Castro, who knew that none of his planes was missing, realized immediately that something was up.

On Sunday, April 16, Kennedy vetoed a projected second strike, a decision that would later be scrutinized by investigators and denounced by the insurgents. The President was still obsessed with keeping down the "noise level" of an inherently noisy operation. Kennedy's decision upset Bissell and another CIA man, General Charles Cabell, both of whom urged Rusk to have the President reconsider. Rusk demurred but gave agency officials the option of stating their case directly to the President. His offer was declined, no new air strikes were launched, and the invasion went forward.

On Sunday evening the insurgent flotilla dropped anchor and the fighters prepared to disembark. Problems arose immediately. In a remarkable oversight, no one in Washington had noted that virtually every approach to the landing beaches was protected by coral reefs. Although insurgent frogmen were able to locate channels, the ships were unable to come as close to shore as had been contemplated, and the frogmen were themselves spotted by Cuban militia. Thus the one element of surprise that remained—the exact timing of the invasion—was lost before the first insurgents had left their transports.

The brigade then encountered all the hazards of a night amphibious landing. Some troops were off-loaded so far from shore that they sank under the weight of their equipment. At dawn, while the brigade was still attempting to unload its heavy weapons, Castro's bombers appeared, accompanied by T-33s armed with .50 caliber machine guns. Four of the insurgents' aircraft were shot down, leaving the bombers free to zero in on the ships. First to go was the *Houston*, loaded with ammunition and gasoline. Then it was the turn of the *Río Escondido,* which exploded in a ball of flame. The remaining insurgent vessels put out to sea.

Deserted by their "navy," the insurgents had only a minimum of supplies with which to face Castro's rapidly consolidating defenders. Nevertheless, the brigade held its own on Monday, April 17, inflicting heavy casualties on Castro's forces. The marshy terrain initially favored the insurgents, because Castro's forces were confined for a time to two roads that led inland from the beaches.

At dawn on Tuesday, April 18, the brigade's remaining B-26s attempted to bomb Castro's principal airfield at San Antonio de los Banos, but clouds obscured the target and the strike was unsuccessful. At the beachhead, Castro's commanders were bringing armor into play. Soviet-manufactured T-34 tanks, parked in a line, fired point-blank into the insurgent lines. Morale within the brigade, which had held up through the previous day's fighting, began to sag.

The collapse began in the small hours of Wednesday, April 19. At 4:32 the expedition sent its last message: "AM DESTROYING ALL MY EQUIPMENT AND COMMUNICATIONS. TANKS ARE IN SIGHT. I HAVE NOTHING TO FIGHT WITH. AM TAKING TO THE WOODS. I CANNOT WAIT FOR YOU."[2] More than 1,100 insurgents were taken prisoner.

Even as the collapse began, President Kennedy, still in dinner clothes, wrestled with the question of increasing the U.S. role. Bissell and Burke proposed a strike from the carrier *Essex* aimed at destroying Castro's jets and restoring a degree of parity in the air. The one aspect of the operation about which Kennedy had been adamant, however, had been minimal American involvement. In a compromise, Kennedy authorized the use of six unmarked jets from the *Essex* to cover a final insurgent air strike from Nicaragua. This limited involvement, initiated at a time when the issue had already been decided, failed in its objective. Because of a mixup concerning times zones, the insurgent B-26s arrived at the beaches an hour before the fighters. Two insurgent bombers— flown, counter to Kennedy's instructions, by Americans—were destroyed, their crews killed.

It was on the morning of April 21 that Kennedy put in that call to Taylor in which he acknowledged that he was in deep trouble over Cuba. A meeting at the White House was arranged for the following morning.

In the Oval Office, Taylor met with Kennedy, Vice President Johnson, and a host of chastened administration gurus. In his memoirs Taylor recalled, "I sensed an air which I had known in my military past—that of a command post that had been overrun by the enemy. There were the same glazed eyes, subdued voices, and slow speech that I remembered observing in commanders routed at the Battle of the Bulge or recovering from the shock of their first action."[3] Two days later Taylor commented to his family that Kennedy seemed bewildered that things could have gone so wrong when the invasion plan had been approved by all participating agencies.

Kennedy went over what was known of the debacle and asked Taylor to lead a postmortem. There was to be a committee—the Cuba Study Group—and the constitution of its membership was curious, to say the least. With Taylor as chairman, it comprised Attorney General Robert Kennedy, Allen Dulles, director of the agency responsible for the Bay of Pigs operation, and Admiral Arleigh Burke, who as a member of the Joint Chiefs had also been one of the players. Taylor was provided with an ad hoc staff and was given two months in which to carry out his investigation. In a key part of his instruction, the President told Taylor that "what I want is your own report, drawing from past experience, to chart a path towards the future."[4] The emphasis was to be on corrective measures, not on scapegoats.

Neither Kennedy nor Taylor could have anticipated that this gloomy meeting was the beginning of an association that would last as long as the Kennedy presidency and that would reinstate the older man as a pillar of Washington's security establishment. The President's top advisers tended to fall into one of two categories. Some qualified for the "Irish Mafia," the Massachusetts-based politicos, led by brother Bob, who were close friends and associates of the new President. A second group, including Secretaries Rusk and McNamara, had been selected by Kennedy largely on the recommendation of other people and in many instances were hardly known to him personally.

Taylor fell into the latter category. To his knowledge he had met Kennedy only once before, in about 1948. Many years later Taylor was pleasantly surprised when his book attacking Eisenhower's defense policies, *The Uncertain Trumpet*, drew a rave review from Senator John F. Kennedy:

> This volume is characterized by an unmistakable honesty, clarity of judgment and a genuine sense of urgency. It is free of rancor and recrimination, but it leaves no room for doubt that we have not brought our conventional war capabilities into line with the necessities. We have allowed important aspects of our national military strength to erode over the past years. . . . It is a book that deserves reading by every American.[5]

When Taylor, then in Mexico City, wrote an appreciative note to Kennedy, he received one in return. "I was more than happy to give your book my endorsement," the candidate wrote. "Its central arguments are most persuasive . . . and it has certainly helped to shape my own thinking."[6]

After Kennedy's election later that year there had been a call from Secretary of State-designate Rusk. Would Taylor be interested in the ambassadorship to France? He was, after all, fluent in French and, as a soldier, might be able to "get along" with de Gaulle. Taylor declined; he had just completed the move to New York City, and he had a commitment to Lincoln Center.

But then came the Bay of Pigs. It was one thing to turn down an ambassadorship; it was another to say no to a President who was in trouble over a military matter. The short flight from New York to Washington would bring Taylor back to the center of power in Washington, not only under Kennedy but under his successor as well. It was an unlikely turnabout for a career that had ended on a negative note after thirty-seven years of remarkable service.

Part One

THE
STUDENT

Chance favors the prepared mind.
—Louis Pasteur
1822–1895

Chapter 1

MISPLACING THE STRAIT
OF MALACCA

America's World War II leadership had strong midwestern roots. Dwight Eisenhower was a product of Abilene, Kansas. Omar Bradley grew up in rural Missouri. Eisenhower's chief of staff, Al Gruenther, was born in rural Nebraska.

Maxwell Taylor represented a command generation different from that of Eisenhower, Bradley, and Gruenther, but his roots were remarkably similar. General Bradley described his family as "plain Missouri farmers, proud, honest, hardworking and poor."[1] The Taylors were never in poverty, but the difference was not great. Maxwell Taylor was the son of a small-town lawyer who ended his career with the Katy Railroad. Money was frequently tight. Taylor would note in his memoirs that when he and his father both contracted typhoid fever in 1906, his father ended up owing the family doctor about one hundred dollars, a debt that took two years to pay off.

Taylor's mother, Pearle Davenport Taylor, was the daughter of a Confederate veteran who had gone into farming. To say that she was a doting mother is an understatement. Her possessiveness was the subject of considerable joking within the family, but the extent of her influence on her only child is not easy to assess. She was certainly instrumental in developing his interest in reading, an interest that he carried through life.

The Taylor line came to Missouri from England via Maryland and Kentucky. One ancestor, Bartholomew Taylor, had been a soldier in the Revolution. John Earle Maxwell Taylor was a remarkable person in ways quite different from his famous son. As a lawyer he represented a vanishing breed: he was called to the bar not by way of law school but by apprenticing himself to another lawyer. He was a model of judicial probity, and the courtesy title of "judge" was never more appropriately applied than to him. Father Taylor passed on to his son a sense of integrity and an abiding interest in politics. One of his stories was of the McKinley-Bryan presidential election of 1896, as seen from Kansas City. Bryan, the Democrat, was so popular in the Midwest that no one could conceive of his losing. The saloons filled up on the day after the election to celebrate the returns—only to empty slowly as the fact of McKinley's victory sank in.

What early influences molded the young Missourian? He was brought up in the Disciples of Christ, an evangelical offshoot of the Presbyterian church that renounced all governing bodies above the local congregation. Except while he was at West Point, first as a cadet and later as superintendent, his church attendance was irregular. Throughout his life Taylor would be a dutiful son, but there is no evidence that he modeled his behavior on that of his strict, humorless mother or on that of his more easygoing, cigar-smoking father. I suspect that the strongest influence on the young Taylor was an amalgam of forces that we call The Home: a place of security and affection where, in Taylor's case, there was also intelligent guidance.

Many of young Max's adult characteristics doubtless grew out of his having been an only child. In the absence of siblings he was thrown on his own resources. One result was that he became an omnivorous reader. According to his parents, the first present he ever requested was an unabridged dictionary. Its cover fell off from use—but he kept the book among his cherished memorabilia.

Apart from his parents, the main influence on the young Max was the maternal grandfather whose name he bore. Milton Davenport worked a small farm between Keytesville and Dalton, Missouri. He had served in the Civil War as a noncommissioned officer in the Confederate armies of Sterling Price and Jo Shelby. Milton had only one arm, but this was the result of a postwar sawmill accident rather than Yankee bullets. In any case, it was he who turned his grandson in the direction of a military career. In Taylor's words,

The perfect day for me was to work with him in the fields during the daylight hours, listen to his Victor phonograph after dinner, and have him refight the battles of The War. He did not glorify the war . . . but his tales had a gripping quality in describing how shared hardships and dangers bind men together in the camaraderie of arms.[2]

It was with his grandfather that Taylor first experimented with firearms. The old veteran still had one of his sidearms—a long-barrel, single-shot weapon called a horse pistol, because its length and weight mandated that it be rested on a horse's neck to be fired. One day, Grandpa Davenport and his admiring grandson loaded this antique with powder and nails and took aim at a crow in a nearby tree. As my father told it, the gun roared, leaves and twigs flew everywhere, and the crow flew away unharmed.

One suspects that young Max was fortunate in his early teachers. None ever succeeded in killing his interest in a subject, and the majority appear to have been dedicated and understanding. He was head of the Army's Far East Command in 1954 when the postmistress of Cyrene, Missouri, wrote to him about her friend Nellie Craig Toombs. Miss Nellie was wondering whether if the General Taylor she kept reading about was the same Max Taylor to whom she had taught English in Kansas City. Indeed he was, the general wrote:

What I learned in your classroom always stood me in good stead in later years and accounted in a large measure for the little difficulty which I encountered in the courses at West Point and in subsequent schools. I remember, in particular, your thorough instruction in grammar based upon parsing and analysis. In later years I became very much interested in foreign languages and found that the principles of grammar I learned at Ashland were equally applicable to the languages of the East and of the West.[3]

Once, in the sixth grade, Max was asked along with his classmates to name his professional ambition. He duly wrote "major general," an answer that understated his eventual rank by two stars but nonetheless reflected his commitment to a military career.

At Northeast High School in Kansas City, Taylor was not only a star student but a keen debater. At about age fourteen, he entered a high school competition with an oration on Robert E. Lee, which, according to family legend, won first prize. The text represents his first preserved writing and is an impressive effort for any youngster, not only for its content but for its error-free syntax. He opened with a rhetorical flourish:

> As in the darkness of the night astronomers find some new star rising in the heavens, so amid the darkness of struggle and strife has risen some great man whose character has shone as the very star of light in the gloom of war and desolation.

The orator then considered the constitutional considerations that led Lee to remain loyal to Virginia, Lee's personal integrity, and the Virginian's devotion to his duty as he perceived it. "The measure of a great general is not ultimate success," Max concluded. Lee's nobility of character was attested to "by the love and devotion given him by his whole army. It can be truthfully said of him, 'In righteousness did he judge and make war.' "[4]

Taylor graduated from high school at sixteen and was voted the "most genuine boy student" by his fellow seniors. In Europe the Great War was in its third year, and the Allied cause appeared precarious. The prospect of American involvement was growing, and Taylor watched enviously as his slightly older peers registered for the draft:

> Very soon I found that I couldn't get a date because I wasn't wearing a uniform and didn't have a draft card. So in 1918 I was really desperate about this thing. . . . I went down and falsified my age by a year, making it eighteen instead of seventeen, and registered for the draft. Then I had a draft card.[5]

Max's immediate interest was in obtaining an appointment to West Point, but he had no political connection through whom to do so. Moreover, his high school curriculum had been weighted toward the classics and languages—he had had four years each of Spanish and Latin and two of Greek—and away from the science and mathematics that were the core of the West Point curriculum. Seeking to remedy this situation he enrolled in a junior college, the Kansas City Polytechnic Institute. To raise a little money he worked in his spare time for the gas company, reading meters in Kansas City's redlight district.

Meanwhile, America went to war. The prospect of his only son's being drafted and shipped off to France may have lent impetus to Father Taylor's efforts to secure him an appointment to one of the service academies. Luck was with him. Congressman William P. Boland, impressed with the young man's scholarship, offered him an appointment to either West Point or Annapolis. Taylor had only to pass the entrance exam.

The two examinations were similar in most respects and probably undemanding by comparison with today's college boards. The examination for Annapolis, however, included a section on geography for which Taylor was not fully prepared. Years later he still remembered having placed the Strait of Malacca in the Middle East, and he suspected that this had been his downfall. He compared his failure with that of the artist James McNeill Whistler, who had been dismissed from West Point after failing chemistry. Had silicon been a gas, Whistler later complained, he would have been a major general. Taylor's variant was that had the Strait of Malacca been in the Middle East, he would have been an admiral. The possibility of Max Taylor's having gone to Annapolis remains an intriguing might-have-been.

The United States Military Academy can be a forbidding sight to a new plebe.

In midwinter West Point is bleak and gray, uninviting to the eye. The hills with their leafless trees come rolling down to the Hudson River, deep green, swollen now and shifting with ice. In dead winter the wind rockets up the valley, and the men march along the road, their chins buried in heavy coat collars. They walk with economy, arms swinging to cadence, eyes up and watchful. It is a gray place all of it, buildings gray, men in gray, the sky itself reflecting gray and bouncing it back.[6]

As Taylor later recalled, he arrived in New York City on October 20, 1918, and, on his father's instructions, spent the night at the Astor Hotel. The following evening he took the Weehawken Ferry to the New Jersey side, where he caught the West Shore Railroad for the last leg to West Point. There was a cadet on the train, the first one Max had ever seen. Taylor found his way to the old West Point Hotel on the edge of the plain, and from a window there watched the graduation the following day of the last of the Academy's "short-term" classes.

In one sense his timing was excellent. America's entry into the war had caused the Academy to be transformed, briefly, into a glorified officers candidate school. The class of 1921 had graduated in seventeen months instead of the usual four years, and Taylor's class of 1922 was initially scheduled to be processed even faster, entering in November 1918 and graduating the following June. The armistice intervened, however, and the class of 1922 returned to the four-year schedule.

In another sense Taylor's timing was not so good. The West Point of 1918 was, in the words of Army Chief of Staff Peyton March, "forty years behind the times," mired in tactical and intellectual doldrums from which not even the World War had moved it.[7] The curriculum was completely prescribed, with heavy emphasis on math and science. Two subjects that might be assumed to be important to a soldier—history and English—were lumped together in a single department. The Academy had the nucleus of a permanent faculty, but most teaching was done by recent graduates.

Rote learning was very much in vogue. In accordance with the methodology of Founding Father Sylvanus Thayer, each cadet was expected to recite the day's lesson before his class and to be graded on each recitation. Most colleges had long since abandoned this rigid methodology, and many bright cadets must have been depressed by this intellectually stultifying environment. Not Taylor. He had missed the war, but he could still have a West Point ring and a military career. Indeed, even in the strict regimen of his plebe year, Taylor found himself with time on his hands. "As I had had most of the subjects taught during the first two years," he later wrote, "I had ample leisure to do a great deal of desultory reading in the small but well-stocked Cadet library, where I continued to indulge my interest in reading widely, if not deeply, in the fields of philosophy and military history."[8]

Whatever his shortcomings in geography, the seventeen-year-old Missourian who entered West Point just days before World War I ended was well equipped to handle the rigors that lay ahead. He was a strong physical specimen, six feet tall and about 155 pounds. His health was good, and he had already developed the remarkable work habits that he would carry through life. He had read extensively about West Point and was prepared for the worst. Most important, he was committed to a military career and intended to make the most of what West Point could provide him.

But was there a darker side to this seeming paragon? Although Taylor rarely if ever accumulated enough demerits to require punishment tours, such delinquencies as he incurred remain dutifully chronicled at the Military Academy today. On one occasion in his Second Class (junior) year he was charged with "allowing disorder and boisterous conduct in the mess hall" after having been directed to maintain good order. There were other malfeasances. Particularly intriguing are the demerits assessed against Taylor for employing "an improper expression at 8:00 a.m." on November 26, 1921. Surely no expression used on a dreary November morning should be cause for reproof, but this was West Point.[9]

For three of Taylor's four years at the Academy, the superintendent was General Douglas MacArthur, one of the Army's rising stars who had distinguished himself in the war just ended. At West Point he established a reputation as a colorful "reform" superintendent. He initiated reforms in the plebe system, promoted cadet athletics, and devised more progressive criteria for the selection of cadet officers. In the face of considerable opposition from the Academic Board, he increased the proportion of classroom time allotted to the social sciences and reduced the heavy emphasis on mathematics.

There are parallels between MacArthur's objectives as superintendent and Taylor's own when he returned as superintendent after World War II. That fact, together with the famous MacArthur charisma, might lead one to think that the superintendent had been a major influence on the young Missourian. In practice, however, that was not the case at all. Taylor would later remark that the only occasion when he caught more than a glimpse of the superintendent was on graduation day, when MacArthur looked him in the eye and handed him his diploma. Taylor believed strongly that the superintendent, by his remoteness, passed up an opportunity to impress his personality on the Corps of Cadets.

Whatever his personal views of the superintendent, Taylor benefited from MacArthur's interest in athletics. MacArthur promoted not only the team sports in which the Academy was a recognized collegiate power, but intramural athletics as well. Max had picked up tennis before arriving at West Point; at the Academy he became a dedicated player. In his First Class (senior) year he was captain of the tennis team. In later years he became an accomplished squash and handball player as well.

Taylor's record as a cadet was impressive. He ranked seventh in his class in "general merit" in his first year, fifth in his second year, and seventh again in his junior year. His lowest rank in any subject was sixty, and that was in mechanical drawing. He was something of a legend as a linguist; he once went an entire year with only perfect scores in Spanish. He graduated fourth in a class of 102 and was a captain on the regimental staff. In the 1922 yearbook, the blurb on Max Taylor emphasized his academics. "He is without doubt," read his accolade, "one of the most learned scholars of the class." The yearbook went on to laud "the literary abilities of this youthful prodigy."

Taylor was not yet twenty-one when commissioned in June 1922, but his high academic standing allowed him to choose his branch of service. His choice was the engineers. Only the top fraction of each class was allowed to choose that branch, which, until recently, had enjoyed not only prestige but premium pay. As a lieutenant of engineers, the Missourian was following in the footsteps of his boyhood hero, Robert E. Lee. But whether his reputation for "bookishness" would be an asset or a liability in an army that thrived on conformity remained to be seen.

Chapter 2

THE OLD ARMY

The Army that Taylor joined on his graduation was subject to divergent currents. On one hand, it was justifiably proud of its role in the Great War just ended, a role that foreshadowed America's emergence as a great power. On the other hand, it was beset with the problems associated with all demobilizations: rapidly rundown budgets, personnel, and equipment. In the years between 1918 and 1922, the Army retrenched from a wartime strength of 3.7 million men to an authorized Regular Army strength of 137,000. The cornerstone of postwar defense policy was not the U.S. Army but the fleet. Although postwar naval construction was inhibited by the same budgetary restraints that affected the Army, America's good relations with its immediate neighbors fostered a belief that the Navy was the first line of defense against any enemies as might appear. Well might Lieutenant Taylor have wished that he had been more precise in locating the Strait of Malacca.

In part because it retained large quantities of equipment left over from World War I, the postwar Army had great difficulty in obtaining funds from Congress for modernization. The National Defense Act of 1920 provided for only nine Army divisions. By 1920 the wartime Tank Corps had shrunk from some five thousand tanks to about seven hundred, and many wartime pioneers in armor, including George Patton and Dwight Eisenhower, had returned to the cavalry and infantry, respectively. Contrary to popular belief, the Army's air arm enjoyed a high priority in the military budget. As early as 1926, the War Department attempted to gain authorization for a total of twelve bomber squadrons, twenty-one pursuit squadrons, and twenty-one squadrons of other aircraft.

At Taylor's graduation the armed forces were grappling with the age-old problem of armies: how to keep usefully employed in times of apparent security. All armies put a premium on training, but styles nevertheless vary. In the British Army, professional life was strongly influenced by the need to garrison the empire and by an officer's strong identification with his regiment. The U.S. Army did not have a far-flung empire or a strong unit identification. An officer's friendships and professional associations were likely to be an outgrowth of the military schools he attended and his choice of branches within the service. Taylor later acknowledged that he found the Army he joined in 1922 "drab and unexhilarating" after West Point. He watched a significant number of his classmates migrate into the worlds of business and finance. The Missourian, however, stayed in uniform, convinced of the worth of the profession he had chosen and sustained, perhaps, by a conviction that his skills must someday be put to good use.

Taylor's first posting was to the Engineer School at Fort Belvoir, near Washington, D.C., but his mind was on matters other than road building and river crossings. In his second year at West Point he had met a Washington belle, Lydia—"Diddy"—Happer. Their introduction had been a spontaneous thing; she had been visiting the cadet brother of an Annapolis friend. Their attraction to one another was reinforced by the discovery that they shared the same birthday, August 26, even to the year, 1901. Diddy had been far more oriented toward hops at Annapolis than at West Point, but Max succeeded in changing that. It was an active courtship, first from West Point and then from Fort Belvoir. The young lady's parents were impressed with Taylor but not with his financial prospects. Her father, a realtor, said that he would not consent to marriage until Taylor had two thousand dollars in the bank.

The young lieutenant began setting aside every nickel toward his nest egg. He starved himself in the course of a two-year assignment with the 3d Engineers in Hawaii, saving most of a monthly salary of about $170. The two were married in 1925 and it would prove an ideal marriage, even though their individual interests were far from identical. Diddy had none of her husband's scholarly interests, and the interest in athletics she professed during their courtship was later exposed as a transparent fabrication. But in the good years and the bad she would be the ideal wife, always supportive and interested in people in a way that helped compensate for her husband's limited interest in social activities.

Like most of their Army colleagues the Taylors spent much of their lives on the move. Not until the general retired from the service would they own a home, and during an Army career of thirty-seven years they averaged nearly a move a year. Such stability as life afforded came from the Army's sense of community, the rediscovery of old friends at new postings, and the strength of their own marriage. Their honeymoon was hardly one to be emulated. Married in Washington on a Monday, the happy couple sailed from New York for Hawaii on Wednesday. Their vessel, however, was not a cruise ship but an Army transport, and the sexes were strictly segregated. Not until the ship reached Panama, about a week after sailing, did the Taylors exchange more than a wave.

Taylor may have been enchanted with his bride but he was less enthusiastic about his choice of branches within the Army. Prestigious though the Corps of Engineers was, the new lieutenant wondered about it as a vocation:

> When I joined the 3d Engineers at Schofield Barracks in Hawaii, the commanding officer was a fine old gentleman named Colonel Schultz. He had been number one in his class at West Point some time in the 1890s. He had served almost every day of his service on river and harbor work and now at the end of his career was commanding an engineer regiment. Well, the old gentleman hardly knew how to get on his horse, but what was worse in the eyes of a second lieutenant right out of the academy, he often wore his spurs upside down. Well, looking at Colonel Schultz on a horse, I said, "Taylor, that might be you twenty years from now."[1]

The question became which other branch he might best transfer to. Although Taylor had become an accomplished horseman at various Army posts, he was not interested in the cavalry, armored or otherwise. It was a bit too social for one of Taylor's financial resources; many cavalrymen, including one George Patton, moved from post to post with their own string of polo ponies. The infantry was "Queen of Battles" and clearly a possibility, but in the end

Taylor's choice was the field artillery, in part because he was interested in the technology. Given this technological interest he might have opted for the fledgling Air Corps. But he was a soldier, not a daredevil. Moreover, pilots had to tend to their planes much as cavalrymen looked after their horses, and an empathy with internal combustion engines would never be one of Taylor's strong points.

So it was that Taylor, in 1926, transferred to the field artillery. While still an engineer, however, he was involved in an incident that would influence his personal relationships for the remainder of his life. In Hawaii, while supervising the blasting of a tunnel, he entered a shaft that was being prepared for blasting. There was no flagman to warn the young lieutenant as he rounded a bend close to the blast site. The ensuing explosion did not cause serious injury, but for weeks afterward he was almost entirely deaf and, even after his condition improved, his hearing remained somewhat impaired. When Taylor retired from the Army in 1959, he declined to accept partial disability on account of his hearing problem, but the problem was real. It made routine social intercourse something of a chore and at times caused him to miss the nuances of a discussion. As a result, he became increasingly prone to handle matters of any importance by means of memoranda.

On his return from Hawaii, Taylor was assigned to West Point as an instructor, first in Spanish and later in French. He was so thoroughly versed in the two languages that he was paid the honor of being assigned the best and the worst students in each language. These five years at the Academy were among the most relaxed of his career. In his later years Taylor would not be noted as a mixer, but in these years at West Point he was something of a social lion. Like most junior officers, he did not rate quarters on the post itself; he and his bride lived in an apartment above a garage in nearby Highland Falls. Among their contemporaries as instructors were Mark McClure and Al Gruenther. The latter was an accomplished bridge player, and although Taylor was never quite in his class, the two were frequently invited to referee bridge tournaments in the New York suburbs. Nor was bridge their only pastime: In those Prohibition days, Taylor and Gruenther devoted weekends to improving their recipe for bathtub gin.

Taylor might have remained a lifelong bridge player (as did Gruenther, who became a world-class player) had he not concluded that bridge was too time-consuming. He dropped the game cold turkey in his late twenties and never played another hand. Given his competitive nature, he may also have suspected that he might never be so good at it as Al Gruenther. He devoted his leisure instead to tennis and handball, his languages, and professional reading.

One of the few kind references to Douglas MacArthur in Taylor's memoirs is in connection with his assignment to the Command and General Staff School at Fort Leavenworth. MacArthur, as Army chief of staff, had noted the slow pace of peacetime promotion and had directed that the Command and General Staff School admit some senior lieutenants as well as captains and above. As a result Taylor was one of five or six lieutenants chosen for the two-year course beginning in 1933. There the Taylor family, which by then included me, occupied one of four small apartments in a converted machine shop near the main school building.

A Leavenworth classmate, George Rehm, recalled the Command and General Staff School as a high-intensity course. Morning classes were followed by independent study, study that could not be postponed because each student was expected to produce a paper or solve a map problem each day. Class rankings were not published because they were believed to have been a factor in two recent suicides. Nevertheless it was widely assumed that final rankings went into participants' service records. Some students studied in pairs, but Rehm and Taylor chose to go it alone. Prior to his arrival at Leavenworth, Taylor had read in French a manual on the employment of artillery by a German officer, one Colonel Brockmuller. He found to his surprise that no one at Leavenworth had heard of Brockmuller, and as a result he was invited to translate the manual from French into English as his graduation thesis.

Out of the 119 members of Taylor's class, no fewer than 62 eventually became general officers. They included some of the principal leaders of World War II: Mark Clark, Matthew Ridgway, and Walter Bedell (Beetle) Smith. In Taylor's opinion, his Leavenworth classmates represented the ablest group of comparable size with whom he was ever thrown into association. One of them,

Carter Magruder, was especially known for his quiet competence. Over the years, he became one of Taylor's closest Army friends.

After Leavenworth, Taylor might have been ordered to any of a half-dozen Army posts with an artillery component. In the event, however, the War Department produced a far more imaginative posting for him. Years before, Taylor had expressed an interest in one of the few postings for language officers in Japan or China. In the intervening period he had solidified his credentials as a linguist with five years teaching French and Spanish at West Point. He was no less interested in the East after Leavenworth than he had been twelve years earlier, and he jumped at the prospect of a tour in Tokyo. So it was that in the fall of 1935 the Taylor family, which by then included my brother Tom in addition to me, set out for Japan aboard one of the creaky Army transports of that day.

In Tokyo, Taylor served both as the assistant military attaché and as a language student. Our home in Tokyo was a two-story frame house in the Shirokane district. We shared a circular compound with the minister of Chile (Chilean dana-san) among others; his residence was much the grandest. Across the way was Taylor's boss, military attaché Colonel William Crane. Alongside our house, growing through a specially constructed hole in the overhanging roof, was a tree reputed to be the oldest in Tokyo.

I was about seven when I was awakened one night by a light that flashed in the window of the second-floor room that I shared with my brother. Scared, I wandered into my parents' room to report that a burglar was trying to enter through my window. Nonsense, came the reply, and that must have been good enough for me, for I padded back to my room and was soon asleep once again. Not until the following morning did I learn that my father had apprehended a burglar in the kitchen. The intruder had climbed up the "oldest tree in Tokyo," checked out my room, and then tried his luck downstairs.

One of the accommodations the Taylors had made over the years concerned religion. Diddy was a Christian Scientist and a faithful church attendee. Taylor himself, although a nominal member of the Disciples of Christ, was best characterized as "Army Protestant." His church attendance was sporadic for most of his life, but he generally made a point of attending Easter services. One spring during our time in Japan some American colleagues urged Taylor to join them in duck hunting on Easter Sunday. He consented, probably with misgivings, for his wife would not allow his failure to make Easter services go unnoticed. But in the end Taylor arose while it was still dark, joined his colleagues, and made his way to a duck blind in some dank marsh. Dawn was breaking and the first ducks had just appeared when the area experienced a mild earthquake of the type to which Japan is prone. The ground trembled, the ducks flew away, and the humiliated hunters returned to their hearths and spouses.

After about two years Taylor had become fluent in Japanese and was able to take advantage of an unusual arrangement in which selected foreign attachés were allowed to observe the activities of Japanese military units, even to the extent of living with them in the field. In Taylor's case the unit in question was the Imperial Guards Artillery Regiment, which the American joined just as it was about to move out for field exercises near Mount Fuji. It was a remarkable cultural experience, one that gave the American a unique insight into relationships within the Japanese military. Taylor later recalled:

> Social relations were patterned after those in the Japanese family with the colonel in the role of paterfamilias. This fact was particularly apparent at the bath hour when, the colonel in the lead, we filed to the bath, which consisted of a large tank of near-boiling water serving the function of the wooden o-furo of a Japanese family. Thereupon, in order of rank, one by one we soaped and scrubbed ourselves outside the tank, then eased ourselves gently into the hot water to parboil, being careful not to agitate it for fear of further raising the temperature. As I had been given a courtesy ranking at the head of the captains of the regiment, I always had the good fortune to get into the tank fairly early in the sequence.[2]

The combination of Taylor's linguistic skill and his field experience with the Imperial Artillery led to a remarkable temporary assignment: six months in China in a key period of the Sino-Japanese War. As Japanese forces advanced southward in the latter half of 1937, most of the American embassy personnel evacuated Peking, leaving only a skeleton staff. The senior staffer remaining was the military attaché, Colonel Joseph W. Stilwell, who stayed behind to monitor the progress of the fighting. Stilwell's relations with the Japanese were almost as bad as those with his superiors in Washington, and he requested the temporary use of a Japanese linguist as translator and assistant.

Taylor jumped at the chance to assist Stilwell, despite warnings that "Vinegar Joe" was not the easiest person in the world to work with. Getting to Peking, however, was an odyssey in itself. Taylor traveled by steamer from Yokohama to the Korean port of Pusan, where he transferred to a train that took him north through Seoul and Pyongyang, and across the Yalu to the border city of Antung in China. There he had to debark for customs inspection, and the Chinese customs, alas, managed to mislay his trunk. Rather than risk being stranded in Antung, Taylor boarded the train for Mukden without a toothbrush to call his own. At Mukden his luck took a turn for the better. He was met there by the American consul, John P. Davies, who said that he had been instructed to expedite Taylor's travel if possible. He promised to do what he could concerning the missing trunk—which eventually made its appearance, just in time for the return trip to Tokyo. In Peking, however, the new arrival had to outfit himself from a local U.S. Marine outlet.

Whatever Taylor may have heard of "Vinegar Joe" Stilwell, in the event the two got along famously. Taylor's task was to accompany Stilwell wherever the Japanese would allow them to go and to facilitate the older man's dealing with Japanese authorities, whom he loathed. Traveling with Stilwell was never dull, as Taylor noted in his memoirs:

> I found "Vinegar Joe" a genial travel companion, full of Chinese lore and glad to talk about the country and people to an interested listener. He had a deep affection for the Chinese, an admiration for their achievements of the past, and a faith in the promise of their future. We rambled together over a good part of North China, traveling by automobile, by crowded troop trains, and not infrequently by foot. We slept wherever the night found

us and led thoroughly unsanitary lives. Stilwell openly despised the rules laid down by Western doctors for staying alive in China; he loved to walk through a Chinese market and pick up fruit to eat after merely brushing off the dust with a sweaty sleeve. Though I knew it was folly, I could do no less and soon became an ambulant case of chronic diarrhea while Stilwell seemed to flourish on our regime.[3]

Despite their grudging willingness to permit a certain amount of legal spying by Stilwell and his companion, the Japanese were xenophobic and highly security conscious. Their soldiers wore no unit designators and as a result the American embassy lacked the most basic data regarding the order of battle of the invading armies. A bit of cultural serendipity allowed Taylor to score a small triumph in this area. Like many a tourist he made an excursion one afternoon to the Summer Palace outside Peking to admire the Great Buddha. There he spotted the kind of graffiti that armies have engaged in since the time of Caesar's legions: three Japanese soldiers had written their names on the back of the Buddha. Not only their names but their unit designators! Taylor's information represented the first inkling that the units in question were in North China.

On one occasion the Japanese announced that they had won an engagement against Chinese forces not far from Peking. Taylor requested permission to visit the site, and for once the Japanese authorities were forthcoming. The American was led to the scene of the battle and was allowed to take some photographs. He counted some two hundred Chinese dead, including the bullet-riddled body of a Chinese general hanging out the window of his staff car. Two months later, Taylor felt an urge to revisit the site. It had been completely cleaned up, with only a great earthen mound as a reminder of the recent bloodletting. On top of the mound, Chinese farmers were planting carrots. To the American officer, this incident somehow seemed to reflect the imperturbability of the East.

Back in Tokyo, Taylor continued his effort to develop an order of battle for the Japanese in China. This meant spending a lot of time at various railroad stations, attempting to spot the odd unit designator among troops entraining for the front:

> I remember standing at Shinogawa-eki, one of the main railroad stations, one day, watching the troops go out. I saw, across the crowd on the other side of the square, a little child on the back of a Japanese woman. He was waving two Japanese flags and the funny thing was that he was blond. I got a little closer, and [I could see] it was my son Tom. I didn't get any closer . . . [but] when I got home I got him and said, "Now, Tom, I saw you." He said, "Yes, Father, I was seeing our boys off to China." I asked, "Why are our soldiers off to China?" He said, "The wicked Chinese are killing our men." He was a thoroughly indoctrinated son of the Emperor that day.[4]

As 1938 turned into 1939, most of Taylor's time was occupied in preparing a report that was effectively the culmination of his four years in Japan as assistant military attaché. Titled "Tactical Doctrine of the Japanese Army," it was a distillation of his months of living with the Imperial Guards, his travels with Stilwell, and his analysis of hard-to-obtain Japanese language publications on military doctrine. The report, which comprised some sixty-eight single-spaced pages, was almost as long as Taylor's first book, *The Uncertain Trumpet*, and it reflected comparable care in preparation. Considering its date and the limited data available to the writer, the report was a remarkable assessment of the enemy that the United States would soon be facing in the Pacific:

> Japanese tactical doctrine insists vigorously on the inherent superiority of the offensive. The object of all maneuver is to close quickly with the enemy where the assumed superiority of the Japanese in close combat can be realized to the utmost. Like the French Army at the outbreak of the World War, the Japanese seem to feel that in the attack there is some mystic virtue which can overcome material weapons in profane hands.

The writer detected a number of weaknesses in the Japanese Army. It had a propensity for frontal assaults, "often with inadequate means," that would not serve it well against a first-class antagonist. Its artillery was inadequate in quantity and defective in

fire control. Most Japanese divisions were lacking in motor transport. "The well-known marching powers of the Japanese infantry
can be counted upon to compensate in a measure for this deficiency . . . but not to the degree of assuring the interception of
an enemy . . . animated by a pressing desire to get to safety." At
the same time, Taylor was impressed with the Japanese aptitude
for night fighting:

> The Japanese Army has a strong partiality for the night attack.
> This form of combat favors the bayonet fighting stressed in the
> training of the infantry and tends to cover the weakness in artil-
> lery and cooperation of the combined arms which foreign
> observers consider to exist. . . . The Japanese are further en-
> couraged in their faith in night attacks by successful experiences
> in the Russo-Japanese War and subsequent operations in Man-
> churia and China.

All things considered, Captain Taylor viewed the Japanese Army
as a formidable force:

> It is an army easily misjudged by the foreign officer who sees
> first of all its straggling columns, slovenly dress and unmilitary
> bearing. Just as there is no glitter to its accoutrements, there is
> little theoretical excellence to recommend its tactics. But it is an
> army which excels in durability and performance. In the same
> way that its infantry "straggles" thirty miles a day and arrives at
> the destination on time and with surprisingly few casualties, its
> command and staff can be counted on to evolve plans and or-
> ders which, without being brilliant tactical combinations, are
> practical and workable schemes for getting a maximum perfor-
> mance from the Japanese soldier.[5]

As Taylor prepared to return to Washington in 1939, he had
considerable grounds for satisfaction. His study of Japanese military doctrine was finding appreciative readers in Washington; it
would be the standard U.S. Army text on this subject well into the
Pacific war. Moreover, he had made himself proficient in Japanese, having mastered not only the spoken language but the *kanji*
form of written Japanese, based on Chinese ideographs. All things

considered, he probably knew as much about the Japanese Army as any American.

His career prospects, however, were bleak. The thirty-eight-year-old captain had spent four years outside the Army mainstream, leaving him essentially a loner in an organization in which advancement often required a "sponsor." He had never served as aide to a general or in close proximity to some rising star, and his friendship with the acerbic Stilwell was a questionable asset. Taylor later acknowledged that his highest career expectation at this time was to make full colonel, and even this would require keeping his copybook clean. He would later recall how he and his fellow officers studied the *Army-Navy Journal*, seeking out the obituaries and speculating on how they might effect a hoped-for promotion.

But the America to which Taylor was returning was changing. Although the Roosevelt administration faced considerable opposition in its attempts to rearm, it was nevertheless upgrading the armed services from the low levels of the 1920s. First priority went to the Navy, but the Army was not ignored. From a strength of less than 150,000 at the time Taylor joined it, the Army had now passed the half-million mark. New equipment was slowing making its way through the pipeline.

If Taylor had run the risk of being forgotten during his four years in Japan, he had also been sheltered there from a heavy dose of intraservice politics. Even as the Nazis and the Soviets readied their nonaggression pact, the Army was choosing sides as to who should succeed General Malin Craig as Army chief of staff. The front-runner was General Hugh Drum, who had been a corps commander in World War I and who in 1939 commanded the Hawaiian Department. Drum was openly campaigning for the top post, but he was by no means the only contender.

A dark horse for the post was Craig's deputy chief of staff, Brigadier General George Marshall. He was by far the most junior of the contenders, but he had some influential admirers. Craig himself favored his deputy, and so did the Army's most prestigious figure, retired General John J. Pershing. Marshall was available, but he was uneasy in the role of candidate. He wrote to an Atlanta journalist who sought to boost his prospects, "My strength with the

Army has rested on the well-known fact that I attended strictly to business and enlisted no influence of any sort at any time."[6] In the end, Marshall's strategy was eminently successful. In August 1939, Roosevelt appointed him over the heads of thirty-two more senior generals to be the new chief of staff.

In the fall of 1939 our family made its way home by sea. The trip seemed endless; we sailed first to Shanghai and there boarded the Army transport *U.S. Grant* for home. The venerable *Grant* was not noted for either speed or comfort. So slow was our progress— there was a layover of two weeks in the Philippines—that we later calculated that the entire voyage from Japan to San Francisco had taken some fifty-six days. Few tears were shed when, during World War II, the *Grant* was used for target practice.

An era was ending as we wended our way across the Pacific. I remember the Chinese boys swimming around our ship at Shanghai, diving for pennies. It seemed to me like a lot of trouble to go to for a few pennies, but then the Chinese were funny that way. As we passed through the tropics, there were movies most evenings on the poop deck, and group singing. I remember songs like "K-K-K-Katy," "Shine On, Harvest Moon," and "The Monkeys Have No Tails in Zamboanga." It seemed hard to believe that halfway around the world Hitler was preparing to invade Poland.

Chapter 3

GENERAL MARSHALL

In July 1986 Taylor was the honored guest at the National Defense University at Fort McNair, where a conference room in the main hall was named in his honor. He had already opted to deposit the bulk of his papers at NDU; eventually the Taylor Room there was to hold much of his military memorabilia as well. By then the general was almost unable to walk, and his attendance at NDU that day would be his last public appearance.

In the remarks he prepared for the occasion, which were read for him, the old soldier's thoughts returned to 1939 and the year he spent at what was then the National War College. "On our first day," he recalled, "we students were assembled in what became Arnold Auditorium to meet and receive advice from a few senior generals . . . seated in the front row. I happened to get a seat in the balcony from which I could see the generals well. To my surprise the first speaker introduced was General George Marshall, the new Army chief of staff. I never ceased to be impressed by him."[1]

Taylor spent a pleasant year at the War College, a member of the last class there until after World War II. He played third base on the softball team and, in the comparatively relaxed academic environment, came to know some of his later associates, including Lyman Lemnitzer, Tony McAuliffe, and Bill Dean. In the end, however, Taylor was destined to graduate in absentia. Matt Ridgway, who was handling Latin America in Marshall's War Plans Division, had been assigned what was viewed at the time as a sensitive undertaking: to initiate a series of missions to Latin America aimed at ascertaining what our allies there might require to meet a military threat from Nazi Germany. Ridgway had instructed Taylor in Spanish at West Point, and they had been classmates at

Leavenworth. Taylor soon found himself in a C-47 over the mountains of Peru. "I'll never forget that experience," Taylor later reminisced. "The Latins would give us these huge shopping lists, which we couldn't possibly fill. At one point I wound up in Peru. Darned if the Peruvian admirals didn't present me with a list of things they needed to combat possible German submarines in Lake Titicaca, a land-locked body of water in the Andes foothills."[2]

Taylor's stint at the War College had compensated to some extent for his isolation from the Army mainstream during his four years in Tokyo. After graduating in 1940, Taylor was assigned to his first troop duty in many years: commander of the 12th Field Artillery Battalion at Fort Sam Houston, Texas. There he participated in his first field exercises as part of a division, little realizing that this was, in effect, his farewell to the peacetime Army:

> Command of the 12th Field Artillery Battalion was an enormous pleasure. . . . The old noncoms who had all the know-how were still there and I had a battalion just unbelievably rich in talent in the noncommissioned officer grades. . . . The experience of these men, particularly my sergeant major, was an enormous help to me. . . . His knowledge of soldiering and the practical side of administration of a unit—looking after families, all the things that went with peacetime service—made him of enormous value to me.[3]

After less than a year at Fort Sam Houston, Taylor had the extreme good fortune to be ordered back to Washington to a position in General Marshall's secretariat. Working for Marshall was hardly a piece of cake, as the Missourian—he was Major Taylor now—would quickly affirm. But Marshall was intent on rewarding people who met his standards, and Taylor was being afforded a priceless opportunity to succeed or fail under the watchful eye of the chief of staff.

Marshall's immediate staff consisted of the secretary of the general staff and a half-dozen assistant secretaries, of whom Taylor was one. The secretary on Taylor's arrival was Colonel Orlando Ward, but he was shortly succeeded by Beetle Smith. It was a challenging position, particularly as the Army proceeded with its first expansion since 1917. It fell to Smith and his assistants to handle the paperwork and to monitor the implementation of the many decisions flowing from Marshall's office.

Although Taylor later dealt regularly with presidents, no other figure would have the influence on him that General Marshall did. The deep respect that Taylor would always hold for Marshall was somewhat unusual, in that Taylor's greatest admiration was generally reserved for combat soldiers. Marshall's combat experience had been largely limited to the Philippines; he had made his reputation within the Army as Pershing's chief of staff in World War I. But almost everyone who worked closely with Marshall felt the force of his personality. Taylor would write in his memoirs:

> General Marshall never spoke anywhere without receiving the undivided attention of every listener. . . . One could never imagine questioning the accuracy of his facts or challenging the soundness of his conclusions on any subject he undertook to discuss. He did not give the impression of great brilliance of mind, as General MacArthur did, but of calm strength and unshakeable will.[4]

Working for Marshall involved coming to grips with some of the general's idiosyncrasies. In later years, Taylor probably related more anecdotes involving Marshall than about any other of his contemporaries. For example, he recalled Marshall's fetish about his door: anyone who opened it was expected to enter and state his business. No mere "peeking" was allowed.

Another of Marshall's preoccupations—keeping confidential information secure—to some extent rubbed off on Taylor. But on one occasion an issue of telephone security nearly cost him his job, or at least the good opinion of his chief. Shortly after Pearl Harbor, Marshall directed Taylor to obtain White House approval for the evacuation of MacArthur from the Philippines. Roosevelt was on a train en route to Hyde Park and FDR's military assistant, General "Pa" Watson, told Taylor that he would pass the substance of Marshall's recommendations to the President by secure telephone. Taylor protested that his chief would not approve the use of a phone for this sensitive matter, but Watson went ahead, noting that the White House link was designed for just such purposes.

When Taylor reported to Marshall what had happened, the latter's reaction was every bit as explosive as the younger man had feared. He excoriated Taylor for his irresponsibility, without, it appears, explaining how a lowly major was to prevent General Watson from communicating with the President as he saw fit. Taylor took Marshall's reprimand so seriously that he went to some lengths to ensure that the chief of staff saw a memorandum that detailed the safeguards built into the White House telephones. Marshall never mentioned the matter again.

The chief was noted for carrying a "little black book" in which he noted the names of promising subordinates. Later, Taylor himself would adopt this practice. With Marshall, however, there was always some question as to whose name was being recorded, for the chief of staff was notoriously bad at remembering names. Once, in the early months of the war, when Marshall was due back from a flight overseas, a question arose as to which staff officer should meet his plane that night. Taylor and a colleague, Colonel Bob Young, decided on a coin flip, and the loser, Young, was left to make all arrangements. The plane was delayed, and it was nearly dawn before Marshall and his baggage were delivered to the chief of staff's quarters at Fort Myer. His duty done, Young turned to his boss to ask if that would be all. "Yes," Marshall replied. "Thank you, Taylor."

While the Army's rising stars were learning the ropes in the old Munitions Building on Constitution Avenue, the beginning of World War II was gradually bringing changes to the Old Army. In September 1939, President Roosevelt had declared a limited national emergency, which led to a small increase in both the Regular Army and the National Guard. The Army found the incremental increase disappointing, yet there was enough budgetary authority to permit the first corps-level maneuvers since 1918. When Roosevelt sent Congress an Army budget of $853 million in early 1940, the amount was more than twice the average budget of the mid-1930s.

After Hitler's invasion of France and the Low Countries, Congress needed no convincing in the matter of rearmament. Following testimony by Marshall in support of a 335,000-man Regular Army, both houses approved legislation providing for an Army of 375,000, supported by a War Department budget of nearly $3 billion. In September 1940, for the first time since World War I, Congress provided for a draft. Thus, although Pearl Harbor would catch the country napping in a tactical sense, moves that vastly speeded the mobilization of the nation's military strength and national resources were already afoot.

The attack on Pearl Harbor found the Taylors occupying a small row house on Military Road in northwest Washington. Along with many others, I recall that day with all the clarity that one reserves for cosmic events. I was in the living room listening to a Redskins football game when the broadcast was interrupted for a bulletin that the Japanese had attacked Pearl Harbor. Perhaps anticipating a career in intelligence, I duly passed this word upstairs, where my parents were cleaning out some closets. One of them remarked to the effect that one of our boys must have had a bomb loose in his rack. I returned to the radio and thought no more about it, but after a time my father thought he had better check in with his office. All telephone circuits were busy and stayed that way. Taylor climbed into the family Chevy and for all practical purposes disappeared for several days.*

From the shambles left by the Japanese bombers came one of Taylor's most enduring recollections of General Marshall. As December 7 came to a close, the War and Navy departments were attempting to sort fact from rumor and to assess the magnitude of the disaster. That evening Marshall determined to summarize the situation for the President as best he could, and he called for a secretary. The day being Sunday, secretaries were in short supply. The only one available was a young lady of conspicuously good looks who had been with the chief's office a very short time and whose machine for taking dictation was equally untested.

Taylor ushered the young lady, whom he identifies in his memoirs only as Miss X, into Marshall's office, and in due course she

* It would be many years before historians would conclude that General Marshall's phobia about telephones contributed to the debacle at Pearl Harbor. After being shown a decrypted Japanese message that clearly indicated that war was imminent, Marshall was urged to telephone General Walter Short in Hawaii. He refused, opting instead to send a warning via the Army's own radio link. His message was delayed, only to arrive after the Japanese attack.

emerged and set to transcribing her notes.† Time passed, and Marshall buzzed Taylor to ask what was taking so long. Taylor checked with the secretary, who at first indicated that she would be finished shortly. A few minutes later, however, she burst into tears. "Oh, Major Taylor," she blurted, "I didn't get a word of it!" In Taylor's words, "I have rarely had a more unwelcome task than to go back to General Marshall and tell him that he would have to do his dictation all over again. On the bleakest day of his life, this must have seemed a final, cruel blow."[5]

As 1942 wore on, Taylor, like others in the chief's office, was eager for a field command. With the rapid expansion of the Army there appeared to be opportunities everywhere. One visitor to the War Department early in 1942 was Taylor's erstwhile traveling companion in China, Joe Stilwell, now a major general. The two had lunch at the old Hogate's restaurant on Maine Avenue, and Stilwell invited Taylor to join his staff in what would soon become the China-Burma-India theater. Taylor accepted eagerly, and in due course Stilwell sent a list of names to Marshall for approval. When the list came back, the names of everyone requested had been approved except one—Taylor's.

The resulting disappointment was short-lived. Marshall had plans for him, although they did not necessarily entail a staff job. He believed much of the "Old Army" to be either too old or too rigid to command troops in battle under the pressures of modern warfare. He did not often discuss his leadership philosophy, but he may have had Taylor, among others, in mind in some comments he made to military writer George Fielding Eliot shortly before Pearl Harbor. In the course of an interview Marshall reached into his desk and handed Eliot a sheet of paper. "I've made a little list," he said.

> I've looked over the colonels, lieutenant colonels, and some of the majors of the Army. . . . I'm going to put these men to the

---

† Although Taylor carefully protects the identity of the delinquent stenographer, she has elsewhere been identified as a Miss Morgan. Leonard Mosley's biography of Marshall contains a section in which the author recounts the problems the Japanese embassy encountered in transcribing the long message from Tokyo breaking relations with the United States. Taylor noted in the margin of his copy, "Japanese Morgan."

severest tests which I can devise. . . . I'm going to start shifting them into jobs of greater responsibility than those they hold now. . . . Those who stand up under the punishment will be pushed ahead. Those who fail are out at the first sign of faltering.[6]

Ultimately, Taylor became a beneficiary of Marshall's interest in a comparatively new form of combat, airborne warfare. The Army was about to reactivate one of its most illustrious World War I units, the 82d Division, as an airborne unit. Its new commanding general, Matt Ridgway, was a close associate of Marshall's. Ridgway was looking for a chief of staff and sent Marshall a list of a half-dozen officers, including Taylor, from which he asked that the appointment be made. Ridgway had known Taylor slightly at Leavenworth; more recently, he had had a chance to study Taylor's report on his mission to Latin America.

Ridgway's list, like Stilwell's, went into Marshall's "In" box. This time, Taylor was was not deleted but was checked as Marshall's choice. The Army was about to send its top Japanese expert to fight the war in Europe.

Taylor's one year with Marshall was undoubtedly the most influential of his career up to that time. He found much in his chief that he strove to emulate: his integrity, his total devotion to his profession, and his intolerance of anything except the highest levels of performance. In addition, I believe he found it instructive to observe Marshall's dealings with Congress, for he came away with a clear impression that the chief of staff must worry about much more than the country's declared enemies.

At the same time, Taylor did not leave the War Department as a Marshall clone. He himself had found the chief intimidating and had observed the paralyzing effect that he could have on others. Taylor later acknowledged that, as he rose in the Army hierarchy, he sought to make himself more approachable than Marshall. His sense of humor helped, but personal relationships, like languages, were something he worked at. As time went on Taylor became less and less "one of the boys," but he cultivated an ability to make people feel at ease when he wished them to be.

Considering the lateness of the hour when the U.S. Army turned its attention to the use of airborne forces, it is remarkable that these troops were able to make the contribution in World War II that they eventually did. As Taylor himself commented more than once, the Americans discovered airborne warfare at precisely the time that the Germans were giving it up as too costly.

Strictly speaking, the Red Army was the real pioneer in airborne warfare. The Soviets had experimented with parachute troops in the 1930s; indeed, the largest airborne exercises before World War II were those staged by the Soviets. Nevertheless, it was Hitler's use of airborne forces early in World War II that drew attention to "vertical envelopment" in the West. In their May 1940 attack on the Netherlands, the Germans employed paratroopers to seize bridges over the Maas and Waal rivers. A year later the Germans launched their largest airborne assault ever against the British-held island of Crete. Against Crete, the Wehrmacht's leading proponent of airborne warfare, General Kurt Student, employed some 25,000 parachute and glider-borne soldiers in seizing a strongly defended island whose adjacent waters were controlled by the Royal Navy. Student's force was roughly handled in the ten-day campaign; it suffered some 3,000 killed and 11,000 wounded. But the British ultimately evacuated the island.

Hitler called the Crete campaign a disaster and told his staff that the day of the paratrooper was over. The Allies, however, were much impressed with Student's achievement. The U.S. Army began small-scale experiments with paratroops in June 1940. The first parachute training was conducted at Fort Benning, Georgia, and Camp Claiborne, Louisiana. After Pearl Harbor, Marshall authorized the formation of six parachute infantry regiments and, when initial experiments seemed promising, two airborne divisions. The first of these, the 82d, bore a famous name. The second, the 101st, was brand new and was to be formed from a nucleus of the 82d.

The commanders of the two divisions were sharply contrasting personalities. Matt Ridgway, forty-six, was a West Point graduate who felt that his professional career had effectively ended when he was sent to West Point as an instructor in 1918 rather than to

France with the Allied Expeditionary Force. But Ridgway was not one to brood and he stayed with the Army. Like Taylor, he was selected for all the "right" schools, most notably Leavenworth and the War College. To a greater degree than all but a few soldiers, Ridgway reveled in life in the field. When commanding troops, he was "out front all day, exhorting, cajoling, teaching."[7]

Bill Lee, the "father" of the U.S. airborne program, was named to command the 101st. A North Carolinian, he was the same age as Ridgway but cut from a different mold. Unlike either Ridgway or Taylor, Lee had served in the trenches in World War I, and, like most veterans of trench warfare, he felt that there had to be a better way to fight. After the war he had spent three years in France, studying the German experiments with airborne forces. Following the German successes in Holland, Lee was able to persuade the War Department to initiate some experiments with parachute forces. By the summer of 1940 the first parachute battalion was training at Fort Benning, using as a test platform a 250-foot steel tower that had seen service at the New York World's Fair. Fortunately for pioneers like Bill Lee, Marshall was intrigued with the possibilities of airborne warfare. By the end of 1941 four battalions were in training at Benning.

The logical next step was expansion to division-size units. But what size division? Lee and others favored a "heavy" division, with ample transport, a traditional artillery complement, and personnel strength close to the standard 14,000-man infantry division. There was little time for experimentation, and the British—the only army in a position to share information on airborne doctrine —had never expected hitting power from an airborne division comparable to that of a standard division. Eventually, ground forces chief General Lesley J. McNair decreed a much lighter force, one initially established at about 8,300 men, divided into a parachute regiment, two glider regiments, plus light artillery and support units. In McNair's words, "An airborne division should be evolved with a stinginess in overhead and in transportation which has absolutely no counterpart thus far in our military organization."[8]

And stingy it was, although in time there would be modifications in both the parachute-glider ratio and in personnel strength. Although individual weapons were the same as in a standard division, artillery was limited to 75-mm pack howitzers. For ground transport, airborne divisions were heavily dependent on the versatile jeep and its various trailers. Both of the country's airborne divisions were sacrificing striking power for mobility.

In the fall of 1942 the Taylor family was reunited at Fort Bragg, North Carolina, proud of the head of the family's new rank of colonel. The family head had passed a rigorous summer training with the 82d at Camp Claiborne, working twelve-hour days, seven days a week, in the sizzling Louisiana heat. He was a fit 175 pounds, but he conceded that keeping up with Matt Ridgway was no easy matter. One of our first family evenings at Bragg was spent with tweezers and candle, helping remove assorted fleas and ticks from Colonel Taylor.

Like their counterparts in the 101st, Ridgway and Taylor had much to ponder. To the extent that anyone could simulate an airborne assault, it would be led by lightly armed paratroopers, who would be followed by gliders carrying the heavier equipment. But until glider-borne artillery could be brought into play, the paratroops would have to depend on rifles and a few machine guns. Ammunition would be in tight supply, a fact that would dictate rigid fire discipline. Communications were essential, but the radios of the day were bulky and could be issued only sparingly. If there was any certainty in a parachute operation, it appeared to be that even the most accurate drop would scatter soldiers over a wide area. At worst, small groups of lightly armed soldiers might have to fight for days independent of any formal unit. Another of the Army's airborne pioneers, General James Gavin, would write:

> Since the beginning of recorded history, soldiers have been drilled repetitively to de-emphasize their individual behavioral traits and force them to adapt to larger combat formations. . . . All this had to be discarded as we sought to train the paratroopers to the highest peak of individual pride and skill. . . . To the soldiers of another generation, it seemed to suggest too little discipline and too much initiative given to individual soldiers.[9]

Overregimentation would never prove to be a problem with the airborne soldiers. The paratroopers were all volunteers. A few were attracted by the extra fifty dollars per month in jump pay, but most would have jumped without any pay at all. Glider troops, who were not volunteers, received no extra pay, despite the fact that there was hardly any activity connected with World War II more hazardous than landing on hostile terrain in a heavily loaded glider. One poster, designed by glider troops, featured a composite photo of wrecked gliders with the caption: "Join the glider troops. No flight pay. No jump pay. But never a dull moment."[10]

The Duke of Wellington once said of a new group of recruits, "I don't know what effect these men will have upon the enemy, but by God they terrify me." From the outset, the airborne soldiers posed major disciplinary problems. They were aggressive and fit and, more often than not, from the "wrong side of the tracks." Their energy was boundless, their contempt for soldiers other than airborne was profound, and their unit pride often resulted in fights that destroyed some bar or brothel. Taylor would tell the story of two paratroopers who had to be separated after one made a slur on the other's manhood. The other challenged him to a parachute "duel": the first to pull his rip cord would be deemed "chicken." Word got around, and there was a clutch of spectators when a C-47 took the two gladiators to an agreed altitude. The two jumped virtually simultaneously, appearing to the spectators as tiny dots as they tumbled toward the landing zone. Both waited so long that Taylor wondered whether either could open his chute in time. Finally there was a flicker of white from one jumper and then from the other. In airborne legend, the winner staggered up to his adversary and shouted, "I always knew you were yellow!"

Taylor, Ridgway, and Gavin all wrote books about their experiences in World War II, and all touched on the disciplinary problems they encountered during this period. Taylor's description was perhaps the most euphemistic. In a masterpiece of understatement he characterized the first paratroopers as "full of the Old Nick." But by the time these generals had turned to their memoirs, time had cast a kindly glow over even the most egregious misbehavior. Many of the worst offenders had contributed to the legends of their divisions, and all too many had been left beneath a white cross in Normandy, Holland, or the Ardennes.

In this atmosphere it was mandatory for the airborne commanders to prove their manhood. All sought to qualify as paratroopers, not only to be in the vanguard but perhaps also to avoid
assignment to the totally unpredictable gliders. Taylor's first jump
was made under the tutelage of jumpmaster Julian Ewell, who
would be associated with Taylor for much of their subsequent careers. As Ewell recalled:

> Taylor took a very compressed [training] course and I wanted to
> be sure that his first jump passed without incident. So I went
> along and jumped right after him. I was watching as he landed
> and a brisk breeze snatched him up in the air and he hit with a
> terrible crash. . . . I landed nearby and ran over to pick up the
> pieces but he bounced up apparently unhurt. He was always in
> good physical condition—which helps.[11]

Taylor admitted to a graceless landing, one that left him with cuts
on his face, but he believed that his earlier experience as a horseman had enabled him to roll with the fall. In an elite corps it was
not unusual for zealots to log a hundred jumps or more. Taylor
made no more than a half-dozen in his military career. Two of
these were combat jumps, which gave him probably the highest
ratio of combat to training jumps of any soldier. But he was never
interested in jumping for its own sake. "Far from getting jump-
happy," he wrote, "I viewed the parachute strictly as a vehicle to
ride to the battle, to be used only when a better ride was not available."[12]

While other paratroopers kept scorecards on their jumps, Taylor
contemplated what would come next. At Benning, the 82d staged
one of the larger practice jumps to date and came down in fairly
good order. The officer in charge remarked after the landings,
"Well, that's it." Taylor, the division chief of staff, turned on him.
"What do you mean, that's it. They haven't *done* anything."[13] As
Taylor would recall, many paratroopers were so jump-happy that
training in infantry tactics was all too often short-changed.

Chapter 4

SICILY

The months at Benning were taxing for the men of the 82d. Not only was the division being split into two, but it was experiencing a wholesale turnover in personnel. Part of this turnover grew out of the need to staff two divisions, but much of it stemmed from a pruning of those soldiers perceived as lacking aptitude for airborne warfare. This latter category covered a multitude of real or supposed shortcomings, including any tendency toward airsickness. Thousands of men left the division, to be replaced by new recruits. The training was punishing, as one young recruit would testify:

> [Our] second day was a copy of the first, except more physical training was added and a little more training on the packing and care of parachutes. The runs lengthened to nine miles every morning before breakfast, and the push-up punishment came more often, even for no reason at all. . . .
>
> Everything was done on the double; but when any of the instructors wanted something done even faster, they would yell, "Hubba-hubba," one time. We were told this was Yiddish for "Hurry, hurry," but I never took the trouble to find out if this were really true.[1]

As chief of staff, Taylor was responsible for much of the division's paperwork. But he had not exchanged a desk in the Munitions Building for one at Benning or Bragg. To the extent that he could, he attempted to put in some desk time the first thing in the morning, go out for training in the field, and return to headquarters at the end of the day to clear up any urgent work that remained. Ridgway reportedly was not entirely pleased with this arrangement and may have preferred a chief of staff who was a full-time manager. In any case, a change was in the offing. When Ridgway lost his chief of artillery to the newly formed 11th Division, he appointed Taylor to the artillery post and found a chief of staff more to his liking. The new billet carried with it the rank of brigadier general, and Taylor thus gained his first star.

With the star went the right to have an aide-de-camp, and the new general did not make his choice lightly. He interviewed more than a half-dozen young officers, including a hell-raising Harvard man, Tom White. When Taylor told White the job was his if he wanted it, the younger man began to have second thoughts; he wanted to fight, and he was not sure that he wanted to be an aide. In White's recollection, Taylor talked him into accepting. "I'm a brand new general," he said. "I've never had an aide before. You've never been an aide. Why don't we try it?" White agreed and would serve as Taylor's aide for most of the war.[2]

Meanwhile, the British Eighth Army gave the Allies their first good news in some time with their victory at El Alamein in October 1942. U.S. forces were preparing their first offensive moves in the war against Germany and Italy. But what should be their objective? Ever since Dunkirk it had been clear to Allied strategists that their armies must return to the European continent. But the perils of an attack across the English Channel were obvious, the price of failure heavy, and the time required to mobilize the necessary resources formidable. Under these circumstances, the British were attracted by the prospect of operations in the Mediterranean, where enemy as well as Allied logistics would be strained. The military weakness of Hitler's Italian partner was an additional incentive.

Strategically, Allied landings in North Africa held out the tempting prospect of trapping Rommel between the British Eighth Army and Anglo-American forces to the west. Moreover, Allied control of North Africa would assist in securing the sea routes across the Mediterranean, would pose the threat of an invasion of Italy, and would reduce the possibility of Spain's joining the Axis. In the end the British carried the day, over the objections of those like Marshall who sought a total commitment to the cross-Channel attack. To command Operation Torch, the invasion of North Africa, the

Allies chose an American then little known to the public, General Dwight D. Eisenhower.

On November 8, 1942, an Anglo-American armada totaling more than eight hundred vessels began debarking troops at Casablanca in Morocco and at the Algerian ports of Algiers and Oran. Although Rommel was in no condition to contest the initial occupation of Morocco and Algeria, this was only a temporary respite. As time went on he would prove as formidable a foe to the Americans as he had to the British. In the end, however, the Allied victory was complete, in part because of Hitler's folly in refusing to permit the evacuation of the Afrika Korps. Although the Allies incurred some 70,000 casualties in North Africa, they captured a quarter-million of Hitler's best troops.

On May 20 Anglo-American forces held a victory parade in the streets of Tunis. One of the spectators was Maxwell Taylor. He had flown to North Africa by way of Brazil to prepare the way for the arrival of the 82d by sea. The division had not been required for Torch, but other operations lay ahead. The bulk of the 82d arrived at Casablanca on May 10, after an eleven-day voyage. From there they were moved by rail to Oujda, in the Moroccan interior. There, in Ridgway's words:

> we trained in a fiery furnace, where the hot wind carried a fine dust that clogged the nostrils, burned the eyes, and cut into the throat like an abrasive. We trained at first by day, until the men became lean and gaunt from their hard work in the sun. Then we trained at night, when it was cooler, but the troopers found it impossible to sleep in the savage heat of the African day. . . . Jumping was a hazard, for the ground was hard, and covered with loose boulders.[3]

Taylor recalled that the troops' one indulgence was the local red wine, which they buried deep in the sand during the day and exhumed by night. When not in training, the officers played volleyball in 120-degree heat. Taylor, for one, also walked for exercise. According to aide Tom White, "He would walk nine miles in two hours, which is almost like running, striding along with very little conversation."[4]

During this period Taylor had an opportunity to renew contact

with the Seventh Army commander, George Patton. Their acquaintance before the war had been limited, a result of their
representing different branches as well as different command gen-
erations. But Patton in North Africa was a genial host. Taylor
would recall an evening at Patton's headquarters when one of his
guests inquired about his secret in leading American troops. Patton, a twinkle in his eye, replied, "I have a surefire formula. First I
take the American soldier and dress him up till he's proud of being
a soldier. Then I get behind him and give him a swift kick."[5]

In North Africa the men of the 82d got their first look at war, for
the sands were littered with the hulks of German and British
tanks. The division had missed the Tunisian campaign, but its staff
was soon deeply involved in planning for the invasion of Sicily. A
mountainous island of some ten thousand square miles, it was a
logical stepping-stone in any campaign against Italy, Sardinia, or
southern Europe. The invasion of Sicily, code-named Husky, was
the first major amphibious strike against Germany or Italy. The
invading force was to comprise six U.S. divisions, including the
82d, plus the seven-division British Eighth Army. The American
airborne component in the invasion was limited to two regiments,
in part because of a shortage of transport aircraft.

The plan called for Gavin's 505th Regiment to parachute behind
the projected amphibious beachhead at Gela to secure it against
counterattack. On either D plus 1 or D plus 2, a battalion of Colonel Reuben Tucker's 504th Regiment, with supporting artillery,
was to reinforce Gavin. The rest of the division would come in by
sea. While Ridgway argued unsuccessfully for the employment of
his entire division in an airborne role, Taylor studied the enemy
defenses. Sicily was defended by some 200,000 Italian troops,
backed by two German panzer divisions. Such a force should have
been more than enough to hold off the invaders, and Taylor later
confessed that the invasion plan "would never have received a
passing mark at Leavenworth." Ultimately, however, Eisenhower
was fully justified in his belief that the Italians would not prove to
be tenacious defenders.

On July 9, as the sea armada headed toward Sicily's southern
tip, Gavin's paratroopers prepared for departure. At about 10 P.M.,
226 transport aircraft, each holding about sixteen soldiers, headed

for Sicily on a route that was to take them by way of Malta. Many of the pilots never saw Malta, for problems arose immediately. Fearing midair collisions, some pilots veered out of formation. Others, with limited night flying experience, became thoroughly lost. Most of the aircraft found their way to Sicily, but few sticks were dropped even close to their landing zones. An estimated 80 percent of the paratroopers were dropped at distances up to sixty-five miles from their designated areas. Few among the thirty-four hundred men were able to locate their units; most fought in small bands and eventually linked up with the Allied beachhead.

Taylor remained in Tunisia, charged with launching Reuben Tucker's 504th as airborne reinforcements on the evening of the second day. Little resistance was expected, for the Allies controlled the air, and the seaborne invasion had met only token opposition. Americans and British alike had found beaches deserted and fortifications unmanned; most inhabitants had greeted the Allied soldiers as liberators. Although there was sharp fighting ahead against the German panzers, a combination of tactical surprise and inept defense had given the Allies a vital foothold on the southern part of the island.

Taylor had no intimation of disaster as the C-47s bearing Tucker's force took off in the choking dust. A few hours later, however, he was awakened with word that aircraft were returning with wounded on board. He hurried to the airstrip where he found perhaps a dozen aircraft, some badly damaged. Although Ridgway had gone to great lengths to warn Allied naval units of the airborne reinforcement plan, the 504th had been mistaken for German aircraft, as a result either of deviation from predetermined routes, trigger-happiness on U.S. ships, or both. Twenty-three aircraft had been lost to friendly fire, and although many of the paratroopers had been able to parachute to safety, many others had not. The 504th suffered a total of 229 casualties, including 81 dead.

There was, of course, an investigation. The Navy declined to accept responsibility and insisted that the problem lay with faulty navigation on the part of the pilots. In the wake of the incident Ridgway wrote, "The responsibility for loss of life and material resulting from this operation is so divided, so difficult to fix with impartial justice, and so questionable of ultimate value to the ser-

vice because of the acrimonious debates which would follow . . .
that disciplinary action is of doubtful wisdom."[6] Taylor, with his
sense for the incongruous, later quoted one wounded soldier as
telling him, "I was glad to see that our fellows could shoot so
good."[7]

Following the ill-starred operations of Gavin and Tucker, the
82d slowly assembled in the area around Gela. Most of the division arrived by sea, but Taylor and part of the division staff flew in
on July 16. Ridgway had some senior casualties to replace, including his assistant division commander Brigadier General Charles
Keerans, who was one of the victims of friendly fire. Whatever
misgivings Ridgway may have harbored about Taylor as his chief
of staff, he appears not to have hesitated in naming him to Keerans's slot.

The division soon marched northward from Gela up Sicily's
west coast, for the most part encountering only light resistance.
Conscious of the defects of the airborne portion of Husky, the
division and its leaders were chafing at the bit. None of its stars—
luminaries like Ridgway and Gavin as well as Taylor—was ever
disposed to lead from the rear, and this characteristic soon
brought a clash of egos. Ridgway has related how, near Trapani,

> I was up with the advance guard, expecting momentarily to get a
> salvo on the road, when I looked around to see General Maxwell
> Taylor, my division artillery commander, standing by my side,
> watching the shell bursts casually, with an artillery man's ap-
> praising eye. . . . It distressed me to see Max up there, for one
> shell could have gotten us both, leaving the division without a
> top command. So I told Max, by God, he was to get back until I
> sent for him. . . . I talked pretty strongly to Max, for I knew he
> had all the courage in the world . . . but someone had to stay
> back at the CP and I knew it wasn't going to be me.[8]

The land campaign in Sicily proved to be undemanding. Taylor
himself called it "as pleasant a campaign as one is likely to have in
a war." One day, in the mountains north of Castelvetrano, Taylor
wanted to check the progress of an element of the division operating on the other side of a ridge. Seeing that his map showed a trail
over the ridge, he and a driver took the shortcut indicated, bounc-

ing into a small village. There, in the village square, Taylor and his driver found themselves among what appeared to be the entire Italian Army. The Italians, however, proved notably unwarlike, strolling about and otherwise indicating disinterest in their visitors. In Taylor's words:

> Since there was no retreating, I rose in my jeep, raised my hand in a military salute and drove by them. In a testimonial to the irresistibility of ingrained military discipline, most of the soldiers struggled to their feet and stared at us as we passed by and out the gate leading down the hill to the next valley. Not a shot was fired.[9]

The airborne portion of Husky proved almost the only negative in a highly successful campaign, one that set the stage for Italy's surrender. But in Ridgway's headquarters and especially in Washington the feasibility of parachute operations came in for scrutiny. Critics in the War Department argued that paratroopers might best be employed in small groups for sabotage operations behind enemy lines. (This is how they were subsequently employed by the Germans, although less from preference than from dwindling resources.) In opposing any reduction of the airborne role, Ridgway and Taylor argued that the deficiencies revealed in Sicily were correctable. All agreed that much remained to be done in the area of joint training with Troop Carrier Command and in navigation.

Hitler was able to rescue the bulk of his two panzer divisions from Sicily, but Allied control of the island made an invasion of Italy feasible and, to many observers, likely. By the summer of 1943, Mussolini's once-feared navy had been rendered impotent by a combination of fuel shortages and weak leadership. Italy itself was under attack from Allied bombers, and Italian morale was sagging everywhere. With this background the Grand Fascist Council convened in July for the first time since 1939. After ten hours of deliberation, it voted Mussolini out of the premiership and replaced him with seventy-three-year-old Pietro Badoglio, the "Victor of Ethiopia."

On July 23 General Eisenhower issued a statement in which he applauded the deposition of Mussolini and indicated that he was prepared to deal with the Badoglio government. But there was some question as to what was negotiable, because the Allies, at the Casablanca conference in January, had gone on record as demanding "unconditional surrender."

Hitler, for one, had a clear understanding of what would ensue. "Undoubtedly . . . [the Italians] will proclaim that they will remain loyal to us; but this is treachery. Of course they won't remain loyal."[10] The Führer had judged his man well, for Badoglio would prove as devious in his dealings with the Germans as he was with the Allies. From the outset, both Eisenhower and Badoglio wanted to see Italy out of the war. As to how this was to be accomplished, however, they marched to different drummers. Eisenhower was prepared to impose unconditional surrender, with all that this implied. But he was willing to leave the door open a crack: if Italy were to assist the Allies against the Germans, the terms of a final settlement with Italy might be considerably softened. Badoglio had a different agenda. He wanted the Allies to spare Rome and to rescue his government from Nazi vengeance. He had no desire to continue the war on anyone's side.

Unlike Hitler, the German commander in Italy, Field Marshal Albert Kesselring, was initially ready to accept the Italian professions of loyalty. He also expected an Allied invasion of Italy. He thought the Naples-Salerno area the most likely invasion site but could not rule out the possibility that the island of Sardinia was next on the Allied agenda. Only after air reconnaissance revealed troop loadings in North Africa well in excess of what might be required for Sardinia was Kesselring reasonably sure that the Italian mainland was the Allied target. The coast near Rome was one possible landing area but there were many others as well. The Germans viewed their two reinforced divisions near Rome as sufficient to safeguard the capital against most contingencies, but they could hardly turn back a seaborne invasion in which the Italians assisted the Allies.

While Kesselring attempted to plan for all possibilities, an emissary from Badoglio, General Guiseppe Castellano, was conducting secret negotiations with the Allies. In late August, there was still some question as to whether Italy would sign an armistice at all. Even less certain was the matter of whether the Badoglio government was prepared to carry on as a cobelligerent against the Germans. On August 31 Castellano met with Eisenhower's chief of staff, Taylor's old friend Beetle Smith, at Cassibile in Sicily. Smith opened the conference by asking whether the Italian was empowered to sign an armistice. The wily Castellano replied by quoting at length from a memorandum that put forth a very pessimistic appraisal of the situation on the mainland. Because of the threat of German retaliation, he said, no armistice could be announced before the main Allied landings. And the Badoglio government had to be certain that the Allied landings were in sufficient strength to guarantee the security of Rome. Because of the inferiority of their equipment, the Italians could not stand up to the Germans alone.

Smith, who was assisted by State Department representative Robert Murphy and British political adviser Harold Macmillan, told Castellano that his proposal was unacceptable. He offered two alternatives: Italy could accept an armistice under the terms previously outlined, or Italy could refuse it. Smith noted that Eisenhower had little room for maneuver under the terms of the Casablanca declaration and that if Italy did not agree to an armistice the problem would be turned over to the Allied governments, which could be expected to impose the harshest conditions. The stakes at Cassibile were high. The Allies had available only about fifteen divisions for Italy and believed it essential that the Germans be obliged to divert some resources to neutralizing the Italians. But for Italy the stakes may have been even higher. Italy's refusal to accept a military armistice, with the possibility that later collaboration with the Allies might favorably modify its terms, threatened an overthrow of the dynasty and the collapse of the Badoglio regime.

The discussions with the Italian emissary had made it clear that Badoglio and his colleagues feared the Germans more than the Allies. In due course Castellano returned to Rome for instructions, leaving the Allies to ponder how the change of government in Italy might yet be turned into an asset. One possibility might be for the Allies to hold out the prospect of securing Rome. Allied planners had considered and then discarded two plans for employing the 82d Division in Italy. Now, at the eleventh hour, Eisenhower's staff drew up a new plan, called Giant II, in which the 82d would launch an airborne assault near Rome and there help Italian units protect the city until such time as the Germans would have to devote their full attention to the Allied seaborne invasion.

On September 1 Ridgway and Taylor were called to General Harold Alexander's 15th Army Group headquarters and informed for the first time of the projected use of the 82d against Rome. In addition to mollifying the Italians, Giant II promised tangible military benefits. Operating in concert with the Italians, the 82d might gain control of the highways on which the Germans would be sending reinforcements against the Allied beachhead at Salerno. The loss of Rome and its environs in turn could even induce the Germans to pull back from southern Italy altogether. Taylor was impressed with the possibilities of the mission but he was very much aware of the pressure that Smith was putting on the Italians. "Little as I knew of the situation in and around Rome," he would write, "I could not believe that the Italians could do all the things to which Castellano was agreeing."[11]

Meanwhile, the Italian emissary was shuttling secretly to and from Rome, clarifying the complexities of the proposed armistice. Militarily, the main prize was Italy's fleet, but questions such as where the fleet would surrender were straightforward compared with the uncertainties surrounding Giant II. Would the surrender of Italy's ground forces prove to be entirely passive, or could the Allies count on a degree of assistance once Rome was secure? The complications in this hectic first week of September ran from the technical—whether or not Castellano was authorized to sign the instrument of surrender—to the uncharted waters of military cooperation.

On September 3 Italy secretly accepted Eisenhower's surrender terms. Italian soldiers throughout Italy were to lay down their arms, and the Italian fleet, merchant marine, and air force were to be turned over to the Allies. The Fascist party was outlawed. It was agreed that, for the moment, a non-Fascist government would look after Italian internal affairs under Allied supervision.

Meanwhile, planning for Giant II proceeded. On the day of the Italian surrender, Ridgway and Taylor met with Castellano and the Allied staff to complete plans for the jump on Rome. In its final form, Giant II called for both parachute and air landing operations at five airfields in Rome's northern environs. At the same time, a sea convoy from Sicily was to move up the Tiber River bringing artillery and antitank weapons. Because of a continuing shortage of transport aircraft, the 82d was to be arrive in increments, with the first 2,000-man combat team landing on the night of September 8–9 at two airfields twenty-five miles from Rome. After what had happened to Tucker's jump in Sicily, Ridgway and Taylor demanded assurances that Italian antiaircraft batteries would not fire on American aircraft. Castellano assured the Americans that they would not.

In treating with Castellano, Taylor was mindful of the navigational problems that had plagued parachute operations in Sicily. To an Italian proposal that U.S. aircraft approach their drop zones from north of the city, Taylor replied that such routes would be hard to identify at night and that the transports should instead navigate up the Tiber. A final decision was deferred. Ridgway, meanwhile, was becoming increasingly skeptical as to whether the Italians were capable of delivering on Castellano's assurances that U.S. aircraft would not be fired on. When the emissary was recalled to consider this aspect, he conceded that the airfields in question were strongly protected and that a cease-fire might not be total.

By this time both Ridgway and Taylor had grave misgivings about the entire operation. Too much depended on the Italians. The plan required not only that they withhold fire but also that they illuminate the drop zones in a prearranged manner. Equally important, they were to provide several hundred trucks, plus gasoline, rations, and support services. The readiness with which Castellano undertook to provide so much, far from reassuring the Americans, only increased their apprehension.

On September 4 the two Americans went to see Alexander and Smith and spelled out their concern. Ridgway proposed that two officers, one from the 82d and one from the Troop Carrier Command, travel secretly to Rome to determine the feasibility of Giant II on the basis of what they saw and were told there. This proposal was approved, as was Ridgway's choice of Taylor as one of the two emissaries. His partner was to be Colonel William T. Gardiner, an

Air Force intelligence officer. Gardiner, age fifty-three, was a Harvard graduate and a private pilot. Before the war he had served a term as governor of Maine. He would bring an Air Force perspective to the talks, and he, like Taylor, was fluent in French, which was expected to be the language of the negotiations. On September 6 Taylor flew from Bizerte to Palermo, where he met with Gardiner. The two had only the most casual acquaintance, but the next two days would be among the most eventful of their careers.

Chapter 5

"SITUATION INNOCUOUS"

During the first week of September, while Allied convoys gathered for Operation Avalanche at Salerno, the 82d Airborne found itself once again in Tunisia. Soon, however, it would be back in Sicily, the island that it had helped capture just a short time before. Having completed the planning for Giant II on the night of September 3–4, Ridgway flew to Bizerte to brief his officers and prepare to return his division to Sicily.

Meanwhile, questions arose as to how much the Italians should be told about the two pending operations. On September 4 Castellano asked Beetle Smith when the amphibious landings would take place and when the armistice was to be announced. Smith declined to be precise but told Castellano that the invasion would take place "within two weeks." This was not especially helpful for the Italians, but Castellano appears to have had other sources of information. On September 5 he wrote to General Vittorio Ambrosio, the chairman of the Supreme General Staff: "I have not been able to get any information on the precise locality of the landing. Regarding the date I can say nothing precise; but from confidential information I presume that the landing will take place between the 10th and 15th of September, possibly the 12th."[1] Because Avalanche was in fact scheduled for September 9, Castellano planted the seed of a serious misconception.

Meanwhile, in Rome, Army Chief of Staff Mario Roatta was provided with a copy of the Giant II plan. In accordance with his government's commitments, he took action to move two additional Italian divisions to the Rome environs, but the pace was leisurely. He did not want to alarm the Germans, and he believed that he had a full week in which to make his dispositions. Even so, he was taken aback by what the American contemplated and by what was expected of the Italian Army. What Castellano had promised seemed far beyond his, Roatta's, capabilities. (British political adviser Harold Macmillan would characterize Roatta as "a travelled and intelligent conversationalist," but also as "a natural coward.")[2] There appears to have been no one in Rome who recognized that Giant II was the sole remaining avenue by which the Italians might yet work their way into Eisenhower's good graces. Badoglio, in particular, was notably passive. To him, Giant II was a lifeboat, not a vehicle by which Italy might redeem itself with the victors.

On September 6 the Italian high command responded to a request from Eisenhower by sending an eleven-man delegation to Allied headquarters at Bizerte. They carried with them several requests for modification of the agreed surrender scenario. In addition, they brought with them a request that Giant II take place two days after the Allied amphibious landing rather than simultaneously. They also emphasized that the amphibious landing should be within striking distance of Rome. This Avalanche clearly was not.

It was with these initial signs of Italian wavering that Taylor and Gardiner departed on their mission to Rome. At a briefing at Fifteenth Army Group headquarters, Allied leaders had decided that unless Taylor sent word to the contrary, the airborne operation would proceed as planned on the night of September 8. Taylor, in Rome, could recommend modification of the operation or its cancellation, as events dictated. Messages were to be sent in code on the facilities of the Italian Military Intelligence Service, but the Americans carried a small radio of their own as well. Should there be any subterfuge on the part of the Italians, the use of the word *innocuous* in any message was to constitute a recommendation that Giant II be scrubbed.

The two Americans departed from Palermo at 2 A.M. on September 7 in a British PT boat. By common consent they wore American uniforms devoid of any sign of rank; such "cover" as they had was to play the part of two enemy airmen rescued from the Mediterranean. Off the island of Ustica, some fifty miles north of Palermo, they rendezvoused with an Italian corvette, the *Ibis*. The two vessels exchanged recognition signals and the PT boat attempted to come alongside the *Ibis*, but there was just enough sea to make this impossible, and the transfer of passengers was accomplished by small boat. Once the Americans were on board, the *Ibis* made its way across the Tyrrhenian Sea to the port of Gaeta south of Rome. Their host on board was Rear Admiral Franco Maugeri, the chief of naval intelligence, who provided a private lunch for the three of them, all the while complaining about the perfidious English. In Taylor's view, Maugeri was all too knowledgeable concerning his and Gardiner's mission. If Maugeri knew so much, how many others had been told of their operation?

The *Ibis* reached Gaeta in the late afternoon, navigating carefully through minefields outside the port. At the dock, curious onlookers watched as Italian sailors prodded the "captive" Americans into a navy automobile. On the outskirts of town, Taylor, Gardiner, and their two escorts were transferred into a military ambulance for the seventy-five-mile drive up the Appian Way to Rome. Ambulance or not, Taylor would later recall the ride as notably uncomfortable. There were also roadblocks, but at each one the ambulance was waved on. It arrived in Rome at about 8:30 P.M., at one point passing a German patrol at close quarters. In Taylor's words, "I could have reached out and touched them."

At the Italian Supreme Headquarters at the Palazzo Caprara, the Americans were warmly greeted on behalf of General Giacomo Carboni, commander of the corps assigned to defend Rome. Two rooms on the third floor had been prepared for the visitors. Carboni himself was not available, however, and it soon developed that his superior, General Ambrosio, was out of town on private business. To their annoyance, the Americans were served a leisurely dinner on behalf of the absent Italian brass, who clearly viewed the situation with no sense of urgency. While Taylor and Gardiner looked at their watches, an Italian translator described General Carboni in glowing terms. According to the Italian, his chief's anti-Fascist views had jeopardized his career under Mussolini.

At Taylor's insistence, Carboni put in an appearance shortly after 10 P.M. In his beribboned tunic and polished boots, he impressed his visitors as something of a dandy. He arrived with a map showing the disposition of his own four divisions around

Rome, but his overall assessment was highly pessimistic. If the Italians were to declare an armistice, the Germans would occupy Rome and the Italians could do little to prevent it.

> Formerly there had been three thousand Germans to the south and eight thousand to the north of Rome. Since the change in government, German forces had come in through the Brenner Pass and also through Resia and Tarvisio, and now there were twelve thousand north of Rome with 120 heavy and 150 light tanks and twenty-four thousand troops to the south. . . . The Germans were well supplied and equipped. They had cut off the gasoline supply of the Italians and the Italians were short of ammunition, only twenty rounds [being available] for some pieces.[3]

According to Carboni, the arrival of U.S. airborne troops would only provoke the Germans to more drastic action. He believed that the Italians would be unable to secure the airfields, cover the assembly areas, and provide the necessary logistical aid to the airborne troops. If an Allied amphibious landing north of Rome were not possible, Carboni said, the only hope of saving the capital lay in avoiding overt acts against the Germans and awaiting results from the Allied landings in the south.[4]

Carboni's pessimism led the Americans to demand to see Badoglio himself. The Italians were reluctant to disturb their chief in the middle of the night, but the premier agreed to receive his visitors. Carboni drove the Americans in his own car to Badoglio's villa on the edge of town, through a city still blacked out from an Allied air raid.

Badoglio, looking "old and tired," received them in his pajamas. He first met privately with Carboni, however, leaving the Americans with the impression that Carboni had used the interval to bring the old marshal over to his way of thinking: that the Italians should do nothing but await rescue by the Allies. When Badoglio did receive the two Americans, he backed his subordinate completely, adding further that the armistice, which was already signed on his behalf, would have to be postponed and Giant II canceled. When Taylor asked whether the marshal realized how deeply his government was committed by arrangements already in place, Badoglio protested that the situation had changed. In the circumstances described by Carboni, Italian troops could not possibly defend Rome.

Taylor tried again. How, he asked, did Badoglio expect Allied leaders to react to this changed situation? The marshal could only reply that he hoped that the Americans would explain the Italian position to General Eisenhower. This Taylor refused to do, but he did indicate that he was prepared to convey to Eisenhower whatever message Badoglio chose to send. The result was a message from Badoglio, penned in the small hours of September 8, advising Eisenhower that it was "no longer possible" for his government to accept an armistice and that Giant II was not feasible "because of lack of forces to guarantee the airfields."[5] Taylor followed this message with one of his own:

> In view of the statement of Marshal Badoglio as to inability to declare armistice and to guarantee fields GIANT II is impossible. Reasons given for change are irreplaceable lack of gasoline and munitions and new German dispositions. Badoglio requests Taylor return to present government views. Taylor and Gardiner awaiting instructions. Acknowledge.[6]

Taylor signed off on this message at 1:21 A.M. He and Gardiner took their leave of Badoglio and returned to the Palazzo Caprara where they turned their messages over to Carboni for transmission. Some fourteen hours remained before the 82d would be on its way to a potentially disastrous drop. In due course, receipt of Badoglio's message was acknowledged by Allied headquarters. But what of Taylor's follow-up? Perhaps some amplification was required. At 8:20 A.M. Taylor sent a second message:

> Summary of situation as stated by Italian authorities. Germans have 12,000 troops in Tiber Valley. Panzer Grenadier Division increased by attachments to 24,000. Germans have stopped supply gasoline and munitions so that Italian divisions virtually immobilized and have munitions only for a few hours of combat. Shortages make impossible the successful defense of Rome and the provision of logistical aid promised airborne troops.[7]

The morning wore on, and the only message for which formal acknowledgment had been received was the first, that from Badoglio. Decoding was a time-consuming operation, and there was even the possibility of an unreported malfunction in transmission. At 11:35 A.M. Taylor sent his third message, one that consisted of only two words: "Situation innocuous."

That morning at his headquarters in Bizerte, Eisenhower received Badoglio's message and the first of the three from Taylor, who had noted that the Italians were apprehensive about the likely Allied reaction. Their concern was fully justified, for Eisenhower was furious at Badoglio's duplicity. He grabbed a pencil to write a reply, broke it, took up another and broke it also before he gave up and dictated his reply:

> I intend to broadcast the existence of the armistice at the hour originally planned. If you . . . fail to cooperate as previously agreed I will publish to the world the full record of this affair. Failure now on your part to carry out the full obligations to the signed agreement will have the most serious consequences for your country.[8]

Reluctantly, Eisenhower directed cancellation of Giant II. In Rome, Taylor and Gardiner waited for a reply to yet another message, this one requesting authority to bring with them an emissary from Badoglio to explain the Italian position. In the absence of a reply, the two agreed to take with them General Rossi, the deputy chief of the Supreme General Staff. At 3 P.M. they received a message from Eisenhower's headquarters directing them to return home. Once more the American officers set out by ambulance across enemy-controlled Rome. This time their goal was Centocelli airfield on the outskirts of the city, where a trimotor Savoia Marchetti bomber was waiting to return them to Tunisia. Far from relaxing, Taylor found this leg the most nerve-racking of the journey. Although the Italians assured him that the flight plan had been cleared with both the Italian and Allied air forces, Taylor by then had little confidence in such assurances. His apprehension appeared fully justified when a U.S. fighter made a pass as the Italian aircraft crossed the North African coast. But the American pilot held his fire.

Remarkably, the drama of Giant II did not end with the return of the two American emissaries. Taylor's first message recommending cancellation was not received and decoded in Bizerte until late in the morning of September 8. With only seven hours remaining until takeoff time for the 82d, Allied commanders were uncertain whether even a priority message to Sicily would be delivered and decoded in time to abort the mission. To be on the safe side, Alexander directed Lemnitzer to fly from Bizerte to the 82d's primary airfield at Licata to assure that there was no slipup. Lemnitzer took off in a British night fighter, squeezed in behind the pilot.

Alas, their navigation was faulty. Not until Mount Etna loomed was the pilot able to verify his location and set a belated course for Licata. On the ground, Ridgway listened to Eisenhower's announcement of the Italian armistice—his signal to take off. Overhead, some sixty C-47s were already aloft, awaiting word to proceed. Lemnitzer and his pilot waited anxiously for an opportunity to land without endangering either themselves or one of the transports. Lemnitzer finally landed and rushed over to Ridgway with word of the cancellation. Almost simultaneously, Ridgway received the radio message to that effect. All things considered, it had been a very near thing.

Taylor made a brief report to Eisenhower at his headquarters near Tunis, then headed for a bunk. He tossed his musette bag into a corner, "where the sound of smashing glass [from] my forgotten bottle of Scotch provided a fitting end to a disappointing mission."[9]

In the course of his long career Taylor would come in for criticism from a variety of sources on a number of issues. Where matters of substance were involved, as in his opposition to President Eisenhower's defense priorities and in matters relating to Vietnam, Taylor would go to some pains to document the bases for his actions. The one remaining area of some criticism—his recommendation to cancel Giant II—caused him no small irritation.

One source of criticism was the acerbic Beetle Smith, who had lobbied hard for Giant II. Even after the war, Smith complained that it had been a mistake to send an airborne specialist into

Rome. What had been needed was a forceful "generalist" who might have told Badoglio, "See here, you signed this agreement— and if you don't live up to it—you will all be lined up against the wall and shot."[10] Robert Murphy, one of Eisenhower's political advisers, appears to have given considerable credence to Italian professions of good faith. Writing in 1964, Murphy recalled that "the Italian Army chiefs who had conferred with us in Sicily denied that they had withdrawn support. It has always been my feeling that our airborne commanders had set their minds against this expedition from the start for standard military reasons and because nobody trusted Italians."[11]

The most categorical criticism of Taylor's actions was by the American naval historian Samuel Morison. In his history of World War II naval operations Morison characterized the cancellation of Giant II as "a great opportunity lost":

> General Carboni had grossly exaggerated the strength of the Germans near Rome and minimized that of the Italian Army in Rome. An air drop on Rome was what the Germans most feared. . . . General Taylor, an airborne specialist, saw the difficulties all too readily and had neither the wit nor the information to call Carboni's bluff. We should resolutely have gone ahead with the drop; Badoglio would not have dared not to cooperate, since he knew that if he did not, his government and his king would be overthrown. It might have failed, as all such operations are very risky, but the certain benefits from its success were vast, out of all proportion to the possible damage from failure.[12]

By any standard, Morison's argument is flawed. To be sure, Kesselring was concerned about an airborne attack; it was one more contingency to worry about, and he probably thought of an airborne operation in terms of the Germans' own inundation of Crete. As for Italian cooperation, it is difficult to imagine a weaker reed on which to risk an elite division. Nothing in his behavior before or after Avalanche suggests that Badoglio could have been browbeaten into fighting the Germans. Indeed, the first thing he and his ministers did after the Salerno landings was to evacuate Rome, leaving the populace to whatever fate the Germans might decree.

A far stronger case could be made that Giant II was harebrained from the start. Barring a sterling performance by the Italians, the 82d would have found itself in an untenable position. The Germans had a paratroop division of their own, with 88-mm guns and armor, along the south bank of the Tiber, well situated to block any move by the Americans from their drop zones to Rome proper. In addition, they had a reinforced panzer division, the 3d, only forty miles north of Rome. Taylor would write in his memoirs:

> Had we decided to go ahead with GIANT II in spite of the refusal of the Italians to cooperate with us, we could never have introduced more than the first night's increment of about 2,500 troops. . . . They would have landed twenty-five miles from Rome with no trucks, few supplies, and limited ammunition. With surprise lost after the first night's landing, and no Italian antiaircraft defense of the airfields, the German air force would never have allowed further reinforcements to arrive from Sicily by air. . . . What [the 82d] could have accomplished under these circumstances I certainly do not know, but I have never regretted the decision which spared these elite troops to serve their country with distinction at Salerno, Anzio, Normandy and elsewhere rather than end their useful days in Italian graves or German prisons.[13]

Cancellation of Giant II, however fortunate, was a disappointment to airborne commanders, for they badly needed a success that would vindicate the employment of airborne forces in large-scale units. In Washington there was serious discussion as to whether, in the wake of Sicily, paratroops could be effectively employed in the invasion of Europe. Marshall was still a believer, but McNair was not, and Eisenhower's position was not yet clear. No one could overlook the fact that no airborne operation in the Mediterranean—American or British—had gone remotely according to plan.

Meanwhile, circumstances had once again separated Taylor from his division. Following cancellation of Giant II, the 82d was employed in a ground capacity to buttress Clark's Fifth Army in the seaborne operation at Salerno. Taylor, however, had by then been tagged as an instant Italian expert and was detailed to the Allied Control Commission that was to deal with the Badoglio government in Brindisi. On September 11 he flew to Taranto in a B-17 bomber, in the company of the British head of delegation, Noel Mason-MacFarlane, and two political advisers, Robert Murphy and his British counterpart, future Prime Minister Harold Macmillan. There was no welcome mat at Taranto; the four deplaned in midday heat at a deserted airfield, surrounded by abandoned German and Italian aircraft. From the north came the sound of firing, indicating that the newly arrived British 1st Airborne Division was encountering some resistance. Walking out to a dirt road, the Anglo-American quartet commandeered a staff car from an indignant Italian colonel and took off on the twenty-five-mile drive to Brindisi. Years later Taylor recalled:

> We were four big men, and the seams of the little car seemed to stretch as it bounced over the road toward Brindisi. We were stopped frequently at road blocks by Italian soldiers who demanded our papers, but we were gaining confidence in our role of Allied conquerors, and scorning all requests for *documenti*, brushed by the barricades.[14]

The Allied mission reached Brindisi in the late afternoon and proceeded to make contact with Badoglio. For three months Taylor acted as chief of staff to the Allied Control Commission, one of the many quasi-political positions he would occupy during his long military career. Harold Macmillan found the American brigadier "charming [and] intelligent"; he noted in his diary that Taylor had studied "Italian in Twenty Lessons" and was "jolly good."[15]

Mason-MacFarlane, known as "Mason-Mac," set up shop in the same medieval castle that housed the Badoglio government, and the members of the Control Commission had splendid quarters overlooking the Adriatic. Much of the commission's time was spent in reviewing proposed appointees to cabinet and other senior positions in the Badoglio government, for these had to be untainted by close association with the Fascists. Taylor recalled that one of his most useful services to Badoglio was of a highly unofficial nature. Shortly after he had arrived, the marshal asked with some embarrassment whether Taylor could find him a set of underwear: he had left Rome with only what he was wearing.

In December the 82d moved from Italy to Northern Ireland, there to begin training for Operation Overlord, the invasion of Normandy. On General Mark Clark's insistence, however, the division left behind Colonel Reuben Tucker's 504th Regimental Combat Team. This detailing of the 504th grew out of a compromise that satisfied no one: Clark wanted to keep the entire 82d in his command, whereas Ridgway wanted to train his division as a unit. For Taylor, all this meant one more move. Beetle Smith made good on his promise to relieve him from the Allied Control Commission, but Ridgway ordered him to remain at Fifth Army headquarters to secure the return of the 504th as soon as possible. Although Taylor was very much in demand, his position with Ridgway was something less than secure. Even as he laid this latest task on Taylor, Ridgway named thirty-six-year-old Jim Gavin to be his assistant division commander, the position Taylor had occupied on a temporary basis. Although both Eisenhower and Ridgway were appreciative of the risks he had run in Rome, Taylor was clearly in danger of losing his identification with the 82d Division.

Clark ultimately released the 504th, and Taylor was free to join the 82d in England. The mobilization for Overlord was in full cry. General Eisenhower had arrived in England to take up his duties as supreme commander. In a period of less than six months he would be prepared to undertake the most demanding operation of the war, an assault across the English Channel against an entrenched and battle-hardened defender.

Part Two

THE
WARRIOR

Where is the prince who can afford so to cover
his country with troops for its defense as that ten
thousand men descending from the clouds might not
in many places do an infinite deal of mischief
before a force could be brought together
to repel them?

—*Benjamin Franklin*
letter to Jan Ingenhousz, 1784

Chapter 6

NORMANDY

At the time Eisenhower took command of the Allied forces destined for Europe there were some 750,000 American troops in Britain. Among them was the newly arrived 101st Airborne Division. The 101st had embarked from New York in August in two venerable British vessels, the Cunard *Samaria* and the P and O liner *Strathnaver*. The latter had broken down en route and had only reached Liverpool a full six weeks after departing New York, its reluctant passengers crammed into every space on the ship. In due course the 101st was billeted in southern England, and some paratroopers could scarcely believe the transition from a leaky steamer in the North Atlantic to a farmhouse in the verdant English countryside. "When I woke up the next morning," one soldier recalled, "I thought I'd passed out on a Hollywood movie set. All around the area were fairy-book cottages with thatched roofs and rose vines on their sides."[1] The same paratroopers who at home would have trashed a bar at the slightest provocation adapted surprisingly well to their new surroundings. Explicit briefings on their "guest" status were certainly a factor, but whatever their motivation, the Screaming Eagles settled into their camps with remarkably little friction.

With the arrival of winter the training pace quickened. The airborne ethic called for officers to do anything, within reason, required of their men; and the 101st's commander, General Bill Lee, would pay a price for this strenuous regimen. In early February, while on a training exercise, he complained of chest pains and was hospitalized. When the diagnosis was a severe heart condition, there could be no question of his leading the 101st into Normandy. The only issue was the choice of a successor. The assistant division commander, General Don Pratt, took temporary command, but there was no thought that his appointment was permanent.

After consulting with Omar Bradley, Eisenhower cabled Marshall on February 9 that "my present thought is to take Brigadier General Max Taylor from the 82d Airborne Division to replace Lee [but] . . . it occurs to me that you might prefer to send an airborne division commander from the States. . . . If not, I am sure Taylor will make a good division commander, and he has the advantage of combat experience." Marshall's reply was a model of brevity: "If you prefer Taylor to Miley or Chapman assign him accordingly."[2]

In the aftermath of Sicily, there was considerable skepticism concerning the proposed use of airborne troops in Overlord. Nevertheless, both Marshall and Eisenhower felt that the Allies should exact the maximum utility from these expensive assets, and both divisions had had their personnel strength increased. But where might these elite divisions best be employed? Generals Marshall and Hap Arnold, reviewing the invasion plans, favored a bold use of parachute forces in the French interior, in a manner that would threaten some of the Seine River crossings or even Paris itself. Acknowledging that such an operation had never been attempted, Marshall nevertheless pressed it as one that would oblige the enemy to make major revisions in his defense plans.

Eisenhower pondered, and in the end opted for a more conservative course. He would employ both American divisions to secure the areas immediately inland from Utah Beach on the Cotentin Peninsula. There was important opposition to the employment of airborne forces at all, led by the senior British airman, Air Marshal Trafford Leigh-Mallory. In his view, the German losses in Crete and the American debacle in Sicily constituted strong evidence that airborne forces in their slow transports could not be permitted to overfly heavily defended areas. Although the air drops for Neptune, the airborne component of Overlord, were designed to take maximum advantage of surprise, Leigh-Mallory was still stressing his opposition to the "very speculative" airborne operation as late as a month before the invasion. If Neptune were not canceled altogether (it involved the British 6th Airborne Division as well as the Americans), Leigh-Mallory wanted all glider landings to be at dusk rather than dawn on D-day. Ridgway, however, argued successfully that the lightly armed airborne units would require their full artillery and communications support if they were to engage the Germans on the first day. Ridgway carried his point, although there was growing concern over the physical obstacles to a successful glider operation. Tall poles erected across possible landing areas—"Rommel asparagus"—were one problem, and the Norman hedgerows were equally hazardous. A typical hedgerow, designed to control cattle, began with a wire fence about three feet high. Dirt was packed in generous quantities around the fence creating a solid ridge; on top of this the farmers planted shrubs and trees that often grew to a height of ten feet or more. For the defending Germans, every hedgerow represented a natural defensive barrier. For an incoming glider, difficult to maneuver with its heavy load, every hedgerow was a potential death trap.

Taylor's appointment to command to the 101st was not entirely unexpected, but there was considerable potential for friction. Not only was the Missourian a latecomer to the paratroops but he had no prior connection with the 101st. Although Taylor later maintained that the 101st gave him a warm welcome, not everyone was pleased at being handed a late-blooming artilleryman from the archrival 82d. Colonel Jerry Higgins, the chief of staff of the 101st, knowing that many division commanders liked to pick their own senior staff, volunteered to request a transfer so that Taylor could have his own man. According to Higgins, Taylor responded to his offer with a bemused expression. "Jerry," he said, "you were selected to be chief of staff of this division by Bill Lee. If you were good enough for him you are sure good enough for me."[3] Incidents like this won quick acceptance for the newcomer.

Taylor took command of his division on March 14 and soon was deeply involved in the planning for Neptune. He was fortunate to be working under two officers with whom he had prior acquaintance. Commanding the VII Corps, which included the two American airborne divisions, was General "Lightning Joe" Collins, who had been one of Taylor's instructors at the War College. The hard-driving Collins had had the unusual experience of having commanded a division in the Pacific before coming to England.

Marshall had suggested to MacArthur that Collins would make a fine corps commander, and when MacArthur pronounced the forty-seven-year-old Collins too young for such responsibility, Marshall called him to Eisenhower's attention. Collins's corps was part of the First U.S. Army, commanded by Omar Bradley. Taylor's contact with Bradley had been limited, but he always credited Bradley with having urged his selection as Lee's successor.

If there was any "secret" to Taylor's wartime success with the 101st—he would insist that no magic was required in leading such fighting men—it was his attention to detail. As division commander he sought to anticipate every contingency and to provide training so realistic as to condition his men for anything they might encounter. In preparing for Overlord, the VII Corps staged two amphibious landings to simulate the forthcoming assault on Utah Beach. The 101st participated in both, replicating, without the jump, the hoped-for linkup between the 101st and the 4th Division advancing from the beach.

Taylor would later maintain that he never "worried" about the performance of his division on D-day. Nevertheless, no untried division had ever been given a more challenging assignment. The practice in World War I had been to allow a new division to "get its bearings" in a quiet sector of the front before making heavy demands of it. In Operation Neptune there would be no "quiet" sector for the Screaming Eagles. They would simply be plunged into the maelstrom, where their youth could prove either an asset or a liability. An officer of the 101st later reflected on this factor:

> Among the paratroopers the average age was nineteen. Officers averaged 22–23 years, while enlisted men were mostly 17- and 18-year-olds. Battalion commanders were in their mid-twenties, while regimental commanders were in their thirties. Our viewpoints were those of young men, and we did not question orders. If told to attack—with or without supporting artillery or air support—we did. Perhaps we didn't know better.[4]

Because Collins's exercise had not included a jump, Taylor pressed successfully for an additional maneuver, code-named Eagle. In this exercise he sought to match closely the forthcoming D-day scenario. Division elements were trucked in darkness to their designated airfields, where more than four hundred aircraft and fifty-five gliders carried 6,000 men to drop zones resembling those in Normandy. The exercise was remarkably successful; an estimated 75 percent of the paratroopers landed in or near their designated drop zones, and forty-four out of the fifty-five gliders made it safely to their landing areas. Still, Eagle identified some shortfalls including, in Taylor's judgment, problems in locating equipment dropped by parachute and in distinguishing friend from foe. To help locate equipment dropped at night he ordered a supply of luminous cord from the United States. For the second problem he had an imaginative solution: heavy-duty metal "crickets" that gave out a loud double chirp when squeezed.

A more serious concern was that of assuring that the maximum number of aircraft made it to the drop zones. A few days after Eagle, Taylor, in a letter to the commander of the IX Troop Carrier Command, noted that twenty-eight aircraft had returned to their airfields without carrying out their drops. Taylor said that if D-day should see a similar failure rate he was prepared to court-martial for "misbehavior in the presence of the enemy" any paratroopers who refused to jump. He hoped that the Troop Carrier Command would consider taking similar action "against pilots who are responsible for failure to drop their loads."[5]

In March, Prime Minister Churchill and General Eisenhower made a joint inspection visit to the 101st. The Screaming Eagles naturally went all out for their visitors, providing not only briefings but a demonstration jump. A dinner hosted by Churchill aboard his special train afforded Taylor his first contact with the Prime Minister. Unaccustomed to Churchill's extreme working hours—the Prime Minister customarily arose in late morning and worked far into the night—Taylor was a bit taken aback by the evening:

> Churchill was just getting up from a nap when we arrived at the train, and he appeared tired and a bit grumpy. However, drinks were soon passed, and he seized upon a large glass of cognac. Soon the color was back in his jowls and the sparkle in his eyes. He began to reminisce about the Boer War, and by the time dinner was served he had us in the midst of World War I. He

remained in superb form throughout the evening, keeping us early-rising soldiers well beyond our normal bedtime.[6]

Ridgway and Taylor were consulted from the outset concerning the execution of Neptune, but the plans were so tightly held that not until mid-May was Taylor authorized to brief his own key officers. And even then no date was given. Recalling the 82d's scattered drop in Sicily, Taylor insisted that his officers familiarize themselves not only with the missions of their own units but with those of neighboring units as well. Working at sand tables, division officers committed to memory the principal terrain features of the Cotentin Peninsula.

Neptune called for the 101st's parachute component, 6,600 men in three regiments, to land in darkness and to secure four causeways leading inland from Utah Beach. It was a vital assignment, for the Germans had flooded low-lying areas behind the landing area, obliging any invasion force to funnel across a handful of causeways to advance. Failure to control these roads would halt the seaborne invasion in its tracks. After securing the causeways, the 101st had two other missions: to protect the southern flank of the VII Corps and in particular to destroy the bridges over the Douve River north of Carentan. For the 101st, Neptune would be essentially a parachute operation. The one area in which Leigh-Mallory's pessimism carried the day concerned the employment of gliders. Because the gliders would presumably come in after the Germans had been thoroughly alerted by the paratroops, the division was allocated only fifty-two gliders, enough for about three hundred men and some artillery. Most of the 327th Glider Regiment became part of the seaborne landing.

For all the obstacles in the way of the cross-Channel invasion, there were also factors operating in its favor. Field Marshal Rommel, in overall command of the German defenses, had not been given time to complete his elaborate system of underwater obstacles or to install antiglider obstacles at all potential landing areas inland. Even more important, Allied intelligence services had been remarkably successful in deceiving the Germans as to the actual invasion site. A welter of conflicting indicators led Hitler to conclude that the Allied target would in fact be Cotentin, but his military leaders were convinced that the principal Allied thrust must be directly across the Channel to the Pas-de-Calais area. Finally, the actual invasion date, June 6, found the Germans in a low state of readiness, in part because their meteorologists had predicted sufficiently inclement weather to preclude a major amphibious operation at that time.

Nevertheless, the forces available to the Germans around Cotentin were formidable. They had three divisions on the peninsula: the 709th in the north and along the east coast, the 243d along the west coast, and the newly arrived 91st at the base of the peninsula. South of Carentan, moreover, was one of the Wehrmacht's elite units, the 6th Parachute Regiment. Properly handled, these forces were capable of repelling any seaborne invasion if the Allies were denied time to consolidate.

In late May, Taylor began a series of visits to the various staging areas, seventeen in all, in which the units of his division were confined in the days immediately preceding the invasion. Taylor sported none of the affectations of leadership—no grenades, no pearl-handle pistols—but he was an extremely effective speaker and transmitted his own sense of purpose. In a series of pep talks, many delivered from the hood of his jeep, he sought to imbue his men with his own sense of being on a historic mission. A former sergeant with the Screaming Eagles, Fred Patheiger, later recalled part of his unit's pep talk. "All paratroopers are hell-raisers," Taylor had said. "During the first 24 hours after you jump, raise all the hell you can."[7]

The division command post in England was the manor house at Greenham Common, near Newbury. The seven airfields that the division would use on D-day were all located within a few miles of one another. The invasion had originally been set for June 5, but weather forecasts were so unpromising that Eisenhower directed a twenty-four-hour postponement, and a message to this effect reached Newbury on June 4. Taylor's reaction was one of keen disappointment, for he feared a loss of the momentum that had been building in the preceding weeks.

Faced with a rare free day, he sought to work off a little energy. Among the visitors from London for the postponed takeoff was

Colonel Frank "Froggie" Reed, a squash partner of prewar years, and Taylor proposed a game at a nearby court. In the midst of one hard-fought point Taylor felt a pop in his left leg. He had torn a tendon. By evening he could hardly walk and was thinking ruefully of the load that he would carry into battle the following day.

June 6 brought other visitors to Greenham Common. Most conspicuous was Eisenhower, who had dinner at the division mess and drove to an airfield that evening to see off the first of the paratroopers. Taylor would enjoy recalling how Ike went from plane to plane, defusing the pre-H-hour tension with the warmth of his personality.

> "What is your job, soldier?"
> "Ammunition bearer, sir. . . ."
> "Where is your home?"
> "Pennsylvania, sir."
> "Did you get those shoulders working in a coal mine?"
> "Yes sir."
> "Good luck to you tonight, soldier!"[8]

Once the visiting was past, Taylor was subjected to much the same combat dress procedure as his soldiers. All were weighed down "like medieval knights in armor," in jumpsuits crammed with ammunition, grenades, first aid supplies, and rations.

> Over the jumpsuits they wore pistol belts, supported by suspenders, to which were attached ammo clips, canteens, shovels, first-aid kits, .45 caliber pistols, bayonets, compasses and musette bags containing extra socks, cigarets, ammo and, usually, a ten-pound antitank mine. They strapped gas masks and trench knives to their legs or boots. . . . Then came the main parachute and its integral harness, which included a large "belly band" designed to hold the backpack snug. Weapons (M-1 rifles or carbines) were jammed inside the "belly band" butt upward at the shoulder, either in one piece or broken down in Griswold containers. Next—for the overwater flight—came a Mae West inflatable life preserver. Lastly came the reserve chest parachute . . . and a steel helmet, held in place by a chin strap and cup.[9]

In all, a paratrooper carried between 125 and 150 pounds of gear into battle. The forty-two-year-old Taylor had a few breaks. He carried an officer's .32 caliber pistol in lieu of a rifle, and he dispensed with the antitank mine and a few other accoutrements. In place of a shovel he carried a bottle of Irish whiskey strapped to his game leg—the one he did not plan to land on.

Takeoff time for Taylor's aircraft was around 10:45 P.M. But night comes late in the English summer, and there was still light as convoys of trucks offloaded the American paratroopers by their waiting aircraft. For most of the 430-odd aircraft conveying the 101st, the 130-mile flight would last for about three hours, much of this consumed in assuming flight formation over England. The routes of both the 101st and the 82d would carry them over the Cotentin Peninsula from the west, away from the Allied sea armada approaching from the east. Taylor's C-47 was part of a forty-five-plane formation, most of which carried elements of the 501st Parachute Infantry Regiment. The division commander would later recall his flight across the Channel as uneventful, with some members of his sixteen-man stick even dozing in their bucket seats. He himself regarded the takeoff with a feeling of relief after the demands of the previous weeks.

As the formation of C-47s approached the Normandy coast at about 1,500 feet, it entered an unexpected fog bank. The fog turned out to be less extensive than feared at first, but it effectively destroyed the V formation, as pilots, unable to check the wing lights of their neighbors, altered speed and altitude. At that moment Taylor had cause for satisfaction that he had trained his division to expect the worst in terms of their drop.

The composite landing area for the two American airborne divisions was some twelve miles long and four to seven miles wide. The goal for Taylor's own stick was Drop Zone C, one of the two southernmost drop zones of the five being used by the 101st and the 82d. There was barely time for a final equipment check as the fog broke and Taylor looked out the open door into the night. "It was a wonderful sight," he recalled, "to stand in the open door of the plane and look across the plains of Normandy in moonlight. The sky seemed to blaze with the flare of rockets and of tracer bullets. Here and there burning planes on the ground cast a glow over the Norman countryside."[10] George Koskimaki, a radioman in Taylor's stick, has given his description of the jump sequence:

> I suddenly noticed the red light appear on the panel over the open doorway and at that moment Jumpmaster Lawrence Legere was the most important person in our group as he yelled, "Get ready!" . . . Next came the order to "Hook up!" The snap of the anchor line fastener clicking into place could be heard the full length of the cabin. Each man made doubly sure he had hooked his static line to the cable running overhead down the center of the ceiling.
>
> Next came the order to "Check your equipment!" Each man checked the connections of the man directly in front of him to make sure all items were secure. . . .
>
> Above the roar of the engines could be heard the call, "Sound off for equipment check!" From far forward could be heard "Sixteen—OK," "Fifteen—OK," "Fourteen—OK," right on down to General Taylor who bellowed, "Two—OK!"[11]

Finally the green light went on. Taylor followed Legere out the door, leading the cry of "Bill Lee!"

The jump had been carried out at about seven hundred feet, so Taylor had little time for sightseeing on his descent. A gust of wind carried him away from his companions across a line of trees where he landed with a jolt, fortunately, on his good leg. He found himself in a field with several cows, who evinced no more than normal curiosity, but like many of his soldiers he had great difficulty in extricating himself from his parachute. Taylor later reckoned that it took at least ten minutes for him to get free, and he accomplished this only by cutting away the harness. (In this he was more fortunate than one of his soldiers, who hacked off the tip of one thumb while cutting his way out of his harness.) He could see no sign of other Americans, and from a neighboring field came the ominous sound of a German machine pistol, "like the ripping of a seat of pants." In his haste to get moving he abandoned the bottle of whiskey so carefully attached at Greenham Common.

Pistol in hand, the division commander made his way along a

hedgerow in what he supposed to be the direction of others in his stick. He saw with some apprehension that he was in an area of new entrenchments: where there were entrenchments there were likely to be Germans. After some twenty minutes he heard the sound of movement along his hedgerow. When he heard the sound of a "cricket," he responded in kind. "There in the dim moonlight was the first American soldier to greet me, a sight of martial beauty as he stood barcheaded, rifle in hand, bayonet fixed, and apparently ready for everything."[12]* The two embraced briefly, then moved off in search of others.

It took the remainder of the short summer night for Taylor to assemble a few dozen soldiers. They represented many units and many skills, and the radio operators, cooks, and clerical personnel far outnumbered the available riflemen. Taylor himself had landed only a mile and a half from his designated drop zone. Most others, it was clear, had been far less fortunate. Those in assembly areas could count themselves lucky to be alive and unhurt. Father Francis Sampson, the Catholic chaplain in the 506th, landed in water over his head and nearly drowned before finding his footing. He then made five or six dives in the course of recovering his Mass kit. Private Donald Burgett watched from the ground as one C-47 came in low and diagonally across the field where he had just landed. The parachutes were just starting to open as the seventeen-man stick hit the ground; Burgett thought they made a sound "like large ripe pumpkins being thrown down to burst against the ground."[13]

Taylor called his officers together in an impromptu assembly area. They decided to stay put until there was enough light to find a landmark and get their bearings. At daylight Taylor had with him perhaps ninety soldiers, including chief of staff Jerry Higgins, division artillery commander Tony McAuliffe, division engineer John Pappas, and Julian Ewell, commanding an infantry battalion. As he marshaled this heterogeneous collection Taylor dropped one of his more memorable aphorisms, paraphrasing

---

* Never one for names, Taylor could not remember the name of this "first" soldier in Normandy. Much later he recalled, "It was a Polish name. I saw him years later. Unfortunately, he'd gotten fat."

Churchill, "Never before have so few been commanded by so many."

Quite apart from the question of numbers was that of location. Every pasture looked the same, and it was daybreak before they could get their bearings. ("Just as dawn was breaking we looked up and saw a large church steeple and knew where we were—Ste. Marie du Mont.")[14] There had been occasional contact with the Germans in the hours immediately following the landings, but the initial German reaction to Neptune was one of confusion and uncertainty, much as Taylor had anticipated. In the words of one author, "The Americans knew what was happening, but few of them knew where they were; the Germans knew where they were, but none of them knew what was happening."[15] One German patrol mistook Taylor's jumpmaster, Larry Legere, and his aide, Tom White, for French farmers. Challenged by the Germans, Legere explained in French that he was returning from a visit to his cousin. As he spoke, he pulled the pin of a hand grenade, which exploded among the unsuspecting Germans.[16]

Given his division's scattered drop, Taylor implemented an earlier understanding: if a unit did not reach its designated drop zone, it would carry out those missions that went with the sector where it found itself. At the same time, he thought it important that a skeleton division headquarters be established at the location specified, a group of farmhouses that went by the name Hiesville. As dawn broke at around six o'clock, he dispatched Colonel Tom Sherburne and a small detachment to Hiesville, while he himself set out with the remainder of the column to secure one of the beach causeways. The Americans were largely unopposed in their march. Robert Reuben, a Reuters newsman who had jumped with Taylor's stick, recalled an incident along the way:

Along the route of march, General Taylor was uncertain of our location. The General, who spoke fluent French, and Legere and I approached a farmhouse to make inquiries. A farmer and his wife came to the door, and I was amazed to find them not at all surprised to see us. *"Bonjour, monsieur,"* said General Taylor. "We are American invasion soldiers. Can you tell us the nearest town?"

The elderly couple acted as if they had an invasion every day. They told us that the next town was Pouppeville and gave us directions in a matter-of-fact manner. Many of our boys were later disappointed to find many of the coastal peasants similarly unemotional. I think they had been waiting so long for invasion that when it came it was almost anticlimactic.[17]

As the little column worked its way east, it periodically had a view of one of the great sights of the war: the vast Allied armada off Utah Beach, the sea filled with landing craft, the air dominated by U.S. fighters. Initially, the only threat to the American paratroopers was from the U.S. Navy, whose flat trajectory shells would occasionally hit and ricochet inland. The column moved on, picking up incremental groups of paratroops as it went.

After a hike of about four miles, Taylor's cooks and clerks made their real first contact with the Germans at around nine o'clock near Pouppeville, at the base of the southernmost causeway. The German garrison put up a stiff defense from the stone houses of the village, and Taylor nearly became a casualty when a badly aimed grenade from one of his soldiers bounced off the side of one house and exploded among the Americans. By noon, however, the Americans had occupied the village, capturing forty prisoners while incurring some twenty casualties. Shortly after occupying Pouppeville, Taylor's group made contact with elements of the 4th Division moving inland from the beach. It was an important junction. Because his headquarters radio had been lost in the jump, he borrowed a radio from the 4th Division to inform Bradley of the linkup and of the light enemy resistance in the immediate area of Utah Beach.

It was just as well that the Germans were confused, for the 101st had undergone a wild night. In the words of one survivor, men landed "in pastures, plowed fields, grain fields, orchards, and hedgerows. They landed at the base of antiglider poles [Rommel's asparagus], in tall trees and small trees. They landed on roof tops, in cemeteries, town squares, backyards, paved roads, and in roadside ditches. They landed in canals, rivers, bogs, and flooded areas."[18] At dawn, of the 6,600 paratroops, perhaps 1,100 were at or near division objectives, but of those most were near some objective other than that specified for their unit.

The division staged two glider landings on D-day, the first before dawn and a second, smaller operation at dusk. A night glider operation had never been attempted before, but both Taylor and Ridgway had insisted that they have use of their division artillery from the outset. In the morning operation, forty-nine of fifty-two gliders made it to the 101st landing zones, making the glider portion of D-day far more precise than the parachute drop. But glider landings were hardly landings at all. Hazardous at all times, the landings on D-day were made more so by poor visibility, natural obstacles, and Rommel asparagus. No glider that went into Normandy ever saw service again, and some were so thoroughly destroyed that the soldiers had difficulty removing their cargo.

Landing casualties were remarkably light under the circumstances, but one fatality was the first American general to ride a glider into combat, Taylor's assistant division commander, Don Pratt. Pratt, who was well respected in the division, was noted for being superstitious. Two days before the invasion Taylor had gone into Pratt's lodgings for a talk, tossing his cap onto his bunk. "Don't do that," Pratt had protested, knocking the cap off the bed. "Don't you know it's unlucky?"[19] Pratt's luck had indeed run out. His pilot, Mike Murphy, recalled that their landing appeared at first to be successful but that the glider then went out of control. "We slid for over eight hundred feet on wet grass and smashed into trees at fifty miles per hour," he recalled. Murphy suffered two broken legs, his copilot was killed, and Pratt died of a broken neck.[20]

The 101st had a threefold mission: to capture the four exits from Utah Beach, to protect the southern flank of the VII Corps advance, and to destroy the bridges over the Douve River north of Carentan. In quickly securing the causeways, the 101st made a major contribution to the success of Overlord. In another mission, however, the blocking of the Douve, the division encountered problems. "Skeets" Johnson's 501st had had the worst drop of any unit and faced the most organized resistance. Johnson gained a toehold on the river at La Barquette but was unable to gain control of the highway running north from Carentan.

Still, the division could hardly have accomplished more in its first day of fighting. It had survived a potentially disastrous drop and had fought a series of sharp small-unit operations to achieve its initial objectives. By evening its organized strength was more than two thousand, and it had access to its glider-borne equipment. In the late afternoon Taylor turned responsibility for the Pouppeville causeway over to the 4th Division and headed his little column in the direction of Hiesville. He limped into the large stone farmhouse that was his command post at about five o'clock, doubtless thinking unkind thoughts about Froggie Reed.

Reports poured into the division headquarters all evening, but at about eight o'clock Taylor had had enough. He told Jerry Higgins, whom he had named assistant division commander in place of Pratt, that he was going to bed, adding, "I don't expect to be disturbed." Higgins was taken aback, because the division's situation was still highly unsettled, but during the night he resisted several temptations to awaken his commander. At daybreak Taylor came downstairs and asked for a briefing. He then turned to Higgins and ordered him to bed, adding that he should not reappear until called. As Higgins later put it, "Taylor realized that he would require a clear mind as the situation approached a critical state, and he disciplined himself into providing that mind."[21]

Chapter 7

CARENTAN

As D-day came to a close, the extent of the Allied foothold was less than Eisenhower had hoped. Instead of controlling beachheads six miles deep as the high command had projected, Allied forces were no more than five miles inland anywhere. The Canadian and British beachheads were in contact with each other, but nowhere else were any of the five invasion forces joined. On Omaha Beach, two American divisions maintained a precarious hold that was scarcely more than one mile deep. Wrecked landing craft, abandoned tanks, and assorted debris of war littered an area where 2,500 Americans had died. At Utah Beach, in contrast, the Americans had found a soft spot in the German defenses. The 4th Division was in firm control there about three hours after landing.

At Hiesville, meanwhile, Taylor sought to learn what he could of the status of his own command and the situation on the peninsula. The fact that all four causeways were secure was cause for satisfaction, but an appalling amount of heavy equipment was missing, including virtually all the parachute artillery. Taylor could expect no support from the 82d, for initial reports from the west indicated that Ridgway was heavily engaged. His drop had been even more scattered than that of the 101st.

Nevertheless, Taylor's confidence in his division was being vindicated in widely scattered areas by small groups of his soldiers. Near Causeway 4, Colonel Pat Cassidy, commanding a battalion of the 502d, ordered one of his noncoms, Staff Sergeant Harrison Summers, to gather some men and clear out a compound of houses the Germans were using as barracks. Summers knew little of the men in his impromptu squad, so when they reached the objective Summers set out on his own. Armed with a submachine gun he kicked open the door of the first house, ducked inside, and opened fire, killing four Germans. There he was briefly joined by a captain of the 82d, but as the two moved toward the second building the captain was shot dead. Summers, alone, slipped into the second barrack where he gunned down six more Germans.

Summers's squad had been spectators thus far, but now Private John Camien joined him. The two went through five more houses, killing thirty more of the enemy. The next building in the complex was the mess hall. Bursting through the door the amazed Americans found fifteen Germans still at breakfast and shot them all. By the time Summers and Camien reached the main barracks they had support from a bazooka team. American rockets set fire to the roof and some fifty Germans had to make a run for it. Many of these were cut down, and most of those who escaped were rounded up later in the day. Four decades later, Taylor participated in an unsuccessful campaign to upgrade the Distinguished Service Cross awarded to Summers to the Congressional Medal of Honor.

Not all clashes were as spectacular as Summers's achievement. Military historian Max Hastings has noted that "all wars become a matter of small private battles to those who are fighting them. . . . This was uniquely true of the struggle for Normandy, where it was seldom possible to see more than 100 or 200 yards in any direction, where forward infantry rarely glimpsed their own armour, artillery or higher commanders, where the appalling attrition rate among the rifle companies . . . rapidly became one of the dominant features of the campaign."[1] Much of the next three days would be spent in collecting the scattered paratroopers, in marshaling the glider forces who had come in by sea, and in clearing out areas of resistance north of the Douve River. Control of the Douve, including the Carentan-Cherbourg highway, was crucial to the division's mission of protecting the southern flank of the VII Corps.

By the evening of June 7 Taylor had determined that he must seize St. Côme-du-Mont on the Carentan-Cherbourg road before proceeding against Carentan itself. As long as the Germans held this village they were capable of threatening the advance from Utah Beach; capture of St. Côme would eliminate this threat and would remove the last important area of resistance north of the Douve. In recognition of this, the Germans had sent a reinforced regiment, the 1058th, to defend the village.

Taylor directed Bob Sink to attack St. Côme on the morning of June 8 and provided him with reinforcements in the form of Ewell's reserve battalion and a battalion of glider infantry. Sink began his attack at dawn, employing four battalions. The morning was one of sharp fighting and repeated German counterattacks. By early afternoon, however, two of Sink's battalions were in St. Côme, while Ewell had secured "Dead Man's Corner" south of the village. The surviving Germans retreated south across the Douve.

Carentan was next. Although it was then a town of only about four thousand, it was an important communications link between the VII Corps's widely separated objectives, Cherbourg to the north and St. Lô to the south. Taylor had anticipated that his division's mission would eventually include the capture of Carentan. On June 8 he met with Collins and informed him that St. Côme and the northern bank of the Douve had been secured. "All right," Collins replied, "now take Carentan."

Bradley and Collins were eager to maintain momentum and to compensate for the slow buildup on the beaches. At the end of D plus 1 only a quarter of the projected supplies were ashore, and the troop buildup was 20,000 short of the two-day goal of 107,000. The Allied beachheads remained vulnerable to counterattack, especially by armor. Indeed, they might have been in serious jeopardy had Hitler not held back the bulk of his panzer reserve and retained the Fifteenth Army in the Calais area as a hedge against any second Allied landing. On June 9 Bradley visited Collins to underscore the importance of Carentan; he told his corps commander that if the 101st encountered problems it should be reinforced.

On that day the 101st launched a two-pronged attack in the direction of Carentan. While the 502d Regiment advanced south along the Cherbourg road, the 327th crossed the Douve near its mouth to attack from the northeast. Taylor had confidence in the 502d, even though it had a new commander. (Colonel George Moseley, its regimental commander, had broken his leg in landing. Taylor, finding him attempting to direct his regiment while being trundled about in a wheelbarrow, had to order him to an aid station.) Command of the regiment went to Colonel John Michaelis, who would eventually become one of three officers of the 101st to achieve four-star rank in the postwar army, the other two being Tony McAuliffe and Taylor himself.

The 327th Glider Regiment was a different matter. Most of the regiment had come in by sea, and its commander, George Wear, was believed by some to have been slow in getting his unit into action on D-day. Several days later Taylor observed Wear's first action against the Germans and did not like what he saw. On the afternoon of June 10 he sent for Colonel Bud Harper, who had been acting as a beachmaster on Utah Beach. Taylor told him that the 327th was his, and outlined his plans for moving against Carentan. Riding south in his jeep, Harper saw Wear's vehicle near Brevands. Signaling it to stop, Harper handed Wear the envelope containing Taylor's order. Few words were exchanged. The forty-two-year-old Harper, who had been an agriculture major at the University of Delaware, would lead the division's glider forces for the remainder of the war.

By June 9 the 101st had three regiments along the Douve. The 502d was on the right flank near Houesville, the 506th was astride the Cherbourg road, while the 327th was at La Barquette. The division plan called for the 327th to make the primary effort from the left, crossing the Douve near Brevands to clear the area north of the town. At the same time the 502d would cross the causeway over the river north of Carentan, bypass the town on the west, and seize a rise known as Hill 30. The 506th had the most intimidating assignment, because the ever-present marshes would keep it largely confined to an elevated road until it reached the outskirts of the town.

There were many private wars. On the afternoon of June 10 one of Michaelis's battalions, commanded by Lieutenant Colonel Robert Cole, began a careful advance down the Cherbourg-Carentan road. Resistance was stiff, and the day even brought an attack by Luftwaffe dive bombers. However, by midafternoon most of Cole's battalion was across the Madeleine River and approaching Carentan. Although enemy fire was increasing, the Americans now had the advantage of being able to move off the road and onto firm ground. Cole told one officer that he was going to order smoke from the artillery and then make a bayonet charge against the farmhouse that was the source of the heaviest enemy fire. At about six o'clock, Cole led elements of three companies in one of the few bayonet charges of the war. At first only about 60 of the 250-man battalion followed Cole and his executive officer, John Stopka. Then more paratroopers sprinted out of the ditches and the charge gained momentum. The Americans overran the farmhouse and kept going, grenading and bayoneting German paratroopers in rifle pits and hedgerows. Cole, who later died in Holland, became the first Screaming Eagle to win the Congressional Medal of Honor.

The battle for Carentan, which lasted three days, was designed to press the Germans from several directions. Taylor wanted to move fast. Although he was baffled at the absence of a major German counterthrust—it was, after all, D plus 3—he was going to make full use of the unexpected grace period. Taylor would later recall his role as scuttling by jeep from one flank of his division to the other, counseling and observing.

While the 502d was heavily engaged on the highway, Harper made tentative contact with forces advancing from Omaha Beach. The Germans, however, had by then concluded that retention of Carentan was essential to prevent a full junction of the two American beachheads and to preclude an American drive across the Cotentin that would isolate German units on the peninsula. Rommel had already ordered the 17th Panzer Division to Carentan, but Allied control of the air delayed its arrival by twenty-four hours.

On the same day as Cole's charge, the 327th moved against Carentan from the northeast, advancing two battalions on either side of the Isigny-Carentan road. Bud Harper opted to approach Carentan through a wooded area along the Bassin à Flot. Three companies crossed the canal on the morning of June 11, but they were able to advance only a few hundred yards before being halted by heavy fire. In the evening, however, the envelopment of Carentan continued. The 506th pressed toward Hill 30 south of the town. Taylor took Skeets Johnson's 501st from a defensive position north of the Douve and threw it into the fight. Johnson was to drive east of the 327th in a wider encirclement of Carentan and link up with the 506th in the area of Hill 30.

By this time fighting had reached the outskirts of Carentan and the town was taking a beating. It was under fire not only from the artillery of the 101st but from naval guns offshore and from V Corps tank destroyers up from Omaha Beach. In the early hours of June 12, Sink captured Hill 30 and sent a battalion into Carentan itself. The wider envelopment also made progress. The 501st moved east of Carentan and made contact with the 506th shortly after Harper's regiment, with Taylor in the van, had driven into town.

The airborne pincers had achieved their objective, but the Germans eluded the final advance. Colonel von der Heydte, commanding the defense, pulled out of Carentan late on June 11 and set up a new line to the southwest. Von der Heydte would be sharply criticized for this withdrawal, for the 17th Panzer was even then moving to relieve Carentan, but considering his low ammunition supply and the pressure from the 101st he may have taken the only reasonable course.

Taylor himself was in Carentan on the morning of June 12. His immediate inclination was to continue the attack. He wanted to establish a defense in depth, and to this end he wanted to continue south and to establish contact with elements of the 82d heading in the direction of Baupte. But the advance south of Carentan was sluggish, reflecting the weariness of troops who had seen a week of near-continuous action. In any case, the immediate threat from the Germans made any further advance moot. At dawn on June 13 the 17th Panzer put in a belated appearance and drove the 506th and the 501st back to the outskirts of Carentan. Taylor brought in Michaelis's regiment as reinforcements but the situation remained tenuous. He would later note that airborne divisions were notoriously deficient in antitank weapons and that he might have had considerable difficulty with the German panzers "had not General Bradley, unsolicited, sent us the reinforcement of a combat command of the 2d Armored Division."[2] Bradley was in fact quite concerned for the 101st, for he had "Ultra" intelligence—decoded German messages—indicating that a panzer attack on Taylor's understrength division was imminent. Bradley later recalled, "This was one of the few times in the war when I unreservedly believed Ultra and reacted to it tactically."[3] By midmorning on June 13 an element of the 2d Armored was in Carentan, and Taylor was conferring with the task force commander, General Maurice Rose. At about two o'clock that afternoon the American tanks turned south in a column with infantrymen deployed on each side.

One of the units of the 101st that had its hands full with the German armor was Fox Company of the 506th. In the words of the company historian:

At 3:00 sharp a fierce rumbling shook the road—big, beautiful Shermans of the 2d Armored came roaring with armored infantrymen trailing them, men fresh from the beaches and spoiling for a fight. Fox men didn't yell a single "Hurrah!" or utter a spoken word. They were simply overwhelmingly thankful.

The tank leaders spotted Fox Company's line and fanned out in front. Those equipped with bulldozer ploughs crashed through hedgerows as if they were stiff paper, permitting others to race through. It was wonderful to watch them at work and many retired to the high ground, the better to watch them. A tank would stop in a hole made by a brother tankdozer, then turn a sharp right or left, wherever the Krauts were, and sweep every foot of the hedgerow. . . . What they missed were mopped up and destroyed by the armored infantrymen. The men were treated to an awe-inspiring show of violence.[4]

The American counterattack drove the 17th Panzer back several miles. By the afternoon of the following day, soldiers of Sink's 506th were running routine patrols in Carentan. One day Taylor and several of his staff were inspecting a country road when they passed one of their soldiers taking a break. To Harry Kinnard he looked no more than sixteen, but he was reclining against a hedgerow, eating his K ration, his feet propped on the body of a dead German. Taylor turned and remarked to Kinnard, "I guess we don't have to worry about our untried division any more."[5]

For the 101st, the worst of Normandy was over. Division surgeon David Gold, weary of his diet of Spam, found reasons to visit the front, where the paratroopers would periodically shoot a French cow for steaks. With the lull in the fighting, Taylor turned his attention to disciplinary matters. He always wanted his division to "look sharp," and it was time to remind his men that they were an Army division, not freelance gunfighters. On about D plus 10 each company commander received a directive from the commanding general stating that all men were to be clean-shaven and in clean uniforms by a certain day. The general would make inspections, and any soldier found in violation would be fined $50 and his company commander $100. Many Screaming Eagles were furious. Here they had "captured Normandy" and this was their reward! Others were philosophical. Sergeant George Koskimaki later recalled:

> For the invasion we had blackened our faces and some had camouflage-painted their uniforms, all to provide concealment in the hedgerow country of France. After the general's order, we got rid of the stubble and grubby clothes real fast. I remember I didn't remove my boots during the first week. When I finally changed socks, I discovered that the bottoms had rotted out of the originals. We must have been fragrant![6]

On June 20, during a break in the action, Taylor scheduled an award ceremony in Carentan itself. Soldiers of all units were on hand when Taylor addressed the formation and awarded the medals. At the conclusion of the ceremony he returned to a makeshift platform and told his soldiers that he would now address a few remarks to the curious who had surrounded the square. In fluent French, beginning with *"Mes amis,"* he explained the reasons for the American presence and thanked the French for their support. In fact, such support was far less than would later be received in Holland, but the effect of Taylor's remarks was gratifying. In Jerry Higgins's recollection, "I have never seen such a transformation in an assembly—from lackluster indifference to enthusiastic applause. They could not believe that a foreigner in a high-level position had such a command of their language."[7]

The 101st's role in the Normandy campaign was largely over. On June 29 it was withdrawn from the Carentan sector and moved north to Cherbourg for occupation duty. It was due some relief. During June the division had suffered more than 3,800 casualties, approximately a third of its strength. (It is a commentary on the risks that the Allied high command was prepared to run that these figures were lower than those estimated during the planning phase in England.) On July 7 Taylor spoke to his men from the roof of a pillbox near Cherbourg. He told them exactly how proud he was of them. "You hit the ground running toward the enemy. You have proved the German soldier is no superman. You have beaten him on his own ground and you can beat him on any ground."[8]

For the Allied high command, the work of the two American airborne divisions, on which such care had been lavished, was a source of great satisfaction. Despite heavy casualties—and those of the 82d were even higher than those of the 101st—the airborne operation was viewed as a major factor in the success of Overlord. Bradley, who had told Eisenhower that he could not order landings at Utah Beach without the airborne drop, was elated. As for Eisenhower, asked many years later what had been his most satisfying moment in the war, he replied that it was when he received word that the two airborne divisions had reached their destinations in Normandy.

In assessing Neptune in his official report, Taylor weighed both the tangible achievements and the intangibles. The most visible benefit clearly had been his division's contribution to an almost bloodless landing at Utah Beach. Less quantifiable was the immense amount of confusion the airborne landings had sown in the mind of the enemy. "An airborne landing at night," Taylor wrote, "has a devastating effect on the enemy. It upsets his command organization and prevents the movement of his reserves and artillery." Although various developments may upset the plans of the attacker, "the disruptive effect of the attack on the enemy" more than compensates.

At the same time, Taylor was not inclined toward complacency. He called attention to the heavy losses in equipment dropped by parachute, estimating these to be in the area of 60 percent. He had harsh words for the Troop Carrier Command, noting that the scattered drop had undone all the careful planning undertaken in England. He himself had little cause for complaint; indeed, he would request the same pilot, Frank McNeese, for the coming operation in Holland. But he wrote that "the confidence of the airborne troops in the Troop Carrier Command has been undermined by the dispersed drop and the conduct of some pilots. This can be restored only if it is known that pilots who failed conspicuously in Neptune have been eliminated and that the proficiency of the groups to navigate accurately through cloud and bad weather has improved."

Taylor found other lessons in the Normandy operation. In his judgment, an airborne division should not be expected to function as a unit for at least twenty-four hours. As a result, the initial impact of an airborne operation must come from "the aggressive action of small groups." Airborne units must be promptly supported by heavier forces. In Taylor's judgment, the previous assumption that an airborne division could maintain itself independently for two or three days should be revised downward. At the same time, the surprise element inherent in an airborne operation should be exploited to the maximum. For this reason, and to minimize the absence of heavy weapons, "it may be more economical of lives to land directly on the enemy than to come down at a distance and close with him in a deliberate approach march and development."

Taylor's final conclusion was rooted in personal experience. "There is an immediate requirement," he wrote, "for a quick release harness." He had not forgotten those ten uncomfortable minutes in the dark with those Norman cows.[9]

He also drew lessons in a broader context. The Americans had favored a cross-Channel invasion in 1943 and had only reluctantly deferred to the British preference for a campaign in the Mediterranean. As far as Taylor was concerned, the British had been right. "We weren't ready to do [Normandy] in 1943," he later recalled. "The Mediterranean operations were good because we needed the experience. Few of our men had ever seen combat."[10]

The 101st command post was located in an apple orchard south of Cherbourg when Bradley sent word that he wanted to visit the division and present some decorations. Taylor directed his G-1, Ned Moore, to pick out the most worthy recipients. Bradley arrived in a Piper Cub that afternoon, and the open-air ceremony went off without a hitch, although Moore had had little time in which to work up the citations. After Bradley had shaken hands with the last soldier, he turned and pinned the Distinguished Service Cross on Taylor. As Moore told it, Taylor was annoyed at being surprised: "I don't think he spoke to me for a week."*

* Taylor also was awarded the British Distinguished Service Order for his role in the capture of Carentan. The citation, signed by General Montgomery, noted that Taylor "personally conceived and directed a river crossing which was entirely successful and permitted elements of the [101st] Division to flank the city."

Chapter 8

THE BRIDGE TOO FAR

On July 10 the first elements of the 101st made their way to Utah Beach where, over the next three days, they were loaded aboard LSTs and returned to England. The two American airborne divisions were almost the only fighting units for which D-day included a round-trip ticket. Most other units remained on the Continent for the duration. But apart from the fact that the 82d and the 101st had both been badly cut up, they also represented a major portion of Eisenhower's strategic reserve and presumably could be deployed more readily from England than from a rehabilitation area in France.

Meanwhile, Allied armies were advancing, but at a far from satisfactory pace. Although Eisenhower had a million men ashore by early July, in only a few areas had the Allied beachheads been moved as far as twenty miles inland. Some observers viewed a ground stalemate—a return to trench warfare—as a very real possibility, particularly with the fastidious Montgomery as ground forces commander. The signs were ominous. For instance, in the preinvasion scenario the British Second Army was to have captured Caen on D plus 1. But Caen did not fall until D plus 33.

Not that American forces were conducting a blitzkrieg. Bradley's First Army moved slowly and fitfully through the swamps and hedgerows of Cotentin in the direction of St. Lô. Losses were heavy and it was not unusual for a division to suffer as many as two thousand casualties in a week's time. Cotentin was an infantryman's war. Both sides sought to make use of their armor, but neither was entirely successful. Tanks were essential for fire support, but the terrain inhibited maneuver. And because the stone houses of the French countryside made natural fortresses, one village after another became the scene of destructive house-to-house fighting. Not until July 18 did St. Lô, by then a smoking rubble, fall to the Americans.

The men of the U.S. airborne divisions were spared this. The 101st was back in its camps around Newbury, attempting to integrate replacements for those who had fallen in Normandy. The division's reputation had preceded it, and the 101st received a warm welcome from its English hosts. Taylor himself had fond recollections of the English summer. On one occasion, Eisenhower visited the division to award the Distinguished Service Cross to several of the Screaming Eagles. One of the recipients was a Private Rogers, and as the citation was being read, Eisenhower asked Taylor why such a brave soldier was only a private. The division commander was caught by surprise, and when Eisenhower asked whether there would be any objection to his promoting Rogers, Taylor could hardly object. After the ceremony he told Rogers's regimental commander, Bob Sink, about his new noncom, and Sink was delighted. A photograph of Sink pinning on the corporal's chevrons received wide circulation.

As Taylor told it, the story should have ended there, but it did not. Rogers fully justified his previous rank by going AWOL and making a spectacle of himself. In Sink's absence he was called before the acting regimental commander, Charles Chase, who promptly busted him back to private. Sink, on his return, was dismayed. "Charley," he protested, "you can't bust Ike's own corporal," which prompted Chase to reply in turn, "Sir, I do not think he intended the title to be hereditary." The story ultimately made its way back to Eisenhower himself, who was both amused and chastened, remarking that henceforth he would leave such promotions in the hands of regimental commanders where they belonged.

When time permitted, Taylor sought to combine business with pleasure. On Sunday afternoons he was likely to invite one or more officers to take a picnic lunch and to visit historic sites, such as Stonehenge and Eton, in the South of England. Jerry Higgins recalled that Taylor never wasted a moment en route. "When conversation lagged he took language cards out of his pocket and refreshed himself in Japanese—just in case the division were deployed to the Pacific after the defeat of Germany."[1]

Notwithstanding the decorations and a general feeling that the division had performed well in Normandy, Taylor was never one to rest on past laurels. Teams from the division staff met with units down to company level for "lessons learned" talks. Communications and antiarmor tactics were high on the list as the division resumed a demanding training schedule, including cross-country marches in which soldiers in full pack were expected to cover twenty-five miles a day.

Meanwhile, the Allied airborne forces were being reorganized. Marshall continued to be intrigued with the possibility of operations deep in enemy territory: if any were to be attempted they would involve several divisions. Quite apart from the size of any such operation, nearly everyone recognized the need for better coordination between the soldiers and the Troop Carrier Command. One organizational possibility was to merge all Allied airborne assets along with their airlift into a single command. Eisenhower was favorably disposed, but he was dealing with a complex situation: the United States would be providing most of the troops but the British felt themselves best qualified for command. Ultimately, Eisenhower approved the establishment of the First Allied Airborne Army. It would comprise an American corps, made up of the 82d, 101st, and 17th divisions, and a smaller British corps, encompassing the 1st and 6th divisions and a Polish brigade.

The new organization had much to recommend it, and Eisenhower's inclination to have it commanded by a U.S. airman held out the promise of improved rapport between paratroopers and pilots. Unfortunately, his choice for command was Lieutenant General Lewis Brereton, a fifty-three-year-old bomber man who had been ousted by MacArthur after losing most of the latter's Philippine-based aircraft on the ground a full day after Pearl Harbor. The high-living Brereton was only marginally interested in matters such as trooplift. In the Holland campaign, where an experienced airborne commander might have asked some of the pertinent questions in the planning stage, Brereton was most interested in assuring that his pilots would not have to fly more than one mission per day.

In appointing Brereton to command the First Allied Airborne

Army, Eisenhower disappointed British General "Boy" Browning, who had been maneuvering to gain the command for himself. Browning was a veteran paratrooper (he was also the husband of novelist Daphne du Maurier), but most of the Americans viewed him as ambitious and arrogant. As a consolation prize, Browning was named to command the forthcoming operation against Arnhem; Matt Ridgway would command the three-division American corps, but for purposes of the Holland campaign had effectively been kicked upstairs. For the first time, American airborne forces would be serving under a British commander.

Amid this administrative turmoil, Allied commanders were attempting to develop the most promising scenario for an airborne operation. Plans were submitted at the rate of nearly one a week. Under one proposal, Operation Transfigure, American and British paratroopers were to have seized points southwest of Paris to block one escape route for German forces. When Patton's advance made Transfigure unnecessary, the participating units moved back to their camps. The story was much the same with Linnet I, designed to drop airborne forces into Belgium to expedite the British ground advance. Taylor's diary reflected the frustration of the airborne soldiers:

Friday, September 1: General Brereton dropped by for lunch. . . . Operation LINNET somewhat uncertain. Discussed the capture of Liege as possible secondary objective. Visited General Browning's headquarters and discussed capture of hostile airfields. . . .

Saturday, September 2: Started making rounds of airfields talking to troops. Was interrupted and called to General Browning's headquarters at 1800. General Browning did not arrive until after 1900 and gave a new mission for Operation LINNET. . . . After returning and briefing the staff on the modified mission word was received cancelling the entire operation and placing the division on a 36-hour alert.

Sunday, September 3: Received TWX cancelling LINNET and unsealing airdromes. Was called to Moore Park at noon and received division mission in the Liege area. General Browning stated that as best known at this date takeoff time would be 1400

September 5. Went to Eastcote with General Williams and selected drop zones from a map. Talked with General Ridgway. All felt there was a slight possibility of taking off on September 4. Returned and gave the situation to unit commanders at 1730 and directed them to brief down to jumpmasters. Operation . . . cancelled at 2200.[2]*

By this time the threatened stalemate in France had long since been broken, and the Allies were conducting a pursuit that was limited primarily by logistical considerations. Nevertheless, it seemed essential that the elite Allied airborne units be put to use. Field Marshal Lord Carver, then a brigadier of armor, would recall the desperate attempts to get the airborne into action. "The airborne high command," Carver observed, "was frightened to death that they would be converted to regular infantry."[3] Paradoxically, success in France had served only to increase jealousies within the Allied high command, jealousies that took the form of competition for supplies, disputes over objectives, and wrangling over strategy.

Montgomery affected the role of the dutiful, often abused subordinate, faithful to orders even from the inexperienced Eisenhower. Monty, however, had concurred only reluctantly in the supreme commander's insistence on a broad advance into Germany, as opposed to a sharp thrust against a single strategic point. Eisenhower almost unfailingly assumed the role of conciliator, but occasionally, against his better judgment, he allowed Montgomery to have his way.

The two men clashed when the Briton heard on September 7 that Patton's army was to be accorded priority in the allocation of fuel for a time. An infuriated Montgomery told Ike that there were not enough supplies for two offensives, without mentioning that a

---

* An anecdote from this period that has enjoyed wide circulation might be called the Flying Condoms Caper. Just before one of the many aborted operations of this period, Taylor allegedly met with one of his regiments for a predeparture pep talk. As he reached his now-go-get-'em peroration, the assembled paratroopers, by prearrangement, released a cloud of condom balloons that wafted through the hangar (or English countryside) to the division commander's discomfiture. For every Screaming Eagle who swears that he was there, I find two to assure me that the incident never took place. Careful study of the aerodynamic qualities of air-filled condoms leads me to conclude that the story is apocryphal.

prime reason for the shortages had been the British delay in capturing Antwerp. Three days later Eisenhower, in response to a request by Montgomery to confer with him at Brussels, agreed to make the trip despite a severely sprained knee that was causing great discomfort. In a meeting held in Eisenhower's aircraft, Montgomery subjected the supreme commander to a tirade on the matter of supplies, implying that Eisenhower was not acting in good faith and that Patton, not Eisenhower, was effectively running the war. Eisenhower listened as long as he could and then leaned forward, put his hand on Montgomery's knee, and said, "Steady, Monty! You can't speak to me like that. I'm your boss."[4]

The two talked on, but the atmosphere was tense. Montgomery urged that his 21st Army Group be authorized to push through Arnhem and on to Berlin. Eisenhower dismissed the proposal, for the Allies lacked the necessary supplies and had no means of protecting the flanks of any such salient. Then Montgomery advanced a more modest proposal, one with Arnhem as its immediate objective. Eisenhower listened. As early as mid-July Eisenhower himself had directed his planners to come up with an airborne operation marked by "imagination and daring." Now, as Ike heard Montgomery out, the supreme commander saw in the Arnhem operation a plan that met his own requirements for bold use of his airborne resources while promising to appease the nettlesome Monty.

The new plan was called Market-Garden, the Market portion being the airborne landings and Garden being the ground advance to Arnhem along an airborne "carpet." Involving as it did three and a half airborne divisions, Market would prove to be the largest airborne operation of the war, which is to say of all time. Its plan, in broadest outline, called for the airborne forces to land near Eindhoven, Nijmegen, and Arnhem to seize and protect the bridges that were essential to keeping open the highway to Arnhem. In Garden, ground troops of the British Second Army were to advance some eighty miles from the Belgium-Netherlands border to Arnhem. Market-Garden had the twin objectives of getting the Allies over the Rhine and into position to threaten the Ruhr. If successful, it would also have the effect of outflanking the Siegfried Line and positioning the Second Army for a drive into the German heartland.

Market represented a far more daring use of airborne forces than had heretofore been made and doubtless reflected the wishes of strategists such as Marshall and Arnold, as well as Eisenhower's desire to appease Montgomery. It also reflected a prevailing optimism in SHAEF† headquarters which saw the Germans as being on the run and believed the end of the war was in sight. On the eve of Market the British estimated that the Germans had no more than fifty to one hundred tanks in the Netherlands and that many of the troops there were of a "low category." According to the British, "It was thought the enemy must still be disorganized after his long and hasty retreat from south of the Seine River and that though there might be numerous small bodies of enemy in the area, he would not be capable of organized resistance to any great extent."[5] In fact, as recently as late August this optimistic assumption would have been closer to the truth. In early September, however, Field Marshal Walter Model, in overall command of the German defenses, directed the 9th and 10th SS Panzer divisions, which had seen heavy action in France, to move to the Arnhem area for rest and rehabilitation.

This move by two elite enemy divisions was reflected in Ultra radio intercepts, much as the move of the 17th Panzer in Normandy had been. Unlike Bradley in the fighting for Carentan, however, Montgomery was not disposed to change his plans. Beetle Smith, Eisenhower's chief of staff, called the relevant intelligence to Montgomery's attention and urged that one of the American divisions be dropped into Arnhem along with the British "Red Devils" in order to counter the two panzers. According to Smith, Montgomery "waved my objections airily aside."[6] Taylor, meanwhile, knew nothing of the two German divisions and would later call it inexcusable that the division commanders who were to lead the fighting were not informed of the likely presence of German panzers.

In its final form, Market called for 20,000 paratroopers, 15,000 glider troops, and 10,000 regular infantry brought in by airlift. The

† Supreme Headquarters Allied Expeditionary Forces.

British 1st Division, commanded by General Roy Urquhart and reinforced by the 1st Polish Parachute Brigade, was to seize Arnhem and the Rhine bridges and prepare airstrips to handle reinforcements. The American 82d, now commanded by Jim Gavin, would land south of Arnhem and seize key bridges in the Nijmegen area. The 101st was to land still farther south to secure some fifteen miles of the corridor and to seize four major bridges at Zon, St. Oedenrode, Best, and Veghel.

Taylor made one key contribution to the planning for Market. After studying the flat, marshy, terrain between Veghel to the north and Eindhoven to the south, he insisted that his entire division be dropped in a compact area between Zon and Veghel so that his battalions would be within supporting distance of one another from the outset. He would land two of his regiments, the 502d and the 506th, by the edge of a forest roughly equidistant from both Eindhoven and Veghel. The 502d would be responsible for objectives at Best and St. Oedenrode, the 506th for those in Zon and Eindhoven. The 501st was to land in two areas north and west of Veghel, and the glider forces would constitute the division reserve.

At the tip of the Allied spear the British 1st Division would be heavily dependent on aerial resupply, for even if all went on schedule British ground forces would only link up with Urquhart's Red Devils on D plus 3. Taylor's report after Normandy had concluded that ideally an airborne division should be reinforced after no more than twenty-four hours. Even if this timing was conservative, three days was not. Moreover, could the British XXX Corps be expected to average more than twenty miles per day over a single road? In one of the planning conferences for Market-Garden, Browning pointed to the northernmost bridge over the Lower Rhine at Arnhem and inquired, "How long will it take the armor to reach us?" "Two days," was Montgomery's reply. Studying the map, Browning replied, "We can hold it for four, but sir, I think we might be going a bridge too far."[7] As for Taylor, he had no time to second-guess the overall strategic plan. In contrast to Normandy, where preparatory time had been sufficient to permit even a practice drop, Market was thrown together in the space of a single week.

As the new D-day approached, the possibility of another dispersed drop like the one in Normandy was very much on Taylor's mind. In Normandy, securing the division's initial objectives required a comparatively small portion of its total resources; the rest could be expended in "raising hell" behind enemy lines. In Holland, however, the British advance depended on the American airborne divisions' controlling their respective portions of the road to Arnhem. And if the 101st should fail to secure the route to be traversed by the British Second Army, it would matter little how the 82d and the British 1st performed up the line; they would be effectively isolated. With recollections of Normandy fresh in his mind, Taylor was uneasy about the forthcoming air drop and indicated as much to Ridgway. The corps commander could offer little comfort. He talked to General Hal Clark, commanding the Troop Carrier Command, on the subject of the training level of his pilots, but they agreed that it was not likely to be better for Holland than for Normandy. In certain cases it was likely to be lower, because of the necessity of employing every available transport and crew.[8]

Assured by the meteorologists that fair weather was in prospect, Brereton decided on the evening of September 16 that D-day would be the following day. On the night of September 16 the RAF dropped 900 tons of bombs on German air bases from which fighters might threaten the Market sky train. On Sunday morning, September 17, nearly 1,500 transports and 500 gliders took off from twenty-four airfields in the South of England, splitting into two great columns as they crossed the North Sea. Those units headed for Arnhem, plus the 82d, took the northern route; the 101st took a more southern course. Operation Market was under way.

The commander of the German First Parachute Army was at his headquarters some nine miles from one of the American drop zones when the Market armada was first spotted. As General Kurt Student recalled, "The 17th of September was . . . a remarkably beautiful late summer day. All was quiet at the front. Late in the morning the enemy air force suddenly became very active. . . . At noon there came the endless stream of enemy transport and cargo planes, as far as the eye could see."[9]

Taylor himself took off at about 10 A.M., with Frank McNeese once again at the controls. American fighters had cleared the Luftwaffe from the skies, but the southern route taken by the 101st was well within the range of German antiaircraft fire. Flying east between Antwerp and Brussels the sky train attracted considerable flak. Then the formation of C-47s turned north into the Netherlands, giving some paratroopers the sight of their lives:

> Men in the planes looked down and, for the first time, saw their earthbound counterpart, the Garden forces whose ground attack was to be synchronized with the air assault. It was a spectacular, unforgettable sight. The vast panoply of General Horrocks' XXX Corps spread out over every field, trail and road. Massed columns of tanks, half-tracks, armored cars and personnel carriers and line after line of guns stood poised for the breakout. On tank antennas pennants fluttered in the wind, and thousands of Britishers standing on vehicles and crowding the fields waved up to the men of the airborne.[10]

Moments later, warning lights in the aircraft flashed on, and paratroopers hooked up. In Taylor's words, "Standing in the door ready to jump behind [Jumpmaster Pat] Cassidy, I saw the plane on our wing hit by ground fire and flames start licking back from the engine. . . . Cassidy was so fascinated by the sight that I had to nudge him to remind him that the jump signal was on."[11] Taylor himself made a soft landing (it was either his fifth or sixth jump and would prove to be his last) and immediately began verifying the location of his units. He need not have been concerned. The drop of the two American divisions was much the most precise of the war, indeed, better than in most exercises. Taylor would have nothing but praise for the pilots of the transports, several of whom made it through to their drop zones despite heavy flak damage. All told, the 6,800 paratroopers of the 101st incurred jump casualties of less than 2 percent and equipment loss of less than 5 percent. Both figures represented a vast improvement over Normandy.

Taylor attached himself to a battalion of the 506th commanded by James LaPrade, one that had as its assignment the securing of the bridge at Zon. As the battalion moved south, however, it was halted by fire from one of the Germans' most formidable weapons, an 88-mm gun. A bazooka round fired by Private Thomas Lindsay took care of the gun, but the delay was crucial. As the Americans rushed to seize the bridge, the Germans detonated it in their faces; Taylor, one hundred yards away, was showered with debris. Destruction of the Zon bridge prevented the 506th from reaching Eindhoven on D-day, but the city was a D-plus-1 objective, and the delay would have been significant only if the British ground attack had been ahead of schedule.

Meanwhile the division's glider components were beginning to arrive. Fifty-three of the 70 gliders landed successfully, carrying 32 jeeps, 13 trailers, and 250 men. Because of the long stretch of highway for which he was responsible, Taylor had felt obliged to give priority to transport, that is, jeeps, in assigning glider cargoes. Not until D plus 3 did the division have use of its 75-mm artillery.

Gliders once again proved the most exciting way to travel. Of those gliders that did not make it, two collided over the landing zone, one fell in the English Channel, and seven came down behind enemy lines. Colonel Ned Moore, Taylor's G-1, recalled that his glider took a direct hit from an antiaircraft round, but its construction was so flimsy that the shell passed through the cabin without exploding. Corporal James Evans of the division artillery had an even more hair-raising ride. Ground fire wounded Evans, his pilot, and his copilot, sending the glider out of control. Evans managed to crawl into the cockpit, figure out the controls, and steady the plunging craft. He then roused the pilot, who was able to return to the controls and make a landing.

By the end of D-day the 101st had gained all of its immediate objectives except for the blown bridge at Zon. The 502d was encountering serious resistance at Best, but that town was a secondary objective. The towns of Zon, St. Oedenrode, and Veghel were in American hands, and the highway between them was clear. The most immediate problem was one of communications. One of the missing gliders had carried British signals personnel, and without them the 101st was unable to establish contact with the oncoming XXX Corps. Not until the following morning, when contact was established with an American signals unit attached to the British, did the 101st get a reading on the delayed British advance.

Taylor spent the night in the outbuilding of a local church. For most of his life the general was a world-class sleeper: neither noise nor stress interfered with his rest, and he later remarked that he slept as well in the barns and farmhouses that he encountered during the war as in his bed at home. He was up at dawn on D plus 2, making a quick trip by jeep to St. Oedenrode before rejoining the 506th outside Eindhoven. He was concerned that the Germans might put up a fight for the city but they did not, and Sink's regiment occupied Eindhoven on the afternoon of September 18. In Taylor's words, "I drove into town in my open jeep shortly thereafter, ducking apples tossed at the Americans by the cheering Dutch population."[12] From the outset the 101st had been receiving valuable assistance from the Dutch underground. The warm welcome at Eindhoven would be long remembered by the men of the 101st.

That evening British engineers arrived to repair the bridge at Zon. Tanks and bulldozers moved up and down the road, clearing wreckage and attempting to keep traffic moving. Taylor received a note from British Second Army commander Miles Dempsey dated that morning congratulating the Americans on their D-day success and adding, "I hope Guards Armd. Div. will join hands with you today."[13] There was no mention of the fact that the British advance was already twenty-four hours behind schedule, but Taylor had little time for developments outside his own area of responsibility:

> *Tuesday, September 19:* At 0600 went to the Zon bridge and watched first Second Army tank roll across. Also visited 501st CP at Veghel in the morning. In the afternoon watched 502d making attack near Best. At 1800 a couple of German tanks rolled up on the outskirts of Zon and began shelling bridge and Div CP. Committed Div reserve battalion to the task of clearing situation and by 2200 everything was under control.[14]

This terse diary entry hardly does justice to one of the many alarms with which the 101st had to deal during Market-Garden. By D plus 2 the Germans had gathered in force at Best and represented a clear threat to the highway. Taylor threw almost the entire 502d against the enemy, precipitating one of the major engagements of the "highway war" and resulting in a timely victory. The 502d, bolstered by Harper's glidermen, killed more than three hundred Germans and captured more than a thousand, along with fifteen artillery pieces.

At almost the same time, a German panzer brigade attempted to sever the highway at Zon. Taylor had only a scratch force with which to defend the road, but fortunately the attack was tentative. Taylor personally led a counterattack by part of a glider battalion with a 57-mm antitank gun. A round from the gun disabled one tank and a bazooka round took care of the other. The Germans did not press the attack and the crisis passed. The incident, however, was typical. No part of the Arnhem road was safe, and no one could be sure of where the next attack might develop. A contributing factor was the slow advance by the British VIII and XII corps on either side of the salient. The British were encountering problems with both the Germans and the marshy terrain, and because of their slow advance there was little reduction in the territory that the 101st was obliged to defend.

Because the 101st did not have the resources to maintain a static defense along its stretch of highway, Taylor sought to keep the Germans off balance with offensive thrusts of his own. The Screaming Eagles were coping, but elsewhere the signs were ominous. In the 82d's sector, near Nijmegen, the Germans put up a tenacious defense of the highway bridge over the Waal. It was not until the afternoon of D plus 4 that the paratroopers gained control of the bridge, and not until D plus 5 that the first units of the XXX Corps were able to cross the bridge and begin the last ten-mile advance to link up with the Red Devils at Arnhem. By then the Germans fully realized that they had only to block a single road to continue to isolate the 1st Division, and this they proceeded to do. Bad weather hampered efforts at aerial resupply, and by D plus 5 the British paratroopers were being hammered between the two German panzers. Not until D plus 6, September 23, did the British reach the Lower Rhine across from the embattled 1st Division. The "bridge too far" could not be saved. On September 25 Browning and Horrocks authorized the survivors to withdraw.

Out of nine thousand men of the British 1st Division and the Polish brigade, fewer than twenty-four hundred made it to safety. In Taylor's words, Market-Garden accomplished all that was expected of it "except victory at the critical point." After the war General Tony McAuliffe recalled that in the initial planning for Market, it was to have been the 101st that dropped into Arnhem. According to McAuliffe, the British requested a switch in assignments because they had already studied the Arnhem area in connection with an earlier operation that had been scrubbed.

Chapter 9

THE ISLAND

If the Normandy pattern had been repeated, the 101st would have moved to a rear area following the setback at Arnhem and from there back to England. But no withdrawal was forthcoming. Even after their sector of "Hell's Highway" was secured by the British Second Army, the 101st and 82d stayed on, attached to the Second Army. Prior to Market, Taylor had been told that his division would probably be relieved in forty-eight to seventy-two hours. Always conservative in his preparations, Taylor had based his planning on a period of thirty days. Even this assumption proved optimistic, for the 101st remained in the battle zone until November 25, a total of seventy days. During this period division elements were in constant contact with the Germans, and even rear-echelon units were within enemy artillery range. Supplies were sufficient to prevent any major shortages, but there were no personnel replacements. October and November were trying months, a fitting preparation for the ordeal to come at Bastogne.

By the end of September there was a degree of stability in the division sector. Skeets Johnson's 501st was defending the area around Veghel. The 502d was at St. Oedenrode and the 506th, at Uden. Harper's 327th was split, with one battalion northeast of Veghel and the remainder in reserve. The division was strengthened by the attachment of several small British tank, antitank, and field artillery units to compensate for its extended stay in the line. On September 27 the troops at Veghel received their first mail from home since D-day. The tempo of the fighting eased somewhat; at one locale, the friendly Dutch converted part of a dairy into a huge shower where grimy paratroopers could clean up for the first time since leaving England.

The campaign was full of surprises. Skeets Johnson, one of the

101st's boldest regimental commanders, had been an intercollegiate boxer at the U.S. Naval Academy who had made an unusual
transfer from the Navy to the Army paratroops after graduation.
One day, in Johnson's sector, two Germans came through the U.S.
outposts with a flag of truce. They had come to bargain for the
return of their battalion commander who had been captured earlier. In return, they offered to return a chaplain of the 502d. The
division history does not record the immediate reaction of Johnson and his officers to this offer to exchange "a bishop for a
knight," but it became clear that the Americans were not prepared
to deal when Johnson ordered that the two Germans, who had not
been blindfolded as they came through the U.S. lines, be held until
further notice.

As word circulated that the 101st would stay on with the British,
the reaction was one of surprise and disappointment. The mood
did not improve when word went around that the division was to
move north to reinforce the British XXX Corps. Nevertheless, on
October 2 the division began to deploy to the area north of Nijmegen between the Waal and the Rhine rivers. The move was not
without its critics in the high command. Brereton wrote to Eisenhower that the practice of keeping the 101st and 82d in the line "is
a violation of the cardinal rule of airborne deployment." He added
that "further combat will deplete them of trained men beyond replacement capacity."[1] Eisenhower agreed and on October 2 wrote
to Montgomery that he had plans for the two divisions and wanted
one released right away and the other as soon as possible. Montgomery agreed in principle but made no move to comply.

Generally for the Screaming Eagles, the most disagreeable part
of the Holland campaign was that part spent on "the island." The
terrain was largely farmland, divided by drainage ditches and
rows of trees. Most of the area was below the water level, protected from inundation by dikes. The soldiers were obliged to live
in shallow foxholes, which more often than not were waterlogged
and which afforded little protection from German artillery. In
contrast to the flat terrain of the island, the German-occupied
north bank of the Rhine was marked by low hills that allowed
enemy artillery to reach the entire 101st sector. Taylor called the
island campaign "a muddy, inglorious defensive conducted under

the constant observation and guns of the enemy."[2] Moreover, although the division had had a clear-cut mission while it was protecting the Arnhem highway, the Allied need to control "the island" was far less clear.

Casualties mounted. Skeets Johnson had more than a hundred jumps to his credit, and in both Normandy and Holland he was heedless of enemy fire. On the island the incoming whistle of one German shell led everyone to hit the deck except Johnson, who was fatally wounded. Taylor attended a funeral service for him the following day, perhaps reflecting that of the four regimental commanders who had gone into Normandy only Bob Sink remained. Moseley had been evacuated, Wear relieved, and now Johnson was dead.

Johnson's death saddened Taylor not only because the Annapolis graduate had been an effective and popular leader but because his death appeared to have been unnecessary. Taylor expected his officers to share the dangers of battle; his soldiers would tolerate nothing less. But he neither expected nor desired that they take unnecessary risks. In Normandy he had chewed out Bob Sink for personally undertaking a reconnaissance that should have been assigned to a junior officer. Taylor expected his officers to be out in front when the tactical situation required their presence there, but he was not interested in macho displays. He constantly reminded his officers that they had an obligation to stay alive and to assist the division in achieving its missions at the lowest possible cost.

One satisfying episode in this period was the rescue of the last survivors of the Arnhem debacle. Sink's regiment, whose operational area extended to the Rhine, heard through the Dutch underground in mid-October that more than a hundred survivors of the British 1st Airborne were in hiding across the river. Taylor and Sink made elaborate plans for their rescue, including plans for a "box" artillery barrage to seal off the proposed embarkation point if the British were discovered. But no artillery was required. In weather typical of this period, the overcast and drizzly night of October 22 proved ideal for concealment. Sink's paratroopers manned a number of British pontoon boats and at a prearranged signal crossed to the north bank. In the course of the night they conveyed 138 British soldiers and 4 American airmen to the relative sanctuary of the island.

At about this time the division command post was located in a partially concealed orchard. Taylor, perhaps acting on fresh intelligence, directed that it be moved before it became a target for German artillery. The signals company was dismayed, for there were scores of telephone lines running from under the trees; one technician estimated that the move would require at least the rest of the day. Then Julian Ewell, who had succeeded Skeets Johnson in command of the 501st, heard two loud explosions that he could not immediately identify, and saw a long, silvery object come burrowing out of the ground about six feet away. ("It just lay there, rocking slightly, putting off a little steam from the morning dew.") As Ewell recalled, the signals men reconsidered their earlier timetable and were able to move those wires in about ten minutes. The consensus was that the Germans had brought up a large-caliber railroad gun, one whose armor-piercing ammunition had failed to detonate in the marshy soil.

One of Taylor's characteristics as a combat commander was his insistence on active patrolling. He considered that the experience gained by officers on patrol was essential to their development, and he regarded the information that they brought back as his most useful tactical intelligence. Patrolling was not a popular activity, however, especially in Holland, where the danger was considerable and the rewards uncertain. Patrols had to contend with mines and booby traps as well as enemy fire; one night reconnaissance by the 502d had resulted in the loss of seven men. It was in part because recent patrols had been cautious and unproductive that a twenty-three-year-old intelligence officer, Lieutenant Hugo Sims, volunteered to lead a reconnaissance aimed at bringing back a prisoner for interrogation. Although it was not unusual for patrols to number more than thirty, Sims chose to limit his group to six.

The plan was fairly straightforward. Sims proposed to cross the Lower Rhine about four miles east of Arnhem and then to work his way north. By daybreak he planned to take over a house just off the Arnhem-Utrecht road and from there monitor traffic during the daylight hours. That night he intended to capture a German vehicle and take it and its driver to the river's edge. From there he would make his way back to the island.

The river crossing on the first night was uneventful. Sims and his band made their way past German outposts without being detected. As they worked their way north, they passed an ammunition dump and carefully noted its location and the types of munitions stored there. Farther along they skirted an enemy motor pool, passing so close that they could smell the bad tobacco being smoked by the Germans.

When dawn broke, Sims and his squad, on schedule, were close to the house where they planned to pass the day. It turned out to be occupied by two German soldiers, but both were asleep, and Sims was able to radio back that he had already seized double his quota of prisoners. As the day went on, the volume of traffic on the Arnhem-Utrecht road increased, and a variety of passersby found reason to drop by Sims's observation post. Six Dutch civilians were "detained" through the period of the mission, and a number of Germans were taken prisoner, all to their considerable surprise.

By late afternoon there were as many prisoners as there were Americans, and Sims prepared to call it a day. He hailed a passing truck—all uniforms must have looked pretty much alike—one that turned out to be carrying fifteen German soldiers. The numbers were getting out of hand, but Sims was undaunted. The paratroopers took their twenty-odd prisoners to the outskirts of Renkum, in the direction of the Rhine. There Sims's German-speaking sergeant delivered a little lecture. The Americans were taking them across the river to where they would not have to worry about the war any more. But anyone making unnecessary noise would be shot immediately.

The paratroopers formed their prisoners into two columns and marched them directly through the town. As they headed for the river, Sims spotted a squad of Germans at an outpost. The one German-speaker among the Americans bantered with them while Sims and the others took them prisoner. At the river bank Sims made a predetermined flashlight signal to the south bank. For the rest of the night Sims and his five comrades supervised the transfer of their thirty-two prisoners to the American side. For this exploit, one of the most remarkable of the war, Sims was awarded the Silver Star.[3]

By the end of October the fighting had subsided but the misery index was on the rise. Heavy rains made foxholes all but untenable. And there were still no personnel replacements. On November 7 Taylor wrote to Ridgway, "Generals Bull and Bonesteel called unexpectedly yesterday. I was a little discouraged to find that the former had no definite idea as to when we would be relieved."[4]

In early November, Ridgway, who had been effectively without a command during the Holland campaign, made an inspection of the 101st sector. One stop for Ridgway and Taylor was a mortar observation post in the belfry of a church overlooking the Rhine, and Ridgway ordered the sergeant there to direct a few rounds at a specified point on the enemy side of the river. The observer acknowledged the order and picked up his telephone. "Joe," he said, "remember the dead horse we used as an aiming point yesterday? This target is about 50 over and 100 left. Ten rounds when you're ready." As Taylor told it, the rounds were in the air almost at once, and their accuracy was above reproach. He and Ridgway went on about their business, but something about basing his sighting on a dead horse bothered the division commander.

Two days later Taylor, accompanied by aide Steve Karabinos and driver Charles Kartus, had occasion to pass the same observation post. Taylor signaled for a stop, hopped out of the jeep, and tracked down the sergeant who had been the observer two days before, chiding him for not using standard fire control procedures in the presence of the corps commander. He then picked out a random target across the river and told his man to fire at it "by the book." The sergeant protested briefly that the Germans had just moved up some mobile guns and that target practice would only stir them up. Taylor waved his objections aside. Employing procedures that, Taylor later admitted, consumed more time than the dead-horse sighting, his mortars eventually found the range.

Meanwhile, as the sergeant had predicted, the Germans were not idle; a self-propelled gun began replying. Steve Karabinos recalled what followed:

I turned to the General and said to him . . . we had better start doubletiming for some cover, which we did. I had hardly said the above when we heard the gun go off again and this time the whistling sound seemed to be right on top of us. By that time we were alongside a building and I was near turning the corner when suddenly I found myself being hurled some five feet through the air, but fortunately behind the building. I then proceeded to pick myself up and come back to the side of the building to see how the General and Kartus were faring. The General was just picking himself off the ground and I asked "How are you, General?" He replied, "The sonsabitches got me in the ass." I helped him to his feet and then picked Kartus up. He was hit in the left arm. . . . I was OK except that my wristwatch got busted. . . .

Since neither of them was seriously hurt, I loaded both into the jeep and hurriedly drove them to the aid station. . . . Both of them got a drink of rum at the aid station, but I didn't get anything because I wasn't hurt. I pleaded my case for a drink on the basis that my wristwatch was busted. The medics insisted that didn't count.[5]

Taylor would later tell the story of how he earned a Purple Heart with self-deprecating humor. Well might he do so, for in the affair of the dead-horse sighting he had violated several of his own precepts. He had exposed himself unnecessarily, he had failed to heed the advice of the most knowledgeable person on the scene, and he had insisted on parade-ground procedures in a combat situation. I suspect that he took the lesson to heart. It was said of General William Tecumseh Sherman that he never acknowledged a mistake, and never repeated one. To a great extent, the same could be said of Taylor.

If the division commander had to be wounded, his timing was excellent. At long last the American airborne divisions were being withdrawn from the combat zone. The first to pull out was the 82d, which began its move on November 11, D plus 55. On November 25 the first segments of the 101st pulled out for France.

As in Normandy, casualties had been heavy. In the first phase, along Hell's Highway, the 101st had suffered 2,110 casualties, including 315 killed. In the second, protracted phase on the island, the division had incurred nearly 1,700 additional casualties, including 375 dead. The total of nearly 3,800 killed, wounded, and missing for the Holland campaign was almost identical with the casualties for Normandy, despite the fact that D-day in Holland had been far less costly. The heavy losses in Holland were an immediate result of the division's extended exposure in the combat zone. At the same time, the 101st inflicted far more damage than it received. Although there is no accurate figure for casualties inflicted, the number of prisoners taken by the 101st—4,800—exceeded the division's total casualties.[6]

Taylor's report on the Holland campaign reflected a general maturing of airborne operations. This time there was no litany of equipment shortcomings or problems with airlift. His report focused on two problems above and beyond the key one, the extended period for which his division had been kept in line. The first concerned replacements. Because no personnel replacements were available for the seventy days in Holland, "the strength of combat units became progressively weaker." If an airborne division were to be kept in combat for more than thirty days, he urged that provision be made for adequate replacements. His second point concerned artillery, which arrived only on D plus 3. He recommended for the future that some artillery should be brought in with the first elements, so that key terrain at some distance from the landing zones might be denied to the enemy.

On the positive side, the Dutch populace as well as the underground had proved to be an unexpected asset. Whereas Taylor had perceived the reaction of the French to the Normandy invasion as bordering on indifference, he was very much taken with the Dutch. In later years he recalled; "We never had to set up military government in a Dutch town. They just moved into the town hall and commenced running their communities again. Far ahead of our advance they sent back valuable information on German concentrations over the domestic telephone lines, which the Germans hadn't had time to dismantle."[7]

The Holland campaign was the only occasion in World War II in which Taylor fought alongside troops of another nationality, in this case the British. He gave them mixed reviews. In Sicily he had been impressed with their staff work; they were "a lot more experienced than we in the actual planning of an operation." In Holland, however, he felt that the British infantry did not measure up:

> They would go into action and just deploy and stay in place. . . . They would lie there and take heavy casualties from shelling of all types, never breaking or retreating, but without the drive to move forward, apparently without the sense of preservation which makes good troops know that they are in danger and that the safest way is to move toward the enemy and not stay put.

The shortcomings of the British infantry did not extend to their artillery. "They were magnificent gunners," he would recall. "They had conserved their artillery, and it was excellent."[8]

While the 101st rested in some old French barracks at Camp Mourmelon near Reims, Taylor received special orders. He was, on Marshall's direction, to return to the United States to participate in discussions concerning the future structure and equipment for airborne divisions. Given the relative quiet on the front, he had no hesitation in leaving. It would afford the first reunion with his family in two years, and he had full confidence in Tony McAuliffe and Jerry Higgins.

Despite the Allied repulse at Arnhem, the belief that Germany was on the ropes was widespread. By mid-September the U.S. First Army had pierced the Siegfried Line at several points, although it had been unable to exploit these gains. Improved supplies were expected to change all this. Eisenhower directed Montgomery to give the highest priority to opening the port of Antwerp, and once this was accomplished the supply crunch could be expected to ease. But the Allies were unduly influenced by their rapid course across France. The high command did not fully anticipate what should have been obvious: that shortened lines of communication, together with a natural desire to defend the fatherland, would lead to stiffer German resistance. Granted a respite by the Allies' supply problems, the Germans were making a remarkable recovery from the debacle in France.

Nor were the Allies the only people interested in Antwerp. Even prior to Market-Garden, Hitler was formulating plans for a massive counterstroke in the West. At a council of war on September 12 he had seized on mention of "the Ardennes." He told his generals, "I have made a momentous decision. I am taking the offensive. Here—out of the Ardennes!" He smashed his fist on the map for emphasis. "Across the Meuse and on to Antwerp!"[9] As the Führer spelled out his plan, his listeners were incredulous that Hitler could propose such a scheme, given the adversity that pressed on Germany from all sides. Yet attacks through the Ardennes had achieved surprise in both world wars. Could not such a result be achieved again? On Hitler's map the German lines were just over one hundred miles from Antwerp. A rapid thrust through the Ardennes could cut off more than one hundred thousand Allied soldiers, deny Europe's largest port to the Allies, and eliminate the immediate threat to the Ruhr. With luck, it might even sow fatal divisions within the Western alliance.

Field Marshal von Rundstedt, who was to have overall charge of the operation, had no faith in the plan. He had no confidence in Hitler's promises of equipment and was far more disposed toward a limited offensive in the area around Aachen. But the Führer was firm. He first set a date of December 10 for the attack, but logistical considerations caused the date to slide to December 16. In any case, there was to be one final throw of the dice.

Chapter 10

FOUR THOUSAND MILES
TO BASTOGNE

While the Screaming Eagles were winning the war in Europe, the Taylor family lived in a rented house off Lee Highway in Arlington, Virginia. The three of us—my mother, my younger brother Tom, and I—followed the war news intently. We lived frugally and deplored the stories of wartime profiteering that were a staple of the Washington press. We had a dependable family car, the same one that Taylor had driven to the War Department on Pearl Harbor day, and a cocker spaniel named Po, after the dog in a Japanese fairy tale who had sniffed out treasure in his master's garden. My mother's volunteer work for the Office of Price Administration entitled us to a "B" gasoline ration for the car, although I have few recollections of other than the most essential driving. Some foods, notably meat, were also subject to wartime controls, but my mother did wonders with egg dishes and tuna casseroles.

Word that our father would be "home for Christmas" at the end of 1944, if only for a visit, was exciting news for Tom and me. It was, however, very much a working visit, and the general would be seeing far more of Pentagon officialdom in his two-week stay than he would of his family. On December 8 he flew from France to Scotland, accompanied by his aide, Tom White. From there he flew to Washington by way of Iceland, arriving on December 10 to a warm family welcome. Almost immediately he plunged into a round of calls and conferences. He spent a half hour on December 11 with Marshall, who praised the combat performance of the airborne troops but expressed annoyance at their being employed piecemeal, in his view, rather than en masse. The following day he met with Secretary of War Henry Stimson, who quizzed him at length about Market-Garden. The primary purpose of Taylor's trip, however, related to the staffing of airborne divisions, in particular the allocation of junior officers. In meeting with senior G-3 personnel, Taylor emphasized that billets such as assistant platoon leader were essential in an airborne division, made so both by past casualty rates and by the dispersion that had accompanied almost all airborne operations to date.[1]

On December 15 Marshall concurred in the bulk of Taylor's staffing recommendations and sent him off to inspect various training installations along the East Coast. Four days later Taylor squeezed in an overnight visit to Dunn, North Carolina, to pay his respects to his still-ailing predecessor, Bill Lee. The following day he flew to Hagerstown, Maryland, where he had his first look at the C-82 transport, programmed to replace the C-47 in the Troop Carrier Command.

Meanwhile, in the Ardennes, von Rundstedt was moving thirteen infantry and seven armored divisions to areas opposite a lightly held sector of the American front line some sixty miles across. Given the Allied control of the air, the secrecy with which this was accomplished remains remarkable. Luck played a part. Although Hitler had no idea that the Allies had broken his military codes, he had ordered radio silence in all matters related to the Ardennes offensive, action that denied the Allies the Ultra intercepts that would have indicated the scope of the German offensive. On December 12 the 12th Army Group's intelligence office concluded that "it is now certain that attrition is steadily sapping the strength of the German forces . . . and that the crust of defenses is thinner, more brittle and more vulnerable than it appears on our G-2 maps or to the troops in the line."[2]

Even as this was written, von Rundstedt had assembled 1,400 tanks and armored assault guns and 1,900 artillery pieces. Hitler had stripped the Russian front to the bone in order that he might attempt to cripple the Allies in the West. The German plan called for the deployment of 200,000 men against a sector manned by 83,000 Americans. At the outset, at least, the Germans would have a similar two-to-one superiority in tanks. In mid-December von Rundstedt was granted the final prerequisite to his offensive:

weather sufficiently bad to ground the Allied air forces for several days.

On December 16, while Taylor inspected airborne units at Fort Bragg, the Germans struck. The day was bitter cold, and the snow on the ground contributed to an early morning fog as the gray-clad German infantry moved forward. Contrary to some accounts, the attackers did not have everything their way. Determined resistance on the northern shoulder by the U.S. 99th and 2d divisions threw the Germans off their schedule. In the center of the salient, however, they made good progress. Von Manteuffel's Fifth Panzer Army had two key targets, a rail center at St. Vith and the town of Bastogne, the latter being a congruence of the major roads of the Ardennes, including one to Antwerp.

Taylor, back in Washington, read of the German offensive but scoffed initially at press reports of its scope. He had concluded that most of the German units that the 101st had encountered in Holland were of indifferent quality, and was inclined to believe— as were Eisenhower and Bradley—that most of the Wehrmacht had lost its fighting edge. On December 21, however, the War Department confirmed that a heavy attack was in progress. Taylor, who had spent the morning visiting the wounded of his division at Walter Reed Hospital, checked in at the Pentagon. There on the situation map was his division, a blue pin in a sea of red. A few hours later Tom White, who was visiting the convalescing Larry Legere at Fort Devens, Massachusetts, was called by his parents. They had just received a telegram from Taylor in Washington, ordering White to return to Washington by the first available transportation. Captain White would not be spending Christmas in Boston after all.

The American high command was slow to recognize the magnitude of the German attack. The commander of the First Army, General Courtney Hodges, at first thought it a limited-objective thrust aimed at diverting his own thrust east. Bradley, shown that von Rundstedt appeared to have committed fourteen divisions to "the bulge," was incredulous. By midday on December 17, however, Hodges had decided to ask for Bradley's strategic reserve, which by this time consisted only of his two convalescing airborne divisions. Because Bastogne was both a highway hub for the region and the headquarters of General Troy Middleton's VIII Corps, both the 101st and the 82d were initially directed there. Shortly, however, the 82d was diverted north to St. Vith, leaving only the 101st with Bastogne as its objective.

December 18–19 was a period of wild confusion for the Screaming Eagles. From a standing start they were expected to move the eighty-odd miles from Mourmelon to Bastogne with all possible speed. Maps were scarce and weapons rarely at hand. Moreover, Taylor was not the only senior officer out of the area. The assistant division commander, Jerry Higgins, was in England delivering a lecture on the Holland campaign, and he had taken several other officers with him. Most would eventually rejoin the division at Bastogne, but their absence placed heavy burdens on the acting division commander, Tony McAuliffe. Julian Ewell recalled that some men went off with little or none of their equipment: "People were tossing helmets and rifles to soldiers already in the trucks."[3] By the evening of December 18, amid the confusion of conflicting orders and choked roads, the first elements of the division reached Bastogne. So, too, did several "orphan" units, including the 705th Tank Destroyer Battalion and a combat command of the 10th Armored Division.

The following day Eisenhower met at Verdun with Bradley, Patton, and their staffs to consider how best to counter the German breakthrough. They agreed that previously scheduled American attacks on the German flanks should be postponed. Although everyone desired to pinch off the Ardennes "bulge" as soon as practicable, only to the south, in Patton's sector, was the situation sufficiently stable to permit an immediate counteroffensive. Patton, however, was raring to go. When Eisenhower asked how soon he could begin a drive to Bastogne, Patton promised to have his army turned around by December 22, scarcely more than forty-eight hours away.

Meanwhile, in Bastogne, the 101st was establishing a defensive perimeter north and east of the town. Tony McAuliffe, whose defiant rejection of a German surrender ultimatum would make him a folk hero in America, was in fact a solid, conventional soldier who went by the book. At Bastogne, he deployed his four regiments in a perimeter defense some seven miles in diameter, obliging the on-coming Germans to divide their advance and creating a backup of vehicular traffic behind von Manteuffel's Fifth Panzer Army. On December 19 McAuliffe directed Ewell to take the 501st on the road to Mageret, make contact with the enemy, and "develop the situation." By that afternoon Ewell was sufficiently impressed with what was coming down the road that he requested permis-sion to establish a defensive line. The situation was much the same to the north toward Noville. Higgins, now on the scene, concluded that Sink's 506th was "way out on a limb" at Noville, but Middle-ton, who had relocated his corps headquarters west of Bastogne, was initially reluctant to authorize a withdrawal. By December 20, however, the enemy had cut the road between Noville and Bas-togne, and McAuliffe ordered the 506th back on his own authority. Even so, it was dark before the last remnants of the Noville contin-gent had made it back to Bastogne. Losses were heavy.

On December 21, the day of Taylor's briefing at the Pentagon, the advancing Germans surged past Bastogne on both sides. By that afternoon the remaining corridor to the west had been sealed, leaving the 101st surrounded. To the east and south, the defensive perimeter was only about a mile from the town. Ammunition for both artillery and small arms was running low, for the rain and overcast had prevented any aerial resupply. By noon of the follow-ing day the 101st's four artillery battalions were down to two hun-dred rounds each, and McAuliffe contemplated a ration of ten rounds per gun per day.

On December 19, division surgeon David Gold had set up his hospital at a crossroads west of Bastogne. Almost immediately, however, there were signs of Germans in the vicinity. Back in the States, Gold had participated in an exercise in which his hospital, three miles from the "front," had been captured by the "enemy." Now he thought, "Christ, this is Louisiana all over again!"[4] That evening a column of German tanks clanked up the road and began firing into and over the hospital. Gold protested under a flag of truce, but in the end had no choice but to surrender his hospital, a serious development for the division. In the emergency, aid sta-tions were turned into makeshift hospitals, but none of the wounded could be evacuated. A church near the center of town served as an aid station for one regiment, the 501st. So crowded did it become that regimental commander Julian Ewell set up an annex in a garage, where the wounded lay wrapped in blankets on top of sawdust. A snowstorm on December 22 once again delayed any aerial resupply.

In the late morning of December 22 four German soldiers with a flag of truce approached a farmhouse near the hamlet of Arlon that served as an outpost for Bud Harper's glidermen. The Americans were so cocky that the first rumor to make the rounds was that the Germans wanted to surrender. For a brief period the men of the 327th left their foxholes, built fires, and even took time to write home. Because Harper was away from his command post, Alvin Jones, his G-3, received the Germans and took their message to division headquarters in the center of town. The language was straightforward:

> To the U.S.A. Commander of the encircled town of Bastogne:
>
> The fortune of war is changing. This time the U.S.A. forces in and near Bastogne have been encircled by strong German armored units. More German armored units have crossed the river Ourthe near Ortheuville, have taken Marche and reached St. Hubert. . . .
>
> There is only one possibility to save the encircled U.S.A. troops from total annihilation: that is the honorable surrender of the encircled town. In order to think it over a term of two hours will be granted beginning with the presentation of this note.
>
> If this proposal should be rejected, one German Artillery Corps and six heavy A.A. Battalions are ready to annihilate the U.S.A. troops in and near Bastogne. The order for firing will be given immediately after this two-hour term.
>
> All the serious civilian losses caused by this artillery fire would not correspond with the well-known American humanity.
>
> The German Commander[5]

Most of the division staff were in the operations room, located in the basement of an old barracks, when Jones arrived and said he had a message from the German commander. "What is it?" McAuliffe asked, awakening from his first sleep in forty-eight hours. "It's an ultimatum, sir," Jones replied. Colonel Ned Moore took the papers and scanned the English text. "They want you to surrender," he said. "Nuts!" commented the stolid McAuliffe, who had just been told that he would get his first aerial resupply that night. By the time McAuliffe got around to composing a reply he had received lots of advice. "That first crack you made would be hard to beat, General," commented Harry Kinnard, the G-3. "What was that?" McAuliffe asked. "You said 'Nuts!' " The others were equally enthusiastic. McAuliffe wrote "Nuts!" on a piece of paper, signed it "The American Commander," and told Harper to deliver that reply.

Harper returned to the farmhouse, where McAuliffe's unconventional message thoroughly confused the waiting Germans. The Wehrmacht officer who was acting as translator inquired, "Is that reply negative or affirmative?" Harper retorted that it was "decidedly not affirmative," adding helpfully that it was the equivalent of "Go to hell."[6]

Appropriately enough, even as the Americans spurned von Manteuffel's surrender demand, the tide was beginning to turn. On the same day that McAuliffe sent his famous reply, Patton was making good on his promise to see to the relief of Bastogne. Undeterred by a swirling snowstorm, he ordered three divisions, including the 4th Armored, to break through to the 101st from the south. "Drive like hell," Patton told his men.

The fickle weather now took a turn for the Allies. U.S. fighter aircraft were out in force on the morning of December 23, seeking the German columns that heretofore had been immune from air attack. Also in the skies were hundreds of C-47 transports, dropping their loads within the Bastogne perimeter, the color-coded parachutes indicating whether they bore food, ordnance, or medical supplies.

> Men watched in awe from their foxholes, others from windows and the streets of the town, and crowds of civilians emerged from their catacombs for what seemed to be a miracle, "resupply coming from the sky." They "applauded, shouted with joy, cried"; they were saved, "lost hope rekindled." To at least one paratrooper, Capt. Laurence Critchell of the 501st Parachute In-

fantry, it was difficult "not to feel a sentimental pride of country."[7]

By this time the Germans themselves were perplexed about Bastogne. It could not be bypassed indefinitely, and as long as it remained in American hands it would be a magnet for Patton's tanks. Hitler insisted that the town be taken no later than December 25.* To achieve this objective clearly would require more than the equivalent of two divisions thus far committed, but von Manteuffel was also expected to drive to the Meuse River. After augmenting his forces in front of Bastogne with a regiment of the 15th Panzer Grenadiers, von Manteuffel prepared for an all-out attack on Christmas Day.

On December 24 McAuliffe distributed a holiday message to his soldiers. After wishing all a Merry Christmas he conceded, "What's merry about all this? you ask. We're fighting—it's cold—we aren't home." But he cited their common achievement in throwing back everything the Germans had thrown at them and then confirmed what most had heard concerning the surrender demand and his succinct reply. He closed on a reassuring note:

> Allied troops are counterattacking in force. We continue to hold Bastogne. By holding Bastogne we assure the success of the Allied Armies. We know that our Division Commander, General Taylor, will say "Well done!"[9]

In the foxholes the men of the 101st shook hands and exchanged Christmas greetings. McAuliffe himself was walking past the local police station, which was being used to house prisoners, when he heard the sound of Christmas carols in German. On an impulse he went inside, and the singing gave way to jeers. "We'll be in Antwerp in a few weeks," one prisoner shouted. "We'll soon be freed," insisted another, "and it is you who'll be the prisoner." McAuliffe waited for them to quiet down and then wished them holiday greetings.[10]

---

* The Screaming Eagles numbered none other than Adolf Hitler among their admirers. The minutes of one of his staff meetings noted, "The Fuhrer again and again stressed the exemplary stubborn defense of Bastogne and said among other things, 'I should like to see the German General who would fight on with the same stubborn, tough resistance in a situation which seemed just as hopeless.'"[8]

The German attack came before dawn on Christmas morning. This time they concentrated on the 502d north of the Marche highway and on the 327th west of Bastogne. At one time German tanks broke through the 327th, and several reached a hamlet just a mile from the center of town. There most of the tanks were destroyed, and the Germans never again came so close to capturing Bastogne. There was heavy fighting through most of Christmas Day, but at the end of it the Germans were obliged to heed the threat posed by Patton's relief force.

Two of the 4th Armored Division's battalion commanders, Creighton Abrams and George Jaques, drove their tanks to within four miles of Bastogne on Christmas Day. The following morning they were considering their next moves when they saw American cargo aircraft dropping supplies for Bastogne. The airdrop so dramatized the plight of the defenders that the two officers vowed to push through by the most direct route. At about five o'clock that afternoon, division headquarters received word of the approach of "three light tanks believed to be friendly." The message brought McAuliffe hurrying to the southern sector, where he found three tanks of the 4th Armored amid much backslapping and handshaking. "How are you, General?" asked Captain William Dwight of the 37th Tank Battalion. "Gee," said McAuliffe, "I'm mighty glad to see you."[11]

While his division was writing one of the great pages in the history of the war, Taylor, with Tom White, was sandwiched among the packing crates on a C-54 crossing the North Atlantic. White would remember the trip all too well, including a snow-delayed departure from Washington:

We finally flew out on Christmas Eve at about ten o'clock in the evening; it was still snowing, but it wasn't a wild snowstorm. In those days planes were not pressurized and we had to fly at ten thousand feet through bad weather, in bitter cold and great discomfort. We flew into Gander, Newfoundland, and from Gander to the Azores where we stopped for refueling and dinner; by then it was Christmas Day. This was the only time I ever saw General Taylor really let his hair down. Instead of his usual two

drinks he had several more, and we talked about many things—
the States, our families, some of our dreams, but nothing military. I had never seen him that way before and I never saw him
that way again.[12]

It was noon on December 26 before the two Americans reached
Orly Field in Paris. From there they traveled by staff car to Eisenhower's headquarters at Versailles, where they saw firsthand the
confusion the Germans had created in rear areas. A handful of
English-speaking Germans had been parachuted behind American
lines where they misdirected convoys, spread rumors, and, by
some accounts, planned to assassinate Eisenhower. So tight was
security at SHAEF that Taylor, despite his uniform and two stars,
was obliged to show his tags to gain admission.

At Versailles, Taylor asked to see Eisenhower's chief of staff, his
old friend Beetle Smith. He asked Smith for a plane from which to
parachute into Bastogne—a request that, had it been granted,
would have caused General Sheridan's galloping return to his
command at Winchester to pale by comparison. Smith, however,
pointed out that the 4th Armored had just broken through to Bastogne and had evacuated most of the wounded. He suggested that
Taylor would do well to go to Luxembourg and check in at
Bradley's and Patton's headquarters and then rejoin his command
by road. Smith had strong praise for the 101st and a chuckle for
McAuliffe's reply to the Germans. He and Taylor agreed that Mc-
Auliffe should be given his own division command at the first opportunity.

Taking leave of Smith, Taylor began a long trek to the front. He
first drove to Mourmelon, where he picked up his combat gear and
some warm clothing. He and White had dinner and headed for
their bunks, but in Taylor's words, "there was too much on my
mind for sleep." He roused White and their driver, Charles Kartus,
and headed into the night toward Luxembourg. Taylor estimated
the drive at about five hours, but he was overly optimistic:

Unfortunately this estimate did not take into account the para-
chutist phobia. The road was cluttered with towns and villages,
most of them with guards [who were] on the lookout for para-
chutists and who wanted to inspect all vehicles driving by. We

soon got tired of these delays and proceeded to drive along without stopping. Luckily, the occasional bullets generated thereby were not fired by sharpshooters.[13]

Arriving at First Army headquarters on the morning of December 27, Taylor was able to meet with Bradley and Patton. He found both confident that the German attack was slowing and that a counterattack would soon be possible. For the final leg to Bastogne, Taylor exchanged his staff car for a jeep and headed north with White in search of the 4th Armored Division. In time they found it and were told of continued fighting on the Assenors road by which Abrams's and Jaques's tanks had entered Bastogne. Yes, Patton's soldiers told them, the road appeared to be open, but there was still plenty of firing. Would the general care to borrow one of their tanks? Taylor declined, on the grounds that he preferred the mobility afforded by a jeep. As they were about to take off on this, the last lap, Taylor spotted a group of war correspondents—Joseph Driscoll of the New York *Herald Tribune*, Norman Clark of the London *News Chronicle*, Cornelius Ryan of the London *Daily Telegraph*, and one Walter Cronkite, representing United Press—warming themselves in a shack by the side of the road. He offered any of them the vacant seat in his jeep, but all four declined.

Bastogne was little more than a mile away, but what remained of a road was littered with burned-out tanks and other debris, and from the woods came periodic bursts of small-arms fire. Charles Kartus, who drove Taylor throughout the war, declared this to be his "scariest" time in the war as he bounded at high speed over and off the road in the general direction of Bastogne. (An American manufacturer of jeeps subsequently used "Taylor's Ride" to Bastogne as a full-page magazine ad for its rugged product. It portrayed Taylor's jeep careening through a group of surprised Germans, its occupants keeping the enemy at bay with deadly pistol fire.)

At the outskirts of the town the Americans ran into a group of soldiers gathering supplies that had been dropped by air. Darkness was beginning to fall as the paratroopers directed their commander to the division headquarters in the center of town. McAuliffe and his officers were incredulous when Taylor informed them that they were heroes; in any case, McAuliffe insisted that the division was ready to go on the offensive. Not everyone, however, would have agreed with this assessment; casualties during the siege had amounted to 105 officers and more than 1,500 soldiers. An officer of the 4th Armored recorded his impressions of Bastogne:

> The wind swept through the broken trees along the roads and the armor in the field, even the tanks that had been hastily smeared with white paint, stood out in sharp relief, cold and naked. The troops built little fires of anything that would burn, even within sight of the enemy, to try to warm themselves. . . . The dead lay frozen and stiff and when the men came to load them in trucks, they picked them up and put them in like big logs of wood. The frozen arms and legs got in their way when they were piling them.[14]

As Taylor resumed his command, his chagrin at having missed the siege was mitigated by pride in the performance of his division and by the knowledge that more fighting lay ahead. Shortly after his return he issued a message to the troops:

> To the soldiers of this division who have lived through the day-to-day fighting in this area it is not possible to appreciate fully just what has been accomplished, but every senior commander knows, the American people know, what the retention of Bastogne has meant in checking the German drive. Bastogne joins with Normandy and Holland as a brilliant feat of arms performed by the 101st Airborne Division.
>
> I wish to congratulate Brig. Gen. A. C. McAuliffe and every officer and man for this job so well done.[15]

Taylor would later speak of his having missed the siege of Bastogne as one of his two disappointments of the war—the other being the cancellation of Giant II against Rome. Whereas a dash through enemy lines such as his on December 27 would be the high point of many a military career, Taylor rarely spoke of it and had to be prodded to include some mention of it in his memoirs.

To him it was a sideshow; the real action had been the eight-day siege.

Late in life Taylor would acknowledge that there was some irony in the his division's most famous defensive effort. In stemming the German advance, the defenders of Bastogne had effectively limited the extent of the German penetration and almost certainly reduced the number of Germans taken prisoner when "the bulge" was finally pinched off at its base. None of this, however, in any way dimmed the luster of his division's "finest hour."

Chapter 11

BASTOGNE TO BERCHTESGADEN

The 101st's campaigns tended to divide into two phases. In Normandy, the campaign took on a different character following the assembly of the division and the capture of Carentan. In Holland, there was a clear distinction between the skirmishing along Hell's Highway and the longer period of fighting north of Nijmegen. So, too, there were two distinct phases at Bastogne. Although the division gained its acclaim for its tenacious defense over the eight-day siege, the Screaming Eagles were in fact in constant contact with the enemy over the next twenty-two days as well. And because the division was on the tactical offensive for much of this period, losses in the period after Christmas would prove to be heavier than those during the siege itself.

In the last days of December the southern corridor to Bastogne was fully open. Supplies poured in; a single day brought no less than 13,500 pounds of Christmas turkey. But the Germans were far from done with Bastogne. Von Manteuffel, whose panzers were already overextended, viewed the reinforced Bastogne corridor as a threat to his forward units. The enclave that once had blocked the German advance now threatened its retreat. On December 30 he launched another heavy attack against the town, only to be repulsed by American armor.

Taylor spent his first few days in Bastogne examining perimeter defenses and talking to his commanders. For the most part he liked what he saw. Frontline units occupied strong defensive positions with good fields of fire. Some extra battalions of artillery that the division had picked up in December strengthened an already formidable defense. But the weather continued to favor the enemy. Poor visibility made the availability of air support a day-to-day proposition, while German night bombers had no difficulty in locating a major road junction such as Bastogne. Meanwhile, the ground was so hard that soldiers sometimes requested help from the engineers in blasting out a foxhole for the night.

Some of the heaviest fighting at Bastogne began just after the New Year. On January 3 Taylor received orders from Middleton to prepare an attack to the northeast in conjunction with a move by Patton's army to cut off the base of the Ardennes "bulge." At the same time the Germans launched attacks on Bastogne from the northeast, north, and northwest. In meeting the threat Taylor employed a technique he had used successfully in both Normandy and Holland: formation of an ad hoc task force under the direction of a senior officer. In this instance he created Task Force Higgins, comprising the 502d and 327th regiments plus other units, including the 705th Tank Destroyer Battalion. After three days of furious fighting in the area around Champs, the German pressure eased and Task Force Higgins was disbanded. Taylor later recalled that "the Germans were strong in tanks whereas our airborne troops were weak in antitank weapons." In these adverse circumstances the 502d passed what he called the sternest test of a soldier in combat: "to stay in a foxhole while an enemy tank runs over it and then attack it from the rear."[1]

Meanwhile, Patton's counteroffensive had bogged down, and orders for the 101st to go on the offensive had to be put on hold. It was just as well. The division represented the tip of a salient, one that was five miles across in some places. To advance, however, it would require support on the flanks. Taylor would have liked to take some high ground in the Noville-Bourcy area northeast of Bastogne, but he was not prepared to attack unsupported. He took advantage of a lull to move the division command post from a barracks in the middle of town ("The German bombers could find it in their sleep") to a small château just outside of town to the southwest. On January 7 he received word that Tony McAuliffe had just been named to command the 103d Infantry Division. The officers of the 101st threw a dinner in his honor, and, because he was going to a "straightleg" outfit, presented him with a pair of paratrooper leggings. It was an emotional farewell; according to Julian Ewell, McAuliffe broke down and cried.

On January 9 the 101st went briefly on the offensive in support of a broader Allied counteroffensive from the south. After two days of hard fighting the offensive was called off because of a German threat elsewhere. The only product was casualties. Taylor's diary entry for January 10 read:

> Visited all regimental CPs in morning. Units progressively proceeding to take their objectives. Attack called off at 1400 by higher headquarters. Gen Patton with several division commanders attended conference at the Hqrs reference the above change in plan. Result was our division pulled back to approximately its line of defense prior to going to offensive, and there set up positions for defense of Bastogne again.[2]

The last major offensive by the 101st began on January 9 as part of the drive northward of the VIII Corps. The week that followed proved bloody and took a heavy toll of the division's most experienced officers. Julian Ewell, commanding the 501st, was wounded, as were no fewer than five battalion commanders. In a letter to Ridgway on January 11, Taylor tallied some debits and credits:

> The unit commanders of the division have all done extremely well in the fighting here. I have recommended for promotion Ewell and Chappuis, who command the 501st and 502d respectively. Their performance has amply justified my expectations. I feel I still have three potential regimental commanders in Lt. Colonel Chase (506), Lt. Colonel Cassidy (502) and Lt. Colonel Kinnard (Division G-3), so I am well situated in that grade. However, the position of battalion commander is becoming increasingly difficult to fill.[3]

The tactical situation presented more than its share of frustrations. The requirement to defend an extended salient made it difficult for Taylor to maintain adequate reserves, much less initiate any major offensive effort. On several occasions Middleton attempted to generate a general offensive. Such plans called for the 101st to remain in place while other units came abreast or took over part of the airborne perimeter to allow the 101st to assemble reserves. In Taylor's recollection, "Over and over again these attacks were called off or stopped because of the failure of our neighbors to come up."[4]

Fortunately, the enemy had never quite known what to do about the Bastogne salient. Earlier, when the German offensive had some momentum, most enemy units had chosen to bypass the town. In the first half of January the Germans renewed their attacks, but generally in piecemeal fashion. Taylor was impressed with the quality of the enemy troops but not with their tactics. When the fighting was over, the 101st had prisoners from nine different divisions, none of which had ever attacked in greater strength than a regimental task force.

At long last the Bastogne campaign was about to end for the Screaming Eagles. On January 16 word came from VIII Corps headquarters that the 101st's sector was to be taken over by the neighboring 11th Armored Division. The 101st would move first into corps reserve and then to a defensive sector in Alsace. Here action was largely limited to patrols across the Moder River while the division assimilated replacements for its heavy casualties. Taylor took great care in the matter of replacements. When conditions permitted, he met with them in small groups. A handout provided to new arrivals suggests the tone of this welcome:

> As Division Commander, I welcome you to the 101st Airborne Division. We are proud of having you in this division and expect you to be proud of joining it. This is the division which, of all the Allied forces, was the first to land on the shores of Normandy. It is the division which cleared the road for the British Army in its rapid advance into Holland last September. Above all, it is the division of Bastogne which broke the back of the German counteroffensive and thus changed the course of the entire war.
>
> To belong to this division is an honor to me and is an honor to you. It is also a responsibility which must be met in proportion to our respective jobs. Your immediate job is to make yourself into as fine a fighting soldier as the veteran who became a casualty and created the vacancy which you are to fill. I want you often to think of this man whom you will never meet. He was a friend of ours whom we knew well and regarded highly. He fell

in battle while fighting gallantly at our side in Holland or in Belgium. It is up to you to be as good a man as he was and that is not an easy order.

The standards of this division are high. You will see other soldiers in American uniform doing things which you will not be permitted to do. You will see dirty soldiers, undisciplined soldiers and men that plainly have little respect for themselves or their organization. That is not the way of this division. Here you will carry your weapon at all times. You will wear your uniform properly. You will render military courtesies except when you are under enemy fire. . . .

In return for your loyalty to the division, the division will look after you. I insist that every officer and non-commissioned officer in this division have as his first concern in life the wellbeing of his soldiers. These experienced leaders will teach you all that they have learned in past campaigns of how to live in the field and in battle. If you listen attentively to their advice you will live long and serve your country well. . . .[5]

The 101st returned to Mourmelon, near Reims, where Eisenhower presented the Screaming Eagles with the first Distinguished Unit Citation ever awarded an entire division. After a period of rehabilitation the division was attached to General Alexander Patch's Seventh Army for the final campaign of the European war. By April the division was in southern Bavaria in what was thought to be a very sensitive area. The Allied high command believed almost to the end that Hitler and some die-hard supporters planned to make their way south from Berlin for a last-ditch stand in a Bavarian redoubt. But German resistance in the south evaporated as it did elsewhere. Units as large as divisions simply vanished, as both sides listened to news bulletins that chronicled the disintegration of one of the most feared armies of modern times.

On May 4 the 101st received its last wartime mission: to occupy Berchtesgaden, Hitler's mountain retreat. Taylor reflected on this prestigious assignment and gave it to Bob Sink and the 506th. If Taylor had a favorite among his regimental commanders it was Sink—a fact that some in the 101st thought remarkable. The two had sharply contrasting styles: the folksy, devil-may-care Sink

From the desk of . . . . .

COLONEL PAUL W. CHILD JR., USA (Ret.)
Director of Publications
Editor of Assembly and
Register of Graduates

ASSOCIATION
OF GRADUATES

11 May 1989

Colonel Paul Miles
Dept of History
USMA

Paul,

Thank you for your note of 10 May regarding the Taylor book. The enclosed version arrived two days ago, and I had planned to get it to you this week.

As you will note, it is an uncorrected proof and may be of limited value to the reviewer. When the finished book arrives, I'll send it right over.

Regards,

Paul

(who once made a parachute jump in loafers, to prove a point) was a very different personality from his cool commander. Years later, however, Taylor would characterize Sink as "among the bravest, most able men I knew—[he] exposed himself to enemy fire more than anyone in the division—but he never got promoted in the war."[6]

On May 9, Taylor had the following message for his soldiers:

It is my pleasure to announce that the war in Europe ended in victory this morning at 0001 hours. It is an occasion for solemn rejoicing and thanksgiving. I call on all of you, regardless of sect or creed, to give thanks to the God of Battles who has brought victory to our Armies and destruction to the enemy. The troops will form today in memorial services for victory and for the remembrance of our Dead who made victory possible.[7]

After a year of bitter fighting, the 101st found itself inundated with placid prisoners in a picture-postcard Alpine setting. While the division had been in France and Holland, orders against looting had had some deterrent effect. In Germany, however, such edicts proved unenforceable, as nearly everyone's thoughts turned to plunder. The wine cellars of Nazi bigwigs were a favorite target, and whole truckloads of rare vintages disappeared overnight. Motor vehicles were also subject to instant requisitioning. It seemed that almost every soldier had a motorcycle, and Taylor himself made use for a time of Hitler's armored Mercedes touring car.

Artifacts of the "Thousand Year Reich" abounded, and many were of great value. Among those seized by the 101st were several silver services belonging to Goering, along with the Reichsmarshal's silver-bound guest book, replete with compromising prewar salutations from visiting Western dignitaries. It was all that Bud Harper could do to keep Hitler's "Eagle's Nest" from being totally dismantled. When his men cleared out the silverware and began carting off larger souvenirs, Harper put the area off limits. Bob Sink assembled a portion of his regiment and was heard to tell them, "Men, you've got to stop this lootin'. The general says that lootin' is damn near stealin'."[8]

Taylor's diary entry for May 10 read, "Left for Field Marshal Kesselring's headquarters, 50 miles to south. Had conference with

K. and returned with Marshal to Berchtesgaden, 1100. Press conference at 1500."[9] Kesselring, the converted airman who had commanded German forces in Italy, was the division's prize prisoner. (Others included panzer commander General Heinz Guderian, labor boss Robert Ley, and propagandist Julius Streicher.) It was Kesselring who almost got Taylor into trouble. Newsmen were clamoring for an interview with the ranking prisoner, and Taylor, after checking with corps headquarters, arranged a press conference with a stipulation that there be no photographs. He and Higgins sat at the same end of the table as the marshal, and Taylor privately thought his prisoner handled the interview very well.

Within days, however, Taylor was receiving calls from Seventh Army. It seemed that a photograph, taken surreptitiously from the far end of the table, projected some drinks that had been provided for the reporters in such a way as to make it appear that Taylor and Higgins were wining their prisoner and having a jolly time together. Taylor was able to convince his superiors that this was not the case, but the subject was a sensitive one, for the American press was up in arms over the alleged coddling of prominent Germans. Nearby, a less fortunate American commander was sacked for allowing himself to be photographed shaking hands with Goering.

At Berchtesgaden, Taylor had occasion to reflect on the quality of the German forces he had faced during the war. His conclusion was that, except in the Bastogne campaign, the 101st had not faced the Wehrmacht at its best. He was interested in inspecting two SS panzer corps that had surrendered in Bavaria. Each had been provided with the best equipment the Reich had to offer, while regular army units had floundered. And each had been held back for a final campaign that had never materialized.

Taylor's greatest headache in this period was the safeguarding of the important art treasures recovered at Berchtesgaden. Most notable was Goering's collection, which included no fewer than five Rembrandts, plus assorted works by Rubens, van Gogh, Renoir, and van de Meer. Taylor later recalled that he took special pains to safeguard Goering's art, even though he never had enough men to protect everything. Most of it was eventually returned to the various European institutions that Goering had pressured into parting with their treasures.

For all the euphoria at Berchtesgaden, Taylor was not among those who believed that the war was over for the 101st. He fully expected that it would shortly be transferred to the Pacific and that he would yet have a chance to make use of his Japanese. Meanwhile, weary of the stream of military tourists through Berchtesgaden, he determined to relocate his headquarters to a less congested area and chose the nearby resort town of Badgastein. Its best hotel, however, was occupied by the staff of the Japanese embassy, who had been moved south from Berlin in the final weeks of the war.

Taylor decided that enemy diplomats did not need the entire hotel. He and Higgins drove to Badgastein, walked into the hotel lobby, and asked, in English, to see the ambassador. There was a phone call but no one appeared, and Taylor again asked for the ambassador. A few minutes later a functionary came down and told the duty officer, in Japanese, that the ambassador was resting and had sent word to let the Americans cool their heels. Upon overhearing this, Taylor exploded—in Japanese. As Higgins recalled the incident, "The effect was electrifying—everyone in the lobby jumped up from their chairs, the duty officer grabbed the phone, and in a very short time the ambassador came hurrying down the stairs, trying to adjust his clothing as he came. Taylor again spoke in Japanese, and the ambassador quickly agreed with his request."[10] A member of the Japanese entourage remarked to Higgins that the American had told them off in "kitchen" Japanese, a form never employed between persons of equal status!

In late June Taylor received a visit from none other than General Marshall, who wanted a day off on his way home from the Potsdam Conference. The division commander hosted a lunch for Marshall and Patton at his headquarters and there heard for the first time of the successful testing of an atomic bomb. Marshall told the two generals that the United States would use such a bomb against Japan "on the first moonlight night in August" and that he expected that perhaps two such bombs would end the war. Marshall's accurate estimate meant that the 101st would not have to serve in the Pacific.

For Taylor the war was over. He took leave of his division at a review at Auxerre, France, and it was a wrench. Later he wrote:

For all their hard-boiled reputation, generals can be terribly sentimental about their units and their men. Standing bareheaded at the foot of the reviewing stand, I received the last salute of these gallant soldiers, their ribbons and streamers recalling our battles together. They had put stars on my shoulders and medals on my chest. I owed my future to them, and I was grateful.[11]

And what did the men of the 101st think of their complex commander? Generalizations are dangerous, but it appears that opinions of Taylor fell within a fairly narrow range and were largely independent of rank. There was nothing avuncular about Taylor, and he did not inspire universal affection. He most often addressed a man crisply as "Soldier," and in Tom White's phrase, "he was not a GI's general." But he did command respect as a cool professional. When fighting was in progress he seemed everywhere, counseling, directing, encouraging. He seemed always to be pressing the enemy, but never expending lives without clear purpose. If the men in the ranks had a beef, it was all that shaving. Their division commander was "very West Point"—not a term of flattery—and the story of how the "Old Man" got his wound in Holland doubtless made the rounds. But he held out the prospect of something that interested every soldier: survival. The rank and file watched their CO in operation and thought, "There is one smart s.o.b. If anyone can get me through this war in one piece, he may be the guy."

The view of Taylor held by his officers was probably not dissimilar. Carl Kohls, his G-4 (logistics), was impressed by Taylor's attention to detail. "I soon learned that he knew more about the operation of each G-section than we did."[12] Bob Sink was impressed with how his division commander almost always managed to seize the tactical initiative. He dubbed Taylor "Mr. Attack," a nickname that enjoyed a brief vogue but never quite seemed to fit a very complex personality. Bradley McKennan, a junior intelligence officer, recalled that the first thing Taylor had done at his headquarters at Greenham Common had been to get rid of the four-poster bed that had been a perk for the CO and to install a regulation cot. "This small matter seemed to impress upon all of us that [Taylor] wanted no more than his officer staff had."[13]

Most felt that Taylor had a gift for making everyone feel part of the team. Where combat conditions permitted, he would ask those responsible for special activities—supply officers, chaplains, commissary officers, medics—to join his staff for the evening meal. There they would be asked to comment on current operations and to tell him of any problems they were encountering. Jerry Higgins thought that the division profited immensely from these exchanges with specialists whose work rarely brought them into contact with the division commander.

Taylor's immediate staff found their general very demanding. Harry Kinnard, who later became a three-star general, recalled that during the Holland campaign Taylor directed him to work up an evacuation plan in case the Germans flooded the island. This was only one of many requirements that came Kinnard's way, and he thought the chewing out he got for being late with it was not really called for. Others noted that Taylor gave task force commanders such as Higgins and Ewell wide latitude in combat operations, but kept a tight rein on the division staff. Taylor was only an occasional user of profanity, and a "By God!" from the CO had a way of gaining his listener's full attention.

Steve Karabinos, one of two wartime aides, thought that Taylor had a curious fault: excessive modesty.

> General Patton's command post was normally ten miles back of the front lines, and he carried his press coverage with him. In an airborne division, [our] command post was [perhaps] one mile away from the point we were attacking. Not too many of the press could jump in with us or were eager to be that close to the action. And by the time it was safe for the press to come in . . . [Taylor] spoke only of the men who carried the brunt of the attack. That was his nature.[14]

As for Taylor, command of the 101st had been the satisfying culmination of a career devoted to the study of war. He credited much of his personal success to the Army school system, which had given him the qualifications for division command without his having commanded anything larger than an artillery battalion.

For much of his later life he would attempt to analyze the qualities that made a successful commander in war. Some people had these undefinable qualities of leadership, others did not. For all his modesty, the late-blooming paratrooper knew that he was one of those who did.

Although Maxwell Taylor was largely unknown to the American public when the war ended, as far as the Army was concerned he was on the fast track. This was not surprising, given his record, but Taylor was well aware that fortune also played a role. He remained on friendly terms with Ridgway but was immensely grateful to have been given a command away from the 82d and Ridgway's eagle eye. He was also fortunate to have served in Europe, his Japanese expertise notwithstanding. Years later he would remark that if you wanted to get ahead in the Army, you had to have served in Europe, whereas if you wanted to advance in the Navy, you had better have served in the Pacific. He noted that of the five Army chiefs of staff immediately after the war—Eisenhower, Bradley, Collins, Ridgway, and himself—"all had some responsibility for Utah Beach on D-day."

So it was that the Army's top Japanese linguist made his reputation in Europe and employed his Japanese only to expel enemy diplomats from a Bavarian hotel.

Chapter 12

THE SUPERINTENDENT

While still in France, Taylor was informed that he had been chosen to be superintendent of West Point. His selection represented an immense career boost, for although there were many two-star generals who had distinguished themselves in the war, only one could be chosen to head the nation's military academy. When Taylor assumed his new post in September 1945, he became the fortieth soldier to head the Academy since its establishment in 1802. There was probably no more prestigious two-star post in the Army. His predecessors included such luminaries as Robert E. Lee and Douglas MacArthur. Indeed, at forty-four, Taylor was the second-youngest superintendent ever; only MacArthur had been appointed at an earlier age. For Taylor, the new assignment represented an opportunity to bring to his alma mater the difficult lessons of World War II. As superintendent he would have a large voice in filling posts in both the teaching faculty and the administration. He would also have a degree of independence unusual in the military, for as superintendent he was answerable only to the Army chief of staff, Eisenhower, and the Secretary of War, Robert Patterson.

The end of World War II was a period of conflicting signals for the American military. On the one hand, the ending of censorship had unleashed a flood of criticism from former GIs, many of whom made it clear that they held their erstwhile commanders in less than high esteem. On the other hand, the prestige of the American military was never higher in the councils of government. Under Truman, one Army officer, George Marshall, became Secretary of State while another, Eisenhower, was viewed in both political parties as Truman's likely successor. Under Marshall, ten of the top twenty positions at State were occupied by persons brought in from the military services. Military men were appointed to some of the most prestigious ambassadorships and occupied positions of influence everywhere: Beetle Smith, for instance, was Truman's choice to head the Central Intelligence Agency; General Lucius Clay headed the U.S. occupation zone of Germany; and on the other side of the world Douglas MacArthur administered Japan as his personal fiefdom. Fortune 500 companies vied with one another for the services of senior defense executives. Taylor was not yet a prime target for corporate recruiters, but in time he would become one.

Few corporations provide their chiefs with more impressive perks than those afforded the superintendent of West Point. The ceiling of Taylor's dark-paneled office overlooking the Hudson was rimmed with photographs of his predecessors—even P. G. T. Beauregard, appointed in 1861, who served only five days before defecting to the newly formed Confederate States of America. The superintendent had the use of a limousine, a lakeside cottage on a remote part of the reservation, and a cabin cruiser for evenings on the Hudson. He was served by three aides.

The superintendent's living accommodations were equally impressive. His residence on the west side of the Plain had been built in 1820, and the iron grillwork around the porches also dated to the period before the Civil War. In the reception room there hung a handsome portrait of a dark-haired, youthful Robert E. Lee, attired in the uniform of a major in the United States Army. If one must live in a museum, there is hardly a more livable one than the superintendent's quarters at West Point.

Tradition is sacred at the Academy, and the organization of the corps of cadets had changed little since Taylor's own graduation. It was larger—there were now 2,400 cadets—but the main unit was still the company, numbering about eighty men. Superimposed on a cadet hierarchy that ran from first captain to the lowliest plebe was an infrastructure of Army regulars, the tactical officers or "tacs," who advised the cadets and who acted as instructors in military subjects. An entering plebe still underwent two months of "beast barracks" during which he was exposed to boot training and general harassment.

The academic year began in September. In Taylor's student days the first-year subjects had been mathematics, English, a modern language, and mechanical drawing. At the end of his first year a plebe was "recognized," that is, addressed by name and accorded the social status of an upperclassman. At the same time he was allowed three weeks' leave, his first extended absence from the Academy. He returned in July for two months of infantry training, after which he began a new academic year. He again studied mathematics as a principal subject, generally passing through calculus and statistics. He also studied English literature, a second year of his language, military topography, and either physics or chemistry. There were no electives. At the end of this, his second year, a cadet again had a period of leave and then generally participated in military exercises with his counterparts at Annapolis. When he returned in the fall, he studied mechanics, English, electricity, and a social science. At West Point, history and political science were combined in a single department.

At the end of his third year a cadet took leave and again went for interservice training. His final academic year comprised courses in political science, law, military hygiene, and military art and engineering. On graduation day he received two important documents: a bachelor of science degree from the Military Academy and a commission as a second lieutenant in the Army or Air Force.

In his nearly four years as superintendent, Taylor would do comparatively little to change the functioning of the corps or the administration of the Academy. The curriculum, however, was a different matter. In consultation with the Academic Board and a group of outside consultants headed by Dr. Karl Compton of the Massachusetts Institute of Technology, Taylor initiated a liberalization of the science-heavy academic load. Language study became one of the few electives offered, with Russian first offered in 1945. Courses in Russian history, U.S. diplomatic history, and international economics were added. Taylor attempted to improve the English department, which had traditionally been weak at the Academy, and he horrified some educators by monitoring the classroom performance of instructors whose teaching was suspect. He was also a physical fitness buff. Signs displayed in faculty areas made clear that no potbelly could set a proper example for the Corps of Cadets.

The chairmen of the various departments at West Point constituted the Academic Board, and as a group they were no more
receptive to change than their civilian counterparts. Larry Legere,
Taylor's Normandy jumpmaster, was a history instructor at the
Academy, and one of his ancillary responsibilities was to coach
the cadet debating team. The debaters had long been limited to a
single off-campus debate each year, but Legere proposed that, in
addition, they be allowed to fly to the West Coast over the spring
break to debate several universities there. When the head of the
Academic Board vetoed the trip, Legere took his case to the superintendent. As an old debater, Taylor needed little persuading. He
approved the trip and made it the first of many.[1]

The new superintendent did not view West Point solely as a
means of providing the fundamentals for a military career. He
sought to inculcate in his cadets the character traits and work
habits that he believed essential to leaders of a citizen army. In
this regard he took a special interest in the workings of the honor
system and was fond of quoting Wilson's Secretary of War, New-
ton D. Baker, on the subject of honor within the military:

> Men may be inexact or even untruthful in ordinary matters, and
> suffer as a consequence only the disesteem of their associates or
> even the inconvenience of unfavorable litigation, but the inexact
> or untruthful soldier trifles with the lives of his fellow men and
> the honor of his government. It is therefore no matter of idle
> pride but rather of stern disciplinary necessity that makes the
> Army require of its officers a character for trustworthiness
> which knows no evasion.[2]

Taylor subscribed to this sentiment completely and, as a result,
kept close watch on the cadet committee that administered the
code. Early in his term, he had received some high-level guidance
concerning the application of the honor system at West Point. Following up on a meeting with Taylor in January 1946, Army Chief
of Staff Eisenhower recalled a gripe relating to the honor system
that dated back to his own cadet days:

> I remember as my most unfortunate experience while I was my-
> self a Cadet, an incident where some light bulbs had been

thrown into the area. The culprits were found by the lining up of the Corps and the querying of each individual as to whether or not he was guilty of this particular misdemeanor. Any such procedure or anything related to it would of course be instantly repudiated by any responsible officer . . . but I do think it important a policy along this line be clearly explained to all concerned at least once a year.[3]

Here Ike was preaching to the choir. Taylor had no intention of permitting misuse of the honor system, and in at least one instance he intervened personally in an honor code investigation. The incident involved one of the lesser members of the varsity football squad who, on his way back to barracks, snatched a Coke off a delivery truck at the mess hall. Because theft falls under the honor code, the offending cadet found himself before the Honor Committee and in danger of expulsion. It was Taylor's practice to allow the committee maximum autonomy, but in this instance he asked to meet with it. His opening remarks dealt with what constituted "theft." Did not the value of the object and the demeanor of the perpetrator have some bearing on the case? He asked about the general reputation of the offending cadet and was assured that it was good. The superintendent asked the committee members to project themselves into a combat situation. Was Cadet X a person they would want to have commanding a unit on their flank? The answer was a resounding affirmative. Taylor then left the committee to its deliberations, confident that a promising career would not fall victim to a bottle of Coke.

But the superintendent's interest in "reform" had self-imposed limits. Although there had long been those who saw the system of "beast barracks" as degrading negative reinforcement and who therefore advocated its abolition, Taylor was not among them. He told one incoming class:

There will be some among you who will feel that your treatment today and during the next few weeks is unreasonably severe. I would remind you that you are entering a career which is not a soft one. It is tough in the same way that war is tough. . . . As a future officer, the West Point cadet is expected to display discipline and the other military virtues to a degree beyond that required anywhere else in the world.[4]

If West Point was to produce military leaders, who might best inculcate the necessary qualities of leadership? The alumni of a certain airborne division were clearly one possibility. At the end of the war the 101st had lost out in some bitter infighting over which airborne division—the 82d or the 101st—would be carried over to the smaller, peacetime Army. Eisenhower had initially chosen the 101st but, needled by Ridgway, had changed his choice to the 82d. Although this development angered the Screaming Eagles, Taylor recognized an opportunity. He enjoyed wide latitude in staffing the Academy, and now he picked some of his ablest wartime associates to serve at West Point. Jerry Higgins became commandant of cadets, with responsibility for day-to-day supervision of the corps. Allen Ginder, a battalion commander who had been seriously wounded in Holland, became one of his aides. Tom Sherburne, a tennis partner as well as a combat artilleryman, was named to command the field artillery detachment; Ned Moore became public affairs officer; and Bob Sink was a "tac." Jokes about the "101st Military Academy" abounded, but Taylor thought his appointments just fine. In the words of one military writer, "Vitality was everywhere evident in the post-war Academy."[5]

Taylor's most controversial change in the curriculum centered on the introduction of military leadership as a regular course of study. During the war he had remarked on the paradox that West Point, with its commitment to developing military leaders, offered no course in military leadership. At the Academy he and Commandant Jerry Higgins set about remedying this. Higgins recommended that the tactical department—which traditionally had dealt with disciplinary, not academic, matters—be given responsibility for a full-time course in military leadership, one that had the same standing as any academic course. Taylor concurred and, in May 1946, a formal recommendation went before the Academic Board.

Higgins later wrote that he could not recall "a meeting of responsible individuals where rancor so filled the air." The head of each academic department spoke in opposition to the proposal.

When Taylor put the matter to a vote, the only affirmative vote came from Higgins. The superintendent then thanked the board members for their time and comments, and announced that the new course would be instituted at the beginning of the next academic year.

> It would be hard to describe the tension and looks of disbelief that arose! The Dean got up and in a very formal tone *informed* the Superintendent that the Academic Department was responsible for all educational courses and that they had decided that the course should not go forward. [Taylor] smiled, rose, and very politely informed those present that he appreciated their *advice*, but that the Superintendent made the decisions—and that he had decided to go forward with the course on leadership.[6]*

Taylor's speeches were not limited to his presentations to the cadets. Like a college president he was constantly on the lecture circuit, speaking to alumni groups, veterans organizations, and civic groups. The fact that he was an accomplished speaker had probably been a factor in his being chosen for the superintendency. Now, as the solidarity of the war years gave way to a reaction against most things military, the War Department was grateful to have in Taylor an articulate spokesman on its behalf. Among the many speaking engagements Taylor accepted during this period was an invitation from a Congressman John Kennedy to speak before a Veterans of Foreign Wars post in Boston. Years later, Taylor would have difficulty in recalling the young congressman who had been his host.

Over the years I followed a number of my father's presentations from inception to delivery. Whatever his audience, he sought to convey just one or two principal points with maximum clarity. His practice was to work up a longhand draft, which his staff turned into a double-spaced text. But he never spoke from the typescript. Rather, the final version of any speech was encapsulated on cards, and it was to these that he would occasionally refer in delivery.

---

* Interestingly, the minutes of the Academic Board show only that the course was instituted; for the record, all members of the Academic Board present indicated their assent.

(Once, when a newsman complimented him on a "fine impromptu speech," Taylor replied with a twinkle, "Young man, I never give an *impromptu* speech.")[7] His presentations were free of rhetorical flourishes and for the most part sparing of excessive military jargon. His sense of humor stood him in good stead, especially when he was called on to introduce an old friend or comrade-in-arms like Al Gruenther or Tony McAuliffe.

A former commandant of cadets, General Robert Richardson, observed during Taylor's tenure that the five years following the end of a major war were "generally the most complex and frustrating that the Academy's authorities had to deal with."[8] The years of Taylor's superintendency were a case in point. There were cadets during his tenure who had used an appointment to West Point as a means of avoiding the wartime draft, and by the late 1940s most of these were looking for a way out.

Getting out of West Point was rarely a problem. Nevertheless the resignation of several prominent football players during Taylor's superintendency was the subject of some embarrassment. A cadet who had entered the Academy during the war years had only to be found academically deficient to make an easy transition to postwar America. Those who preferred to keep their academic records clean had an opportunity to resign or to be found deficient in aptitude or conduct. In the academic year that ended in June 1946 a total of 185 cadets either resigned or were separated for reasons unrelated to academic or physical proficiency. A year later this figure was 172; by June 1948 the total was down to 105; and by June 1949 it was 67.[9]

Taylor was never disposed to brood over things that were beyond his power to change. Cadets who had sought out the Academy as a means of avoiding the war were welcome to leave. In a letter to a congressman, he noted that there had been an upsurge in resignations, and he acknowledged that the Academy had been a safe haven for some:

> I am reasonably sure that a certain number [have] been guilty of using the Academy as a hideout. It would probably be more accurate to say that some designing parents have used the Acad-

emy, for it is rare to find calculating or unpatriotic motives among young men of cadet age. However, neither the Academy nor the War Department is responsible for this condition, nor can they rectify it.[10]

Notwithstanding his focus on leadership and curriculum reform, Taylor would have been largely out of public view in the late 1940s had it not been for the Academy's role as a power in intercollegiate football. When he arrived at West Point, Taylor inherited one of the greatest teams ever fielded by Army. It had gone undefeated in both 1944 and 1945, downing not only archrival Navy but also Notre Dame, scoring a total of 107 points against the Irish in the two years while allowing none. For the first time in decades, Army football players were popular heroes. The team's premier running backs, Doc Blanchard and Glenn Davis, shared the cover of *Time*.

Alas, there was a downside to Army's football prowess. It was essentially a wartime aberration, growing out of the simultaneous appearance at West Point of some gifted athletes and the fact that its rivals were fielding teams composed of ROTC students and other draft-exempts. No one at West Point expected the honeymoon to last, but the two crushing victories over Notre Dame raised an intriguing question: might this not be the time for Army to "dump" Notre Dame, the midwestern powerhouse that had, over the years, allowed the cadets only eight wins in thirty-six games?

Except for the revenue it produced, Army had no business playing Notre Dame. Even in those days of relative athletic purity, West Point athletes faced a more demanding academic schedule than did most of their football rivals. The requirement for three years' military service after graduation made it all but impossible for the service academies to lure athletes with professional potential. Conversely, Notre Dame's football squad for the year 1947 included forty-two players who went on to play professionally. Nevertheless, West Point took sports in general, and football especially, very seriously. Competitive athletics carried the imprimatur of no less a personage than Douglas MacArthur, whose words adorned the wall of the massive cadet gymnasium:

> Upon the fields of friendly strife
> Are sown the seeds
> That upon other fields, on other days
> Will bear the fruits of victory.

For Army, and especially its Old Grads, it was inconceivable that their alma mater be other than a first-rank power in the sport that was so often compared to war itself. It was also unacceptable that Army play anything but winning football.

All this brought Army football fans around to the matter of Notre Dame. The Fighting Irish had some of the most fervent alumni in the land. In addition, millions of football fans who had never been near South Bend, Indiana, proclaimed themselves "subway alumni." Nuns lit candles for the team, and New Yorkers scrambled for the tickets that allowed them to cheer the Irish and to boo the Black Knights from West Point.

By the time Taylor became superintendent, relations with Notre Dame were less than warm. Army coach Red Blaik was not fond of his Notre Dame counterpart Frank Leahy, who had been charged with encouraging unsportsmanlike play and had been censured by the National Collegiate Athletic Association for recruiting violations. But these were minor irritants by comparison with the Lujack "kidnapping." A memo to the superintendent in the fall of 1946, which apparently originated in the Academy's Athletic Council, gave the Academy's side of the story:

In 1942 Congressman Schneider of Pennsylvania appointed to the Military Academy one Johnny Lujack, an outstanding young man from Connellsville, Pennsylvania, and a star football player. There was quite a ceremony when Mr. Schneider visited the town and presented the letter of appointment to Lujack, who proudly accepted it and at once began preparing for the West Point examination. Mr. Leahy . . . enticed the boy away. He was given a summer job in Chicago . . . with the usual football scholarship at Notre Dame to follow. Even the boy's mother, who was more than indignant at the turn of events, did not know where he was for some time. When the matter was called to Father Cavanaugh's attention, he brought Mr. Leahy to West

Point. The latter at first denied all knowledge of what had taken place, but when faced with evidence provided by the boy's mother, he had to admit that he was lying. Father Cavanaugh was deeply distressed, but the harm had already been done, and Notre Dame kept the boy. Today he is their greatest star.[11]

After some preliminary discussions at West Point, Taylor took the matter up with a onetime Army football player named Eisenhower. It was the unanimous opinion of the Athletic Council, Taylor wrote, that the Notre Dame game had outlived its usefulness. In his most candid discussion of this sensitive subject he listed three objections to continuing the series:

    1.   Notre Dame's presence on Army's schedule each year limited flexibility in scheduling.
    2.   Notre Dame "will usually play football out of the Cadets' class." Playing the Irish "has ceased to be fun."
    3.   "In the eyes of a large portion of the public it pits West Point against the Catholic Church. . . . Our coaches and players are now being flooded with threatening and often scurrilous letters and postcards. Some are jokes, others are not."[12]

Eisenhower concurred in a suspension of the series but suggested that there be a final game in either 1947 or 1948. With his chief's approval in hand, Taylor drafted a letter to Father Cavanaugh in which he based the proposed suspension on scheduling considerations but also touched on the problems posed by "extreme partisanship." He emphasized that what he was advocating was a suspension, not a termination, of football relations. Although Father Cavanaugh was distressed, he may not have been entirely surprised.

Despite the impending suspension, throughout the last two months of 1946 Cavanaugh and Taylor remained in amicable communication, working on the text of a joint press release and fretting about the optimum timing. The original release date was to have been December 31, but indications that the press was on to something led the two to break the story the day after Christmas. The joint announcement was a bit disingenuous, noting only that the game was in danger of "escaping the control" of the two institutions and that Army needed greater flexibility in scheduling. There was no mention of Johnny Lujack, his mother, or the fact that Army might never win another game from the Fighting Irish.

Other than the break with Notre Dame, Taylor as superintendent did nothing to deemphasize big-time football. Later, he would have second thoughts. Two years after his departure, ninety cadets, including thirty-seven varsity football players, were discharged from the Academy in a cheating scandal that shook the Academy to its foundations. At the root of the affair was the foolish practice of giving identical tests on different days—a stressful situation for any school operating on an honor system. But the fact that most of those involved were varsity athletes was confirmation that the pressures of the playing field, on top of the demands made of all cadets, were more than some athletes could handle. In his memoirs Taylor would write, "It has always been a cause of deep regret that as superintendent I did not perceive clearly or soon enough the potentially baneful influence of big-time football."[13]

Both during and after his tenure Taylor was widely characterized as a "liberal" superintendent. He neither accepted nor rejected this label, beyond commenting that "it is a bit like speaking of a liberal warden of Sing Sing." To some extent it was a matter of style. Taylor was young and vigorous, and so were the officers he brought with him. They symbolized a new generation of military leadership, and they were eager to pass on the lessons of the war just ended. The superintendent's structural reforms were modest, and he left untouched traditional areas such as "beast barracks," daily recitations, and a football team that had grown apart from the corps. But his view was that he had not come to "fix" the Academy: it had never been "broke."

As superintendent of West Point, Taylor became at least a probationary member of the eastern Establishment. For the first time, he and his wife rubbed elbows with the rich and famous. At Quarters 100 they played host to President Truman and various members of his cabinet; ex-president Herbert Hoover; IBM chairman Thomas Watson; the Eisenhowers; and scores of miltary luminaries such as Bradley, Montgomery, and Alexander. The proximity of New York City allowed Mrs. Taylor to indulge her interest in music and the theater, while even her husband developed a taste for some opera. The general became a regular at the Council on Foreign Relations and gave one presentation himself, on the Normandy campaign.

Taylor's still youthful good looks were a subject of much bantering within the family. While in Washington just prior to his dramatic return to Bastogne, he had been taking his daily constitutional when a passing motorist pulled over. "Sonny," he asked, "can I give you a lift?" "Sonny" was not above reminding us of this tribute. His wife would tease him about the attraction he held for women—older women, especially. Once, at the opera, Taylor was told at intermission that Mrs. Vanderbilt wished to see him in her box. When he returned, his wife asked what she had wanted. "She wanted to give me her private number," the general replied.

Taylor's period at West Point was one of transition in terms of American military thinking. On one hand, the Soviet Union was emerging as an expansionist threat every bit as menacing as Hitler's Germany. On the other hand, America's nuclear monopoly appeared to be the ultimate deterrent. Taylor's writings in this period represent his attempts to identify a few strategic priorities. In his view, the United States clearly had lost the advantage of geographic isolation that had allowed it to remain apart from European conflicts when it so chose. The long-range bomber was even then a threat to North America, and he believed that the first weeks of any new conflict might well determine the outcome. Interestingly, as early as the 1940s Taylor had doubts as to whether a world war constituted the principal threat to the peace:

> Can we say dogmatically that nations will never again resort to force except to achieve the complete physical destruction of the enemy? Long before we are called upon to face World War III, there may well be degrees of localized warfare such as occurred in 1937 on the Russo-Manchurian border, in the Spanish Civil War, or recently on the Greek frontier. Even more indirect forms of war must be considered. . . . Our principal military strength-in-being lies in air and naval power and our potential

for generating a great economic war effort. But where could these have been used to save Czechoslovakia?[14]

The main security issue to which Taylor addressed himself in this period was the question of universal military training. It had been endorsed by President Truman, but such was the postwar backlash against everything military that no serious attempt was made to enact the legislation required. Taylor addressed this backlash, commenting on one occasion that "since the dawn of history, the man at arms has stood alongside the priest and the judge among the leaders of mankind. Where the soldier has not been respected, it has been an historical sign of decadence in the country concerned."[15] He did what he could in the losing fight for universal military training:

In addition to its many direct and indirect military advantages, universal military training would present a tremendous opportunity to train loyal recruits for our American system. No man can serve any cause, even though his service is rendered reluctantly at the outset, without coming to feel deeply about its importance. . . . In my judgment, two of the great byproducts of universal military training [would be] the creation in the minds of our young men a realization of what they owe to their country and . . . of what they must do to guarantee its survival.[16]

The fall of 1948 saw the publication of Eisenhower's wartime memoir *Crusade In Europe*, which included a generous reference to Taylor's secret trip to Rome. In the words of the supreme commander, Taylor "carried weighty responsibilities and discharged them with unerring judgment, and every minute was in imminent danger of discovery and death."[17] In a letter to Eisenhower that covered several subjects, Taylor thanked his chief for the mention, adding that "my family and I will cherish your words throughout the years." Ike did not allow the matter to end there. He wrote in reply:

With respect to the little notation I made about you in my book; there should have been a much fuller description of that incident and of the later actions of [your] grand Division during the War. My trouble finally became one of selection and I had to meet the problem on a policy rather than a personal basis.[18]

Chapter 13

BERLIN TO PANMUNJOM

Taylor had hoped to stay at West Point for a full four-year term and thus to present diplomas to the class that had entered at the time of his arrival. The Army decreed otherwise, however, and in January 1949 he returned to Germany for the first time since receiving the surrender of Kesselring and Guderian. As chief of staff of the European Command, with headquarters in the university town of Heidelberg, Taylor had a firsthand view of the evolving policies of the Allied powers toward their recent enemy.

The official American attitude toward the erstwhile Third Reich had changed dramatically during Taylor's years at West Point. Initially, the four occupying powers—Britain, the United States, France, and the Soviet Union—had embarked on the occupation with the avowed intent of punishing the Germans for having served as Hitler's instrument. But the wartime collaboration among the Big Four did not carry over into the occupation, and, as the Soviets proceeded to carve out a sphere of influence in Eastern Europe, it became clear the Germany itself would be a key prize in the emerging East-West competition.

For four years the American military governor had been General Lucius Clay. He had come to the post determined to get along with the Russians and to punish the Germans. This attitude soon changed as he came to conclude that Soviet objectives in Germany were essentially the same as their objectives in countries such as Poland and Czechoslovakia, which they had succeeded in bringing under their domination.

The yearlong blockade of isolated Berlin by the Soviets and East Germans in 1948–49 probably grew out of Moscow's dissatisfaction with its inability to dominate postwar Germany and its irritation at having a Western bastion deep in East Germany. If the

Soviets expected to force the Western Allies out of Berlin, however, they miscalculated badly. In part because the blockade was
imposed in stages, the governments of Britain, France, and the
United States had time to develop a coordinated response. With
the United States providing the bulk of the aircraft, the Allies eventually were able to airlift as much as 13,000 tons of food and fuel
per day to three airfields in the Allied sectors of Berlin. Month
after month over the long winter a train of cargo aircraft made
their runs. In May 1949 the Soviets indicated that they were prepared to end the blockade and eventually did so without any concession from the West.

From his position as chief of staff to U.S. forces commander
General Clarence Huebner, Taylor watched Berlin developments
closely. In a letter to Eisenhower he commented that he was enjoying his work at Heidelberg, although he missed West Point.

> After spending thirteen intermittent years there, [West Point] is
> still the nearest approach to home that we have in the world. I
> hope to regain close contact with the Academy eventually
> through at least one of my sons. Tom, who is with me here in
> Germany, seems to have the makings of a future cadet so that I
> shall probably be ringing Congressional doorbells in Washing-
> ton in two or three years.[1]

By 1949 the Allies were in the process of returning West Germany to self-government. Even as the Soviets were ending the
Berlin blockade, Germany's new political parties elected seventy-
four-year-old Konrad Adenauer Chancellor and established a new
capital at Bonn. Clay retired as military governor for the United
States and was replaced by a high commissioner, financier John J.
McCloy, with offices in Frankfurt. McCloy wanted a commandant
for the American sector of Berlin who could handle both political
and military responsibilities. The Pentagon was at least as powerful a voice as the State Department in matters relating to occupation policy and McCloy requested the appointment of Wedemeyer,
Gruenther, or Taylor. Taylor, who had come to know McCloy
slightly at the Council on Foreign Relations in New York City, was
at the top of the list. Once in Berlin, he would "wear two hats." As
U.S. Commander, Berlin (USCOB), he would report in strictly mil-

itary matters to General Thomas Handy in Heidelberg; in political matters, he was responsible to McCloy in Frankfurt.

Berlin, even before the Wall, was the symbol of a divided Germany and a divided Europe. It was also a considerable geographic area, for its 342 square miles made for a city only slightly smaller than Los Angeles. Berlin's total population was about 3.4 million, of whom two thirds lived in the three Allied sectors. Although the Eastern and Western sectors had separate municipal governments, separate police forces, and incompatible currencies, certain services were inevitably shared. An elevated railway, the S-bahn, covered the entire city but was operated out of the Soviet sector and was therefore susceptible to interruption. West Berlin was also dependent on the Soviet sector for electric power, although steps were already under way to make the Allied sectors self-sufficient.

The city's importance, even in 1949, grew out of its role as a showcase for the competing values of East and West. West Berlin, although beset with problems, showed the Germans at their energetic best, rapidly rebuilding a shattered economic infrastructure. The press was free and highly competitive. Its mayor was feisty Ernst Reuter, a onetime Communist turned socialist, who enjoyed nothing more than thumbing his nose at his former mentors. By the time I visited West Berlin in 1950, physical reconstruction had progressed so far that one had to seek out evidence of wartime destruction. Not so in the East. As soon as one passed into the Soviet sector the atmosphere changed. There were few amenities, few shoppers, and few vehicles. Only propaganda posters were to be found in abundance.

Taylor took up his duties in Berlin in September 1949. He was perhaps as qualified as anyone for this sensitive post. In the first place, he had put World War II behind him. He had never felt any hatred for Germans as such, even when they were shooting at him. Now he could only respect the energy with which they were rebuilding their country. His facility with the German language was just fair, for he had studied it intensively only since arriving at Heidelberg. But it was improving rapidly. Most important, his ability to inspire teamwork would find ample scope in beleaguered Berlin. The Soviet blockade had already backfired, having fostered a bond between the Berliners and their Western occupiers, and Taylor's confrontational style in dealing with the Soviets would strike a responsive chord with the populace.

Berlin was administered by the four powers through a *Kommandatura,* which in theory comprised Taylor and his British, French, and Soviet counterparts. The Soviets, however, had walked out of the *Kommandatura* in 1948 and showed no sign of returning. While the Western commanders went about the business of running the city, their meetings now featured an empty chair for the Soviets. One area in which the Soviets continued to participate, however, was in the administration of Spandau prison. The guarding of Spandau, where Rudolf Hess, Albert Speer, and other top Nazis were incarcerated, continued to rotate among the four occupying powers.

When the Soviet blockade ended in May 1949, the city's residents had breathed a collective sigh of relief in the belief that a return to the preblockade status quo would permit the city to rebuild. The euphoria was short-lived. The Soviets resorted to a series of tactics—closing land routes for "repairs," imposing power outages, kidnapping prominent Berliners—designed to achieve by harassment the dislocation that the airlift had prevented during the period of full blockade. As a result, Taylor found himself delivering diplomatic-style protests to his Soviet counterpart, General Kotikov. Little came of these protests, but they allowed the Western commanders to build up a record and permitted Taylor to demonstrate by his own demeanor that the Allies would not be bullied out of Berlin. On one such visit Taylor noted a large carved elephant on Kotikov's desk. He went out of his way to admire it and then spoiled the Russian's day. "In my country," he noted helpfully, "the elephant is the symbol of our most reactionary party, the one regarded as implacably hostile to the working class." Poor Kotikov. In Stalin's day one did not take chances, and on Taylor's next visit the elephant was nowhere to been seen.

Although the West had scored an impressive political victory with the lifting of the blockade, Berlin's economy remained precarious. Part of the problem went back to the war's end, when the Soviets had repatriated entire factories to the East. A more recent problem related to competing currencies. The West German mark was worth six or seven times more than the East German mark, making trade with the East difficult. When it came to selling in the West, Berlin's geographic position imposed transportation costs that often priced the city's products out of the market. Unemployment was high, in part because of a continuing influx of refugees from the East. In February 1950, for example, 25 percent of the city's labor force was unemployed.

In retrospect, one knows that the city's economy was about to turn around and that Berlin was about to become a full partner in the West German "economic miracle." Meanwhile, Taylor found himself something of an aid administrator and champion ribbon cutter:

> I derived great pleasure from supervising the economic program and watching the city rise from the rubble of its bombed-out buildings. In my [period] as USCOB, I got to know far more about the factories, utilities, transportation system, schools, churches and labor unions of Berlin than I ever knew about any American city. There was always some new construction project to open or some newly finished one to dedicate, and either event called for the presence of the American commandant as the representative of the Marshall Plan program.[2]

Although relations between the Western occupiers and the Berliners were generally good, I was present for one plant inspection that nearly turned ugly. One day, Taylor and a small group of American and German civilians inspected a factory being equipped under the Marshall Plan. As the Americans headed back to their cars, they found the way blocked by a group of young Germans, who surrounded the party and began denouncing the American occupation and blaming it for the shortage of jobs. Taylor told the youths, in German, that if they would designate a spokesman he would listen to him. There followed a dialogue that lasted perhaps five or ten minutes in which Taylor attempted to respond to their complaints. The Germans were by no means convinced, but when Taylor abruptly terminated the dialogue and headed for his car, they made no move to obstruct him.

The Allies left no stone unturned in making West Berlin a thorn in the side of the Communists. The Free University catered to refugees from the East and was a bastion of political conservatism. A powerful radio station, RIAS (Radio in the Allied Sector), broadcast the news that East Germans never found in their own media, and Taylor himself pushed the construction of a Times Square-type news display on Potsdamer Platz that was visible far into the Soviet sector. Allied intelligence agencies were so numerous that they became the butt of jokes to Berliners of all political stripes.

The most serious threat to the peace during Taylor's tour in Berlin came in the spring of 1950. The East Germans announced that on Whitsuntide—May 28—a rally of the popular front Free German Youth would be followed by a mass invasion of the Western sectors. There were only about thirteen thousand police in West Berlin, and Taylor and his French and British colleagues were faced with the likelihood of having to call out their own garrisons under circumstances in which the Communists could easily provoke an incident. As the propaganda from East Germany intensified, Taylor inaugurated a crash program in nonlethal means of crowd control, including tear gas, water cannon, and electric shock techniques. A week before Whitsuntide he briefed the officers of the U.S. Army garrison, employing the same positive reinforcement techniques as in his pre-Normandy appearances before the 101st:

> From now on our attitude is: We don't expect anything serious in town; we don't expect to have to use any of our troops; we are confident that the police and the Germans can meet this threat, but, of course, if our calculations go wrong, we are more than ready. . . . Bear in mind that the ideal situation is for this week to go off without use of any of our troops, without any serious disorders for the police, [and on] Monday night everybody's happy and no heads broken. . . . I don't have to point out that, first, we are not going to send our troops out on the streets armed with bullets in their clips unless it is a rather serious situation. . . . I just ask each and all of you who have direct command of troops to look into your conscience and say, . . . "Am I absolutely sure I left no stone unturned to be sure my men are properly instructed?"[3]

In the end, there was no "invasion" of the Western sectors. From a helicopter, Taylor watched a parade by more than one hundred thousand East German youths, all of whom took care to remain in the Soviet sector. In a press conference Taylor apologized to reporters for "a rather dull weekend" and then drove home his moral:

Why did the communist putsch fail to materialize on Sunday? Because the West Germans and the Western allies showed by word and deed that they would not give an inch to the communist threat, and were prepared to go all out to defend their rights in this city. It is a formula that has always worked against the communists in the past, and one which recommends itself for wide application in the future.[4]

Not long after Whitsuntide, however, West Berlin was once more on the alert. This time there was no immediate threat of invasion but a development halfway around the world that set the city on edge. The Communist world was far more monolithic in 1950 than it would be after Stalin, and the North Korean invasion of South Korea in June raised immediate questions regarding other exposed Western bastions, of which Berlin was by far the most vulnerable. No military threat to Berlin materialized, but the Communist attack in Korea tended to underscore the sense of isolation felt by many residents.

Taylor left Berlin in February 1951 for his first assignment in Washington since before the war. His brief sixteen months in Berlin, however, had made a considerable impression. In particular, he was impressed with Moscow's skill in making maximum use of proxies. In a briefing for the visiting chief of naval operations, Admiral Forrest Sherman, he noted that "we must always bear in mind that if the Kremlin ever decided to blockade Berlin again, we would be quite sure to find German guards on the barricades, with no Russians in sight."[5] At the same time, he had come to appreciate the critical role played by the man in the street; he recognized that the Western position in Berlin rested entirely on the continued support of the populace. At Whitsuntide the Allied commanders had at their disposal only seven battalions of military police, but the residents of the Western sectors were so zealously anti-Communist that Taylor accorded them a large measure of credit for the failure of the march.

Taylor left Berlin convinced that the Soviets were prone to bluff. If the Allies were to insist on exercising the rights they held in Germany and Berlin under the occupation, the Soviets could be expected to back down. In part this conviction reflected the fact that the United States alone possessed nuclear weapons, but he remained convinced, even in the decades of nuclear parity, that Soviet policy included a large element of bluff.

Taylor returned to Washington to work for his old corps commander in Normandy, Joe Collins, who had succeeded Bradley as Army chief of staff. Collins had chosen Taylor to be his G-3: assistant chief of staff for operations and training. The Taylors moved into one of the stately homes on "Generals Row" at Fort McNair, residences so alike in size and design that occupants had been known to walk into the wrong house.

At the Pentagon, the Korean War eclipsed all other problems. The Army had never faced a situation quite like it, for at the strategic level it had proved to be something of a comedy of errors. The Communists had erred badly in assuming that they would have a free hand on the Korean Peninsula. But President Truman's decision to confront the Communists in Korea was an intuitive reaction, and the United States had no contingency plans for fighting a localized conflict. Ridgway would recall, "I don't think that at that time American doctrine contemplated limited war. The concept had always been all-out war."[6]

Washington initially contemplated so limited a role that American participation could be largely confined to air, sea, and logistical support. It quickly became apparent, however, that the poorly trained forces of the Republic of Korea were no match for disciplined North Korean infantry, backed by Soviet-manufactured T-34 tanks. Within weeks the United States was ferrying troops from garrison duty in Japan to the Korean front, with mixed results. For one thing, the American troops were not of uniformly high caliber: some 43 percent of enlisted men in the Far East Command had scored in the two lowest categories in the Army's classification tests. Nor was their equipment as good as much of the enemy's. Hastily committed with weapons dating from World War II, the first American divisions in Korea were hard-pressed to keep from being driven into the sea.

For the first year of the war MacArthur, the theater commander, had virtually a free hand. The daring thrust behind the enemy at Inchon on Korea's west coast was begun on MacArthur's own initiative; the Joint Chiefs in Washington concurred with some misgivings. But success begat confidence, and Washington upgraded its war aims. No longer was U.S. policy merely to restore the status quo at the thirty-eighth parallel. In September 1950 the Chiefs authorized MacArthur to destroy North Korea's armed forces, crossing the thirty-eighth parallel as the situation required.[7]

With North Korea's own forces in full retreat, the question of outside intervention became critical. As early as October, China began warning that it would challenge any move by UN forces to advance to the Yalu. These warnings were discounted at first, but as MacArthur continued his northern advance, and as his supply lines lengthened, his vulnerability to a Chinese riposte caused unease in Washington. MacArthur was not concerned. Meeting with Truman at Wake Island, he dismissed the Chinese threat.

By late October, MacArthur's divided forces were encountering isolated groups of Chinese with disturbing frequency. Then, on November 26, Chinese armies totaling more than three hundred thousand struck the Eighth Army's exposed northern salient. A Republic of Korea (ROK) Army corps collapsed, and soon the UN forces were in full retreat. Not until they were south of Seoul did these forces, now commanded by Ridgway under MacArthur, stabilize the line. MacArthur, meanwhile, was publicly venting his belief that his problems derived from Truman's policy of limiting the war to Korea. When MacArthur permitted a Republican congressman to read into the Congressional Record a letter critical of administration policy, Truman had had enough. On April 10, when Taylor picked up his morning paper at Fort McNair, he saw in the headline that MacArthur had been dismissed. Although close to Collins, Taylor "hadn't the foggiest notion" that MacArthur's ouster was imminent.[8]

One of Taylor's first assignments as G-3 had been to review the directives sent MacArthur, and he had concluded that MacArthur, in driving almost to the Yalu, had not exceeded the broad grant of authority under which he operated. Nevertheless, he was critical of MacArthur's campaign on two grounds. On the strategic level, Taylor agreed with the Administration that nothing was to be gained from expanding the war in Korea. The big stake in northeast Asia was not Korea but Japan. For the United States to get into a major war, declared or otherwise, in a secondary theater struck Taylor as unwise. In addition, he was skeptical of the value of driving north to the Yalu in the first place. Problems would increase proportionately with the UN advance:

> The thing that one boggles at . . . is what would have happened if [MacArthur] had succeeded. Suppose that he had got to the Yalu and the Chinese had not intervened . . . then what? Instead of having a 125-mile front which is roughly the present line at the Demilitarized Zone, he would have had almost 400 miles and he'd have had a million armed Chinese across the Yalu looking at him. What he'd have in his rear one wouldn't know, but at least he would have the elements of a major guerrilla movement in all the fragments of North Korean units that would have been lying around in the mountains.[9]

Fortunately for the United States, the situation on the ground gradually stabilized. Under Ridgway, the Eighth Army held south of Seoul, recaptured the capital, and gained hard-fought ground up the waist of the peninsula:

> Ridgway rallied the Eighth Army after the Chinese had sent it scurrying out of North Korea, found it reluctant even to make contact with the enemy, restored its confidence in itself, and sent it northward to defeat the Chinese and push them back across the thirty-eighth parallel. He accomplished these things partly through his own example of confidence, displayed on many tours of the front. He did it also by insisting upon very high standards of discipline, whereby he in time gave the Eighth Army professional qualities such as few American forces of comparable size have sustained.[10]

Taylor would later characterize Ridgway's accomplishment in stemming the UN retreat as one of the finest feats of arms of the twentieth century.

The war in Korea was bringing about a significant U.S. military expansion, particularly in the Army. At the outbreak of the war the Army had comprised ten divisions, four of them in Japan, and total personnel strength had dropped below 600,000. Following the Communist attack, the four understrength divisions in Japan had been committed in Korea. Within the period of a year, largely because of the draft, the authorized strength of the Army had risen to 1.3 million. Actual strength had increased to fifteen divisions, six of which were in Korea. The Army had more than doubled in size and was obtaining new equipment in significant amounts for the first time since World War II.

In the Pentagon, Taylor was discovering a kindred spirit in the thirty-nine-year-old Secretary of the Army, Frank Pace. A graduate of Princeton, Pace had been Truman's budget director before moving to the Defense Department. Pace and Taylor both saw a build-up of the ROK Army as the means of avoiding protracted U.S. military involvement in Korea. Both were less interested in a Mac-Arthur-style total victory than in an outcome that would deter future Communist adventures. On top of these shared professional views, both were accomplished tennis players and fitness buffs.

Pace and Taylor were not alone in their interest in building up South Korea's forces, but the rapid unfolding of the war in its first year had largely precluded long-range planning. In May 1951, Taylor made his first visit to the Hermit Kingdom since he had taken a train through Korea to join Stilwell in 1937. The primary purpose of his trip was to evaluate the capabilities of the ROK Army, which had heretofore performed so poorly. Although he found considerable skepticism among Americans concerning the ROKs, Taylor was undismayed:

> It took very little investigation to find out what was wrong with the ROKs. They had been asked to do too difficult things with inadequate training under conditions which would have tested the best troops in the world. Recruits who only a few weeks

earlier had been working in the rice paddies and had never seen a gun were being thrown into intense combat with results that could be expected.[11]

Whether the Americans on the scene shared this view, the Korean War was nevertheless becoming sufficiently unpopular in the United States that an effort to build up the South Koreans was imperative. Over the next year or so the United States would expand its military advisory group in Korea (KMAG), revamp the South Koreans' own training facilities, and increase the number of Korean officers at service schools in the United States. In July, Ridgway estimated that if all went well and if the war continued at its more stable pace, the ROK Army might become completely effective in three years.

Meanwhile the war itself had entered a new phase. In June 1951 the Soviets had proposed a cease-fire, and the following month armistice negotiations began. These were to continue over a period of two years, with frequent interruptions and continuing attempts by the Communists to use the negotiations as a propaganda forum. It was only in November 1951 that the two sides reached general agreement concerning a demilitarized zone and a mechanism for investigating alleged violations.

In January 1952 the UN delegation at Panmunjom proposed the repatriation of prisoners by each side in accordance with the wishes of the prisoners. The issue was fraught with peril for the Communists, because sentiment among both the North Korean and the Chinese prisoners was overwhelmingly opposed to return to Communist rule. The resulting impasse brought about a rupture in negotiations in October 1952. Not until six months later, following the death of Stalin, were the talks resumed.

With an armistice at least a possibility, the character of the war itself changed. Ridgway had succeeded MacArthur in Tokyo; his successor as commander of the Eighth Army was James Van Fleet, who had played a major role in raising Greek forces to a standard that had permitted them to defeat Communist guerrillas there. Although Van Fleet was eager to take the offensive, the Joint Chiefs were not inclined to approve actions that promised little return for the probable expenditure in lives. The prevailing note was one of uncertainty. There were allies to be consulted and a restive American public to be appeased.

In August 1951 Taylor was a beneficiary in a reorganization of the Army staff, one that provided the chief of staff with two deputies. One, for plans, was heavily committed to the business of the Joint Chiefs. The other, for operations and administration, was concerned with the day-to-day running of the Army. The latter position went to Taylor, and with it came a third star and the status of a betting favorite to make chief of staff himself one day.

For one who had never had a "sponsor" as a junior officer, Taylor now found himself in a position to assist those he knew to have proved themselves in battle. After delivering a speech at the Command and General Staff School while deputy chief of staff, Taylor heard that there were several ex-officers of the 101st in the graduating class and arranged to meet with them.

He questioned each of us as to our orders and assignment preferences, counseling each of us. My own orders had been changed from the XVIII Airborne Corps to a new job, that of making airborne personnel assignments in the Department of the Army. I stated my preference for Bragg. I was told of the importance to my career of a tour in Washington—the usual litany. [But] subsequently I received a call from the Pentagon— carry out your original orders! [Later] I saw General Taylor's note in my file, querying as to my assignment, and then a scribbled note: assign him to the XVIII Airborne Corps![12]

As deputy chief of staff Taylor became Collins's representative in the working out of a painful episode: the expulsion of ninety West Point cadets for cheating, an affair that went back to the period of Taylor's superintendency. Although the honor code would hardly permit other than expulsion of the offending cadets, the waters were considerably muddied by football coach Earl Blaik, who argued publicly that the entire unpleasantness could have been resolved by means short of dismissal. The Secretary of Defense had appointed a special board, chaired by Judge Learned Hand, to investigate the situation. One of the board members was General Troy Middleton, Taylor's corps commander in the Bastogne campaign and more recently president of Louisiana State University. The board confirmed that cheating had taken place and recommended unanimously that the offending cadets be dismissed. Ultimately, the ninety were permitted to resign.

Most of the cadets involved were not disposed to contest their separation proceedings. Taylor thought this a wise decision, believing as he did that the other cadets would not accept the retention of any of the ninety in the Corps. But what was the Academy to do if an ousted cadet were reappointed by his congressman? In practice, none of the ninety ever reentered West Point, although a number went on to receive degrees elsewhere and a few even gained commissions through other channels. Most either resigned or received administrative discharges. The fullest expression of Taylor's views on this subject was in a letter to Herbert Johnson, who had written him on behalf of a group of the ninety who acknowledged their involvement in honor code violations:

> [Your letter] represents one heartening aspect in this sad affair. The frank admission of guilt and wholesome spirit of repentance which I find therein confirm my first impression, that those involved in this affair, while openly admitting their violation of the Cadet Code of Honor, are not fundamentally men of bad morals or character. They have, however, fallen into evil ways; they have not, in the words of the Cadet Prayer, preferred the "harder right instead of the easier wrong," and in their failure have brought sorrow upon themselves and upon the Military Academy.
>
> I am also glad to note that you recognize the inevitability of drastic action on the part of the authorities in order to restore the honor system to its indispensable place in the ethical structure of Cadet life. Indeed, many of your group have made partial amends for past offense by the straightforward way in which you have assisted the authorities in investigating this matter.[13]

After the cribbing scandal came a war-related controversy. Was there or was there not a shortage of artillery ammunition in Korea? As the fighting had become more static, artillery had assumed additional importance. In the fighting for Bloody Ridge in the summer of 1951, artillerymen of the 2d Division fired more than 153,000 rounds. Neither in this instance nor subsequently was any rationing imposed, but the effect was a serious depletion of theater reserves. The rate of expenditure bothered Ridgway, who concluded that the phenomenal rate of fire was due either to extravagant waste or to a misuse of artillery, or to both. Van Fleet defended his rate of fire, at first through the chain of command. But he then committed the unforgivable sin of "going public." He spoke openly to the press of ammunition shortfalls; and in a letter that was circulated by Eisenhower's campaign organization he blamed the Pentagon for limiting the ROK Army to ten divisions. At Collins's direction, Taylor sought to monitor the ammunition train that began in an American factory and ended at some battery dug in behind a Korean hill. He concluded that although the flow was at times irregular, there was always enough ammunition to meet the requirements of the tactical situation.

In openly supporting Eisenhower in the hotly contested presidential election of 1952, Van Fleet broke with the long-standing tradition that senior Army officers should stay out of partisan politics. Few of his colleagues emulated Van Fleet, although most military professionals, unhappy over developments in Korea, probably favored Eisenhower over Adlai Stevenson in 1952. Taylor was not among this number. Privately, he expressed dismay at his old commander's failure to disavow Senator Joe McCarthy, particularly after McCarthy's slashing attacks on General George Marshall. He said that if he voted, it would be for Stevenson.[14]

As early as September 1952 there were rumors that Taylor would be the new commander of the Eighth Army. Ridgway had given way to Mark Clark in Tokyo, yet Van Fleet's relations with Clark were no better than they had been with his predecessor. The Truman administration was thoroughly fed up with Van Fleet, yet reluctant to sack him in a clear act of retribution. The election of Eisenhower raised the possibility that Van Fleet might be kept on, but it was not to be. On February 11, 1953, the White House announced that the new commander of the Eighth Army would be Maxwell D. Taylor.

Chapter 14

KOREA

Of all the world's nationalities, few have found the road to independence more beset with peril than the Koreans. For centuries they were victims of their own misrule. Then, when the protecting hand of China was withdrawn at the end of the last century, Korea found itself the target first of Japanese militarism, then of Communist expansionism. For the first half of the twentieth century the Japanese saw to it that Korea remained the Hermit Kingdom. When the Japanese were finally expelled at the end of World War II, the ensuing vacuum was filled by a Soviet satellite regime in the North and an autocratic, Western-oriented regime in the South. Three years of fighting between 1950 and 1953 moved only slightly the postwar dividing line across the waist of the Korean Peninsula.

By the time Taylor took command of the Eighth Army, the situation on the ground was analogous to those periods in Europe during World War I when neither side could justify a frontal attack against its entrenched foe. The United Nations Command totaled some 770,000 men, including seven 20,000-man American divisions. The South Koreans had twelve divisions of about half that size, while the other nations of the UN Command had units ranging in size from the 24,000-man Commonwealth Division to token forces.

Opposed to this predominantly U.S.-South Korean force was a Communist army of more than a million. Approximately three quarters of it was Chinese, with the North Koreans now in a distinctly subordinate role. Both sides had serious logistical problems. The Communists were dependent on supplies from China and the Soviet Union, supplies that had to be moved to the front in the face of U.S. air superiority. The Eighth Army had an even longer supply line but compensated for the distance to the United

States by using Japan as a rear staging area. It is just as well that such an area was available, for the Eighth Army did not travel light. Taylor himself would tell the story of his inspection of a U.S. quartermaster depot in Seoul. Pointing to one group of sacks, he asked the depot commander what they contained. Tobacco stems for homing pigeons, was the reply. When Taylor expressed surprise that the Eighth Army pigeons were smokers, the depot commander explained. The Quartermaster Department had discovered, he said, that homing pigeons like to line their nests with the tobacco stems during the mating season!

By the time Taylor had taken over the Eighth Army, the UN supreme commander in Tokyo was General Mark Clark. Clark received his instructions from the Joint Chiefs in Washington, who, in the case of non-American contingents, acted on behalf of the UN Security Council. The field commander for the UN forces was Taylor, who also had operational control of the Republic of Korea's forces. His control of the ROK Army would prove especially important as differences emerged between Washington and Seoul over the desirability of an armistice.

On taking command in Korea, Taylor made his first order of business an inspection of the front. The existing line of contact ran just north of the thirty-eighth parallel.

> My tour of the front gave me my first opportunity to get a good look at the enemy positions facing us. They formed a continuous scar across the landscape from coast to coast, a zone pockmarked with shell and bomb craters testifying to the weight of firepower on our side. Whereas we put our trenches and observation posts boldly on the tops and forward slopes of the hills, the enemy were obliged to keep most of their positions on . . . the backside of the hills. . . . Where the terrain obliged them to live in positions which we could observe, they built many alternate shelters and trenches and moved about frequently to avoid our artillery fire and bombing.[1]

Although the American press was fond of referring to "Chinese hordes" and "human wave tactics," Taylor was not impressed with the numbers on the enemy side. He believed that there was a limit to the number of troops the Communists could support in Korea, and, although generally not given to "gut" feelings, he suspected that the Communists may have reached this ceiling. The main challenge he faced was that of accepting a defensive role. His task was to defend the Eighth Army's lines "with minimum losses consistent with maintaining the integrity of the position."[2] In practice, this would mean that he had to get authorization from Washington to attack in more than two-battalion strength. Nevertheless, he was soon able to make a public statement that doubtless gratified his superiors in Washington. On March 12 he issued a press release to the effect that the Eighth Army had all the artillery ammunition it required.[3]

The new Army commander inherited a far more effective force than he would have found a year earlier. Ridgway and Van Fleet had done as much for the morale of the Eighth Army as they had for its combat capabilities; even the ROK Army was gaining confidence with each passing month. Nevertheless, Taylor found the Eighth Army's patrolling inadequate. To underscore the importance he attached to tactical intelligence, he inaugurated a practice of bringing the leaders of selected patrols to his headquarters for debriefing. Although warned that some of his officers regarded this as a greater ordeal than the reconnaissance, the Army commander continued the practice right up to the armistice.

Taylor's cost-effective approach to his defensive line was soon put to the test. On March 23 the Chinese sent elements of two armies against Old Baldy and Pork Chop Hill on the western sector of the Eighth Army line. After several days of sharp fighting, much of it against the U.S. 7th Division, the Communists gained their immediate objectives. The new commander of the 7th Division, Arthur Trudeau, was preparing to counterattack against Old Baldy when Taylor restrained him. The Army commander flew to 7th Division headquarters by light aircraft and went over the proposed attack with Trudeau and his staff. After concluding that regaining Old Baldy was not worth the probable casualties, Taylor took personal responsibility for canceling the counterattack. Drawing on this incident, he ordered a study of all Eighth Army outposts, with a view to determining in advance of any attack which ones were essential to the UN defensive line and merited a counterattack if lost.

Although he found defensive warfare frustrating, Taylor was eager to find out all he could about the enemy he faced. Whereas the Eighth Army made extensive use of artillery, the Chinese were fighting an infantry war. Taylor later recalled:

During most of the time I was there we never got a round of artillery from them. This was an infantry show and the activity was [against our] outposts. The Chinese would simply . . . work their way across no man's land, often without being detected and sometimes taking days, then form in spite of our patrolling, and launch an attack on an outpost with very little warning. They would just saturate our position with human bodies, rapidly, always at night, so as to limit the effectiveness of our automatic weapons and our artillery. As a result we eventually fortified our outposts so that our men could stay right in their positions and call down our own artillery fire upon them.[4]

One of Truman's last actions as President had been to warn China that American patience with respect to an armistice was not inexhaustible. Shortly thereafter, India had proposed a compromise on the key issue of prisoner repatriation. It upheld the American insistence that there be no forced repatriation of unwilling prisoners, while accepting the Communist position that a final resolution of the "nonrepat" issue should be deferred to the peace conference expected to follow an armistice. On March 30 Chinese Foreign Minister Chou En-lai, returning from Stalin's funeral in Moscow, noted that prisoners refusing repatriation might be turned over to a neutral state so that the prisoner-of-war issue would not obstruct an armistice. Chou's statement suggested that agreement on an armistice might be near, and it propelled the new Eisenhower administration into a feud with its nominal ally, President Syngman Rhee.

Ultimately, Taylor would spend far more time worrying about irresponsible actions by the South Koreans than about military initiatives by the Communists. By 1953 Rhee was about seventy-seven, although no one was really sure. His hair was white and his face wrinkled. His eyes were watery and his hands shook. But he had spent most of his adult life fighting for Korean independence, and the idea of accepting an armistice that did not include the unification of Korea under his rule was anathema. Only a year before, when the Eighth Army had crossed the thirty-eighth parallel in pursuit of the vanquished North Korean army, his goal had appeared within reach. Then China's intervention had ended the dream.

Van Fleet had characterized Rhee as "worth his weight in diamonds" as a wartime leader of his people. Even though Rhee now devoted his remarkable energy to opposing U.S. policy, Taylor, too, found the old man appealing:

> He was a curious mixture of an Old Testament prophet . . . and a shrewd Oriental politician. . . . He knew how to play on the heartstrings of the American officials who visited him, often posing as a confused old man, devoted to his country but needing help to lead his people out of the wilderness. To win sympathy, he could pretend to have trouble with the English language (which he spoke almost perfectly) and to suffer from physical infirmities which vanished when he took off with me on a strenuous tour of the front.[5]

Taylor used all of his considerable charm on Rhee in this period, to little avail. He sought to ignore the government-sponsored demonstrations against an armistice organized by the government, but it was not easy, for the streets of Seoul were filled with chanting demonstrators, often carrying anti-Communist slogans written in blood.

On March 28, 1953, the Communists agreed to an earlier UN proposal for an exchange of sick and wounded prisoners. To Rhee, the implementation in April of Operation Little Switch—the exchange of the sick and wounded—loomed as a red flag. The Korean leader was becoming a barometer of the truce negotiations, quiescent when the talks were going badly, vituperative when an armistice appeared in sight. Clark, who was less tolerant of the old man than Taylor, later described how his relations with Rhee were excellent "right up to the moment the United States indicated clearly it intended to go through with an armistice. . . . Then I became the whipping boy for his bitterness and frustration."[6]

Taylor was fortunate in this sensitive period to have had excellent relations not only with his military superiors but with his other American colleagues in Korea. Ambassador Ellis Briggs was an urbane career diplomat who had no illusions in dealing with the wily Rhee. C. Tyler Wood, the U.S. aid administrator, was an experienced manager who was fully aware of the political implications of American aid. Ambassador Briggs later recalled:

> Ty Wood's, Max Taylor's and my views did not always coincide, but our recommendations for action—sometimes relayed to Washington for approval—were never reached without open discussion among ourselves, frequently followed by a joint call on President Rhee.
>
> I emphasize "joint," for the old gentleman developed an uncanny ability to identify the point at which divided views might lie. He endeavored to exploit such situations by inviting us in, one or sometimes two at a time, hoping to face the third with a *fait accompli.* President Rhee never took it amiss, however, when having invited General Taylor to discuss some military matter loaded also with economic or political gunpowder, the General would turn up with Briggs and Wood in attendance. "Since it would doubtless save time," General Taylor would say politely, "to have my colleagues learn directly from Your Excellency what are the President's views."[7]

With the resumption of armistice talks in late April, Rhee told Clark and Taylor that he would never turn over to the enemy any North Koreans who did not desire repatriation. Nor would he permit any member of the proposed Indian custodial force to set foot in Korea. The Americans were sympathetic on the first point; indeed, many American lives had been lost while the UN Command adhered to the principle of no forcible repatriation. The gambit with regard to the Indians, however, was totally unacceptable, representing as it did an attempt by Rhee to set aside two years of talks aimed at bringing about an armistice.

With so much at stake, the UN Command planned secretly to deal with several worst-case scenarios. Plan Everready, drafted in Taylor's headquarters and approved by Clark, attempted to deal with three contingencies: a refusal of ROK forces to respond to UN directives; an attempt by ROK forces to initiate unilateral action, that is, to "march North"; or a situation in which ROK forces or the civilian population became "openly hostile" toward UN forces. The last of these contingencies would have involved draconian measures. President Rhee would be invited to make a visit that would take him out of Pusan, the temporary capital, and UN officials would arrest his most troublesome followers. If Rhee were to continue to refuse to accept the armistice terms, "he would be held in protective custody, incommunicado."[8]

On June 4 the UN and Communist sides reached agreement on all major points concerning prisoner repatriation. Three days later, Rhee underscored his threats of unilateral action by promulgating special security measures throughout his country, recalling South Korean officers from U.S. training schools, and stepping up his "march North" propaganda in domestic radio broadcasts. On June 17 he told Ambassador Briggs that U.S. offers of economic assistance and a mutual security pact were insufficient if they required South Korean acquiescence in an armistice. Later the same day, while Taylor looked on, Rhee delivered a speech at ROK II Corps headquarters in which he denounced an armistice and repeated his determination to go it alone.

This time Rhee was not bluffing. The following day he played his trump card, ordering South Korean guards to release 27,000 North Korean nonrepats—an essential element in the armistice equation—who promptly vanished into the Korean countryside. The Communists, furious, broke off negotiations once again. Rhee's allies were scarcely less denunciatory; Clark told Rhee to his face that release of the prisoners constituted a "unilateral abrogation of your personal commitment." Taylor agreed with Clark but said very little. He took pains to assure that his personal relations with the old man were disturbed as little as possible. Plan Everready was left to gather dust.

While commanding the Eighth Army, Taylor occupied a small but comfortably furnished bungalow in a onetime Japanese military compound in the center of Seoul. He had left his family at home, but he did have with him Po, our venerable cocker spaniel. Taylor generally brought his pet along when he joined his staff for dinner in the headquarters mess. The clicking of Po's toenails in the hall heralded the general's arrival, and the assembled company typically responded by adjusting scarfs and preparing to rise when the Army commander entered. The little dog was such a reliable signal of his master's arrival that, on a rare occasion when he wandered into the mess alone, he padded into the dining room to find the Eighth Army staff standing crisply at attention.

The dog was Taylor's one domestic indulgence. He was determined that the prospect of an armistice would otherwise not take the edge off the Eighth Army as a fighting force. Shortly after his arrival he ran into an old 101st comrade, Ned Moore, and in the course of conversation inquired about Moore's wife, an Army nurse. Not only was she well, Moore advised, but she was on her way to Korea and would be stationed near Seoul. "No she won't, Ned," Taylor replied. The following day he issued orders that no military spouses, on whatever business, would be permitted in Korea. Ultimately, the order was carried out in a way that made Moore the toast of the town: in most instances, officers and their employed spouses were rotated to Japan. As Moore later recalled, "I didn't have Vivian but I got a lot of free drinks."[9]

If there was no emergency at the front, a typical day for Taylor began with staff briefings at around 8:15. These would often be followed by a helicopter trip to visit one or more units along the 125-mile front line. Alternatively, the morning might entail special briefings, visits by VIPs, or teleconferences with Clark in Tokyo. Lunch provided a break, but it was hardly a gourmet occasion. Most often it was a sandwich and a glass of milk taken during Taylor's Korean-language lesson. A typical afternoon often included one or more ceremonial occasions, such as presentations of awards or the activation of a new ROK unit, and routine correspondence. Fitness was never to be neglected. At four-thirty or five on almost any afternoon, the commanding general was to be found on either the handball or tennis court.

Most evenings he worked on his Korean, a language so complex that it resists any casual acquisition. Taylor was modest about his Korean-language capability, but Ambassador Briggs would later testify to how he put it to good use:

It was the President's custom, at fairly frequent intervals, to accompany the Commanding General on trips to inspect the troops who remained on the south side of the Demilitarized Zone long after the fighting had stopped. On those occasions he used often to address the soldiers and to express most graciously in English the gratitude of his country for the timely assistance rendered in 1950, without which the ROK might have been overwhelmed. . . . Having spoken in English, he would turn to General Taylor, and with a most humble and ingratiating smile would ask if he might now say a few words to his own troops in their own language, "because not all of them had learned English. . . ."

The second speech, in Korean, was to the effect that notwithstanding fainthearted allies who . . . had declined to back up his demand for victory, his country would know no real peace until the hated Communists were ejected by force and Korea's white flag . . . flew all over the territory from Cheju-do to the Yalu. Prolonged cheers.

After listening to the dual efforts on a number of occasions, General Taylor remarked to the President one day that, being a student of languages, his work had convinced him of a remarkable truth: namely, the extreme difficulty of rendering in one language exactly the thoughts expressed in another language, even though the speaker commanded a high degree of proficiency in each.

The diminutive President did not bat an eye. But hereafter, when General Taylor was present with him on the platform, the Korean speech was a closer approximation of the one just made in English. It was definitely a score for General Taylor.[10]

Taylor was eager not only to keep his army busy but also to keep his headquarters staff on its toes. At his mess he inaugurated a practice of biweekly debates after the evening meal. Usually he would select two officers to prepare affirmative and negative arguments on an agreed topic. After each protagonist had made his presentation and had an opportunity to rebut his opponent, the issue would be put to a vote. The commanding general voted only to break a tie.

Early in 1954, with Dien Bien Phu already under siege, Taylor proposed the topic "Resolved: That the United States should intervene militarily in Indochina." The officer tapped by Taylor to defend the negative was an old 101st comrade, Colonel Larry Legere. As Legere later recalled, he and his opponent both made their cases and the issue was put to a vote. The result was a tie, and all eyes turned to the head of the table for the tie-breaking vote. Taylor pondered a moment, then voted with the negative.[11]

Because neither side was able to make dramatic gains of territory, there is a tendency to view the final months of the Korean War as uneventful. Nothing could be further from the case. The Communists were eager to be perceived as the victors following the armistice, and they were prepared to sacrifice thousands of lives to achieve a propaganda advantage. Taylor, in contrast, was expected to maintain the integrity of his defensive line with minimum casualties. He was also obliged to consider the prospect that his Korean "ally" might, on Rhee's order, either repudiate the authority of the UN Command or conceivably launch a unilateral march North to unify the country.

In early June the Communists launched what proved to be the last major offensive of the war, singling out the ROK II Corps for large-scale attacks aimed at gaining enough territory to rationalize claims of victory. The Communist objective was a bulge in the Eighth Army's center in the area of Kumsong. In the course of a ten-day offensive by three armies, with strong artillery support, the Communists succeeded in driving ROK forces back an average of 3,000 meters along a 13,000-meter section of the front. The extensive use of artillery was a departure from normal Chinese practice, and Taylor suspected that enemy forces were expending their ammunition reserves in anticipation of an armistice. He was almost continuously at the front, assuring that the ROK forces were adequately supported.

The front was then quiet for several weeks, as if in recognition of the UN Command's preoccupation with Syngman Rhee. Then, on July 13, the Kumsong area flared again. Assaulted by elements of five Chinese armies, ROK forces fell back behind the Kumsong River, which Taylor regarded as essential to his defenses. In Tokyo and Washington the situation was viewed as sufficiently serious for Clark to order the 24th Division, then in Japan, to Korea. Taylor would later emphasize that he had never requested reinforcements (he had two divisions in reserve and considered them more than adequate). But he had a lot of people looking over his shoulder.

By July 15 the Chinese offensive had run out of steam. The following day Taylor ordered the ROK II Corps to counterattack and to restore its position along the Kumsong. After four days of sharp fighting the line was restored and the battle of the Kumsong salient was over. Taylor always suspected that a major objective of the Communists in this eleventh-hour offensive was to convince the ROK military leadership of the folly of any unilateral march North.

As his duties permitted, Taylor participated in the orchestrated pressure on Rhee to accept an armistice. In a press conference on July 5 he expressed confidence in his ability to extricate non-Korean UN forces from the front line if the South Koreans were to continue fighting after the armistice. In his memoirs, however, Taylor would emphasize that he was glad not to have had to deliver on his promise of a painless UN disengagement.[12]

Rhee, having succeeded in gaining U.S. agreement to virtually all his demands, including massive economic aid, a mutual defense treaty, and a twenty-division ROK Army, agreed in mid-July not to offer any further obstruction to an armistice. The armistice was signed at Panmunjom on July 27 without a word being exchanged among the various signatories. The following morning Taylor set out in his helicopter and inspected the entire front from the air:

> The communist troops were already out in force, standing on their battered hilltops, waving flags and banners bearing communist slogans and shouting songs of defiance and victory. They had prepared for this day for months, intent upon impressing the world that they were the victors and we the vanquished—a reminder that for them the conflict had not ended with the shooting. Our men watched this propaganda display in silence, merely glad that the ordeal of battle was over.[13]

The end of the fighting brought little easing of Taylor's lot. He faced the difficult military challenge of maintaining a high degree of readiness under conditions of a cease-fire. Implementation of the armistice terms was logistically demanding. Shortly after the armistice, Operation Big Switch—the exchange of prisoners—got under way. Between August 5 and September 6 the UN Command delivered 75,000 prisoners to the Communists, and the enemy returned 12,000, most of them Koreans and Americans. A visitor during this period, Congressman Gerald Ford of Michigan, recalled that "this was a terribly sad sight, although we were all thrilled to have our prisoners returned."[14] Among the last to return was the highest-ranking American prisoner, General Bill Dean, who had been captured in the first weeks of the war. Taylor gave him the red-carpet treatment, noting that the greatest pleasure for the normally retiring Dean appeared to be to converse with friends in English.

Although Taylor had seen his share of devastation during World War II, he was particularly touched by what he saw in Korea after the armistice. Whereas Germany had brought destruction on its own head, South Korea had not. A combination of compassion and a desire to keep his soldiers usefully occupied led him to inaugurate the Armed Forces Aid to Korea (AFAK) program, under which the Eighth Army provided equipment and expertise to supplement Korean labor and matériel in the immense task of reconstruction.* He had little patience with Americans who complained of the corruption that was rampant in postwar Korea, corruption that ranged from the pillage of military depots to graft at the top levels of the government. Taylor tightened procedures where he could, but he regarded the situation he faced in Korea as normal for a war-devastated Confucian society.

Although the AFAK program was Taylor's pet project, he looked for other ways to help the populace. Urban areas in Korea were a jumble of squalid, jerry-built slums, which in the winter were

---

* Stephen E. Ambrose, writing in *Eisenhower*, vol. 2 (New York: Simon and Schuster, 1983), p. 108, indicates that Eisenhower was the father of the AFAK program, but that "it held no interest for . . . Taylor." There is no basis for this assertion. Indeed, Taylor's enthusiastic backing for the AFAK program went far beyond implementing his instructions from Washington.

highly vulnerable to fire. In December 1953 the port city of Pusan was virtually leveled by fire. Taylor spent two days there, encouraging U.S. Army units to "adopt" Korean children who had been burned out of their orphanages. Elsewhere, he directed an old friend, IX Corps commander Carter Magruder, to assist displaced farmers in returning to their land behind the demilitarized zone. It was an unenviable task, for the areas in question were riddled with uncharted minefields and unexploded ordnance. In the end, however, the farmers returned to their plots.

On a Sunday morning early in 1954 Taylor decided to attend church services at the Eighth Army chapel, only to be informed, on arriving unannounced, that the chapel was already full. One suspects that word got around fairly quickly that the commanding general had been turned away, and the chief of chaplains may have opened a letter he received the following day with some trepidation. He need not have worried, for Taylor was at his whimsical best:

> I would like to report an incident which, while constituting a personal disappointment, is probably a matter for general felicitation. Arriving at the Eighth Army Chapel this morning at 11:02 a.m., I found it so completely full that I was turned away at the door. As I have always looked forward to the day when the Eighth Army jails and hospitals would be empty and the churches full, I am most happy to find that at least the latter condition is being fulfilled.
>
> Meanwhile, I have a request to make which I hope you will consider reasonable. As a leading sinner in this community, bedeviled by problems with forked tails . . . would you kindly reserve me a seat on future Sunday mornings? For my part, I shall undertake to see that you are notified in advance when my attendance is impossible.[15]

Early in 1954 Taylor almost became one of the last casualties of the Korean War. The signing of the armistice had been boycotted by South Korea, and the resulting cease-fire had brought no diminution in government-inspired propaganda for a march North. Taylor was being briefed at a ROK Army headquarters at Taegu in mid-February when a young Korean major entered the conference room by a side entrance, bearing a sheaf of papers. In Taylor's words:

> As he headed toward my seat below the podium I remember thinking that he probably had a message for me. Suddenly he stopped a few yards away and whipped out a pistol which he waved menacingly in my direction. For a moment everyone was paralyzed except General Kang [Mun-bong] who dropped the pointer which he had been using and leaped on the back of the would-be assailant. Then everyone came to life in a confused melee directed at disarming the culprit, who when subdued turned out to be Major Kim Ki-ok, a march-north fanatic.[16]

Knowing that the incident might be exploited by the Communists, Taylor attempted to keep it out of the media. His appointments diary for February 18—a schedule that was presumably available to most personnel at Eighth Army headquarters—makes no mention of his even being in Taegu and instead lists a number of headquarters appointments. But word quickly leaked out. ROK Army Chief of Staff Chung Il-kwon submitted his resignation, which Rhee refused. Taylor himself put the incident to good use, calling on Rhee the same day and pointedly suggesting that the real culprit was less Major Kim than agitators in higher places who persisted in depicting the Americans as obstacles to Korean unification.†

Much of Taylor's time in the year following the armistice was taken up with economic projects, VIP visits, and implementation of Eisenhower's commitment to build up the ROK Army to twenty divisions. At the same time, however, he sought to draw some conclusions from the fighting just ended that might prove useful in the future. The result was a detailed commentary on various as-

† The affair should have ended here, but it did not. General Kang, who saved the day at Taegu, subsequently had the bad judgment to become involved in the assassination of the head of one of Rhee's many competing intelligence organizations; he was sentenced to a long jail term. His wife sought to interest prominent Americans in his case, and Taylor was one of those who responded. Over the years he wrote to Rhee and others suggesting that, whatever Kang's role in the assassination, he might be an appropriate subject for clemency. Following Rhee's overthrow in 1960, Kang received a pardon.

pects of the Korean fighting, which he passed on to Chief of Staff Matt Ridgway in the spring of 1954.

Taylor's report comprised five sections, two of which noted the paramount role of infantry in the war and the unique importance of logistics. With respect to the first point, Taylor emphasized that Korea had been an infantryman's war. ("Whereas many of our expensive weapons could find only intermittent employment, the infantryman always had a job.") As for the importance of logistics in a war fought far from home, Taylor noted that "the conduct of the war placed a heavy requirement upon the Engineers and the other technical services, who invested labor and supplies representing hundreds of millions of dollars in developing . . . a support system."

The remaining three sections included important reflections of Taylor's own thinking. In his view, the character of the war had largely nullified the Air Force's bombers, the Navy's capital ships, and the Army's tanks. "The enemy reduced the effectiveness of our weapons by his tactic of closing at short range [and] burrowing into our positions." Most significantly, we had not seen fit to employ nuclear weapons, even at a time when we enjoyed a monopoly. In future conflicts, as a result of a tacitly agreed canceling out of "special weapons," he wrote, the United States might be "forced to rely again on conventional means" of achieving its objectives.

Another section dealt with the implications of the war in terms of manpower. The U.S. high command had been surprised first by the quality of the North Korean Army and then by the Chinese. "In the last weeks preceding the armistice, it was a sobering experience to find that hundreds of thousands of Chinese were still willing to give their lives without stint, repeatedly attacking our lines in the face of devastating artillery fire within hours of the signature of the armistice." Taylor then asked a rhetorical question: Can the West compete with such ruthless employment of military manpower? He had no answer, beyond concluding that "whether he is communist or western-trained, the Oriental soldier is henceforth an important factor in reckoning world military power."

Closely related to the capabilities of Asian soldiers was the cost of maintaining a Western army in a country like Korea:

The desire to live at war in accordance with American standards at home, while thoroughly understandable, was costly to indulge. In its most obvious form the desire showed itself in the ice cream factories, snack bars, post exchanges, and other "plush" excrescences. It manifested itself in a different form in the excessive consumption of munitions in support of insignificant actions on the theory that the soldier should get everything it takes to make him safe as well as comfortable.

Taylor concluded that the weapons of all three services should be studied to see whether they paid their way. "Expensive and complicated gadgets of infrequent use should not be allowed to absorb resources needed to support the most flexible weapon in our arsenal, the infantry soldier."[17]

In personal terms, his period as commander of the Eighth Army was a career plus for Taylor. He had commanded a force of nearly a million men under arms with a high degree of professionalism. Working under strict guidelines from Washington, he had carried out his defensive mission with great skill, notwithstanding the fact that he was obliged to parry some of the fiercest Chinese onslaughts of the war. He had avoided Van Fleet's error of making Rhee's political objectives his own and had demonstrated a sensitivity to the political problems his own government faced in prosecuting the war.

The influence of the Korean War on Taylor, however, went far beyond its immediate outcome. In Korea, the United States and its allies had achieved a stalemate under circumstances in which the enemy enjoyed every conceivable advantage except air superiority. Korea appeared to be confirmation that the United States could confront Communist aggression virtually anywhere in the world and bring about at least an acceptable conclusion. Just as a demonstration of Western unity had kept the East German youths out of Berlin at Whitsuntide, so had a similar demonstration of common purpose blunted a blatant case of Communist military aggression. Korea was half a loaf, but it was better than none.

Part Three

THE STRATEGIST

I have conceived of many plans, but I was never free to execute one of them. For all that I held the rudder, and with a strong hand, the waves were a good deal stronger. I was never in truth my own master; I was always governed by circumstance.

—*Napoleon*

Chapter 15

CHIEF OF STAFF

By early 1954 some key Army personnel changes were in the wind. In Washington it was widely rumored that Ridgway's bad relations with both Eisenhower and Secretary of Defense Charles E. Wilson presaged early retirement. Although Taylor had long been rumored as a probable successor to Ridgway, an earlier vacancy was likely in the position of chief of the Far East Command, which was a stripped-down version of the post once held by MacArthur. In April 1954 Ridgway wrote Taylor that, in the event of General Ed Hull's retiring from the Far East Command, "the great probability is that you would succeed him."[1] Taylor noted in reply:

> In the meantime I am certainly not restless in my present assignment. Apart from the inevitable separation from the family, which I like no more than any other soldier in Korea, the command of the Eighth Army has been and is a most satisfying professional experience. . . . I am prepared to stay in Korea just as long as you think I'm useful.[2]

Later in 1954 Taylor, who had gained his fourth star during the Kumsong battle, was appointed head of Army forces in the Far East and moved to Tokyo, where his wife, Diddy, joined him. In February 1955, however, Taylor was summoned to Washington amid considerable speculation that Ridgway would soon be stepping down. Although rumor had it that Taylor was to be offered the position of chief of staff, he himself believed that the trip was to discuss his succession to the overall Far East Command. His wife was an interested spectator as her husband packed his bags, and the two worked out a simple code by which he could transmit any important news. If he was to succeed Hull and remain in Tokyo, Taylor would cable that Lucille Hull sent her regards. Similarly, if he *were* to be offered the chief of staff post, it would be Penny Ridgway who sent her best.

Taylor's first call was on Ridgway, who was not privy to the deliberations about his own successor; as far as Ridgway knew, the only subject to be discussed was the succession to Hull's command. Thus Taylor dutifully cabled that Lucille sent her regards. On February 23, however, Taylor met with Secretary Wilson, the onetime chairman of General Motors, who would be best remembered for his judgment that what was good for his old firm was good for America. "Engine Charlie" (so called to distinguish him from "Electric Charlie" Wilson at the General Electric Corporation) began with a rambling monologue on conditions in Asia and then began to question his visitor. Was Taylor prepared to carry out the orders of his civilian superiors even though he might disagree with them? Taylor did not care for this line of questioning. He doubtless framed his replies carefully, however, for at the end of the interview Wilson informed him that he was under consideration as Ridgway's successor and should meet with the President the following day.

Taylor's meeting with Eisenhower on February 24 was his first contact with his old chief since Ike had taken office, and the President greeted him warmly. Once the conversation turned to substance, Ike's line of questioning was not unlike Wilson's, but again Taylor passed muster. Eisenhower said that he would nominate him for chief of staff after he had served briefly as Far East commander. Remembering the arrangement with his wife, he sent a second cable conveying Penny's regards—thereby sowing considerable confusion in Tokyo. Meanwhile, Taylor met yet again with Secretary Wilson, who had some suggestions about who should be his vice chief of staff. Taylor responded that a prerequisite to his taking the job must be the authority to choose his own deputy. In what would prove to be one of Taylor's few victories, Wilson backed down.

Taylor's prospective appointment was announced in May, and the reaction was generally favorable. The New York *Times* said that "we do not have a change in the quality of the officers upon whom we can call for our national defense," and offered "our warmest good wishes" to both the outgoing and incoming Army chiefs.[3] The Taylors said their farewells in Japan in early June and returned to the United States by way of Europe. The new chief of staff was particularly eager to update his knowledge of NATO, where an old friend, General Al Gruenther, was supreme commander. Regrettably, the Eisenhower administration had come up with a strategic rationale seemingly designed to discourage meaningful military contributions by the member nations. Under Eisenhower, NATO forces were regarded essentially as a "trip wire" in case of hostilities with the Soviets. Because an attack on NATO would draw a nuclear response from the United States, it was said, NATO's inferiority in conventional capabilities need not be a source of concern.

The Taylors arrived in Washington in late June, and on June 30 the Missourian was sworn in as the Army's twentieth chief of staff.* Maxwell Taylor had reached the top of his service, but he assumed his new duties at an especially difficult time. The 1.4-million-man Army that he inherited was to be cut back by 300,000 in 1954 and by an additional 80,000 the following year. At the same time, its sixteen divisions were deployed from South Korea to West Germany and could be required to deal with threats growing out of more than forty mutual assistance treaties.

A decade before, the chief of staff's responsibilities were fairly straightforward, in that they entailed "running" the Army under the civilian authority represented by the Secretary of the Army. Since 1948, however, a major portion of any service chief's time had been consumed by his responsibilities as a member of the Joint Chiefs of Staff, the principal advisory body to the Secretary of Defense and through him the President. The JCS had been created in 1947 as a step in the direction of "unifying" the services. In practice, each service continued largely autonomous, but the Joint Chiefs had considerable say in the allocation of the defense budget.

In the event of disagreement within the Joint Chiefs, Taylor could in theory appeal to the Secretary of Defense. In the Eisenhower administration, however, such an appeal was a waste of

---

* The post of chief of staff was created only in 1903; prior to that date the senior Army position was commanding general. If the two positions are considered to be analogous, Taylor was forty-first in a line that began with George Washington.

time. In Ridgway's words, "Mr. Wilson came in with an extensive ignorance of the military establishment and a well-established dislike for the Army."[4] In the event of an appeal by any service from a decision of the Joint Chiefs, Wilson could be counted upon to back the chairman, Admiral Arthur Radford. If Wilson had a strategic perspective, it was a faith in massive retaliation; he was once heard to observe, "We can't afford to fight limited wars. We can only afford to fight a big war, and if there is one that is the kind it will be."[5] If the facts of a situation did not fit the secretary's prejudices, he decreed that they did. In November 1956, at a time when the Air Force did not have the craft to airlift a single division, Wilson proclaimed airlift to be adequate. General Jim Gavin, who headed the Army's research and development under both Ridgway and Taylor, would recall:

> Mr. Wilson tended to deal with his chiefs of staff as though they were recalcitrant union bosses. . . . I have known General Ridgway, after weeks of painstaking preparation, to brief Mr. Wilson on a problem with lucidity and thoroughness. At the conclusion Mr. Wilson would gaze out of the window and ask a question that had no relevance whatsoever to the subject of the briefing. Among his aides this was known as taking the briefer "on a trip around the world."[6]

Although the tour of the Army chief of staff had traditionally been for four years, Wilson planned to keep the incumbent on a tight leash. In a memo to outgoing Secretary of the Army Robert Stevens, Wilson wrote, "It is my understanding with the President that this appointment would be for a period of two years," as was the case with the other chiefs.[7]

Taylor's colleagues on the JCS were a diverse lot. Nate Twining, the Air Force chief, was a West Pointer who had switched from the infantry to the Air Corps in the 1920s. He had spent the first part of World War II in the Pacific and then had commanded the Fifteenth Air Force in Italy. Four years older than Taylor, Twining was a "big bomber" man to whom Taylor would never be close, but Twining enjoyed good personal relations with his colleagues and would in time be elevated to chairman.

Chief of Naval Operations Arleigh Burke was a 1923 graduate of the Naval Academy and almost exactly Taylor's age. He had gained a reputation with both the Navy and the public as an aggressive destroyer commander during World War II. In tapping Burke as CNO, Eisenhower had reached well down the seniority list, but if he was seeking a Radford clone he must have been disappointed. Taylor would find Burke a congenial colleague, and it was not unusual for the two to thrash out some issues independent of the other chiefs.

Paradoxically, the most divisive member of the JCS was its chairman, fifty-nine-year-old Arthur Radford. In the Navy he had made the transition from battleships to carriers much as Twining had moved from the infantry to the Air Force. During World War II he had commanded carrier groups in the Pacific. Radford first became known to the public, however, as a leader of the so-called admirals' revolt against what they perceived as a reduced role for the Navy relative to the Air Force in strategic bombing. When the Truman administration scuttled the Navy's long-sought supercarrier in favor of the B-36 bomber, there was anger throughout the Navy, but CNO Louis Denfield urged his colleagues to accept the Administration's decision. A number of senior admirals spurned Denfield's advice and supported Radford in attacking the diminished strategic role for Navy aviation. In a massive lobbying campaign, marked by leaks and charges of corruption in the B-36 procurement process, the taciturn Radford became a rallying point within the Navy and a thorn in the side of Harry Truman. Equally important to Eisenhower and Wilson, Radford was a staunch supporter of Nationalist China, and as such his appointment was agreeable to the Taft wing of the Republican party.

The chairman of any panel must often play the role of conciliator. Among Eisenhower's Chiefs, representing as they did differing strategic perceptions as well as competing service interests, some talent at accommodation was especially desirable. Radford, however, was not interested in consensus building. Taylor would call him "an able and ruthless partisan, who did his best to impose his views upon the Chiefs."[8] Radford could do so because he had a blank check from "Engine Charlie" Wilson. According to Taylor's count, only three times in four years did Wilson fail to support the chairman on a split vote within the JCS.

The Chiefs normally met in regular session at 10 A.M. each Wednesday and Friday in a secure area in the bowels of the Pentagon known as "the tank." The agenda was normally agreed on two days in advance. On the day of each meeting the operations deputies for all the services would meet and dispose of matters that did not require the attention of their principals. The items that finally made the JCS agenda were not always controversial, but tough ones could linger for months—or perhaps never be addressed at all.

Secretary of the Army Wilbur Brucker had been appointed at almost the same time as Taylor. A garrulous onetime governor of Michigan, he had been general counsel for the Defense Department and was a nominal protégé of Wilson's. Taylor considered a close relationship between the civilian and military leaders of a service to be essential, and he offered to withdraw as chief of staff if Brucker preferred to have his own man. Brucker declared himself more than happy with Taylor, however, and the older man became a vigorous if not always effective supporter of the Army in Pentagon councils.

Members of Taylor's immediate staff sought as best they could to assess their new boss. Almost all remarked on his intensity, and some found him almost as aloof as his own mentor, George Marshall. Before reaching a decision on any matter of consequence he insisted on being briefed on all possible ramifications of the question under consideration. These briefings, in turn, were the subject of innumerable dry runs—Pentagon dwellers today even speak of "pre-dry runs"—within the staff. An officer who could not handle questions growing out of his initial presentation was likely to find himself reassigned. Similarly, anyone who wasted the chief of staff's time would have difficulty in getting on his calendar a second time.

Having gained the right to choose his own vice chief of staff, Taylor chose Williston (Willie) Palmer, a gruff artilleryman who was one of the Army's senior bachelors. Palmer's temper was legendary, as was his reputation for parsimony. In one instance he issued a directive over Taylor's signature that discouraged the exchange of official Christmas cards. The Washington *Post* ran a cartoon depicting Taylor as Scrooge, but insiders recognized Palmer as the culprit. Nevertheless, Palmer knew the Army inside out, and Taylor looked to him to handle virtually all aspects of routine administration, leaving himself free to cope with JCS and other substantive matters. As Palmer later put it, "I just stayed out of his business."[9]

The first problem that Taylor moved to address as chief of staff was that of the Army's image. Never a glamorous service, the Army was in low popular esteem as a result of the indecisive outcome in Korea and the accumulated grievances of thousands of draftees who had been roped into that conflict. In his first meeting with his staff, Taylor spoke of the need to project the Army's "true character" to the public, the Congress, and the other services. In a memo the following month he was more specific, providing a list of what he described as "principles which I want the Army to live by":

- The Army is openminded and progressive, seeking qualified advice and looking constantly forward. . . .

- In its interservice relationships, the Army is a loyal member of the Defense Team, quick to defend its own legitimate interests but scrupulous in not trespassing on those of the other services. . . .

- The Army respects the dignity of the individual and provides for the moral and physical wellbeing of its men. It is a decent, clean-living society which does not tolerate vice, dissipation, or flabbiness.[10]

Taylor had long been dissatisfied with the appropriately named olive-drab uniform that the Army had worn largely unchanged since World War I. In 1956, after many private "fashion shows," he introduced a snappy new uniform vaguely reminiscent of the field green of the German Army. Over the years the new uniform would prove quite popular, although there were problems at the outset. Pentagon staff officer Donald Seibert recalled how Army regulations initially prohibited the wearing of the new uniform after 6 P.M., a hardship for those who worked late at the office but wanted to go somewhere in the evening. Seibert brought about a change through an unusual channel:

This [regulation] was the subject of a heated conversation one evening at a cocktail party at the Fort Myer Officers' Club. A striking lady happened to overhear the conversation, joined us, and asked me to repeat the problem. . . . I told her the gist of the conversation. She kept nodding and saying, "Of course, that's absolutely right."

"It's ridiculous."

"It puts an awful burden on people."

"That should be changed. Let's talk to Max about it."

With that she grabbed my arm and started dragging me across the room to General Taylor, the Max she wanted to talk to about it. . . . The Chief of Staff was talking to General Eddleman and General Woolnough as we came up.

"Max, you've got to listen to this young man. There's something that needs to be changed right away," she said.

General Taylor raised his eyebrows quizzically and looked at me. My two bosses glared at me. Though I tried to evade the issue and leave, Mrs. Taylor insisted that I tell the General about the problems the current uniform regulations created for Pentagon action officers. . . . He thanked me and told me that he would look into it. I beat a hasty retreat followed by the glares of General Eddleman and General Woolnough. Shortly thereafter the regulation was changed, whether as a result of this conversation I do not know.[11]

In terms of Army capabilities, Taylor's most ambitious project as chief of staff was a reorganization of the standard Army division. While in Korea he had concluded that the old triangular division, based on three large infantry regiments, was outmoded. In 1954 he had used one of the new South Korean divisions to experiment with a new structure, one adaptable to either a conventional or a nuclear battlefield. His preliminary conclusion was that modern battlefield communications permitted a division commander to control up to five subordinate units.

As chief of staff, Taylor directed his deputy for operations, General Clyde Eddleman, to look into the matter of division organization and come up with something better. The result was the pentomic division, based on five reinforced battalions called battle groups. The theory was that a division commander would have more options for deployment with a greater number of subordinate units at his disposal, especially under conditions that placed a premium on dispersal. The Madison Avenue "pentomic" designation reflected the fact that the new division had a tactical nuclear capability in the form of a battery of Honest John rockets. The new organization was also felt to be better adapted to a battlefield that might see the employment of tactical nuclear weapons.

As luck would have it, the first unit to be reorganized as a pentomic division was the newly reactivated 101st Airborne. The "new" 101st, commanded by its World War II artillery chief, Tom Sherburne, had total personnel strength of about 11,500 and was "air mobile," via helicopter, as well as pentomic. The military correspondent for the Baltimore *Sun*, Mark Watson, wrote:

> The three-regiment composition of the division is gone. Instead there will be five "combat groups" of five 240-man companies each, plus a "support group" of all field supply and maintenance elements such as engineer, ordnance, signal, etc. . . . The five-way distribution at group and company levels aims both at better dispersion and better mutual support.[12]

Taylor decreed that the new structure be tried for five years, but the pentomic division never caught on. In maneuvers, many division commanders were unable to maintain effective control over five battle groups. There were also complaints that a pentomic division lacked the offensive punch of its predecessor and that Honest John rockets were less versatile than artillery. But another problem was that the new structure impinged on promotions. Eddleman told Taylor that "everyone in the Army dislikes it for two reasons: One is that it has no staying power and the other is that there is no command for lieutenant colonels."[13]†

Taylor had inherited his deputy for research and development,

---

† Criticism of the pentomic structure left Taylor unconvinced. Five years later, when he was heavily engaged in his investigation of the Bay of Pigs, Taylor wrote to several colleagues of his concern that the Army was abandoning the pentomic concept prematurely. "It will be little short of a miracle," he wrote to General Bruce Clark, "if the United States gets by the next three or four years without some form of war breaking out. In such a period we should try to keep our defense structure stable and be ready at any moment to man battle stations." Taylor to Bruce Clark, June 16, 1961, Taylor Papers.

Jim Gavin, from his predecessor. Gavin was no longer the wunder-kind of World War II, who, in getting his first star at age thirty-seven, may have been the Army's youngest general. As research chief, Gavin had a mixed record. Some found him more interested in initiating projects than in monitoring their progress. Others believed that he tended to intellectualize problems to such an extent that he was unable to make firm recommendations about development. Although he and Taylor agreed on most substantive issues, friends of the chief of staff felt that Gavin, in congressional testimony, had implied that Taylor was not an aggressive enough advocate for the Army.[14]

In December 1957 Gavin testified that Taylor had informed him that he was not being considered for promotion to the Continental Army Command, a post that would have carried with it a fourth star. The next month Gavin announced his decision to retire, adding that he believed he could contribute more to the Army from the outside. General William Westmoreland, who was then secretary of the General Staff, recalls that Taylor asked him to speak to Gavin and to urge him to reconsider. Westmoreland did so, but when he proved unsuccessful it seemed to him that his chief was not unduly concerned.[15]

By this time the Taylors had moved into venerable Quarters One at Fort Myer, overlooking Arlington National Cemetery and the Potomac. The rambling brick structure at the end of Generals Row, where Major Taylor had waited on General Marshall in the first year of World War II, was the country's most prestigious military residence.

The post of chief of staff carried with it a heavy entertainment schedule. Two formal dinners in a week were not unusual at Quarters One, and for every dinner in there was a dinner out. Taylor accepted these obligations but regarded them as unproductive time, for he did not mix business with social occasions. Invitations to dinner at Quarters One generally specified 8 P.M., dress was most often black tie, and guests were expected to be prompt. They were met at the door by an aide resplendent in Army blue. New arrivals would linger briefly at a diagram of the evening's seating arrangements before being escorted into the living room, where they were greeted by the host and hostess. Cocktails would be served until 8:45, when dinner was announced.

The guest books from the Taylors' years at Quarters One read like a Who's Who of official Washington. They are predictably heavy with the military but are also studded with the names of prominent legislators, diplomats, and journalists. Among the signatures are those of John Foster Dulles; Charlie Wilson; Wernher von Braun; Generals McAuliffe, Gruenther, and LeMay; Senator "Scoop" Jackson; and Congressman Jerry Ford. Often there was a guest of honor, usually a VIP visiting the capital. At some time between courses Taylor would rise, ask for attention, and deliver some remarks about the guest of honor. It is unfortunate that there is no record of these remarks, for the chief of staff was a charming host. If the guest of honor was an old Army friend, the ribbing could be hilarious. For others, the host's comments were a model of urbane good humor. Dinner was often followed by several selections by the Army Chorus, a fine men's ensemble that had been established at Taylor's direction.

If the chief of staff's guest list had an "Establishment" bias, there were also exceptions. The most frequent "guest," on formal as well as informal occasions, was Mrs. Taylor's younger sister, Mary Happer. Mary's ebullient enthusiasm made her everyone's favorite. Sergeant Bob Blackwell, in charge of the staff at Quarters One, would recall many years later how Mary would make for the kitchen right away to greet all the staff and ask, "What's for dinner?" John Service was a senior State Department China hand who had run afoul of Joe McCarthy at the peak of the senator's power and was eventually discharged from the government on unsubstantiated loyalty charges. Although the association between Taylor and Service dated back to the period of Taylor's autumn in China with Joe Stilwell, Service was nevertheless pleasantly surprised to be invited to a party at Quarters One at the height of his public notoriety. The China scholar recalled that "most of our Foreign Service friends stood by us—but they generally demonstrated their continuing friendship in more private ways."[16]

Even after a trying day Taylor applied himself to being a good host, and he expected others to be on their good behavior as well. On one occasion General Curt LeMay spent most of the evening in a corner seemingly scowling at the guests. As Taylor saw the last of his guests out at the end of the evening, he turned to aide De-Witt Smith and remarked incredulously, "Did you see that horse's ass, LeMay?"[17]

Taylor was prone to comment, particularly after some grueling social occasion, that people are always honored for the wrong things. So it was with a project, launched during Taylor's tour as chief of staff, to build a home in Washington for Army officers' widows and daughters. Taylor's name would occasionally be linked to the Army Distaff Hall, located near Walter Reed Hospital, but the driving force behind the project was in fact his wife. Mrs. Taylor marshaled support from groups of Army wives on those occasions when she accompanied her husband on visits to Army posts. She shook down her friends for donations to cover fund-raising expenses. The general admired and applauded, but it was his wife who had perceived a need and moved to meet it.

By the time Taylor became chief of staff he had largely given up handball and squash, but his zeal for tennis was undiminished. Several afternoons a week he was to be found playing doubles on a new complex of tennis courts behind Generals Row—courts that he himself had prodded the post commander to install.

Tennis with the chief of staff was not a casual undertaking. Fellow players arrived promptly or were not invited back. The general insisted on providing new balls. Once play began, all courtesies were observed but it was understood—in a variation on Clausewitz—that tennis was war conducted with different weapons. The intensity level was high.

Taylor's one weakness on the court was an erratic forehand. In compensation he had a flat, accurate backhand, a fine lob, and an excellent net game. His serve was unusual in that it entailed a slow windup in which he studied his opponent, sighted along the handle of his racket, and then delivered a spin serve that was most often annoyingly well placed. He was always attacking. Given an agile partner such as DeWitt Smith, Don Williams, or Jack Owen, the chief was a formidable doubles player and would continue to be well into his sixties. At about age seventy-three he still had the shots but his years were showing. Rather than play at a level he considered unsatisfactory, he quit the game and never looked back.

Chapter 16

THE VALLEY OF INDECISION

President Eisenhower took office with a double commitment: to bring the Korean War to a speedy conclusion and to avoid such inconclusive ground wars in the future. But how was the United States to deal with future Communist aggression? Out of the belief that there must surely be some way in which the United States could capitalize on its technological superiority came the strategic doctrine of "massive retaliation." Secretary of State John Foster Dulles characterized it as the capacity to retaliate "instantly by means and at places of our choosing." Administration spokesmen made it clear that the means in question included nuclear weapons.

It was not that the Administration ruled out the possibility of limited war. But Eisenhower and Wilson contended that it was first of all the responsibility of America's allies to deal with localized aggression. As Eisenhower wrote in his memoirs:

> [One] important guideline was that United States security policy should take into account [our] system of alliances. Since our resources were and are finite, we could not supply all the land, sea and air forces for the entire Free World. The logical role of our allies along the periphery of the Iron Curtain, therefore, would be to provide (with our help) for their own local security, especially ground forces, while the United States, centrally located and strong in productive power, provided mobile reserve forces of all arms, with emphasis on sea and air contingents.[1]

Although Ike's doctrine was politically appealing, it did not stand up to close analysis. Implicit in it was an assumption that any country worth defending already had effective armed forces of its own—an assumption that ruled out many strategic or resource-rich areas outside of Western Europe. Nor did it reflect the lessons of Korea, where even a total mobilization of forces by an ally necessitated a large-scale infusion of U.S. forces. Worst of all, it placed the United States in the position of being a likely bystander in the many cases of Communist aggression that fell short of justifying nuclear retaliation.

Part of the problem was that Eisenhower had surrounded himself with businessmen as counselors (his cabinet had been characterized as "ten millionaires and a plumber"), and defense expenditures were no longer viewed as having a special priority within the budget. In Eisenhower's view, it was essential that the United States be able to counter the Soviets, but only if this could be done without straining the economy. From here it was but a short step to reliance on nuclear weaponry. Nuclear weapons provided, in Wilson's vernacular, "more bang for a buck." Lest there be any misunderstanding, NSC directive 162/2, promulgated early in the Eisenhower administration, specified that the United States "would consider nuclear weapons to be as available for use as other munitions" in the event of war.[2]

To be sure, there was uneasy acknowledgment even in NSC 162/2 that not all confrontations lent themselves to resolution by nuclear weapons. Because of the post-Korea distaste for conventional warfare, however, the NSC endorsed "covert measures" short of conventional war as a means of dealing with secondary threats. The new strategic doctrine was soon reflected in the defense budget. By fiscal 1955 the Army budget was the smallest of those of the three services, barely half of what it had been during the Korean War.

When Taylor returned to Japan before being sworn in as chief of staff, he perceived a slight trend away from the Administration's commitment to massive retaliation. To take advantage of any such movement, and perhaps to stimulate strategic thinking within the Joint Chiefs, he formulated a paper titled "A National Military Program," in which he sought agreement on some priorities. He contended that a sound military program for the United States must provide for, in order of priority, (1) deterrence of general war, (2) deterrence of local aggression, (3) defeat of local aggression, and (4) victory in a general war. Implicit in this prioritization, especially the low priority accorded general war, was Taylor's conviction that war with the Soviets would be deterred by the U.S. strategic arsenal. Also implicit in this listing was Taylor's conviction that, although the United States was in a position to *deter* a general war, it was likely to have to *fight* smaller wars.

The paper is of interest both as a reflection of Taylor's own thinking and as the opening gun in what would become a running battle with Eisenhower and his advisers. Taylor's paper, with its emphasis on strategic objectives as opposed to the missions of the individual services, challenged not only the Administration's strategic doctrine but its budgetary process. Like his predecessors, Eisenhower allocated the defense budget among the various services. How each chose to spend its allocation was to a considerable degree up to that service, and the tendency of each was to go for the most modern equipment consistent with its mission. Taylor would have had all services orient their weaponry in terms of the most likely threats, and he assessed the threat of nuclear war as slight. He coordinated his "National Military Program" paper within the Army staff and then presented it at a meeting of the Joint Chiefs held in Puerto Rico in March 1956. In his words, "My colleagues read this Army study politely and then quietly put it to one side."[3]

Taylor had been fully briefed concerning the Army's minority position within the JCS before he became chief of staff. Indeed, he had the advantage of viewing his predecessor's frustration and had been considering how he might achieve more acceptable results. Whereas Ridgway had barely been on speaking terms with Wilson and enjoyed only slightly better relations with Radford, Taylor had come in with a clean slate. He admired the persistence with which Ridgway had argued the Army's cause, but he had never considered his fellow paratrooper the most articulate advocate for their common strategic view. Always an optimist, Taylor hoped that his own powers of persuasion would be more productive. In this he was badly mistaken.

Far from winning his colleagues to his own military program, Taylor found himself from the outset fighting a series of rearguard

Cadet Taylor in his 1922 photo for the West Point yearbook.

The Taylor family, with retinue, in Tokyo. The author is in the foreground; in the background is the residence of the Chilean minister.

Taylor and Joe Stilwell (fourth and second from right) in China in 1937.

The final page of the message pad that Taylor took
with him on his clandestine mission to Rome.

Taylor listens intently as Badoglio reads Italy's declaration of war against
Germany at a press conference in Brindisi.

"It was history encapsulated," wrote Taylor's granddaughter Alice, of this dramatic photograph: "the gallant old country, which had held on alone, now with a vibrant new power at its side."

The smiles at the time of Churchill's first visit to the 101st before D-day disguised some high-level misgivings concerning the use of airborne forces in Normandy.

The Lecaudey farmhouse, Hiesville, where Taylor spent D-day night.

Two days after D-day in Normandy, Taylor studies a map in his jeep, named Diddy.

General Omar Bradley awards Taylor the Distinguished Service Cross in a ceremony near Cherbourg in July 1944. Colonel Ned Moore, reading the citation, is at the left.

Takeoff for Market-Garden. The jumpmaster is Colonel Pat Cassidy.

Taylor talks to a group of soldiers near Herveld during Market-Garden.

The 101st passes in review at Bastogne on January 18, 1945. Taylor is eighth from left.

Field Marshal Kesselring at Berchtesgaden, flanked by Jerry Higgins and Taylor.

President Truman arrives at West Point for dedication ceremonies at the Franklin Roosevelt home in nearby Hyde Park.

Taylor, in Seoul, Korea, delivers a speech commemorating the establishment of the United Nations.

Korean President Syngman Rhee's courtiers look on impassively as Taylor prepares to make a test run in an American jeep presented to Rhee for his seventy-eighth birthday. Mrs. Rhee is in back.

actions. One of these was his campaign to retain some vestige of a missile program for the Army. With commendable foresight, the Army had brought Wernher von Braun and his German rocket team to the United States after World War II. At Huntsville, Alabama, von Braun and his colleagues had produced a prototype 240-mile surface-to-surface missile in 1953, and three years later the Army had its first operational Redstone missile unit. After developing the Redstone, which also put America's first satellite into orbit, von Braun's team set its sights on a 1,500-mile missile, the Jupiter. Successful testing of the Jupiter underscored the fact that the Army had stolen a march on the Air Force in missile development and put the Army on a collision course with the Air Force in the area of intermediate-range missiles. For the Army to go the next logical step—to deploy such missiles—would undercut the rationale for the Air Force's bombers and its intermediate-range missile, the Thor.

In November 1956 Secretary Wilson moved to settle the issue, giving the Air Force sole jurisdiction over deployment of intermediate missiles. In an additional rebuff to the Army, he directed it to limit its research and development to missiles with a range of no more than twenty miles. This was a bitter pill, but the Army bided its time. Eisenhower was known to be dissatisfied with Wilson, and in October 1957 the secretary retired, to be replaced by Procter and Gamble executive Neil McElroy. The Army promptly requested authorization for feasibility studies on a 500-mile missile, and McElroy concurred. Long after Taylor had retired, the Army developed what eventually became the successful Pershing family of missiles.

Missile development took a toll on the shrinking Army budget, however, and it was only peripherally concerned with the Army's stated concern for brush-fire wars. Taylor's research director, General Jim Gavin, told Congress in 1957 that "because of the need to support the big ballistic missile program . . . we have had to cut back on the other things such as a new family of tanks."[4] In that year, some 43 percent of the Army's budget for research and development went to missiles and nuclear weapons. Only 4.5 percent went to new vehicles and 4.3 percent to artillery. Taylor himself was bothered by this breakdown, although to some extent it reflected decisions made under his predecessor. He acknowledged in 1959 that "the big money has gone for the weapons which are limited in employment to general war situations."[5] But the Army's dilemma persisted. Missiles were clearly the weaponry of the future, and the Army had the most competent missile engineers. Moreover, as long as the Wilson-Radford thinking was dominant, all services were obliged to prepare for nuclear war. Radford's preoccupation with nuclear weapons went beyond a belief that the West could not compete with the Warsaw Pact forces in conventional warfare. He sought to eliminate any consideration of conventional warfare from Pentagon planning.

One problem with the Army's modernization campaign was that it lacked influential backers on Capitol Hill. The Air Force had spokesmen such as Senators Stuart Symington and Henry Jackson: Symington had been an aggressive Secretary of the Air Force under Truman, while Jackson's constituency was so dependent on Air Force contracts that he became known as "the senator from Boeing." Similarly, legislators with an important shipyard in their home states became strong advocates for Navy programs. All this translated into clout on important budgetary matters. The Army could not compete. Not only did it have the smallest budget among the services but its scattered suppliers made for minimal political leverage.

Taylor had placed a longtime colleague, Carter Magruder, in charge of Army procurement and, in Magruder's words, left him alone. The choice of Magruder as his deputy for logistics reflected a determination to run a tight ship in procurement matters, for the stolid Magruder was the despair of anyone who sought favors from the Army. When offered the use of a plush lodge by the Army's largest single supplier, the Chrysler Corporation, Magruder would not go near it. Another supplier put on a large reception in New York City that fizzled when no one from the Army showed up. The organization in question complained to the chief of staff that its partnership with the Army in the defense of America was being endangered by Magruder's attitude. Taylor called Magruder in and asked what was going on. He heard his colleague's explanation and thanked him. Nothing more was said about it.[6]

One of the inherent weaknesses of the JCS is that its principals are rarely allowed to be military statesmen, applying their wisdom and experience to critical security problems. Rather, they are primarily representatives of their own services and, as such, are expected to defend the bureaucratic interests of their service, regardless of what their strategic inclinations are. As chief of staff, Taylor had one advantage in that the "Army" view of the nature of the Communist threat was widely shared by thoughtful observers outside the Defense Department. Even so, however, this support meant little in terms of Pentagon hardball. As a result, the Army followed the principle that a service that is a constant loser in "the tank" generally finds other rules by which to play the game—as Taylor would discover. He arrived in Washington prepared to abide by the rules, but some key members of the Army staff had had far longer to assess the problem than he, and they were prepared to carry on the fight outside Pentagon channels.

In the spring of 1956 came the first of the Army protests that came to be called the "colonels' revolt." The dissidents, who included Donovan Yeuell, Lyal Metheny, and George Forsythe, were convinced that a major portion of the Army's problems within the Eisenhower bureaucracy could be traced to inept public relations. For the most part, they supported Taylor's badly received National Military Program and were eager to push it. They perceived support in Congress for Army programs as a largely untapped asset. What would Taylor's attitude be? According to Forsythe, the chief of staff made it clear that his "colonels" were on their own. In Forsythe's recollection, "General Taylor told us that we were in a dangerous assignment and that if we were ever 'uncovered' he 'wouldn't know us.' We understood that full well, because if his efforts were to continue, he had to be at arm's length from [us]."[7]

One of the Army's first public relations initiatives was to rebut an Air Force story in the Washington *Post* concerning the relative merits of the Air Force's Talos and the Army's Nike antiaircraft missiles. Subsequently, "the colonels" passed to the New York *Times* a series of position papers highly critical of the Air Force and the doctrine of massive retaliation. One of them carried the sarcastic title, "A Decade of Insecurity Through Global Air Power." Another contended, "We continue to pour excessive manpower and money into an Air Force which has been substantially neutral-ized [by the Soviet Union's growing nuclear strength] and which pleads for more money, more money, more money."[8]

Secretary Wilson was furious at this public airing of defense disputes. However, as the Yeuell group had predicted, there was considerable sympathy for the Army's cause on Capitol Hill. The *Times* articles caught the attention of, among others, Senators Lyndon Johnson and John F. Kennedy. It was left to Wilson to pick up the pieces. On May 21 Taylor and Twining held an unusual joint news conference in which they respectively disowned the Army papers and the Air Force counters that they had inspired. The following day Taylor circulated a memo to his key deputies in which he indicated "strong disapproval" of public statements that might "fan the flames of controversy." The memo stated that there were "ample means within the Department of Defense for rectifying of differences."[9] The memorandum effectively dissociated Taylor from the leaks, but without disavowing the contents of the papers in question. As George Forsythe recalled:

> We were all sent out of the Pentagon immediately, to *great* assignments, incidentally. . . . When my group was reassigned, the Army staff was delighted. We were a small "super" staff and among the many obstacles that faced us was the unwillingness of the Army Staff to take a new approach to the vital role of the Army in the age of nuclear weapons and indirect aggression. . . . As soon as we were fired they treated us like lepers and kept their distance. It wasn't until later when [Taylor's] concept of the flexible response was accepted by [President Kennedy] and the Army's friends in Congress that the groups of "revolting colonels" grew by scores.[10]

Having cautioned his subordinates, Taylor sought to work through the system. Almost immediately he faced a major challenge. Radford's position with the President was sufficiently strong that in July 1956 he set forth a proposal calling for an 800,000-man cut in military manpower and the recall of most U.S. forces stationed overseas. The session of the Joint Chiefs devoted to Radford's initiative sparked the most direct confrontation between Taylor and his colleagues up to that time:

It was clear to me that the admiral's plan would destroy the world-wide forward strategy which the U.S. had pursued since World War II, undermine our alliances, and eliminate the Army as an effective instrument of land warfare. Hence, I arrived carefully prepared with a written rebuttal drawn up with the help of some of my ablest staff officers. . . . The argument was summarized in the following terms: "The Chairman's concept represents a program which prepares for one improbable type of war, while leaving the United States weak in its ability to meet the most probable type of threat. It fixes the form of possible military reaction, with a resultant loss of flexibility and adaptability for the political and military policy of the United States. It will frighten and alienate our friends. It will play the Russian game directed at getting our forces out of Europe and Asia. It substitutes the concept of 'Fortress America' for our former strategy based upon forward deployment of deterrent forces."[11]

In Taylor's own words, his presentation was received in "strained silence." None of his colleagues offered support, and Radford did not undertake any defense. But in the end it was Radford who had miscalculated, for sources friendly to the Army view again leaked the substance of Radford's proposal to the New York *Times*. The resulting uproar, especially within NATO, obliged the Secretary of Defense to offer assurances that no significant reduction of U.S. deployments in Europe was contemplated. The incident hardened the enmity between Taylor and Radford, however, and almost certainly led the Defense Department to block publication by Taylor of an article for *Foreign Affairs* in which he urged a greater emphasis on deterrence toward the Soviets and the development of improved capabilities to deal militarily with lesser threats.

Taylor took pride in his powers of persuasion, and his near-total inability to bring his colleagues around to his own views concerning the threat of limited war began to take a physical toll. In early 1957 he experienced severe back pains, pains that his doctors could not diagnose with certainty but that we in the family attributed to stress. For a period of several weeks sitting was so painful that he arranged a lectern in his office so that he could do his paperwork from a standing position. After some unsuccessful experiments, he discovered that sitting on a board (especially in cars) and sleeping on a hard mattress or a board brought considerable relief. In time the pain disappeared as mysteriously as it had come, although Taylor would insist on a hard mattress for the rest of his life. The episode is of interest primarily as a demonstration of how stressful were the relations with Wilson and Radford: they succeeded in bringing on stress symptoms where the Germans, North Koreans, and Chinese had failed.

Even in this career nadir Taylor was a model of self-control. Two of his closest associates, Carter Magruder and Lyman Lemnitzer, would later say that they never saw him lose his temper. Others did see him angry, but it was always a passing phenomenon. Clyde Eddleman, his deputy for operations, recalled that "if he lost his temper or flared up occasionally, he would apologize when he cooled off";[12] the fires were quickly brought under control, the iron will reasserted itself, and the episode was soon forgotten. By contrast, when Eisenhower lost his temper he would burn for hours.

Although Taylor was a Democrat by upbringing, he, like most senior officers, was zealous in his attempts to keep the Army "out of politics" in the partisan sense. To most soldiers, this entailed distancing the service from contentious domestic issues, particularly those that were potentially divisive. By 1957 the Army was racially integrated, the day of segregated units having ended during the Korean War, when replacements had to be employed where they were needed. Nevertheless, Taylor looked on uneasily in 1957 as demonstrations against school desegregation in the South raised the possibility that the Army might be employed in the role in which it was least comfortable, that of assuring "domestic tranquillity."

In September 1957 Arkansas governor Orval Faubus employed the Arkansas National Guard to defy a federal court order and to prevent the entry of nine blacks whom the court had ordered admitted to Little Rock's Central High School. President Eisenhower found the entire business distasteful, but he had no intention of permitting Faubus to flout the law. He first attempted to win over the governor, but was eventually obliged to act when the mayor of Little Rock said that he could no longer maintain order.

Traditionally, the federal government employed the Regular Army only as a last resort in domestic disturbances. Taylor himself favored the federalization of the National Guard to deal with Little Rock, but he reckoned without Secretary Brucker. Brucker had no use for the National Guard, and it was he, not Taylor, who was in the command channel. The President called Brucker on September 24 to order that troops be sent to Little Rock and asked Brucker which unit should be sent. Brucker suggested the 101st Airborne. That day, Eisenhower put the Arkansas National Guard under federal control and ordered one thousand troopers of the 101st to Little Rock.

The crisis passed, but not before Taylor had spent a few sleepless nights. The local commander in Little Rock was General Edwin Walker, who even then had a reputation within the Army as a right-wing maverick. Clyde Eddleman ordered his deputy, Earle Wheeler, to Little Rock with authority to replace Walker if necessary. According to Eddleman, Wheeler was appalled to find the troopers of the 101st with live ammunition in their rifles. He directed that weapons were to be unloaded, and in the end there was no firing at Little Rock.[13]

Elsewhere, the Army began to score a few points. The most serious international situations to confront the Eisenhower administration had been the Hungarian revolution, the Suez crisis, and the intervention in Lebanon, none of which was susceptible of resolution by nuclear weapons. Nor had U.S. allies proved able to provide the military resources required. Within the Joint Chiefs, the Navy as well as the Army was coming to view the might of the United States and the Soviet Union in terms of mutual deterrence, although the Navy was committed to strategic weapons in the form of the nuclear submarine. The Air Force was least receptive to change. Eager to keep its bombers in service even as it developed long-range missiles, the Air Force rejected mutual deterrence as heresy. Within the Air Force—a service not noted for profound strategic thought—the growth of Soviet nuclear power only accentuated the need for more nuclear weapons and delivery vehicles so that the West could remain "ahead."

Although Eisenhower had been easily reelected in 1956, his defense policy was drawing heavy criticism. George Kennan, writing in 1954, concluded that "the day of total war has passed. . . . From now on, limited military operations are the only ones which could conceivably serve any coherent purpose."[14] Henry Kissinger came into national prominence in 1957 with his book *Nuclear Weapons and Foreign Policy*, in which he argued that "deterrence is greatest when military strength is coupled with the willingness to employ it."[15] Because Eisenhower's stated willingness to employ nuclear weapons was widely discounted, the Administration's ability to deter war depended on conventional forces as well.*

The most perceptive writing in this period came from nonmilitary scholars. Members of the Joint Chiefs, even if disposed toward strategic analysis, were constrained both by their positions within the Administration and by the requirement to espouse the needs of their own service. Taylor had been arguing for preparedness for limited war since becoming chief of staff. Given the support he received from scholars like Kennan and Kissinger, he can be absolved to a degree from the charge of parochialism. But the Army chief was also bothered by an aspect of massive retaliation that was not widely discussed. A strategy based on the counterpunch of massive retaliation was by definition *defensive*—however massive the counterpunch. Taylor never liked to surrender the initiative, be it in strategic or tactical terms. To him that was a lazy man's defense.

In its planning for any new war the Army made a distinction between strategic and tactical nuclear weapons. Taylor and his colleagues maintained that the strategic arsenals of the United States and the Soviet Union effectively offset each other, but that tactical nuclear weapons were another matter—and potentially far more disruptive of world peace. Because these were short-

---

* During the Lebanon crisis of 1958, U.S. forces offshore included an Army unit armed with dual-purpose Honest John rockets. Because of their nuclear capability the Honest Johns were not even landed lest their presence be interpreted as indicating Washington's willingness to employ nuclear weapons in that sensitive region. Taylor viewed the episode as one more example of the fallacy of overreliance on nuclear weaponry.

range weapons, generally useful for distances under two hundred miles, the other services were happy to leave them to the Army. Yet because of their relatively low yields and the fact that they were "battlefield" weapons, a nation that possessed tactical nuclear weapons was far more likely to employ them than to employ strategic weapons that would probably bring instant retaliation.

One of Taylor's less recognized contributions in this period was to point up the problems inherent in nuclear weaponry of any size. "The more one reflects upon the use of atomic weapons in limited war situations," he told students at the Army War College in 1958, "the more one is impressed with the limitations which we would want to impose on their employment. The so-called tactical weapons are small only by comparison to the megaton yields of the so-called strategic weapons. They are highly destructive to friendly peoples and friendly countries."[16]

And where did the President himself stand in all this? There is little evidence that he focused on the doctrinal differences that divided his Chiefs. Surrounded by fiscal conservatives led by Treasury Secretary George Humphrey, Ike was preoccupied with reducing expenditures, and he addressed strategic questions from a managerial prospective. Taylor himself would recall:

> He was loath to make decisions in the military field, and very frequently, as he told me personally, would decline to decide things for Secretary Wilson. . . . On the other hand, he was detached from considerations of what you might call military strategy by being President. He also was not entirely current with the weapons development that was going on, which was a major field of conflict within the Joint Chiefs of Staff. He also really believed, or acted as if he believed, that general nuclear war was indeed the only kind of war we need to think about. . . . He didn't think that [a major conventional war] would be possible now that nuclear weapons were available. In that he was wrong.[17]

Actually, by the last years of the Eisenhower presidency the Administration's strategic perceptions were moving closer to those of Taylor, Kissinger, and Kennan. General Andrew Goodpaster, Eisenhower's staff secretary, would later recall:

> In the latter part of his administration, probably under the impetus of Foster Dulles, Eisenhower was almost driven to recognize that there was more to it than just the nuclear weapons, that problems were arising in the so-called "third world" that [required] conventional military strength and a conventional military position. . . . The President was reluctant to acknowledge that. I think part of that reluctance came from a concern that he would lose the ability to keep a limit on the buildup of military forces.[18]

Part of the problem, too, was one of communication. In his four years as Army chief of staff, Taylor never met with Eisenhower alone. The President's wishes were interpreted by a succession of defense secretaries who, while successful managers outside government, had little understanding of weapon systems and even less grasp of strategic issues. A more activist President would not have permitted such a situation to arise. But Eisenhower chose to treat the symptoms only, leaving it to his defense secretaries to do something about the "Pentagon problem."

In the fall of 1958 preparation of the fiscal 1960 budget promised yet another row among the Chiefs. The services had already accepted substantial cuts, but budget director Maurice Stans had decreed that additional cuts of $3 billion to $4 billion were required. Eisenhower asked Secretary McElroy to identify where additional cuts could be made and then sought to sugarcoat the pill with a White House dinner for the Chiefs. Virtually all the leaders of the Administration—including Vice President Nixon, Treasury Secretary Robert Anderson, and Stans—were present. After dinner in the main dining room, the President led his guests into the library for talks. There was little mention of budgetary specifics. Rather, the conversation turned to a discussion of general economic conditions, the problems facing the Treasury, and the need for greater "team play" on the part of the Chiefs. After brief pep talks from the President and Secretary Anderson, the Chiefs were invited to respond.

When Taylor's turn came, he did not argue against the overall budgetary ceiling but against the prevailing division of the budget among the services on the basis of a fixed percentage. He noted that this practice failed to take account of the completion of the Air Force's reequipment phase or the need for Army modernization. No one took open exception to Taylor's presentation. They did not have to, for there was no danger that the Army's heresy would gain acceptance at this late date. In the end, the 1960 budget followed the same pattern as the former ones. Writing his memoirs in the early 1970s, Taylor recalled:

> Today I can look back with comparative detachment on those turbulent years fraught with well-nigh continuous conflict with my colleagues of the JCS and Defense Secretaries Wilson and McElroy. They were wearing times, quite different from anything I had known in my previous service. While I never particularly minded the conflicts with my Pentagon peers, I felt keenly the increasing coolness of my relations with the President.[19]

A compensating factor in these difficult times was the strong support he enjoyed from most of his Army colleagues. Many felt that Taylor had restored the Army's sense of purpose at a time when it was held in open contempt by Eisenhower's top appointees. Clyde Eddleman, Carter Magruder, and George Forsythe were among those who felt that Taylor had "saved" the Army. General Al Wedemeyer, who had never been a close associate of Taylor's, wrote in 1959, "As a fellow West Pointer, I feel that you have been a symbol of the ideals of the Academy, etching in the hearts and minds of [all] our sacred motto—Duty, Honor, Country."[20]

Nevertheless, Taylor's tour as chief of staff represented his first brush with failure since Holland, in a career that had appeared to have no valleys, only peaks. His ambitious plans for a national military program had been summarily brushed aside. The 870,000-man, sixteen-division Army that he left behind was down from the 1,100,000-man, eighteen-division force that he had inherited from Ridgway. The pentomic division organization on which he had lavished such attention would be short-lived. His tangible achievements were in the area of damage control. He had kept the Army in the missile field and had even secured authorization for a 500-mile missile. He had frustrated the efforts of Wilson and Radford to make deep cuts in Army personnel.

Amid the honor guards and other trappings that accompany the

retirement of any chief of staff there was, in Taylor's case, a gnaw-
ing frustration. But there was also the satisfaction that comes
from the belief that one has fought the good fight and that in time
vindication would come.

In the spring of 1959 General Andrew Goodpaster, the Army's
liaison officer with the White House, raised a delicate question
with the President. In his judgment, Goodpaster said, Taylor's
planned retirement represented a great loss to the Army. Should
he not be retained in some capacity? Eisenhower promised to give
the matter some thought. Although it was the "Army's turn" to
provide a successor to Twining as chairman of the JCS, Eisenhower could hardly have considered appointing a man whose
strategic views differed so sharply from his own. In due course,
however, he asked Goodpaster to sound out Taylor concerning the
post of supreme commander to NATO.[21] It was a generous offer,
for the NATO position was arguably as prestigious as that of JCS
chairman. Taylor, however, was not tempted. He was convinced
that the Administration's defense policies were fundamentally un-
sound, and he was determined to take his case to the public.

Chapter 17

"A FRIGHTENING AND TIMELY BOOK"

Taylor's retirement, after forty-one years in uniform, might have been a traumatic time. Since World War II he had spent most of his time on assorted Army posts, with their well-tended lawns and fifteen-miles-per-hour speed limits. Since 1942 he had had the services of at least one aide, and as a three- and four-star general he had become accustomed to the domestic staff that was one of the perks of his rank. All this combined to make for a certain isolation from the real world. Within the family there were rumors that the general still expected to ride the New York subway for a nickel. He had to learn to drive all over again.

In the event, there was no cause for alarm. After a week's holiday the Taylors moved into temporary lodgings in the old Westchester Apartments in northwest Washington. There the general began work on *The Uncertain Trumpet,* with occasional interruptions for media appearances.

Eisenhower was about to leave the presidency with his personal popularity intact but his policies, foreign and domestic, under heavy fire. The U-2 affair, in which the Soviets had exposed administration attempts to cover up the loss of a spy plane over the Soviet Union, was only the most recent embarrassment. In part because of the country's continued affection for Ike as a person, dissenters such as Taylor, who opposed administration policies but who did not deal in personalities, were much in demand by the media. Within two weeks of his retirement, Taylor was the interviewee on "Meet the Press."

YATES McDANIEL: Why did you step down when you did?
TAYLOR: As you can imagine, there are a variety of reasons,

some of them personal, some of them official. I would say that in the four years I was chief of staff I pressed as hard as I could to obtain a thorough reappraisal of our national military strategy. I was only partially successful. I feel that in four years I have done all I can as part of the defense team. . . . I now go out and perhaps I can contribute from the outside.

LAWRENCE SPIVAK: General, you and the President seem in conflict over the size of the Army. What is your answer to the President's question [when] you recently put in for more troops: "Where will I put them?"

TAYLOR: We have just lost one of our four Strategic Army Corps divisions because of lack of military personnel. The first step, of course, would be to build up the Strategic Army Corps and also to replace foreign nationals occupying military spaces abroad.[1]

On the day he retired, Taylor had written to a number of senior retired officers, including Douglas MacArthur, concerning his mixed results as chief of staff:

I wish that I could report all objectives taken during my four years as Chief of Staff. Unfortunately, such is not the case. However, I do have the feeling that the country has acquired an [increased] realization of the timeless essentiality of the Army in assuring our national security. The folly of basing our military strategy on Massive Retaliation as a cheap means of security has been more and more apparent. It is hard to believe that a fundamental change in military policy is far away.[2]

MacArthur's reply was warm. "You need have no regrets," he replied. "Your record as Chief of Staff was outstanding and has earned you the admiration of all Army men."[3]

The exchange continued what can only be characterized as an ambiguous relationship between the two men. In public Taylor spoke of the older man with unfailing respect; his misgivings about MacArthur's ego and his controversial advance to the Yalu were reserved for a few intimates. MacArthur, for his part, had spent his retirement years in near seclusion in the Waldorf Astoria in Manhattan, granting few interviews and largely keeping his thoughts to himself. In 1954, however, he had granted an extended interview to Scripps-Howard reporter Jim Lucas in which he spoke bitterly of the "great betrayal" in Korea. Although the general's greatest ire was reserved for the British—whom he accused, incredibly, of passing his military plans to the Chinese—there was venom enough to go around. Among his own countrymen, Truman was "the little bastard"; Ridgway was "a chameleon"; Eisenhower was "a naive and honest man who does not want to offend anyone." As for Taylor, who was commanding the Eighth Army at the time of the interview, he had been "one of the most promising cadets at the academy" when MacArthur had been superintendent. MacArthur had foreseen a great future for him. But Taylor was "a careful and extremely ambitious young man" who would do nothing to jeopardize his career:

He will never make a move without contacting higher echelons. Such a man has a definite value. Certainly, he is just what they want in Korea now. But when such a man is finally cornered and forced to make his own decision—as such men inevitably are—they sometimes come up with some weird ones.[4]

A "weird decision" that Taylor had come up with as chief of staff had been to try to bring MacArthur "back into the Army." The older man had all but severed connections with his former service, but Taylor, after taking some soundings among former MacArthur associates, made arrangements to call on him and assure him that the Army continued to value his counsel. Gradually, the chief of staff's correspondence came to include exchanges of holiday greetings with his old superintendent in the Waldorf Astoria.

MacArthur specified that the lengthy Lucas interview not be published prior to his death, and this restriction was observed. When it was published in 1964, Taylor felt only pity at the old man's bitterness. Unlike Truman and the British embassy, he declined all comment.

While Taylor worked on his book at the Westchester, he was weighing several employment possibilities. He was not interested in defense-related employment; long before it became a scandal, he had had doubts concerning the propriety of senior Pentagon officials' moving into defense-related businesses. One of those who inquired about Taylor's plans, however, was a West Point graduate who had left the Army for finance, General William Draper. Draper wanted to step down from one of his positions, that of chairman of the Mexican Light and Power Company, the principal utility in the Mexico City region. Because the position was highly political—the company's rate structure was closely supervised by the Mexican Government—Draper was looking for a successor who was not only a manager but a negotiator, and preferably someone fluent in Spanish.

Once his book was complete, Taylor accepted the offer from MexLight. In September he and his wife moved to Mexico City, where they occupied a Spanish-style villa on the prestigious Via Reforma. There he lived his most relaxed existence in years. The company largely ran itself, and Taylor had ample time for tennis and the opera. They were at home to visitors. But they were not out of the limelight, for excerpts from *The Uncertain Trumpet* had appeared in *Look,* and the book itself was out by the end of the year.

The Uncertain Trumpet was a short book, totaling about forty-five thousand words. The title came from 1 Corinthians: "For if the trumpet give an uncertain sound, who shall prepare himself to the battle?" There was nothing of a sensational nature in the text. It had few personal references to either Eisenhower or Wilson, and even Radford was treated with respect. The book was oriented toward issues, and its argumentation was uncomplicated. For those who had known Taylor's policy recommendations while still in uniform, the book held few surprises. Nevertheless, it set forth a new strategy for the U.S. military, that of "flexible response."

The book's main contention was that U.S. military programs were based on obsolete premises and that Eisenhower's strategy of massive retaliation was bankrupt against an adversary armed with equally destructive weapons. The flexible response strategy Taylor proposed instead was based on a diversified military arsenal, one that would restore the country's ability to meet military challenges over a wide spectrum. Against an adversary armed with nuclear missiles, the author pointed out, security could come only through deterrence—which meant having a retaliatory strategic force of finite numbers but enjoying sufficient protection to be capable of surviving a first strike.

Even so, such a retaliatory force would be effective only against general nuclear war. It would have little if any effect on localized aggression, which, for just this reason, was likely to become the most serious challenge to the West. Taylor argued that the United States must vastly improve its ability to deal with these threats, primarily but not entirely through increases in the Army's conventional war capabilities. He also sought increases in the defense establishment's tactical air and trooplift capabilities, functions that traditionally had held minimal interest for the Air Force.

The Uncertain Trumpet had other concerns besides weapon systems. Taylor was also sharply critical of the defense bureaucracy. Speaking at a book-and-author luncheon, he characterized the National Security Council as a notoriously uncertain trumpet:

> It is a task of the National Security Council to determine the aims we should pursue as a nation and then to devise a national strategy for the attainment of these aims. . . . Unfortunately, in my experience no such clear guidance has been obtained from the National Security Council. The documents bearing upon military strategy which it has produced have been so general in language as to mean all things to all people.[5]

One of Taylor's characteristics was that he expected organizations to do what they were chartered to do. He might have been surprised to learn that Eisenhower thought no more of the NSC than he did; Eisenhower considered it a debating society that had been imposed on him by his predecessors. Like most presidents, he preferred to thrash out important matters in smaller, less structured groups.

If the NSC was an anachronism, what of the Joint Chiefs? In his new role as Mr. Fixit, Taylor had some proposals here as well:

> The most important organizational change which I would propose would be to separate the responsibilities of the Joint Chiefs of Staff which can be dealt with by committee methods from those which require one-man responsibility in order to get acceptable results. Having made this separation, I would dissolve

the JCS as it now exists and replace it by a new advisory body called provisionally the Supreme Military Council. The service Chiefs of Staff would lose their Joint Chief hats and would return to their services to act exclusively as Chiefs of Staff to their respective department Secretaries.[6]

Although the views here expressed would undergo modification over the years, they reflect Taylor's lifelong interest in organizational solutions to intransigent problems. This interest, in turn, was an outgrowth of his personal philosophy. Most people, he believed, want to do good work. They are prevented from doing their best by ineffective leadership, defective organization, or both. Whatever his position, Taylor sought to provide the necessary leadership and to rectify organizational shortcomings.

Meanwhile, under Taylor's successor as chief of staff, Lyman Lemnitzer, the Army continued to take its hits. In October 1959 its elite missile team, led by von Braun, was transferred to the new National Aeronautics and Space Administration. Writing to Secretary Brucker from Mexico, Taylor characterized this as "unhappy news" but added that "it was probably inevitable and . . . may in the long run best serve the interests of the country."[7]

Early in 1960 *The Uncertain Trumpet* was attracting sufficient interest that it appeared likely that Taylor would be called to testify before Congress concerning the circumstances that had led to his retirement. The Democrats controlled both houses of Congress, and the general could anticipate a receptive audience. Brucker—seemingly more a partisan of the Army than of his party —wrote in January that "it is too early in this session of the Congress to tell definitely whether the wind is blowing 'strongly' or 'gently' in our favor, but I *do know* the Congressional wind is with us."[8]

Except in publications with an Air Force bias, *The Uncertain Trumpet* received good reviews. Both the New York *Times* and the New York *Herald Tribune* gave it top billing in their Sunday book review supplements. George Fielding Eliot, writing in the *Herald Tribune*, called it "a frightening and a timely book." Its author, according to Eliot, had revealed "the blind, insensate bondage in which today's freedom of choice is trammeled by the dead decisions of the past."[9] Jack Raymond, writing in the *Times*, had some stylistic criticism ("The editing has not entirely eliminated Pentagon jargon") but was largely favorable. Raymond called *The Uncertain Trumpet* "an important, rewarding, sometimes exciting book." He picked up on Taylor's mention of his preappointment "loyalty" interviews with Wilson and Eisenhower:

> Regardless of the merit of his complaints and recommendations, there are some charges in this book that American public opinion surely will want to explore—the charge, for example, that from the beginning of the Eisenhower Administration it was "suggested" that the Joint Chiefs "belonged to the Administration in power and were expected to be the spokesmen for its military policy."[10]

Taylor enjoyed his good press, but he was not carried away. In a letter to Field Marshal Sir Gerald Templer, who had written favorably concerning the book, Taylor replied, "Strangely enough, there has been no effort in the United States to rebut this line of argument. At the same time, there has been no rush to take the necessary fiscal actions which are necessary to implement it."[11]

As Brucker had anticipated, Taylor was soon in Washington elaborating on the themes in his book. On February 4 he testified before the Senate Preparedness Subcommittee in both open and closed session. Out of uniform his testimony was far more blunt than it had been as chief of staff. He called for "heroic measures" to build up the nation's defenses. Otherwise, he said, "from about 1961 on the tide will run against us":

> To change the trend will require men, money and sacrifice. The alternative is military inferiority—and there is no living long with communism as an inferior.[12]

Under questioning, Taylor suggested a defense budget of roughly $50 to $55 billion, as opposed to the $41 billion being proposed by the Administration for the upcoming fiscal year.

The following day, in the late afternoon, as Taylor crossed Connecticut Avenue to his rooms at the Mayflower Hotel, he demonstrated his customary caution in waiting for a taxi to pass. Alas, the driver never saw Taylor, who escaped serious injury only by spinning away at the last moment. As it was, he was knocked down and his left arm was broken; he spent several days at Walter Reed Hospital while his arm was set and his abrasions attended to. One of the get-well notes was from Dean Acheson: "It was a high price to pay for telling the Congress the facts it needs so much to know. I hope in a few years it will seem more worth paying than it does now."[13]

Back in Mexico City, Taylor met with company officials concerning the details of the latest rates proposal to be submitted to the Mexican Government. But he continued to follow developments at home closely and on occasion would raise some matter with one of his military colleagues. Writing to Vice Chief of Staff George Decker, he called attention to the proposal of a senior medical officer, General James Forsee, to send American surgical teams "into the backward countries of Asia, Africa and Latin America, for the purpose of treating the sick and instructing the local medical profession. . . . His concept is quite similar to the work of our Army doctors in Korea as part of the AFAK Program."[14] Shorn of its military sponsorship, the proposal anticipated one aspect of Kennedy's later Peace Corps, but for the moment it foundered on budgetary considerations.

Elsewhere, Taylor took time to argue the cause of Sylvanus Thayer, the most influential early superintendent of West Point, for inclusion in the Hall of Fame. In letters to the electors he wrote:

> Thayer was unusual in that, though basically trained in the humanities, he became the great early exponent of technical education in the United States. By making West Point the first engineering school, he provided a center of training for many of the men who opened up the West. . . . Although we think of West Point graduates primarily in terms of their military achievements, the list of those who made their mark in engineering, railroad and road building, exploration and mapping is a significant testimony to the influence of Thayer's teaching.[15]

Taylor watched the unfolding U.S. election campaign with guarded interest. Candidate Kennedy was an acknowledged fan of Taylor's; not only had he praised *The Uncertain Trumpet* but he had indicated on several occasions that he planned to seek military advice from soldiers like Gavin and Taylor. But Taylor was not yet sold on Kennedy. He had had occasion to observe Nixon as Eisenhower's Vice President and thought he had handled himself well. Decision making in a Nixon White House, he thought, would be far more efficient than under Eisenhower. At the same time, he shared the widespread distrust of Nixon as a political hit man. A family letter from Mexico included some of Taylor's political reflections:

> Somehow I can't get very joyful over the coming U.S. elections. . . . Surely, out of a hundred and seventy million Americans there ought to be two gentlemen with better qualifications than Mr. Nixon and Mr. Kennedy. Personally, I would rather pick one of the vice presidents for president. However, there is some slight reassurance in the fact that our Government is no longer that of a single man, but of a large group. I hope that the victor will be able to surround himself with able supporters to compensate for his inadequacies—assuming that he recognizes having some.[16]

Many years later, he elaborated on the thoughts expressed in this letter. Had he been a voter in the Democratic primary, Taylor speculated, he probably would have supported Lyndon Johnson, whom he had seen frequently as chief of staff and for whom he had developed considerable respect. As the campaign went on, however, he developed admiration for Kennedy as well. The fact that Kennedy had called on Gavin for advice during the campaign was a good sign. So, too, were his kind words for *The Uncertain Trumpet.* Taylor was an infrequent voter during his lifetime, and he did not request an absentee ballot in 1960. But by election day he was pulling for the Democrats.

Meanwhile, Taylor found himself back on the job market. In September the reasons for the Mexican Government's footdragging on rate increases became clear: it had decided to nationalize MexLight. In a speech that ran more than three hours, President

Lopez Mateos announced that his government had purchased a majority of MexLight's voting stock and would shortly take over management. It could not be characterized as a friendly takeover, but in the end the Mexican Government paid a mutually agreed price for the remaining company stock.

Taylor was not long among the unemployed. Even as Lopez Mateos announced the nationalization of MexLight, Taylor's name had surfaced before a committee seeking an executive to direct construction of Lincoln Center for the Performing Arts in midtown Manhattan. Taylor knew next to nothing about music, but John D. Rockefeller III was not looking for an artistic director. In the words of the center's official history, "Taylor's keen analytical mind, his firmness in executive decisions, his ability for clear verbal expression [and] his reputation for fairness and integrity were qualities needed for the executive leadership of Lincoln Center."[17]

After a trip to New York to discuss terms, Taylor agreed to a five-year contract as president of Lincoln Center. If he had any concerns about how his appointment might be received, they were soon dispelled. The New York *Times* editorialized:

> New York's good fortune in having had John D. Rockefeller 3d to lead the Lincoln Center for the Performing Arts in its formative years is now doubled with the addition of Gen. Maxwell D. Taylor. . . . His known talents for administration, his enthusiasm, energy, his broad intellectual interests and his feeling for diplomacy will all find their use in this large task.[18]

In November 1960 the Taylors made perhaps the thirtieth move of their marriage as they transferred from Mexico City to Park Avenue in Manhattan. The cooperative apartment they purchased there—old but spacious—was the first home they had ever owned. Taylor assumed his position as president of Lincoln Center on the first of the year and was immediately immersed in key decisions relating to construction financing and the role of the center in the forthcoming World's Fair. In mid-January he was in Washington at a ceremony in connection with Secretary Brucker's retirement, when he was passed a note to the effect that the new Secretary of State, Dean Rusk, was attempting to reach him. It was three days before the two made contact with each other, but when they did

Rusk surprised Taylor by offering him the post of ambassador to France. The general was not seriously tempted; he had just signed his contract with Lincoln Center and was enjoying the new challenge.

Then came the Bay of Pigs.

Chapter 18

THE NEW FRONTIER

Once he had agreed to President Kennedy's emergency request that he come to Washington, Taylor took only twenty-four hours to pack a bag, catch the shuttle, and check into the apartments for transient general officers at Fort Myer—only a stone's throw from the chief of staff's quarters that he had vacated two short years before.

At a meeting on April 21 President Kennedy chaired a discussion of what form the Bay of Pigs investigation should take. At one point it was suggested that the four principal panelists—Robert Kennedy, Admiral Arleigh Burke, Allen Dulles, and Taylor—should act as equals on the panel. Taylor responded that it was his understanding that he would chair the investigation, and it was on this basis that he had come to Washington. The discussion moved on. As Taylor later recalled, the President asked him when he could begin work, to which he replied that he could not start immediately because of a speaking engagement at Harvard that evening. Kennedy, doubtless sympathetic, offered him the use of a White House plane for the trip with the understanding that he would begin work the following day. Taylor then pointed out that he had a long-term obligation to Lincoln Center as well. The President promptly put in a call to John D. Rockefeller III, explained the problem, and asked for a leave of absence for Taylor, mentioning "two or three months" as the likely time frame. Taylor thought at the time that "this had a rather ominous sound."[1]

Two days later Taylor and his colleagues were unwelcome guests at the CIA headquarters in Langley, where they began interviewing survivors of the invasion who had been flown up from Florida. Within a week Taylor had come up with some preliminary findings, and these early judgments would not change significantly during the weeks of testimony that followed. His first reaction was that there appeared to be more than enough blame to go around. Although the CIA had been the most obviously inept, Kennedy had been badly served by the Pentagon, the State Department, and his own staff. A more specific indictment, which again applied to all agencies, was that everyone treated the invasion as business as usual. No one took responsibility for assuring that everything related to the invasion had the highest priority—that it was not to be *allowed* to fail.

Under different circumstances, the investigation itself might have turned out to be nearly as great a disaster as the Bay of Pigs. All the principals except Taylor had turf to protect. Two of the four, Dulles and Burke, bore a degree of responsibility for the failure, while Bobby Kennedy was watching out for his brother's interests. Yet the investigation moved ahead in remarkable harmony. Taylor commented in early May that the one bright spot was that no one was seeking to evade responsibility.

Although the final report was not complete until June, Taylor and his associates briefed the President on their preliminary findings on May 16. It was an awkward occasion. Taylor delivered the main presentation himself, occasionally referring to maps and charts. Planning for the operation had been uniformly bad, he said, in part because there had been no real study of sentiment in Cuba toward the Castro regime. The CIA had been deluded by the anti-Castro zeal of the émigrés. Subsequently, it had failed to recognize that an amphibious military operation was far beyond its capabilities. The Joint Chiefs, for their part, had demonstrated a lamentable unwillingness to call attention to the operation's inherent pitfalls.

Some of Taylor's harshest comments were reserved for the State Department. Although doubtful whether the invasion could have succeeded under optimal conditions, he was critical of the additional impediments placed in its way by the diplomats. In Taylor's view, the world would correctly assume that the United States was somehow behind the invasion, and State's insistence on keeping American personnel in the background accomplished nothing. As one official observed, "The trouble was that we were acting like an old whore and trying to pretend that we were just the sweet young girl we used to be."[2]

Taylor's final report paralleled the May 16 presentation but in more painful detail. If the President and the State Department were remiss in their preoccupation with plausible denial, the Chiefs had been grossly inattentive. By acquiescing in the Bay of Pigs plan, the report read, the Chiefs "gave the impression to others of approving it although they had expressed their preference for [a different site] at the outset, a point which apparently never reached the senior civilian officials."[3] In later years Admiral Burke would put the matter succinctly: "What the chiefs could have done is pound the desk and insist. We stated our case and then shut up. We should have been tough, but we weren't."[4] Dean Rusk, for his part, would recall, "I served the President badly by not going to him and forcing him to ask the Joint Chiefs: What would you need if we were to do this [invasion] with American forces?"[5]

But the primary culprit remained the CIA. Its first error was one of political assessment. According to a report prepared by the agency's own inspector general, no one in the CIA had seriously addressed the question of whether it was feasible to overthrow Castro. Indeed, such intelligence as was available indicated not only that he was firmly in control but that he enjoyed a high level of popular support. The agency was no more effective at the operating level. Equipment was found to have been inadequately tested, just as the presence of coral reefs offshore had been ignored. Although Castro's jet trainers were known to be combat capable, no one seemed to have considered that the Cubans might put them to good use. Basic military precepts were ignored in the area of logistics, leading the insurgents to load virtually their entire stock of ammunition on one vessel, the ill-fated *Rio Escondido.*

Quite apart from these lapses, senior CIA officials thought nothing of dissimulating at the top levels of government in pursuit of their project. Kennedy told Taylor that he had been repeatedly assured that, if worst came to worst, the insurgents could "melt away" into the mountains. But there were no mountains, because the landing site had been moved to the Bay of Pigs area from the Trinidad target area well to the east. Questions concerning attitudes in Cuba were quickly deflected. When Richard Goodwin, a Kennedy aide, asked Bissell why he thought the Cubans would rise up, the CIA man avoided the question. "Don't we have a [National Intelligence Estimate] on that?" Bissell asked of an assistant. The reply was affirmative, but no such estimate was produced.[6]

The Cuba Study Group unanimously concluded that although the immediate cause of defeat had been lack of ammunition, there were "soft spots" everywhere, including the numerical weakness of the assault force, the paucity of air support, and the ad hoc operational planning.[7] The investigators concluded further that the proposed operation could not have been carried out without visible U.S. involvement and that for this reason among others it should have been transferred to the Defense Department. But before proceeding at all, the panelists said, the project should have had a thorough review to ascertain that it was "in the national interest." Taylor himself was never sure of how he would have voted on a military operation to overthrow Castro. Even after the Cuban missile crisis the following year, he tended to regard Castro as more of a nuisance than a threat.

The report of the Cuba Study Group had some interesting bureaucratic ramifications, the most important of which was to take some of the heat off of the CIA. When Taylor had arrived in Washington, the agency's future was very much in doubt. White House sources quoted the President as considering a dismantling of CIA, which would virtually terminate covert activities and divide the agency's analytical functions between State and Defense. By the time the Cuba Study Group submitted its report, however, there was no more such talk. In conversation with the President, Taylor had emphasized that he should not throw out the baby with the bath and that the CIA's covert activities, properly handled, represented an important cold war asset.

One interesting aspect of the Cuba Study Group was its broad mandate. Its charter went well beyond establishing responsibility for the Bay of Pigs, as President Kennedy's letter to Taylor indicated:

It is apparent that we need to take a close look at all our practices and programs in the areas of military and paramilitary, guerrilla and anti-guerrilla activities which fall short of outright war. I believe that we need to strengthen our work in this area. In the course of your study, I hope that you will give special attention to the lessons which can be learned from recent events in Cuba.[8]

Given the shortcomings that his investigation had revealed, Taylor urged the establishment of a senior interagency group to keep tabs on sensitive parts of the world and to consider the options available for dealing with them. He envisaged its performing some of the functions of the Operations Coordination Board, which Kennedy had abolished, but with a far more restricted cast. The Special Group (Counterinsurgency) that ultimately emerged had a far more restricted mandate than what Taylor had proposed, but it provided a central coordinating council for sensitive security affairs and it proved far less prone to leaks than the overstaffed Operations Coordination Board.

The most improbable result of the Bay of Pigs inquiry was the beginning of a warm friendship between Taylor and Robert Kennedy. Superficially the two had little in common. One was a farm boy from Missouri, the other a representative of the country's most powerful political family. They were a generation apart in age. And whereas the older man had spent virtually his entire life in uniform, his younger colleague was on the political fast track. But the investigation had revealed a remarkable similarity in approach and style. Bobby would speak with admiration of Taylor's "intellectual ability, his judgment, his ideas." The general, for his part, was equally impressed with Bobby:

> In sifting out the facts of [the Bay of Pigs] . . . Bobby was a thorough and incisive interrogator of witnesses, quick to identify a "snow job," impatient with evasion or imprecision, and restless in his determination to get at the truth. . . . In working with Bobby, I was deeply impressed with his attitude towards his brother, the President. It was the reversal of the normal fraternal relationship of a big brother looking after a younger one. In this case Bobby, the younger brother, seemed to take a protective view of the President, whose burdens he tried to share or lighten.[9]

In part because of this immediate rapport with the younger Kennedy, Taylor could forget about any return to Lincoln Center. Bobby was, after all, the chief recruiter for his brother's administration. In mid-May he sounded out the general about taking over the directorship of CIA. Taylor declined but did not slam any doors. In late May he commented privately that "they are really putting on the heat" for him to take a position with the Administration and that there was talk of reviving the position of military adviser that had been held by Admiral Leahy during World War II. He saw his return to Washington as inevitable and bemoaned the financial loss it would entail. But the die was cast.

> Some time in early June the President for the first time called me in and said that he was personally aware of the discussions I had been having with his brother. He rather pressed me on the CIA question but again I insisted that this was just not my dish. . . . I really felt that I would be justified in coming back to the government only if I utilized my military experience. This led to further discussions with Bobby.[10]

The following month Colonel Julian Ewell, one of the World War II Screaming Eagles, heard that his old boss was at the Pentagon wrapping up the Cuba report. Ewell went by to pay his respects and ended up having a good chat; the general did not seem to be packing his bags for a return to Manhattan. A few days later the phone rang. Would Ewell be interested in serving as executive officer for a new office, that of military representative of the President? Ewell interpreted this as a command as well as a request, and was soon in the process of establishing a small office on the third floor of the Executive Office Building next door to the White House.[11]

A statement from the White House advised that Taylor would be taking up his new duties on July 1 and attempted somewhat gingerly to define his functions:

> As military representative, General Taylor will be the staff officer advising and assisting the President with regard to . . . military matters. In his new role, General Taylor will not be interposed between the President and any of his statutory advis-

ers or advisory bodies such as the Secretary of Defense, the Joint Chiefs of Staff or the National Security Council. But he will maintain close liaison with them and give his personal views to assist the President in reaching decisions.[12]

Taylor had misgivings about his new role—he was never entirely comfortable in arrangements outside the conventional chain of command—but he saw his job in terms of two functions. The first was simply to provide for Kennedy the basic military knowledge that Kennedy's predecessor, Eisenhower, had acquired through a lifetime in the armed forces. The second was to act as a strategic adviser, with a special interest in areas such as Berlin and counterinsurgency. However diplomatically he carried out his responsibilities, his relations with the Chiefs were likely to be strained. Taylor himself remarked, "I am sure the Joint Chiefs of Staff resented my appointment very deeply because it was plainly a reflection on their recent performance. They had to live with it, however, and they did live with it."[13]

Something else with which they had to live was the equivalent of a Sunday school lesson from the President, delivered at Taylor's instigation. On May 27 the President called on the Chiefs at the Pentagon to discuss their relationship to him. He reminded them of their duty as advisers to the commander in chief and expressed the hope that their advice would come to him direct and unfiltered. He added explicitly that this advice should not be purely military, because most of the problems with which they dealt had political, economic, and psychological aspects. Although he expected the Chiefs to present their military views without hesitation, he regarded them as more than military specialists and looked to them to help him fit the military dimension into the overall context of any situation.

The new "milrep" recruited a tiny staff, made up of Ewell and four other officers, one from each of the three services and one from CIA. He used his staff as "ears," to monitor issues as they surfaced in the White House and worked their way toward the Oval Office. He was determined to remain apart from White House politics, weighing in on an issue only at such time as it reached the

President. This practice flew in the face of bureaucratic consensus building, but it was Taylor's way.

An immediate challenge was to develop means by which the government might deal with confrontations that fell short of conventional war, as in the case of Cuba. There had been a group—the so-called 5412 Committee—that handled such actions, but Taylor was not satisfied with it. A major problem was that it was an ad hoc group, one whose expertise vanished once its principals returned to their own agencies. Taylor favored, as its replacement, a permanent committee composed of the deputy chiefs from State, Defense, and CIA, operating with a full-time chairman and reporting directly to the President. Its functions would include the direction of cold war strategy, the staffing of an indications center, and the supervision of covert operations.

Taylor had expected that he would have more problems with the White House staff than with the Pentagon, and this certainly proved to be the case with the successor to the 5412 Committee. Neither the national security adviser, McGeorge Bundy, nor the State Department looked with favor on a proposal that promised to infringe on their own responsibilities. Moreover, both the Pentagon and the CIA maintained their own indications centers and had no interest in a competitor. In Bundy's recollection, Kennedy "took Taylor's organization charts up to his bedroom and left them there."[14]

Not surprisingly, the mechanism that grew out of Taylor's initiative fell considerably short of what he originally had in mind. Nevertheless, in January 1962 the Administration established the Special Group (Counterinsurgency), with Taylor as chairman and a membership that included Bobby Kennedy, the chairman of the JCS, and senior representatives from State and CIA. For much of the 1960s the Special Group (CI) proved a useful means of focusing the attention of various agencies on problems that cut across departmental lines. To Taylor's satisfaction, the threat that a problem should be referred to the Special Group was often sufficient to prompt an effort by competing agencies to resolve their problems at the staff level.

Of all the issues that came Taylor's way as military representa-tive, the most pressing seemed that of Berlin. As early as January 1961 Soviet Premier Khrushchev had spoken openly of his inten-tion to take unilateral action with respect to Berlin, to "eradicate this splinter from the heart of Europe." The Berlin issue had fea-tured prominently at the summit conference in Vienna, one that saw Kennedy very much on the defensive in dealing with the abra-sive Soviet leader. At Vienna, Khrushchev said that Moscow in-tended to sign a separate peace treaty with East Germany—one that not only would formalize the end to World War II but also would terminate the postwar agreements that guaranteed the Al-lies access to divided Berlin. The Soviets appeared eager to pro-voke a confrontation.

Khrushchev's threat triggered a predictable burst of activity in Washington, where the Kennedy administration was determined to preserve Western rights with respect to Berlin even at the risk of war. The President was aware that he was being tested by the Soviets and that, in the wake of the Bay of Pigs, both his ability and his resolve were suspect. He was handicapped, however, by the fact that long reliance on massive retaliation had left the West largely unable to challenge the Soviets without an implied threat of recourse to nuclear weapons. The President was nevertheless determined to take a stand, and he immersed himself in the prob-lem:

> He reviewed and revised the military contingency plans, the conventional force build-up, the diplomatic and propaganda ini-tiatives, the Budget changes and the plans for economic war-fare. He considered the effect each move would have on Berlin morale, Allied unity, Soviet intransigence and his own legisla-tive and foreign aid program. He talked to Allied leaders, to Gromyko and to the Germans; he kept track of all the cables; he read transcripts of all the conferences; and he complained (with limited success) about the pace at the Department of State, about leaks from Allied clearances and about the lack of new diplomatic suggestions.[15]

Not the least of Kennedy's problems in developing an appropri-ate response to Khrushchev was the fact that everything had to be

The new Army Chief of Staff and his proud parents.

The Army Chief of Staff holds a press conference in November 1958.

This 1961 Jim Berryman cartoon in the Washington *Star* focused on Taylor as a lonesome soldier surrounded by Harvard men.

Taylor addresses a few remarks to President Kennedy after taking the oath as chairman of the Joint Chiefs of Staff.

Taylor, with JFK, reviews, in November 1962, some of the forces that had been mobilized for the Cuban Missile Crisis.

Below, right: Taylor and Diem during the Taylor-Rostow mission in 1961.

A grim Taylor leads the Joint Chiefs of Staff in President Kennedy's funeral cortege.

Presidential consultant.

TWENTY-FIVE CENTS

JULY 28, 1961

A SOLDIER & THE WHITE HOUSE

TIME

THE WEEKLY NEWSMAGAZINE

R. Vickrey

PRESIDENTIAL
ADVISER
TAYLOR

$7.00 A YEAR

VOL. LXXVIII NO. 4

Taylor and Secretary McNamara (partly obscured) demonstrate their support for General Khanh at an unidentified location in South Vietnam.

Field inspection in Vietnam.

The ambassador talks with son Tom during an inspection of the 101st Airborne Brigade in Vietnam. General Westmoreland is in the background.

This poster, with its unflattering likeness, was widely disseminated in connection with Taylor's 1965 appearance before the Commonwealth Club in San Francisco.

Taylor's last public appearance, at the dedication of the Taylor Room at the National Defense University in Washington, July 1986. The general is flanked by his wife and the author. Behind them are the author's son Jim, Sergeant Hurley Cargill, the author's daughter Katherine and wife Priscilla, and Lieutenant General Richard Lawrence, NDU President.

done jointly with Britain, France, and West Germany. The British had no intention of risking war over Berlin, while de Gaulle, although indignant over Khrushchev's provocation, declined to take it seriously. West Germany's position was equivocal. Taylor would recall how, at a White House dinner for Defense Minister Strauss, Dean Acheson had pressed Strauss as to how far his government was prepared to go on behalf of Berlin. Taylor backed up Acheson, remarking to Kennedy that he would be willing to see his Army son Tom in the lead jeep of a force relieving Berlin, but that he would expect a German to be in the jeep as well.[16] Kennedy, for his part, continued to take a firm line. In a TV address he emphasized that Berlin's freedom was not negotiable, and in this instance Taylor made a rare contribution to a presidential speech:

I hear it said that West Berlin is militarily untenable. And so was Bastogne. And so, in fact, was Stalingrad. Any dangerous spot is tenable if men—brave men—will make it so.[17]

Agreement on a coordinated response was still lacking when events took a dramatic turn later that summer. On August 13 the East Germans began construction of the Berlin Wall, catching the Administration completely by surprise in the process. Although there was talk of a military response, neither Kennedy nor Taylor gave it serious thought. The Wall was on Communist territory, and even if the Allies were somehow to dismantle it, the East Germans could raise another a short distance away. What did bother Taylor was a new set of East German regulations restricting access to West Berlin. Seeking a counter, he proposed that the Allied commanders in the city notify the Soviets that they were coming as a group to discuss the Wall and that they would employ a crossing point of their own choosing. This particular proposal was coolly received by the Western commanders, but the Administration was working on a still more dramatic response. On August 17 Taylor met in the Oval Office with the President, along with Rusk, Bundy, and Lemnitzer. There Rusk recommended sending a military convoy to Berlin as a means of asserting our rights and of reassuring the Berliners. The normally hawkish Taylor had misgivings:

General Lemnitzer and I both pointed out that from a military point of view it was an unwise thing to do. Unless we reinforced the garrison in West Germany, putting additional troops in an indefensible area would reduce the forces immediately available to General Norstad. . . . When . . . political considerations were determined to be overriding, it [sic] overcame our objections.[18]

This was far stronger medicine than Taylor's own proposal involving the sector commanders. Theodore Sorensen would call it Kennedy's "most anxious moment during the prolonged Berlin crisis."[19] Still, a 1,500-man U.S. Army battle group sent up the autobahn on the night of August 19 passed through without incident. Khrushchev's bluff had been called; the convoy reached Berlin and the crisis subsided. The Berlin issue would continue to fester, but it would be handled gingerly by both sides.

By this time Taylor was sufficiently in the President's confidence that it fell to him to carry out a political errand on behalf of the White House. An article on the Bay of Pigs in the September issue of *Fortune* left the President, in Taylor's words, "hopping mad." Among other things, author Charles Murphy charged that Eisenhower, unlike Kennedy, had recognized from the outset the need to employ U.S. forces in support of the Cuban Brigade, and that Eisenhower's advisers, unlike Kennedy's, had fully recognized the threat posed by Castro's jet trainers.

Kennedy asked Taylor to rebut the *Fortune* piece and he attempted to do so, getting his staff to document errors in the article. In a meeting in New York with Murphy, publisher Henry Luce, and the *Fortune* editorial board, Taylor set forth the case for the White House. In the discussion that followed Murphy conceded on a point or two; on other matters he insisted that he had reliable information contrary to the White House line. The result was largely a standoff, but the meeting restored a degree of civility to relations between the White House and the *Time-Life-Fortune* empire. It also left Taylor somewhat puzzled at the President's sensitivity to media criticism.

The *Fortune* article was not the only holdover from the Cuba investigation. Eisenhower had refrained from criticizing Kennedy in the period immediately following the Bay of Pigs, and in late June, Kennedy asked his milrep to brief the ex-President on the investigation. Taylor was far from pleased at this prospect; on the helicopter en route to Gettysburg he asked Allen Dulles whether he would mind throwing Taylor's hat into Ike's office and observe how it was treated. In the event, however, Ike was extremely cordial and even expressed pleasure at Taylor's return to government.

If the recruitment of Taylor was a boon for the Kennedy administration—the President spoke of him as "absolutely first class"—the feeling was mutual. The Kennedys, in bringing Taylor back to Washington, had restored the spring in his step and had given him an almost unprecedented opportunity to implement security reforms that had been spurned by the Eisenhower administration. In return, they had gained a total commitment from the country's foremost soldier. Taylor had no private agenda, no aspirations to greater authority. He gave his advice with total candor, but whatever policy was determined on in the White House had his total support.

Whereas in four years as Army chief of staff he had had virtually no contact with Eisenhower, as milrep he had uninhibited access to Kennedy, an access he was careful never to abuse. Their rapport was sufficiently good that Kennedy would needle him about the "military mind," a subject about which Taylor would himself joke at times, but about which he was also sensitive. At one point in 1961 he asked if I had a copy of Barbara Tuchman's *The Guns of August,* which he borrowed, complaining that the President was always citing it as evidence that generals like to "box in" their political leaders with war plans that leave little room for maneuver. He needed to prepare a defense.

As chief of staff, Taylor would come home after a hard day with the prospect of spending the evening at some onerous formal dinner. Not so under the New Frontier. Taylor became a regular at Hickory Hill, the Bobby Kennedy home in McLean, Virginia, where visitors were lucky not to get dumped in the pool. There he played tennis, bantered with Bobby and Ethel, and raised the average age of the guests. "You never knew who would be there for tennis," he recalled. "You could end up with either Donald Dell or Donald Duck." There were also weekends on Cape Cod, and he described one weekend there in the summer of 1962:

> We had quite a 4th of July up at Hyannis Port with the Robert Kennedys. In addition to the Kennedys there were a number of guests, all of the same energetic type as the Kennedys themselves. I took the B course for the day which was only moderately strenuous by comparison to the A. It included tennis morning and afternoon, a swim, a boat ride, a walk on the beach, and several jogs to the house where we were staying, located about a mile from the center of the community. Had I taken the A course, I would have done the same plus a round of golf and a game of touch football.[20]

Following one weekend at Hyannis, which Mrs. Taylor did not attend, Ethel Kennedy provided a full report on the general:

> First, he is an extraordinary houseguest—he never ate one single meal at our house. Thinking it over it was probably because he had to summon all his military bearing for that first luncheon out on the Marlin. He choked his way through the children's spaghetti and meatballs and sand while all sorts of wet, screaming babies ran between his legs. He then played *four* sets of tennis. . . .
>   He riveted us all [with] his exploits in Normandy until Bobby was heard mumbling something about Seamen 2nd Class not being called on to jump in The Great Invasion.[21]

The total informality at Hyannis was unlike anything that Taylor had experienced in the staid Washington society in which he normally moved. On one occasion, coming off the Kennedy boat, he looked back and saw the first lady, alone, struggling with a great load of picnic supplies. With no one else in sight, he chivalrously asked if he could be of assistance. The offer was gratefully accepted.

It was a happy time, but the functioning of the Kennedy White House occasionally drove Taylor to distraction. He was appalled at the lax security; anyone who looked vaguely familiar had access to the most sensitive documents in Washington. Nor was he impressed with the staff support provided the President; he thought that Kennedy went into many meetings not fully prepared:

I was always trying to prepare papers in advance showing pros and cons, and giving the President something that he could have fresh in his mind before he ever went into a conference room. But the President just wouldn't take the time even to look at these papers until the last minute, when he would grab them and rush off to a major conference. . . . Bobby tried to explain to me that my motives were good but [my methods] wouldn't work with John F. Kennedy. His mind just didn't work that way. He carried into the room a certain general knowledge of the subject and developed his own thinking largely by discussion.[22]

Taylor's own way of dealing with conferences could hardly have differed more from that of the President. If a meeting could be avoided he avoided it, for his bad hearing made group sessions a strain, and there was always a danger of misunderstanding in the give-and-take of discussion. When the subject matter was important and his attendance clearly required, he prepared exhaustively and almost always went into the meeting with a "position." Because he had already anticipated the pros and cons in reaching his own position, he was rarely swayed by the exchanges of conference. And because perhaps half the attendees at any Washington meeting are people with nothing else on their calendar that day, Max Taylor gained a reputation for strong opinions. What would endear him to two presidents, however, was his behavior in bureaucratic defeat. Whatever course his President eventually adopted had his full support.

For all his misgivings about White House procedures, Taylor's personal relations with his colleagues were excellent. There had been a potential for friction with national security adviser McGeorge Bundy, but Taylor soon made it clear that he was not a rival. As events unfolded, it became understood that Taylor's turf encompassed Berlin, the Pentagon, and a piece of Southeast Asia; the rest of the world was Bundy's. The two stayed out of one another's way to the extent possible, but each regarded the other as an ally rather than a rival. Taylor would later characterize Bundy as the most influential national security adviser of the several with whom he worked over the years.[23]*

By the end of 1961 Taylor's own work had developed a certain pattern. About two days a week were taken up by Special Group (CI) and its offshoot, the supersecret Mongoose Committee, which was charged with implementing covert activities against Cuba. Bobby was active in both, and this was not necessarily a blessing. He had been by far the most active participant in the Bay of Pigs investigation, and Taylor had nothing but admiration for his zeal in ferreting out the facts. Regarding the Special Group, however, Taylor sometimes had to remind him of who was chairman. When the group was just getting organized, Bobby strongly urged that Arthur Goldberg be made a member. Taylor, who had an aversion to large committees, refused. Bobby successfully pressed the others to vote for Goldberg's participation only to have Taylor cheerfully ignore the vote. "Well, shit," snapped Bobby, "the second most important man in the world just lost another one!" He left the meeting, slamming the door behind him.[24]

Taylor's association with Operation Mongoose, a spin-off of the Special Group, was comparatively brief, which is perhaps unfortunate. Mongoose was a CIA program, strongly supported by the Administration, aimed at making life miserable for Castro. In effect, it was a means of "getting even" for the Bay of Pigs. Beginning in the summer of 1961 CIA-financed Cuban exiles mounted hit-and-run raids against sugar mills, bridges, and similar installations in their homeland. Little was accomplished, however. In the words of one author, "The United States eventually spent nearly $500 million for a series of pinpricks that served only to strengthen a regime that used the raids as a rationale for . . . [turning] Cuba into a fortress."[25] Taylor, given time, would not have condoned such an unproductive employment of covert assets, but his association with the Mongoose Committee ended with his return to the Pentagon in 1962.

If Taylor's committee work took up about two workdays, the

---

* Bobby Kennedy, in a 1964 oral history interview, remarked that "every decision that the President made on foreign policy was cleared through Maxwell Taylor" (Edwin O. Guthman and Jeffrey Shulman, eds., *Robert Kennedy in His Own Words* [New York: Bantam Books, 1988], p. 255). Taylor himself never made such a broad claim, and Kennedy was probably referring to key security decisions.

rest of the week was taken up with activities that came his way as milrep. One of these came along in September 1961 when the President asked him to take a trip to Southeast Asia. South Vietnamese President Ngo Dinh Diem was asking for an increase in American assistance and Kennedy wanted Taylor and Walt Rostow to check it out. Theirs would prove a fateful mission.

Chapter 19

VIETNAM: CHANGING A LOSING GAME

The Kennedy administration knew from the outset that it had inherited major problems in Southeast Asia. Clark Clifford, Kennedy's transition adviser, has recalled hearing that outgoing President Eisenhower was especially concerned about the deteriorating situation in the area. Clifford suggested to Kennedy that he get Eisenhower's views directly, and, as a result, Southeast Asia was at the top of the agenda for the final meeting of the incoming and outgoing presidents. Clifford's notes included the following:

> President Eisenhower said, with considerable emotion, that Laos was the key to the entire area of Southeast Asia.
>
> He said that if we permitted Laos to fall, then we would have to write off all the area. He stated we must not permit a Communist takeover. He reiterated that we should make every effort to persuade member nations of [the Southeast Asia Treaty Organization] or the International Control Commission to accept the burden with us to defend the freedom of Laos.[1]

"In the snows of January," William Bundy has written, Vietnam was Kennedy's "fifth crisis," ranking behind Cuba, Laos, Berlin, and the Congo.[2] The situation in Laos looked especially bleak. The United States was supporting the right-wing forces under General Phoumi, but not even U.S. training and equipment had turned Phoumi's army into an effective force. Its writ ran only in the southern part of the country, whereas the northern and central regions were falling increasingly under the control of the Communist Pathet Lao, who were supplied from North Vietnam.

Basically, the Kennedy administration had three choices. It

could live with the status quo, the de facto partition of a poor and landlocked country that was, Eisenhower to the contrary notwithstanding, not very important in terms of U.S. interests. It could introduce U.S. forces directly into Laos and perhaps Thailand, in an attempt to turn the tide. Or it could resort to negotiations in the hope of securing Soviet and Chinese acquiescence in a government that, although neutralist, would not be overtly threatening to its neighbors.

The Joint Chiefs, seeming converts to Eisenhower's "domino" theory, favored direct American intervention. Although Army Chief of Staff George Decker had reservations, a majority of the Chiefs favored the landing of U.S. troops in Thailand, Vietnam, and parts of Laos itself. If this did not lead to a cease-fire, they favored the use of tactical air strikes against the Pathet Lao and even the use of tactical nuclear weapons if necessary.

Laos was the first substantive issue to which Taylor addressed himself as military representative, and he found himself once again at odds with the Chiefs. He was unimpressed with the fighting qualities of Phoumi's army and was reluctant to commit U.S. forces on behalf of a regime that was doing so little for itself. "Laos has been causing us trouble and late nights," he wrote in May. "It is singularly hard to do something for a country which does nothing for itself. Whereas the South Vietnamese will really fight, these Laotians turn tail at the first threat of a Viet Minh."³ Moreover, he was only a qualified believer in the domino theory. He considered Thailand worth defending, for he believed that it was important to contain the Communists at the Mekong River, a natural defensive barrier. Laos, however, was a different matter; neither politically nor geographically did it justify a major U.S. effort.

Taylor found the President a receptive listener. The Bay of Pigs had made Kennedy suspicious of the advice he received from the Chiefs, and his military representative's assessment served to confirm his own instincts. "Thank goodness the Bay of Pigs happened when it did," Kennedy remarked to Ted Sorensen in September. "Otherwise we could be in Laos now—and that would be a hundred times worse."⁴ But although the President was leery of direct American involvement in Laos, he did not want to see his Cuban debacle followed by a Western pullback throughout Southeast Asia. He told Dean Rusk, "If we have to fight in Southeast Asia, let's fight in Vietnam. The Vietnamese, at least, are committed and will fight."[5]

Indeed, Vietnam appeared a far more promising venue than did neighboring Laos. President Ngo Dinh Diem was no democrat, but he had solid nationalist credentials. He himself was courageous and honest; his country's Japanese occupiers had considered him for the post of "Premier," but had passed over him in favor of someone more malleable. After the war Ho Chi Minh himself had sought to recruit Diem for his cause, only to have Diem go his own way. In the late 1950s Diem became the recipient of considerable U.S. assistance, but he was never anyone's puppet.

Diem gradually brought a degree of order to his half of a country that had been left divided by the 1954 Geneva Conference. His greatest success was against the sects. With considerable advice from a CIA counterinsurgency expert, General Edward Lansdale, Diem bought off the Cao Dai and the Hoa Hao and then turned on the largest of the private armies, the French-supported Binh Xuyen. In a war within a war, Diem defeated the 40,000-man Binh Xuyen army, destroying parts of Saigon in the process.

With the Communists largely quiescent, a government led by the stubborn, uncharismatic Diem suddenly seemed viable. It seemed so even after the Viet Cong insurgency revived. Eisenhower called Diem the "miracle man" of Asia. Vice President Lyndon Johnson, visiting Saigon at Kennedy's request in May 1961, called Diem "the Churchill of the decade . . . in the vanguard of those who stand for freedom."[6]

Taylor's own involvement with Vietnam began in June 1961, as he was wrapping up the Cuba report. He was outside the President's office one day when Kennedy emerged, carrying with him a June 9 letter from Diem requesting U.S. assistance in increasing his army from 170,000 to 270,000 men. "What do I do about this?" he asked, handing the paper to his military representative. Taylor said he would look into it. Working closely with senior White House staffer Walt Rostow, he prepared a memorandum for the President on the alternatives that faced him in Vietnam. Their memo, dated July 27, offered three basic choices:

- To disengage from the area as gracefully as possible;

- To find as soon as possible a convenient political pretext and attack the regional source of aggression in Hanoi;

- To build up the Vietnamese to the greatest extent possible while preparing to intervene with U.S. military force if the Chinese come in or the situation otherwise gets out of hand.[7]

Meanwhile, what of Diem's request for a military increase? Taylor endorsed, in August, a recommendation that Washington support a 30,000-man increase, to 200,000, while the Administration considered the broader implications of Saigon's request. As evidence of increased Communist infiltration grew, Kennedy told his milrep to plan a visit to Southeast Asia. Thus prodded, Taylor assembled a group from the various security agencies. Walt Rostow represented the White House; he had strong views on the containment of communism in Asia as well as in Europe. Ed Lansdale, a longtime associate of Diem's, would also go along, although there is some question as to whether he constituted an official CIA representative. Representatives of State and Defense completed the official party.

At a predeparture conference Kennedy went beyond his formal letter of instructions to Taylor, which charged him with recommending "courses of action which our Government might take at this juncture to avoid a further deterioration in the situation in South Vietnam." He specifically directed Taylor to examine the feasibility of U.S. intervention; of establishing a more limited American military presence; and of any other possible courses of action. But the President implicitly ruled out disengagement. As Taylor himself would put it, "The question was how to change a losing game and begin to win, not how to call it off."[8]

The Taylor-Rostow mission departed on October 16 by White House jet, making a stop in Honolulu for meetings with CINCPAC chief Admiral Harry Felt and his staff. The stopover served only to underscore the divisions among American officialdom concerning the best course in Vietnam. Felt conceded that renewed Viet Cong activity had made for a critical situation, but whereas the Joint Chiefs favored the introduction of U.S. combat forces, Felt opposed the introduction of anything beyond engineer and helicopter units.

The White House mission reached Saigon on October 18, and the omens were not good. New, company-strength Viet Cong attacks on government outposts had inflicted heavy casualties on Diem's forces. The CIA, meanwhile, had upped its estimate of main force Viet Cong strength from about 4,000 in April 1961 to 16,000, of whom perhaps one fifth had been infiltrated into South Vietnam from the North. Even the forces of nature added to the misery index; the most severe floods in decades had ravaged the Mekong delta. "Flying over it," Taylor recalled, "you couldn't see anything but a few little housetops sticking up."[9]

On arriving in Saigon, each member of the mission had specific areas of responsibility. Taylor himself started with President Diem. He had visited Diem on one of his two previous visits to Saigon and had not found him an easy person to deal with. Little had changed in the interim. As Taylor recalled:

Diem was a short, rather stocky Vietnamese, sixty years of age but with no sign of gray in his jet-black hair. He had a grave but pleasant face with the dreamy eye of a mystic and the quiet dignity of a mandarin trained to rule. He moved and spoke deliberately and was highly skilled in steering a conversation in the direction he wished it to go and in avoiding questions which he was not ready to answer. Our interview that day was similar to the one I had had before and those which I was to have later. It was interminably long, about four hours, and consisted principally of a monologue by Diem in French, to which I made an occasional interjection. . . . Meanwhile, Diem smoked cigarettes incessantly and talked in somnolent tones that sorely tested the powers of attention of his overseas visitors, drowsy from too frequent changes of time zones.[10]

Taylor's notes on the interview indicated that Diem put considerable store on a program of road building that was to provide access to Viet Cong base areas in the central plateau. When Taylor moved the subject to the need for more vigorous action by his army to defend his country's frontiers, Diem questioned the feasibility of such tactics. He digressed instead on the possibility of creating depopulated zones between the Communist-dominated border areas and the principal population centers. As for U.S. combat forces, Diem said that he did not require them at the moment but conceded that if Viet Cong strength continued to grow he might have to reconsider. If American forces were to be employed, he said, he wanted assurances that they would be there for the long pull.

Taylor made other calls as well. On a previous visit he had come to know General "Big" Minh, who shared his zeal for tennis. Minh had been Diem's senior general in the war against the sects but had subsequently fallen into disfavor. In his meeting with Taylor, Minh was highly critical of Diem and pessimistic about his country's future. He reiterated a charge that American officials would hear with growing frequency: that Diem favored Catholics over other sectors of the population.

As they went about their calls, Taylor and his colleagues were increasingly convinced that a dramatic move—some form of U.S. presence—was required to deal with a growing malaise. All recognized that the problem was as much political as military, but whereas the Vietnamese body politic resisted any quick fix, the military threat was at least tangible. The Defense Department representatives were convinced that prompt military intervention represented the only means of saving South Vietnam. State Department representatives William Jorden and Sterling Cottrell believed otherwise, that it was an open question whether the country was salvageable even with increased U.S. military help and, hence, that Washington should go slow in any commitments to the Diem government. Despite this hedging, the consensus within the mission was that some U.S. forces were required at once, if only for psychological purposes.[11]

On October 25 Taylor and his colleagues left Saigon, first for Bangkok and then for the resort town of Baguio in the Philippines. If they had flown directly to Washington and attempted to draft a report there, they would have been subject to a variety of bureaucratic harassments. Wherever possible, Taylor liked to return to Washington with a completed report and recommendations already agreed upon.

The mission report, which was cabled to Kennedy from Baguio in summary form, included both general conclusions and specific recommendations. A key conclusion was that in Vietnam in particular and Southeast Asia in general there was "a double crisis in confidence: doubt that the U.S. is determined to save Southeast Asia [and] doubt that Diem's methods can frustrate and defeat Communist purposes and methods."[12] Turning to specific remedies, Taylor and Rostow recommended that joint action with the Vietnamese be undertaken to improve the quality of military intelligence; that the number of U.S. military advisers be increased; and that three squadrons of U.S. helicopters be provided in order to improve the mobility of Diem's forces. The most controversial provision, however, concerned the dispatch of eight thousand U.S. combat troops. The report made the following recommendations:

> The U.S. Government will offer to introduce into South Vietnam a military task force to operate under U.S. control for the following purposes:
>
> (a) Provide a U.S. military presence capable of raising national morale and of showing to Southeast Asia the seriousness of the U.S. intent to resist a Communist take-over.
>
> (b) Conduct logistical operations in support of military and flood relief operations.
>
> (c) Conduct such combat operations as are necessary for self-defense and for the security of the area in which they are stationed.
>
> (d) Provide an emergency reserve to back up the armed forces of the GVN in case of a heightened military crisis.
>
> (e) Act as an advance party of such additional forces as may be introduced if CINCPAC or SEATO contingency plans are invoked.[13]

Taylor's covering letter to this report was cautious, but it included some words that he would come to regret. He acknowledged that if the first U.S. troop commitment proved insufficient, "it will be difficult to resist the pressure to reinforce." But he downplayed the threat of escalation by Hanoi in response to a U.S. troop commitment. "North Vietnam is extremely vulnerable to conventional bombing. . . . There is no case for fearing a mass onslaught of Communist manpower into South Vietnam and its neighboring states, particularly if our air power is allowed a free hand against logistical targets."[14] The letter made clear that important decisions concerning Vietnam would have to be made as time went on, and that it might be necessary to take the war to the source of the aggression:

> While we feel that the program recommended represents those measures which should be taken in our present knowledge of the situation in Southeast Asia, I would not suggest that it is the final word. Future needs beyond this program will depend upon the kind of settlement we obtain in Laos and the manner in which Hanoi decides to adjust its conduct to that settlement. If the Hanoi decision is to continue the irregular war declared on South Vietnam in 1959 . . . we will then have to decide whether to accept as legitimate the continued guidance, training, and support of a guerrilla war across an international boundary, while the attacked react only inside their borders. Can we admit the establishment of the common law that the party attacked and his friends are denied the right to strike the source of aggression, after the fact of external aggression is clearly established?[15]

In the words of one author, "In sending out his most hawkish advisers, Kennedy presumably expected them to come up with hawkish recommendations, and that is clearly what he got."[16] The recommendations, however, were subjected to scrutiny. McNamara and the Joint Chiefs saw them as no more than a first step; they emphasized that South Vietnam could be saved only by the introduction of U.S. forces on a substantial scale. The State Department argued against sending in ground forces and expressed reservations concerning Diem's durability. In the end, both Rusk and McNamara endorsed most of the Taylor-Rostow recommendations with the conspicuous exception of the introduction of U.S. forces. Kennedy approved the compromise in a meeting on November 11, and the United States embarked on what was seen as a "limited partnership" with the Diem government.

The Taylor-Rostow mission was a milestone in the gradual U.S.

involvement in Vietnam, but its importance is sometimes exaggerated. Like a snapshot, its recommendations were an attempt to deal with a set of circumstances encountered at a specific moment in time. It did not commit the United States to send combat forces to bail out Diem, for even if Taylor's recommendation for 8,000 troops had been approved, they represented far less than the six divisions envisaged by the Joint Chiefs as necessary for a "military solution." The real significance of Taylor's report lay in its conclusion that Vietnam was not Laos and that the Diem government was one with which the United States could work. Nor was this so controversial a conclusion as it might have been in 1963; in 1961, Diem embodied important assets as well as significant liabilities.

The Taylor-Rostow report not only linked Washington with the Saigon Government but also brought into the open a dichotomy in Washington that would persist throughout the 1960s. The split was not between "hawks" and "doves" but was at least trilateral. On one extreme were the hardliners, most but not all of whom were in the Pentagon, who favored decisive military measures in Vietnam. On the other extreme were people from the State Department and academe who tended to feel that Vietnam was of little importance, or that Diem was not worth supporting, or both. In between were the "gradualists"—including Kennedy, Taylor, Rostow, and Rusk—who believed that Vietnam was too important to ignore but who sought to achieve U.S. objectives there initially without major military involvement and subsequently with the minimal application of force. In time, Taylor would have second thoughts about "gradualism," and some of these applied to the recommendations of the Taylor-Rostow mission:

> We could have done a lot of things differently. If in 1961 I'd known how the situation would be in 1965, let's say, I wouldn't have come back recommending that we "fly the flag" with a little logistic force in South Vietnam. I would have said, "Let's get several divisions and get in there fast and clean this thing up and come home again."[17]

But how important *was* Vietnam to the United States? The Kennedy administration thrived on crisis management; long-term policy rarely received priority attention at top levels. As for Taylor, he would later spend much time reflecting on how to define America's vital interests, that is, the issues for which the country should be prepared to expend lives and treasure. One reason for this preoccupation was the casual way in which the United States had allied its fortunes with those of South Vietnam. It had done so because President Kennedy had pronounced its defense vital, an understandable conclusion given Western setbacks in Cuba and Laos and given the fact that subversive "wars of national liberation" had become Moscow's preferred vehicle for military expansion. But all this would be difficult to explain to American draftees in Vietnam. Even Taylor would at times be defensive about the fact that the United States had undertaken so important a commitment without a clearer definition of what was at stake.

As 1961 turned into 1962, Taylor was heavily involved in overseeing the implementation of his recommendations. Questions were also emerging about how to quantify progress in a guerrilla war with no fixed front. As the number of U.S. military advisers grew, the trickle of data became a river. The pertinent statistics were not easily interpreted. Did a drop in the number of Communist-initiated incidents mean that "we were winning" or that the enemy was regrouping? Rostow complained that "it was almost as though there were forty different wars, one in each province."[18] For whatever reason, the outward manifestations of deterioration eased somewhat in 1962; the total number of Communist-instigated incidents was down 18 percent in the second half of the year.

Meanwhile, Taylor had other matters to consider in addition to Vietnam. The future of Berlin was no closer to resolution in 1962 than in the previous year, and a related problem was that of Franco-American relations. In March, Taylor made a trip to a number of NATO countries, including France. He was shocked by what he saw, commenting later that "one had to go to Paris at that time and talk to French officials to realize the bitterness that had grown into the relations between our two governments."[19] De Gaulle was not merely dissatisfied with France's role within NATO, he was convinced, in Taylor's view, that the United States and

Britain were conspiring to relegate France to a secondary status in Europe. Taylor proposed on his return that the United States end its opposition to France's independent nuclear deterrent in return for French cooperation within NATO, but nothing came of this proposal.

Also in regard to NATO, the Administration was looking into the question of a replacement for General Lauris Norstad as supreme allied commander. Norstad had been on the job for six years and had hinted at retirement; more important, his relations with McNamara and his "whiz kid" associates were notably cool. For the second time a president sounded out Taylor about the top NATO post, and for a second time Taylor demurred.

In late July the White House announced that Lemnitzer would be going to NATO and that Taylor would be his successor as chairman of the Joint Chiefs of Staff. It was a logical move, for there was widespread recognition that the President's chief military adviser should be part of the chain of command, not outside it. For the most part, media reaction was favorable. The New York *Times* observed that Taylor "combines a brilliant combat record with unusual attainments as a scholar and a diplomat. His views on the necessity for increasing our capacity to deal with limited war and guerrilla tactics . . . are bound to stir controversy within the Pentagon."[20] As for Lemnitzer, the St. Louis *Post-Dispatch* called him "fully qualified" for the NATO post but added that he was lacking "the articulateness in councils" that Kennedy required.[21] As for Taylor, his recommendation was that the post of milrep not be filled.

One immediate result of Taylor's new appointment was a spurt in sales of *The Uncertain Trumpet.* Would he, as chairman, attempt to ram through the concept of a single chief of staff that he had advocated in his book? The answer was no, in part because Congress, and especially the chairman of the House Armed Services Committee, Carl Vinson, showed no disposition to accept it. Lemnitzer was also opposed to any major change, noting that decision making in the Pentagon had vastly improved under McNamara. Still, the Administration took no chances. Stories attributed to "informed administration circles" insisted that Taylor had softened some of the views expressed in his book, including those concerning a single chief of staff.

At his confirmation hearings in August, Taylor affirmed that he was not moving to the Pentagon to reorganize it. The Eisenhower administration's preoccupation with massive retaliation had been reversed, and conventional forces were being given due priority by Kennedy and McNamara. Taylor emphasized that he had no intention of substituting conventional forces for the nuclear deterrent. In response to a question from Senator Leverett Saltonstall of Massachusetts, Taylor underscored the importance of the West's nuclear arsenal:

> In my judgment, if an attack on Western Europe comes, we must use whatever weapons and forces are necessary to defeat it. To meet a massive attack today, because of the lack of adequate conventional forces in the West, it would be necessary to resort to atomic weapons early in the conflict.[22]

One of his more persistent questioners was Senator Margaret Chase Smith of Maine:

> SENATOR SMITH: Have you any intention to transform the role of the Chairman of the Joint Chiefs of Staff . . . [into] a single Chief of Staff?
>
> GENERAL TAYLOR: I not only do not intend to try, I couldn't succeed if I tried. . . . I will do my best to make the system function as it is.[23]

Although there was considerably more questioning of Taylor than of Earle Wheeler, who was at the same time being confirmed as Army chief of staff, the interrogation was never unfriendly. The vote on his confirmation was unanimous, and Taylor prepared to take on his new duties on October 1. On that day, at the White House, Bobby Kennedy administered the required oath while the President looked on. For the first time, a chairman had been confirmed who was not the head of one of the armed services. Max Taylor was back, but what would be his reception in the Pentagon?

Taylor had been briefed extensively on a variety of pending defense matters even prior to confirmation; once he was confirmed the pace slackened briefly. Berlin and Vietnam were never far from his thoughts, but he looked forward to a quiet autumn, to be disturbed only by his move from Fort McNair to the JCS residence at Fort Myer. He wrote to son Tom:

[We] went to West Point with a plane load of old Army hands for the Penn State game yesterday. It was really a wonderful outing, perfect weather, beautiful parade, and then the most satisfactory of football games against Penn State. The only untoward incident was when one cadet in the front rank of an unreported company passed in review plainly out of step. I turned to [General Westmoreland] and asked how this could occur and he had no answer. Later he came up happily to report that the cadet's fly zipper had broken and he was struggling to maintain his pants along with keeping step. I replied coldly that I thought that keeping in step was more important.[24]

Back in Washington, both inside and outside the Pentagon, there was more than the usual amount of speculation as to how the Chiefs would function under their new chairman. Columnist Joseph Alsop put the matter succinctly:

It was not difficult for Gen. Taylor, alone in the Executive Office Building, with no corporate responsibility, to give the President the kind of clear, pointed, unfuzzy military advice the President wants. It may be different when he is in the Pentagon, only the first among four equals, among whom there are also wide divergencies of outlook and interest.[25]

The Chiefs would at times prove a challenge to the new chairman, who would have to choose between harmonizing their differences and forwarding split papers up the chain of command. On assuming the chairman's position, Taylor had little time to work out a working relationship with his colleagues before being plunged into one of the major crises of the Kennedy years.

Chapter 20

CONFRONTATION IN CUBA

The Cuban missile crisis, Harold Macmillan told the House of Commons, represented "one of the great turning points of history."[1] Robert Kennedy characterized the episode as having "brought the world to the abyss of nuclear destruction and the end of mankind."[2] Arthur M. Schlesinger, Jr., has proclaimed that it was John Kennedy's combination of "toughness and restraint, of will, nerve and wisdom, so brilliantly controlled, so matchlessly calibrated, that dazzled the world."[3]

Not everyone was quite so dazzled. Taylor, over the years, would take satisfaction in his own and his colleagues' role in forcing a Soviet stand-down in Cuba, but he was disinclined to dramatize the affair. He remarked to an interviewer in 1964 that he "never had any great concern over World War III arising from [the missile crisis], or over our ability . . . to eject Khrushchev from Cuba. He was doing this right in our front yard."[4]

The crisis began only days after Taylor had moved from the White House to the Pentagon. He was hosting a black-tie dinner at his quarters at Fort McNair on the evening of October 15 when one of the guests, Defense Intelligence Agency director General Joseph Carroll, asked to speak to him in private. According to Carroll, the intelligence community had acquired photographs demonstrating conclusively that the Soviets were installing offensive missiles in Cuba. Although such a development had been rumored for several months—Senator Kenneth Keating of New York was among those who claimed that missiles were already in place —the Administration had denied this. Not only had Soviet spokesmen assured Kennedy that only defensive weapons were being provided to Castro, but there seemed little point to the Soviets' sending offensive missiles. If detected, such weaponry could jeopardize the very existence of Moscow's Cuban ally. As if to confirm the conventional wisdom, the CIA concluded that any such deployment was contrary to past Soviet practice and therefore was unlikely.

On the following day, October 16, Kennedy was briefed on the U-2 photography at the White House while McNamara, Taylor, and others examined the same photographs at the Pentagon. The country's top leaders, civilian as well as military, found themselves propelled into the arcane world of high-altitude imagery. In Theodore Sorensen's recollection, "Barely discernable scratches turned out to be motor pools, erector launchers and missile transporters, some with missiles on them." To the President the missiles looked like "little footballs on a football field."[5]

The threat, however, was profoundly disturbing. Only a month before, the Soviets had assured President Kennedy that no offensive weapons were being sent to Cuba. With their 1,100-mile range, the missiles that the Soviets were now known to be providing could reach military installations throughout the South and Southeast, to say nothing of cities such as Washington, Dallas, and St. Louis. Nuclear warheads were nowhere in evidence, but it was assumed that they were somewhere on the island. The intelligence estimate was that a complex of sixteen to twenty-four missile launching sites could be operational within two weeks. Many years later, Soviet officials would acknowledge that there were forty-two missiles in Cuba and that they could have been armed with nuclear warheads in four or five hours.

Kennedy called a meeting of his top security aides that same morning. Taylor, who had found the President and his advisers in such disarray after the Bay of Pigs, would describe a very different picture at the onset of the missile crisis. "Kennedy gave no evidence of shock or trepidation" growing out of the threat posed by Soviet missiles in Cuba, but showed "deep but controlled anger at the duplicity of the Soviet officials who had tried to deceive him."[6] The two meetings that day—tape-recorded by the President—were devoted primarily to the consideration of military options and show Taylor to have favored air strikes in conjunction with a naval blockade:

> We must do a good job the first time we go in there, pushing 100 percent [destruction?] as closely as we can with our air strike. . . .

I would also mention among the military actions we should take that once we have destroyed as many of these offensive weapons as possible, we should prevent any more from coming in, which means a naval blockade. . . . And also a reinforcement of Guantanamo and evacuation of dependents. So, really . . . I'm thinking in terms of three phases. One, an initial pause of some sort while we get completely ready and get the right [word unclear] on the part of the target, so we can do the best job. Then, virtually concurrently, an air strike against, as [Secretary McNamara] said, missiles, airfields, uh, nuclear sites that we know of. At the same time, naval blockade. At the same time, reinforce Guantanamo and evacuate the dependents. I'd then start this continuous reconnaissance. . . .

Then the decision can be made as [to whether] we're mobilizing . . . as to whether we invade or not. I think that's the hardest question militarily in the whole business—one which we should look at very closely before we get our feet in that deep mud in Cuba.[7]

Kennedy's immediate response was to call for additional photography and to form an ad hoc committee to develop alternative courses of action for dealing with the missile threat. The fourteen-member Executive Committee (EXCOM) that he established included senior personnel from State, led by Secretary Rusk. Defense was represented by McNamara, Deputy Secretary Ros Gilpatric, Assistant Secretary Paul Nitze, and Taylor as the only representative in uniform. McGeorge Bundy was the senior White House representative. Some of the most influential participants, however—people such as Bobby Kennedy, Dean Acheson, and Douglas Dillon—were included because of their close personal association with the President.

So began, for the President and his chief advisers, the first phase of the thirteen-day Cuban missile crisis. This initial seven-day period, during which EXCOM sought to develop the most appropriate response to the Soviets, was conducted in strict secrecy and would last until Kennedy's television address to the nation on October 22. Taylor was himself active on two fronts during this first week. He and his EXCOM colleagues were in session much of each

day to consider policy alternatives. At the same time, he supervised preparations within the Pentagon designed to implement
whatever decisions might come out of EXCOM, up to and including a possible invasion of Cuba.

The missile crisis is one of the most thoroughly analyzed episodes in recent decades and will be considered here only in broad
outline. Within EXCOM, a consensus toward the center quickly
emerged. There was little support for a solely diplomatic response,
such as an appeal to the United Nations or the Organization of
American States (OAS). Nor was there strong support for an invasion, although a number of participants, Taylor included, feared
that an invasion might ultimately be required. On October 17
and 18, EXCOM was in almost continuous session in Under Secretary of State George Ball's seventh-floor conference room at State.
President Kennedy did not attend these meetings—his presence
was felt to inhibit discussion—but Bobby was in almost constant
attendance. There was no formal chairman, and those participating did not always reflect the institutional views of their departments.

Initially there was strong support for air strikes, either against
the missiles alone or against missile sites, airfields, and radar installations. General LeMay, called in by the committee, argued
that an air attack was essential and would provoke no reaction on
the part of the Soviets. LeMay himself favored an invasion, and he
probably refrained from urging one more strongly only because
he knew that the other Chiefs were not behind him.[8] Taylor, for
his part, could see no feasible alternative to air strikes; he believed
that the Soviets, if warned, would hide the missiles and thereby
necessitate an invasion, the contingency that he most sought to
avoid.

The air attack option was favored not only by the Chiefs but by
others, including Dean Acheson and CIA director John McCone.
Unfortunately, the Air Force could not assure that air strikes
would destroy all the missiles. There were other liabilities. Air
strikes were certain to result in casualties, and if these included
Russian military personnel, the Soviets might be inclined to dig in
their heels. In a worst-case scenario, local Soviet commanders

might assume that they were engaged in a general war and fire nuclear salvos at the United States.

Was there an acceptable alternative to air attack? Even before the missile sites were discovered, the possibility of some form of blockade against Cuba had been bruited about as a means of preventing Castro from building up his conventional weaponry. Now, the pros and cons of a naval blockade came in for scrutiny within EXCOM. To be sure, even a blockade entailed significant risks. It was of dubious legality in terms of international law and could itself be viewed as an act of war. A blockade might require U.S. warships to employ force against Soviet vessels on the high seas. But worst of all, in Taylor's view, was the fact that any blockade carried with it a built-in delay that might allow the Soviets to conceal their missiles on the island.

Bobby Kennedy was influential in leading EXCOM away from air strikes and toward a blockade. In a meeting on October 18 Kennedy—who was treated with a certain deference in committee deliberations—raised the "Pearl Harbor" issue. Speaking with emotion, the President's brother insisted that "America's traditions and history" would not permit the contemplated air strikes. Whatever the provocation, Bobby insisted, those who favored them were "advocating a surprise attack by a very large nation against a very small one."[9] This argument did not impress Taylor, who would later point out that the President had explicitly warned both the Soviets and Castro of the dire consequences of their attempting to establish an offensive base in Cuba. The furthest he would have gone to meet Bobby's argument would have been to provide brief warning, enough to allow personnel to take cover but not enough to permit the missiles to be hidden.

The consensus, however, was for a limited blockade, or quarantine. Although not without risk, it at least held out the possibility that the missiles might be removed without bloodshed. It could be proclaimed at any time and enforced by the Navy in comparatively short order. Finally, a quarantine did not have to be the last word; if it failed to achieve its purpose there might still be time for air strikes. Taylor was outvoted but unconvinced. "It was not clear to me," he later wrote, "what we would do if the Soviets stayed outside the blockade zone, opened a vituperative propaganda campaign against the United States, called for negotiations, and continued to develop their weapons systems in Cuba."[10]

In Taylor's recollection, the President was undecided until October 21, when EXCOM was briefed by General Walter Sweeney, Jr., whose Tactical Air Command would have the responsibility for taking out the missiles if the air strike option were adopted. Sweeney's frank admission that any such operation—even if carried out by hundreds of aircraft—would not guarantee the destruction of all missiles reinforced an already perceptible inclination on the President's part toward the quarantine option.

The mechanism agreed upon within EXCOM was a quarantine limited to missiles, one that all participants hoped would be sanctioned by the OAS under the Rio Treaty. The narrow scope of the quarantine was disturbing to some EXCOM members; McNamara and Taylor, among others, urged unsuccessfully that it encompass oil as well as offensive weapons.[11] In any case, the decision to proceed with a quarantine triggered an immense amount of preparatory work throughout the government, work that had to be accomplished in secret. While the President briefed key congressional leaders, the Justice Department drafted a quarantine proclamation. The State Department had a key role: it had to prepare to brief the country's principal allies on what was happening, as well as attempt to obtain OAS support for a quarantine. Yet the heaviest burden of all fell on the Defense Department, which had to prepare for a variety of military contingencies.

Taylor's work pattern at this time was to arrive at his office shortly before seven in the morning and there to receive a ten-minute briefing on overnight developments. He would then depart for either the State Department or the White House. The Chiefs whom he left behind met in almost continuous session. Because there was no single chief of staff, as Taylor had once advocated, the pitfalls of leadership by committee were avoided by empowering each service chief to deal with his own service in the name of the Chiefs. The Army's Earle Wheeler monitored the movement of two airborne divisions to staging areas in Florida. The Navy's George Anderson oversaw the deployment of nineteen ships to the Caribbean to implement the blockade. The Air Force's LeMay kept one quarter of the Strategic Air Command's bombers in the air and had all missiles ready to fire. The chairman kept in touch by secure telephone.

Taylor would later remark, "If I was classified as a hawk in EXCOM, I was definitely viewed as a dove in the arena of the Joint Chiefs of Staff."[12] He had the unenviable task of passing on to the Chiefs the rationale for actions that he and his military colleagues regarded as insufficient. At issue was not just the President's decision against air strikes. The Chiefs viewed the blockade as proposed by EXCOM as minimal; it would cover only offensive weapons, whereas the Chiefs, like McNamara, thought it should be broader, at least to include oil.

On Monday, October 22, the secret phase of the crisis ended when President Kennedy went before a startled nation on television. He denounced the transformation of Cuba into an offensive bastion, noting that "the purpose of these [missile] bases can be none other than to provide a nuclear strike capability against the Western Hemisphere." He then referred to Soviet Foreign Minister Gromyko's assurances that weapons being provided to Cuba were solely defensive, adding, "That statement . . . was false." He went on in clipped, measured tones to outline the proposed quarantine, characterizing it as one of several "initial steps":

> To halt this offensive build-up, a strict quarantine on all offensive military equipment under shipment to Cuba is being initiated. All ships of any kind bound for Cuba from whatever nation or port will, if found to contain cargos of offensive weapons, be turned back. This quarantine will be extended, if needed, to other types of cargo and carriers.[13]

The President's speech began a period of intermittent communication with Moscow. The initial Soviet response was to bluster. The Soviet Union would ignore the "illegal" U.S. blockade, Khrushchev replied; the volatile Soviet leader accused the United States of pushing mankind "to the abyss of a world missile-nuclear war." Meanwhile, reconnaissance photography indicated that work on the missile sites in Cuba was continuing, as was the assembling of IL-28 medium bombers. On the positive side, however, the OAS gave unanimous approval to implementation of the proposed quarantine, which went into effect on October 24. It was an uneasy time for Taylor and his colleagues:

> As I regarded the night following the President's speech a very critical period, I slept that night in my Pentagon office for the only time in the crisis. It was not that I feared that we were on the brink of nuclear war but I still harbored a feeling that Khrushchev had some card up his sleeve. . . . As I was still apprehensive of a move to hide the missiles, I awaited eagerly the results of the first series of photographs which would show their condition following the President's speech. These were not available until October 24 and 25. To my relief, these photos showed no sign of a move to disperse the missiles; instead, they gave evidence of ineffectual camouflage.[14]

On Thursday, October 25, came the first hints that Moscow might be wavering. Three Soviet vessels suspected of being missile carriers stopped in midocean and changed course for home. The following day, the Lebanese-registered ship *Marucla* became the first ship to be stopped and boarded at the quarantine line. There was no resistance, her cargo was judged to be inoffensive, and she was allowed to proceed.

On the evening of the twenty-fifth President Kennedy received the communication from Khrushchev that ultimately would provide a basis for resolving the crisis. It was a strange letter, almost certainly drafted by Khrushchev himself. Taylor commented, "I would agree with those who have described it as the letter of a man either drunk or distraught, or both." Nevertheless, it included Moscow's first acknowledgment that intermediate range missiles were in fact in Cuba and a disingenuous rationale for Moscow's earlier deception:

> You are mistaken if you think that any of our armaments in Cuba are offensive. However, let us not argue this point. . . . These missiles are a means of annihilation and destruction. But it is impossible to launch an offensive by means of these missiles, even nuclear missiles of 100 megaton yield, because it is only people—troops—who can advance. Without people any weapons, whatever their power, cannot be offensive.

Interspersed among these rambling professions of peaceful intent was a formula for a resolution of the crisis:

> If the President and Government of the United States would give their assurances that the United States would itself not take part in an attack upon Cuba and would refrain from such action; if you recall your Navy—this would immediately change everything. . . . Then the necessity for the presence of our military specialists in Cuba will be obviated.[15]

For each step forward, however, there appeared to be a step backward. Khrushchev's conciliatory letter was immediately followed by another, which Taylor read as "the authentic voice of the Politburo"; it linked any removal of Soviet missiles to the withdrawal of U.S. Jupiter missiles from Turkey. Of great concern was the fact that work on the missile sites in Cuba was now proceeding around the clock. The downing of a U-2 reconnaissance plane over Cuba in the early hours of Saturday, October 27, seemed ominous; to the Soviets, concealment of their activities at the missile sites had apparently been of such priority as to justify first blood. In retrospect, Taylor characterized this day as probably the most discouraging point in the crisis. President Kennedy might have agreed. "How can we send any more U-2 pilots into this area tomorrow unless we take out all of the SAM sites?" he asked. "We are now in an entirely new ball game."[16] Not for several decades would it be known that the downing of the U-2 had resulted from a decision by a local commander and had caused considerable distress in Moscow.

One of the rules of EXCOM was that no notes were to be taken, but the Saturday afternoon session on October 27, like that of October 16, was held in the White House cabinet room and recorded. The discussion was far-ranging, encompassing the U.S. missiles in Turkey as well as the implications of an unwillingness on the part of the Soviets to settle on the basis of Khrushchev's first letter. The transcript for that day shows Taylor in two roles, that of a spokesman for the Chiefs as a body and as an individual participant within EXCOM. In the former capacity his views were largely predictable:

TAYLOR: Mr. President, the Chiefs have been in session during the afternoon on—really the same basis as we have over here. This is—the recommendation they give is as follows: that the big strike—OP Plan 3-12—be executed no later than Monday morning the 29th unless there is irrefutable evidence in the meantime that offensive weapons are being dismantled and rendered inoperable; that the execution of the Strike Plan be part of the execution of 3-16, the Invasion Plan [censored] days later. (Pause)

ROBERT KENNEDY: That was a surprise. (Laughter)[17]

Two immediate problems facing EXCOM were the approach of a Soviet vessel, the *Grozny*, to the quarantine line, and the requirement for continued aerial reconnaissance over Cuba at a time when air defenses there were clearly potent. Taylor did not address the matter of the *Grozny*, but both he and McNamara emphasized the importance of continued surveillance:

McNAMARA: The first question we have to face tomorrow morning is, are we going to send surveillance flights in? And I think we have basically two alternatives. Either we decide not to send them in at all or we decide to send them in with proper cover. If we send them in with proper cover and they're attacked, we must attack back, either the SAMs and/or MIG aircraft that come against them, or the ground fire. . . .

TAYLOR: I'd say we must continue surveillance. That's far more important than the ship. . . . We can't give up twenty-four hours at this stage. . . .

THE PRESIDENT: I would think we ought to take a chance on reconnaissance tomorrow, without the cover, because I don't think cover's really going to do you much good. You can't protect—well—hide them from ground fire (mixed voices) tomorrow, and you don't get an answer from [UN Secretary General] U Thant, then we ought to consider whether Monday morning we—we—uh—I'm not convinced yet of the invasion because I think that's a much—I think we may . . .

TAYLOR: I agree with that. My personal view is that we (mixed voices) and also *ready* to invade but make no advance decision on that.[18]

Meanwhile, the President had decided to ignore Khrushchev's second letter and to accept his communication of October 26 as the basis for a solution. To underscore yet again the seriousness with which the United States viewed the situation, Kennedy sent his brother to Ambassador Anatoliy Dobrynin to press for a favorable response. Bobby held out one small olive branch. The President had in fact ordered the removal of U.S. missiles from Italy and Turkey "some time ago"; it was the Attorney General's belief that soon after the Cuba crisis was resolved, "those missiles would be gone." Bobby Kennedy returned to the White House. "The President was not optimistic," he would later write, "and neither was I."[19] Taylor was among those who had no knowledge of Bobby's offer to Dobrynin.

Meanwhile, in "the tank" at the Pentagon, Taylor chaired what was in effect a council of war. The Chiefs were present, as were those who would command various components of any invasion: the commander of the 2d Fleet, who would direct the seaborne invasion; the commander of the airborne forces to be dropped near the missile sites; SAC commander General Thomas Power; General Sweeney of the Tactical Air Command; and several others. In the words of one participant:

> I can well remember that General Taylor dominated and was in complete control of this meeting. He did all of the speaking, except for the brief responses he received when he addressed each of the other members of the JCS and [various] commanders. The objective . . . was to ensure that all participants in the forthcoming Cuban operation understood their missions and tactical roles, and particularly that there was no question concerning the timing of the passage of command from one commander to another.
>
> At the conclusion of this meeting, General Taylor directed seven of the attendees to meet him in his office the following morning at 7:00 A.M. for the purpose of giving him a final briefing, if necessary, on the various aspects of the operation, to include any changes that might have been required.[20]

Taylor, recalling the Whitsuntide youth march against West Berlin, recognized that Communist regimes often appear most unyielding just before yielding. So it was in October 1962. On Sunday morning, October 28, Ambassador Dobrynin sent word to Rusk that a message was en route in which Khrushchev agreed to dismantle the missiles under adequate supervision and inspection. The most volatile period of the missile crisis was over, but not everyone was pleased. In Bobby Kennedy's recollection, two of the Chiefs were "really mad." Bobby quoted LeMay as suggesting that the missile sites be bombed anyway, and Navy CNO George Anderson as saying, "We've been sold out."[21]

At the time of the missile crisis, I was in Bangkok, Thailand, where I was attached to the U.S. embassy. Information on developments in Washington was sparse, but in early November we had a letter from the general:

> All the brass in Washington have been under very great strain the last two weeks since the discovery of the Soviet missile bases in Cuba. . . .
>
> Today we finally got the break we had been working toward. It looks as if we have scored a real victory, although we can never be sure that we are out of the woods. The night before last the President received a letter from Khrushchev, which has not yet been published, which was very favorable. We met the next morning in the National Security Council [sic] to consider it, just in time to receive a new letter broadcast out of Moscow, which tossed in the question of our bases in Turkey.
>
> Now this morning we have a third letter, which seems to give way before the stern reply which the President sent to Khrushchev last night. However, it is too early to be sure that this is the last word.[22]

In his copy of Bobby Kennedy's *Thirteen Days*, which he regarded as a good account of the crisis, Taylor made a marginal notation, "RFK skipped issue of IL-28s." Although Khrushchev's October 28 letter is often regarded as the end of the confrontation in Cuba, the crisis in fact continued into the following year, as Castro resisted some of the understandings worked out between Moscow and Washington. He initially refused to return the IL-28 bombers, which he claimed were Cuba's property, or to permit in-country inspection of missile sites as promised by Khrushchev. On November 11 Taylor wrote:

We have not decided exactly what to do about the IL-28 bombers. I am always surprised to find myself counseling prudence with some of my fire-eating civilian colleagues; but now that they think that Mr. K is chicken, a lot of them are showing boldness which could not be found in town a few weeks ago.[23]

After weeks of wrangling, Castro agreed to surrender the bombers, but he never did permit neutral inspection of the missile sites; the Administration had to settle for aerial photographs of exposed missiles on the decks of Soviet ships. November was almost as hectic as October, but it culminated with Taylor's taking President Kennedy to visit some of the military bases that had been on standby during the missile crisis. There, he wrote, "We . . . saw lots of fine-looking soldiers, sailors, marines and airmen."[24]

Over the years, Taylor would often reflect on the implications of the missile crisis. In contrast to many Kennedy loyalists, he resisted romanticizing it. His greatest satisfaction was that the Kennedy team, with many of the same players as had launched the Bay of Pigs, had performed so efficiently. He remained puzzled as to Khrushchev's motivation in so provoking the United States. He tended to agree with those who believed that the Soviets were attempting to compensate for their inferiority in intercontinental missiles, but he was never totally convinced. The U.S. preponderance in strategic weapons was so overwhelming at that time that nothing the Soviets might place in Cuba could materially affect the balance.

Some of the lessons he drew from the missile crisis had strong domestic overtones. As the 1960s turned into the 1970s, and leaking classified information to the media became a favorite Washington pastime, the secrecy that had been maintained during the first week of the Cuban crisis seemed especially impressive. Arguments that the media have an obligation to ferret out government secrets left Taylor unmoved: "Don't quote the First Amendment to me," he remarked in a 1983 interview. "I don't give a damn."[25] Also instructive, in his view, was the irrelevance of nuclear arsenals in the missile crisis. He saw the U.S. superiority in nuclear weaponry as contributing little to the outcome in Cuba. Rather, it was the proximity of strong conventional forces that caused Khrushchev to back down. By rhetoric alone, however, the Soviets had scored some points through "nuclear intimidation." Taylor feared that the same rhetoric on some future occasion might paralyze action in Washington.

Although delighted that the Cuba affair was resolved by means short of war, Taylor never felt a need to apologize for his advocacy of air strikes. He had argued in favor of bombing "until my commander in chief took another decision. And I'm glad he did, because it proved to be enough."[26] Any reservations he had about the episode centered on whether his country had settled for too little. In an interview in 1964 he suggested that JFK might have demanded the ouster of Soviet troops:

If we had the knowledge then that we have now, I think we would probably have asked more of Khrushchev. We thought we were asking at the top level of demand when we asked him to get those strategic weapons out. . . . I think we could probably have gotten even more had we insisted on the withdrawal of all his ground forces [there were about 20,000] at the same time.[27]

In the final weeks of 1962, however, few were inclined to deny the Kennedy administration its greatest cold war triumph. Although there was no on-site verification of the removal of the missiles, television viewers throughout the West were treated to aerial photographs of missiles and bombers being shipped back to the Soviet Union.

The Soviets also claimed victory at the time, and although such claims were given short shrift in the non-Communist world, they have recently come in for a closer look. To the Soviets, the U.S. promise not to invade Cuba—one that Washington was happy to give—may have represented a significant concession. And Castro, in the words of one author, "won the prize he had sought so long—an effective, though informal, guarantee of Cuban independence."[28] The U.S. removal of Jupiter missiles from Turkey would ultimately give the entire episode an aura of quid pro quo. But all this would come later. The fact was that the Soviets had been caught red-handed in a provocative act and were forced to back down. The final word on the missile crisis may have been that of the Soviet Politburo, which two years later deposed Khrushchev as Premier, placed him under house arrest, and consigned him to oblivion.

Certainly there was no doubt in Taylor's mind as to who had "won." And he was not inclined to let Castro rest easily with a promise of no U.S. invasion. The U.S. commitment, he would point out, was conditional on neutral inspection of the missile sites. Because Castro had not permitted their inspection, an essential condition of the U.S. promise had not been met. Taylor was not promoting an invasion, but he liked the idea of making Castro sweat a little.

Chapter 21

CHAIRMAN OF THE JCS

On October 7, 1962, Taylor wrote to his son Tom:

> On Monday I was sworn into my new office [chairman of the
> Joint Chiefs of Staff] by the Attorney General in the presence of
> the President and a goodly company including mother, grand-
> mother, Mary [Happer], and lesser lights from the Cabinet and
> the Pentagon. An hour later I was at my desk in the Pentagon
> with the feeling that I had never left the place.[1]

One of his first acts as JCS chairman was to order an increase in
aerial reconnaissance over Cuba, and within a matter of weeks he
was propelled into the all-absorbing period of the missile crisis.
Only as Cuba simmered down did he settle into his new routine.

His feelings on returning to the Pentagon were decidedly mixed.
On one hand, his appointment placed him at the top of his chosen
profession and represented vindication of the views that had led to
his break with Eisenhower. On the other hand, a return to the
Pentagon, with its 7,000 offices, seventeen miles of corridors, and
25,000 workers, had little appeal. Taylor would miss his almost
daily contact with President Kennedy—Curt LeMay was somehow
not the same—and he had no illusions concerning his popularity
with his fellow Chiefs. Not only was Taylor the first chairman to
be brought back after retirement, but his appointment meant that
the Army would have two chairmen in succession. Under Truman
and Eisenhower, the position had rotated automatically among
the services.

With the missile crisis easing, Taylor had a chance to take the
measure of his colleagues. Army Chief of Staff Earle "Bus"
Wheeler had been deputy to Norstad at NATO before becoming
chief of staff in the same musical chairs that had seen Taylor ap-

pointed chairman. The urbane, articulate Wheeler had a reputation as an accomplished staff officer, and it is likely that Taylor had a role in his selection. The CNO, George Anderson, was a Navy aviator who had succeeded Arleigh Burke. Although Anderson had excellent professional credentials, he had made himself unpopular with the Administration, first by opposing McNamara's plans for a joint Navy–Air Force fighter and then by complaining of Kennedy's micromanagement of ship dispositions during the confrontation off Cuba. He would shortly give way to Admiral David McDonald.

The enfant terrible of the JCS, however, was Curtis LeMay. He personified the Air Force's insistence on retaining a large bomber force even after strategic missiles had become the backbone of the U.S. strategic deterrent. His preoccupation on the JCS was to gain authorization for more than the three B-70 prototypes authorized by McNamara. Kennedy—eager to dump LeMay, whose one-dimensional approach to military matters was anathema—was unwilling to pay the political price. LeMay had influential backers on Capitol Hill, and Kennedy ultimately decided that he was less of a problem on the reservation than off.

In any case, by 1962 the service chiefs were little more than bit players. Robert McNamara had descended on the Pentagon like a scourge, bringing with him management techniques that in the view of many diminished the traditional roles of the services. Whereas defense secretaries such as Charlie Wilson and Neil McElroy had had little impact on the Pentagon outside the budget process, McNamara's interests extended across the board. He, too, had read *The Uncertain Trumpet,* and in his first year in office he had implemented one of its main recommendations, a breakdown of the budget by "program elements," or function, rather than by service. Now, for instance, the country's strategic retaliatory capability was viewed as a combination of the Navy's Polaris submarines and the Air Force's missiles and bombers. In search of a "rational" defense policy, McNamara cut the Air Force's strategic bomber force, curbed the number of nuclear-powered carriers for the Navy, and told the Army to settle for the M-16 rifle rather than the M-14 it preferred. Fifteen years younger than Taylor, McNamara was intelligent, incisive, and confident. Having given up the presidency of Ford to join the Kennedy administration, he had every intention of making his mark on the Pentagon.

McNamara would later say that he "very much wanted" Taylor to be chairman.[2] Before Taylor accepted the appointment, however, he met with the secretary to work out some terms of reference. Potential areas of friction had little to do with strategic issues, for the secretary and the chairman were in broad agreement on strategy and doctrine. The Chiefs, however, were paranoid concerning the Defense Secretary and his "whiz kids," and Taylor won a couple of concessions. McNamara agreed to some controls over the number of projects that would be laid on the Joint Staff by his special assistants. As for the secretary's advisory role, Taylor gained agreement that the Chiefs would not be prevented from exercising their statutory responsibility to advise the President.

The second point was especially important, for Taylor himself still smarted from his treatment by Wilson and McElroy. He did not believe in stifling dissent, and in the Cuba confrontation that immediately followed his appointment, Taylor had made sure that the Chiefs as a group met with the President on two occasions. Not that the Chiefs were easily pleased. "We . . . felt we were not in the decision-making process at all," LeMay later complained. "Taylor might have been, but we didn't agree with Taylor in most cases, so we felt that the president was not getting unfiltered military advice."[3]

Taylor's own relations with McNamara were to prove remarkably harmonious. Not only did the two men share most objectives in the area of strategy and administration but their styles were similar. Both liked clear-cut decisions and had a visceral dislike of "waffling." Both tended to go into issues in detail, although Taylor was less disposed than McNamara to assemble a mass of statistics in support of his position. In late October, Taylor wrote that he had been able to get out for some tennis for the first time in two weeks. "My boss, Secretary McNamara, is one of the most indefatigable workers I have ever seen."[4]

After Taylor had been on the job for more than a year, he was moved to compare the operation of the JCS then with its operation under Eisenhower. He commented that policy-making was far more open under Kennedy and McNamara; he characterized his old nemesis, Radford, as having told Eisenhower only what Ike wanted to hear. Equally important, he said, under Kennedy the Air Force had replaced the Army in the position of a "permanent" minority on the JCS. He said that LeMay was a problem because he was "not bright" and because he frequently came to meetings with a chip on his shoulder and would have to be mollified by all present. He added, however, that he had no desire to muzzle Le-May as he himself had been muzzled.

Notwithstanding McNamara's pervasive presence in the Pentagon, there was never any question as to who was running the Joint Chiefs. General Bruce Palmer, whose book on Vietnam is occasionally critical of Taylor, notes that he was "clearly the dominant figure" on the JCS.[5] Jack Raymond, the defense writer for the New York *Times*, commented that "Taylor is something special in American military history—a fighting hero, an acknowledged intellectual and a keenly political person with no apparent personal political ambitions. He runs counter to the prevailing image of professional soldiers as inarticulate men of narrow interests."[6]

In terms of an average workday, Taylor's schedule was little different from his years as Army chief of staff. He had moved back to Fort Myer, into quarters overlooking the river and the city, almost next door to Quarters One. He was still an early riser and in good weather would walk through Arlington Cemetery before being picked up by his regular driver, Bob Blackwell, and driven to the Pentagon.

The JCS normally met Mondays, Wednesdays, and Fridays in the windowless, gold-decorated "tank" on the second floor. There, two of the walls were covered with maps of the world, while a third was dominated by a board showing the Chiefs' travel schedule for the next several months. The fourth wall had only a clock. Much of the room was taken up with the rectangular mahogany table at which the Chiefs carried on their work, but there was seating also for the "horse-holders" and two lecterns for briefers. Although seating protocol varied from time to time, one frequent attendee at JCS meetings, General Bruce Palmer, has recalled that the Air Force chief of staff normally sat on the chairman's immediate right. Palmer thought this odd, because both Taylor and Le-May were somewhat deaf in one ear, and this arrangement put their "bad" ears side by side. Bernie Rogers, Taylor's exec, thought that Taylor's tolerance of the smoke from LeMay's ever-present cigars represented one more example of his iron self-control.

One of Taylor's principal complaints as chairman would concern the functioning of the 400-man Joint Staff. In theory it was a staff of "purple suiters"—officers who put aside any service bias while serving the chairman of the JCS. In practice, however, the services rarely sent their best people to the Joint Staff, and those whom they did send were not disposed to take positions that might put them at odds with their own service. Taylor found the work of the Joint Staff under Admiral Herbert Riley deficient in quality and often biased toward Navy positions. Had time permitted he would have undertaken a major shake-up, but as an interim measure he brought over some of his own people from the White House. The chairman's Staff Group examined every paper to come before the Chiefs and provided Taylor with advice independent of the Pentagon bureaucracy.

In the late 1960s, after Taylor's departure as chairman, much of the JCS agenda would be taken up with matters relating to Vietnam. In 1963 and 1964, however, the issues were more diverse, although equally contentious. Roles and missions were the touchiest issue, for the Air Force saw its strategic mission being usurped by the Navy's missile submarines, even as the Army moved into light aviation in its search for mobility on the battlefield. Each service's perception of its mission found its way into the Joint Strategic Objectives Plan (JSOP), a planning document that projected the most likely military threats to the United States, outlined a strategy to counter them, and proposed force levels to achieve this. Taylor strove valiantly in his two years as chairman to make the JSOP less of a wish list, but any progress appears to have been modest.

Almost as contentious as roles and missions was the staffing of the various unified commands that constituted most of the country's fighting strength. During the Korean War, the Army had been the "executive agent" for the Joint Chiefs in directing the war. Now, a dozen or so unified commands around the world directed U.S. forces in their geographic areas of responsibility. Taylor generally favored rotating the heads of each unified command among the three services, except for a few very specialized ones, such as the Strategic Air Command. This was not easy, and CINCPAC, in Honolulu, proved especially intractable. The Navy maintained that the Hawaiian Islands were surrounded by water and that CINCPAC was a traditional Navy billet. In this matter the Navy had its way. As the Vietnam War escalated, the Defense Department would find itself in the position of running a ground and air war through a Navy command thousands of miles away.

NATO strategy was very much on the front burner during Taylor's tour as chairman. To some member nations, "flexible response" implied a deemphasis of nuclear weapons that would either leave Western Europe exposed or, equally ominous, require a heavy NATO investment in conventional weaponry. At worst, it raised the specter of a conventional war along the Rhine in which NATO would provide the manpower and the battlefield. No reassurances from Washington could entirely allay NATO uneasiness concerning the U.S. nuclear deterrent, but the attempt had to be made. One possibility was to agree on the circumstances in which nuclear weapons would be used and the procedures under which the weapons themselves would be released to NATO field commanders. But this raised legal problems, because of statutory prohibitions on the release of nuclear weapons outside U.S. control. Ultimately, the only progress toward greater NATO participation was in granting the NATO staff access to information on nuclear weapons effects and in enlarging the NATO role in targeting. NATO would ultimately modify its reliance on massive retaliation, but not until 1967, long after Taylor's departure as chairman.

For much of 1962 Vietnam was marked by an uneasy calm. By midyear the number of American advisers was up from seven hundred to about 12,000—a point at which even President Diem expressed uneasiness about the U.S. presence. Within the United States Government, it was estimated that of the 85 percent of the populace that lived in the countryside, roughly 47 percent were under government control, 9 percent under Viet Cong control, and 44 percent under neither.[7] The Saigon Government, meanwhile, had embarked on an ill-conceived program of "strategic hamlets" under which peasants were resettled, often under duress, into defended communities. Such a program held out the promise of a higher degree of government control in the countryside but was hardly calculated to win the allegiance of the people most affected. One author notes, "Although some U.S. officials in the field appreciated that most strategic hamlets were ineffective in insulating peasants either militarily or politically from the Viet Cong, the officially received wisdom in . . . Washington was that, on balance, the program was a success."[8]

Progress on the battlefield was difficult to measure, in part because of the mind-set of the senior U.S. military man on the scene, Paul Harkins. Harkins, who had been commandant of cadets at West Point for part of Taylor's superintendency, had subsequently served as his chief of staff in Korea. In February 1962, in one of the actions growing out of the Taylor-Rostow visit, the U.S. military mission in Vietnam was upgraded to a four-star billet. The Joint Chiefs chose Harkins to head the new Military Assistance Command (MAC/V), possibly on Taylor's recommendation. One of Harkins's colleagues has characterized him as "an imposing figure, though . . . not regarded within the Army as an intellectual giant."[9] Others were less charitable, largely because of Harkins's lack of receptiveness to anything that challenged his own unfailing optimism. Westmoreland, who spent several months as Harkins's deputy, was startled to hear him tell McNamara in 1964 that he believed that Vietnam could be pacified within six months; he characterized Harkins's forecast as "incredible."[10] Taylor, however, would rely on Harkins not only for progress reports on the war but on the sensitive subject of Diem's political prospects. It was typical of Taylor to place heavy reliance on the advice of the man on the spot. In the case of Harkins, it proved a fateful error.

The assumption that Vietnam was on an upward trend was rudely shattered in the spring of 1963. The issue was ostensibly one of religion. Although there was little religious persecution in South Vietnam, the Diem family regarded the country's Catholics, perhaps 10 percent of the population, as its political base, and South Vietnam's Catholics benefited from government largesse out of proportion to their numbers. Buddhist organizations, not surprisingly, became centers of political opposition. Diem might have lived with this situation, much as contemporary Poland coexists with the Catholic church, except for the zeal of his underlings. In May 1963 Buddhists in the old capital of Hue were celebrating the birthday of the Buddha when provincial authorities—possibly acting on behalf of Diem's scheming brother Ngo Dinh Nhu—decided to enforce a little-used ordinance against the flying of religious flags. This action triggered demonstrations, and the army moved in. Several Buddhists were killed and others wounded.

Diem's opponents now had martyrs, and soon they would have more. On June 11 Saigon was the venue for the first of several self-immolations by Buddhist priests, events that shocked the world and lent credence to charges of religious persecution under Diem. Had the Kennedy administration wished to cut its losses in Vietnam, it was now presented with an opportunity. But outside the State Department there was little sentiment in favor of abandoning South Vietnam, and even at State the sentiment was more anti-Diem than opposed to a U.S. role in South Vietnam. There were even glimmers of encouragement. A special assessment by the CIA in July indicated that the unrest in Saigon might be a local phenomenon:

Thus far, the Buddhist issue has not been effectively exploited by the Communists, nor does it appear to have had any appreciable effect on the counterinsurgency effort. We do not think Diem is likely to be overcome by a Communist coup. Nor do we think the Communists would necessarily profit if he were overthrown by some combination of his non-Communist opponents. A non-Communist successor regime might initially be less successful against the Viet Cong, but, given continued support from the U.S., could provide reasonably effective leadership.[11]

On June 27 the White House announced the appointment of Henry Cabot Lodge, Jr., as ambassador to Saigon. At the time, Taylor was among those who applauded the appointment of this prominent Republican to the politically sensitive Saigon post. As time went on, however, he would have grave doubts. The former senator was ineffective in administering the large and still growing U.S. diplomatic mission, and his passion for secrecy alienated Harkins. More important, he quickly allied himself with those who felt that the goal of a stable South Vietnam could be achieved only if Diem were deposed.

The summer brought new unrest. On August 20 Diem declared martial law and initiated the controversial "pagoda raids." In the small hours of August 20–21 the Special Forces of Diem's brother Ngo Dinh Nhu occupied principal Buddhist centers in Saigon, Hue, and other urban areas. Inevitably, there were injuries and arrests. Even allowing for the anti-Diem bias of most Western newsmen in Vietnam, the invasion of religious shrines by Nhu's troops smacked of Hitler's Germany and underscored the Saigon Government's insensitivity to world opinion.

Within the State Department, "dump Diem" sentiment intensified. Although Secretary Rusk reserved judgment, in so doing he was largely isolated within his own department. Under Secretary George Ball considered Asia an area of secondary importance and begrudged the attention accorded Vietnam at the expense of NATO. Averell Harriman, a Kennedy favorite, was nominally the department's Soviet expert but in practice dabbled wherever he chose. He was able to place a kindred spirit, Roger Hilsman, in charge of the Far East Bureau. Together they set about considering how best to disengage from Diem.

Hilsman was an anomaly. A West Point graduate, he had served in Burma during World War II and "considered himself a counter-insurgency expert."[12] Taylor would recall:

> It just shows what happens when you put a West Pointer in the State Department. [Hilsman] was quite capable of going over to the Cabinet Room [at the White House] and getting up before a map with a pointer, explaining how the military side of the operation should be run, based on his guerrilla experiences in Burma. It became a very sore point in some quarters. It just amused me . . . but it drove Bob McNamara nuts.[13]

With Harriman's assistance, Hilsman drafted an instruction to Lodge stating that the United States "cannot tolerate a situation in which power lies in Nhu's hands. Diem must be given a chance to rid himself of Nhu and his coterie and replace them with the best military and political personalities available." Because there was no prospect that Diem would jettison his brother, this preamble was largely window dressing. The message went on:

> We must at same time also tell key military leaders that U.S. would find it impossible to continue support GVN militarily and economically unless above steps are taken immediately which we recognize requires removal of [Nhu and his wife] from the scene. We wish to give Diem reasonable opportunity to remove Nhus, but if he remains obdurate, then we are prepared to accept the obvious implication that we can no longer support Diem. *You may also tell appropriate military commanders we will give them direct support in any interim period of breakdown central government mechanism* [emphasis added].[14]

Implicit in the message was that Diem would be replaced by some form of military junta, but there was no discussion of who might compose such a junta. The United States was, in effect, encouraging the ouster of Diem with no clear idea of who or what was to follow.

It was one thing to play at kingmaker; it was far more difficult to put the weight of the U.S. Government behind any one scenario. For Hilsman's cable to become policy would require the concurrence not only of the interested Washington agencies but of President Kennedy himself. It was, however, a summer weekend, and many senior bureaucrats were out of town. One of the absentees was Dean Rusk; his deputy, George Ball, was on the golf course when Harriman and Hilsman arrived with their cable. Ball approved of its tone but insisted that the message be approved by the President. Ball later recalled that selected paragraphs were read to Kennedy at Hyannis, but Deputy Secretary of Defense Roswell Gilpatric would testify as to how the Defense Department was bypassed:

> The first inkling I recall receiving about the proposed message came in telephone calls late that Saturday afternoon and evening from Forrestal and Krulak at the White House. Although it was immediately evident to me that the proposed message was highly controversial and one whose dispatch should have awaited the return to Washington of the President and the Secre-

taries of State and Defense, I did not protest beyond nonconcurrence for [the Defense Department] after being assured that the message had been approved by Ball . . . and cleared with the President at Hyannisport.[15]*

Having studied the August 24 cable over the weekend, a steely-eyed Taylor met on Monday first with McNamara and subsequently with the Chiefs. All were furious at the weekend performance and their anger carried into a White House meeting later in the day. Kennedy opened the meeting with some sharp words for Ball, Harriman, and Hilsman for their handling of such a sensitive matter. The delegation from State was soon locked in a fierce debate with McNamara and Taylor, who were supported by CIA director McCone and Vice President Lyndon Johnson. Little was decided, and the debate appears to have been as much over procedure as over substance. "My God," Kennedy confided to a friend, "my government is coming apart!"[16]

Having authorized Lodge to give the dissident generals a green light, the Administration waited. The Vietnamese generals had much at stake, and they had no easy time reading the signals from Washington. Harkins, who was in regular contact with Taylor, cabled on August 31 the substance of a meeting with Vietnamese Army Chief of Staff Tran Thiem Khiem. According to Khiem, "The generals were not ready as they did not have enough forces under their control compared to those under [Diem] and now in Saigon. He indicated that they, the generals, did not want to start anything they could not successfully finish."[17]

In the absence of a successful coup, Washington found itself in the unenviable position of having to deal with a regime that had some knowledge of a U.S.-backed coup against it. When Diem lifted martial law in September, he seemed in better control of his government than Ambassador Lodge was of the U.S. mission. He and Harkins were barely speaking, while the embassy and the CIA station vied in leaking their views to eager young journalists. Typi-

---

* Hilsman would later claim, in a memoir titled *To Move a Nation,* that the cable had been cleared with Taylor personally at a Washington restaurant. Taylor flatly denied this.

cal of the colored reporting that ensued was this assessment by David Halberstam for the New York *Times:*

> In the embassy, officials feel that the political situation is critical, that it will deteriorate quickly and that a government dominated by Ngo Dinh Nhu could not win. There are not known to be any optimists, or what are now called "diehards," in the political section.[18]

Given this dissension and the continued uncertainty surrounding any coup, Kennedy asked McNamara and Taylor to visit Vietnam in late September. Some have speculated that one purpose of the trip, in the President's view, was to make the Defense Department more sensitive to the need for continued pressure on Diem. In any event, McNamara and Taylor made a grueling ten-day visit during which they were exposed to the divergent views of a divided mission. There was one bit of comic relief, when word was passed to Taylor that General "Big" Minh, one of the purported coup leaders, had an important message for the two Americans. Because Minh was an accomplished tennis player, with whom Taylor had played on previous visits, a game was scheduled at a local club. In Taylor's words, "The game took place all right, with McNamara sitting uncomfortably on the sidelines in the sweltering heat, but at no time did we get a serious discussion started with Minh, whose sole interest that afternoon seemed to be tennis."[19]

In retrospect, McNamara and Taylor were almost certainly misinformed concerning the extent of progress against the Viet Cong, but they left Saigon with no illusions concerning the precarious political situation. Of their principal conclusions, the first was probably inaccurate, while the others reflected an unpromising range of possibilities:

  1. The military campaign has made great progress and continues to progress.

  2. There are serious political tensions in Saigon (and perhaps elsewhere in South Vietnam) where the Diem-Nhu government is becoming increasingly unpopular.

  3. There is no solid evidence of the possibility of a successful

coup, although the assassination of Diem or Nhu is always a possibility. . . .

4.   It is not clear that pressures exerted by the U.S. will move Diem and Nhu toward moderation. Indeed, pressures may increase their obduracy. But unless such pressures are exerted, they are almost certain to continue past patterns of behavior.[20]

As for specific recommendations, McNamara and Taylor proposed that no additional strategic hamlets be built until existing ones could be better protected. Their report called for "clear and hold" military operations, rather than terrain sweeps, "which have little permanent value."

The report concluded that "the security of South Vietnam remains vital to United States security"—strong language, and ominous in that it would inhibit any discussion of disengagement. But it also recommended steps in the direction of what would later be called Vietnamization. It urged that "a program be established to train Vietnamese so that essential functions now performed by U.S. military personnel can be carried out by Vietnamese by the end of 1965. It should be possible to withdraw the bulk of U.S. personnel by that time."[21] Alas, political developments in South Vietnam would shortly make a mockery of this projection.

Before leaving Saigon the two Americans made a farewell call on Diem. It would be the last time either would see him. The secretary and the general contrasted the perceived military progress with the continuing political deterioration. McNamara spoke of the possibility of containing the Viet Cong by 1965, but on condition that Diem's government implemented political reforms that would increase administrative efficiency and allay political tensions. Taylor found Diem's reaction discouraging:

I wish that I could say that our words evoked some signs of a desire for reconciliation or even an inclination to accommodation. . . . While smoking the usual chain of cigarettes, he defended his acts point by point and was obviously not about to capitulate to this latest delegation of Americans, even though they were from the Pentagon, which he viewed as friendly, and not from State, which he viewed as hostile. Altogether it was a depressing evening, the refusal of this stalwart, stubborn patriot to recognize the realities which threatened to overcome him, his family, and his country.[22]

Back at Fort Myer, Taylor was awakened by a call from the Pentagon in the small hours of November 1. The report was that a coup was under way in Saigon. Taylor went to his office earlier than usual that morning and read the cables. A group of generals led by Minh and Ton That Dinh had seized communication centers and attacked the presidential palace. Diem's fate was unknown. Later that day Taylor went to a White House conference called to consider the situation in Vietnam. Shortly after the meeting began, word came that Diem and Nhu were both dead, with the generals calling their deaths suicide. "Kennedy leaped to his feet," Taylor would recall, "with a look of shock and dismay which I had never seen before."[23]

The coup in Saigon and the murder of Diem also had a profound effect on Taylor. He was appalled that a clique in the State Department could have triggered a fateful policy switch at a time when counterinsurgency in Vietnam appeared to be making progress. He was only slightly less critical of the CIA, whose Saigon operatives he considered accomplices in Diem's murder. Beyond this, Taylor felt a degree of personal responsibility for the inept manner in which the Kennedy administration had dealt with Diem. He had a weakness for stubborn patriots, be they German, Korean, or Vietnamese.

In contrast to the defense secretaries with whom Taylor had dealt under Eisenhower, McNamara was not only willing to make tough decisions but at times seemed to court them. One of the continuing interservice issues with which Taylor struggled as chairman was an ongoing dispute between the Army and the Air Force over "roles and missions." The issue had grown more heated as the Army moved into both fixed-wing and helicopter aircraft in search of greater battlefield mobility.

Realizing that someone other than the service chiefs of staff had to resolve this issue, Taylor undertook to do it himself. He assembled a small working group from among the Joint Staff, the chairman's Staff Group, and his personal staff, whom he directed to come up with a formula that clearly spelled out Army and Air Force responsibilities. Taylor studied the result, approved it, and took it up to Secretary McNamara, who read it and said, "Max, I'll approve it right now." Taylor, however, counseled caution. The issue was a sensitive one, he pointed out, and the secretary might want to keep it around for a while before approving it, if only to avoid any suggestion that it had been rushed through.

According to Taylor's exec, Bernard Rogers, McNamara agreed, and put the paper in his safe. Its recommendations proved so controversial that the paper never saw the light of day.

When Taylor died in 1987, Senator Edward Kennedy offered words of praise on behalf of the Kennedy family. Passing over more contentious topics, he praised Taylor's work on behalf of the limited nuclear test ban treaty of 1963. Without Taylor's support, he said, this first step toward arms reduction might not have become a reality.

Early in 1963 President Kennedy chose to press for some step toward disarmament despite the fact that U.S.-Soviet relations were less than warm in the wake of the Cuban missile crisis. As always, the stumbling block was verification; the Soviets were unwilling to permit on-site inspection of test sites, which made any comprehensive ban unenforceable. Nevertheless, Kennedy joined with British Prime Minister Harold Macmillan in proposing new talks on a test ban treaty. Progress was slow, but in July, Khrushchev made a speech in East Berlin in which he endorsed a ban on atmospheric testing.

Such a partial ban fell short of what Kennedy had in mind, but even a limited accommodation faced formidable opposition in the Senate. Leading members of the Joint Atomic Energy Committee predicted that anything other than "a reasonably foolproof testing agreement . . . [could be] a greater risk to the national security than an arms race."[24] The chairman of the House Armed Services Committee, Richard Russell, was opposed to the treaty. So, too, were an impressive array of onetime public figures, including atomic scientist Edward Teller, former AEC chairman Lewis Strauss, and retired admirals Radford and Burke.

Clearly, the position taken by the incumbent Chiefs would be critical, and Taylor urged that they be brought into the discussions at an early stage. Which superpower would be the more hurt by a ban on atmospheric testing? Although the United States would be affected to some degree, it was arguable that the Soviets, who lagged in weapons technology, would be at a greater disadvantage. Nevertheless, given the recent Soviet duplicity concerning missiles in Cuba, the Chiefs viewed any agreement with what Taylor wryly called "controlled enthusiasm."

Testifying in August before a joint session of interested congressional committees, Taylor reported that the Chiefs had "actively participated" in the planning for the treaty and approved it. Their approval, he said, came without any "arm twisting" by the Administration. He cited a joint statement by the Chiefs that "while there are military disadvantages to the treaty, they are not so serious as to make it unacceptable."[25] In the end the Chiefs' position was a big plus for the Administration. Senator George Smathers, a Democrat from Florida, observed that Taylor and other administration witnesses had "clearly and effectively expelled most of the doubts which many of us had about a treaty." He added that "even the most skeptical Senator would have trouble opposing it."[26]

The Senate ratified the treaty on September 24.

While at Lincoln Center, Taylor had fallen into the habit of a brief postlunch nap. At the Pentagon his staff was on notice that when his door was closed he was not to be disturbed for anything except the most dire emergencies. On November 22, 1963, he had just stretched out on his sofa following meetings with a German NATO delegation when his buzzer went off. It was the Pentagon's communications room, the National Military Command Center. General Tibbetts apologized, but said that they had just received word from Dallas that President Kennedy had been shot and was probably dying. Stunned, Taylor first buzzed Secretary McNamara, calling him out of a conference on the budget. He passed along the bare details and then sent word to the Germans that he would be delayed in rejoining the conference.

Taylor called an immediate meeting of the Chiefs in his office, where McNamara joined them. Taylor was at first concerned that the shooting might be part of a plot to overthrow the government.

Word of the assault was passed to the unified commands, and their level of readiness raised one notch. Taylor then rejoined the Germans, telling them of the assassination attempt but withholding word, passed to him during the afternoon, that the President was dead. A few days later, Taylor, on foot, would lead the Chiefs in the cortege that wound its way from Pennsylvania Avenue across the Potomac to Arlington Cemetery.

Over the years, my father would often be asked for his assessment of the young President who had brought him back to government. He had no facile reply. He was prone to note that he had seen several Jack Kennedys—from the President in shock following the Bay of Pigs to the Chief Executive moving confidently to deal with the threat of Soviet missiles in Cuba. On a personal basis, Taylor found Kennedy delightful; he enjoyed the President's sense of humor and admired his patience. "I never saw President Kennedy, young and naturally impatient as you would assume him to be, ever get into [a] snappy mood with the people around him."27

As to Kennedy's style in office, Taylor could not help contrasting decision making under Eisenhower and under Kennedy. During the Eisenhower administrations the White House staff sought to "protect" the President at all cost; Ike, in Taylor's view, never wanted to take actions himself that might have adverse consequences. He did not wish to resolve disputes, he wanted them settled elsewhere. Kennedy, by contrast, expected to be involved in decision making and had no desire to defer action once alternative courses had been considered.

In later years Taylor would occasionally acknowledge disappointment at reports of President Kennedy's sexual adventures ("I never saw any naked women running around the White House"). But his admiration and respect for Kennedy never wavered, and Taylor would date many of his country's subsequent woes from November 22, 1963. In mid-1964, just prior to his departure for Saigon, Taylor had several conversations with Elspeth Rostow, who interviewed him at his quarters for the Kennedy Library's oral history series. All went smoothly until the subject of the assassination arose. According to Rostow, Taylor then broke down; for several minutes there was nothing on her tape except the sound of an occasional passing car. Once he had composed himself, the interview continued.[28]

More than a decade later, at a family dinner, the subject turned to political dissent in the country under Nixon. Taylor had recently returned from a speaking engagement at a small New Jersey college, where hecklers had prevented him from speaking. He commented that Kennedy, had he lived, was the one person who might have preserved a degree of national cohesiveness. Then his voice broke; it was a moment before his normal self-control returned. Surrounded by his family, he had let his defenses down.

Chapter 22

SAIGON

A week after President Kennedy's funeral, the Joint Chiefs had their first meeting with his successor. On the surface, all appears to have gone well. In this initial conference Lyndon Johnson indicated that he planned to continue his predecessor's defense policies, including the U.S. effort in Vietnam. Taylor, for his part, had had considerable dealings with the new President, first as Army chief of staff and more recently as milrep and chairman. He considered Johnson "sound" on security issues, including Vietnam; whereas Kennedy had indicated mixed feelings concerning Diem, Johnson from the outset had opposed any undercutting of the South Vietnamese President. Nevertheless, his first meeting with Johnson as President may have been traumatic for Taylor. His exec, Bernie Rogers, noted that for at least fifteen minutes after returning to his office Taylor simply sat in his chair, preoccupied. Rogers had never seen him in quite this state before.

This first meeting with LBJ focused on the President's responsibilities in a nuclear emergency, but Taylor felt that, given all the material being thrust at him, the new President should have a more detailed explanation of what was involved. He sought, and obtained, a second appointment in which to go over in detail the "black book" of nuclear options that follows the President wherever he goes.

One of Johnson's first acts as President was to ask Taylor to undertake a trip to India and Pakistan. The request was a vote of confidence in Taylor's diplomatic skills, but he was handed a no-win situation. India, which had been subjected to numerous border violations from China, was dissatisfied with the level of aid it was receiving from the United States and was turning increasingly to the Soviets. Pakistan thus perceived an increased security threat from India and was upset about its own level of support from Washington. As a result, President Ayub had set about improving his country's relations with India's enemy, China. Taylor's trip, in December 1963, was a gesture of continued U.S. support for Pakistan, but the State Department insisted that, in the interest of even-handedness, he should visit India as well. Ultimately, Ayub turned down a U.S. proposal for a joint military exercise to be held in Pakistan, and the Taylor mission was of little consequence.

As 1963 turned into 1964, Taylor toyed with the idea of retirement. He had returned to Washington to help out a President who was in trouble; he had no personal obligation to his successor. He could, if he were to leave, number some significant achievements, including an upgrading of the role of the JCS chairman. The New York *Times*'s Hanson Baldwin quoted "informed sources" in the Pentagon as saying that Taylor, as chairman, had come "as close to being a *de facto* single chief of staff as any man can without a legal change."[1] He had overseen implementation of the new Strike Command—a force that combined most of the Air Force's tactical aircraft with Army assault forces and facilitated contingency planning for areas such as Cuba. And the handling of the Cuban missile crisis underscored the fact that the Kennedy-Johnson security team was no longer the gang that couldn't shoot straight. Still, Taylor stayed on.

In April 1964 General MacArthur died. Taylor had continued to have reservations about MacArthur's strategy in Korea, but when interviewed by a television network on the day of the general's death, he was equal to the occasion:

> The death of General MacArthur is a tragic loss to his friends, to the military profession, and to his country. He was one of the truly great men of the century. Basically he was a soldier, proud of his profession, but he transcended the limitations of any professional background. He was essentially a leader of men who appealed not only to his own people but to those against whom he had waged war and defeated in war.[2]*

---

* Two years earlier MacArthur had made his last visit to West Point, where he delivered an emotional farewell. "Today marks my final roll call with you," MacArthur had closed, "but I want you to know that when I cross the river, my last

Meanwhile, Vietnam refused to go away. In Saigon, General Minh was proving as hesitant a President as he had been a conspirator. The initial euphoria that had accompanied Diem's ouster was followed by a period of irresolution and uncertainty. Rather than capitalize on his own considerable popularity, Minh chose to share authority with a committee of officers who were themselves divided by divergent motivations and personal jealousies. In the view of a South Vietnamese diplomat, "The central problem was . . . the generals themselves. The members of the junta had no cohesive vision of government or society, no real thoughts about how to rebuild the nation."[3] They were agreed that all vestiges of the Diem regime must be destroyed, and they sacked key civil officials and military commanders. But there was no political stability. Some officers who had supported the coup against Diem felt insufficiently rewarded. Others felt threatened by any new "anticorruption" drive.

One senior officer missing from the new ruling group was a thirty-seven-year-old corps commander, General Nguyen Khanh. Khanh had risen to the rank of lieutenant colonel under the French and subsequently had helped put down an early coup against Diem. The result had been a series of promotions culminating in his appointment to corps commander, but this had not prevented him from participating in the plot against his mentor. Yet he had not been a member of the final coup group: they did not trust him. In the words of one author, Khanh was

> a jaunty figure with darting eyes and a goatee, [who] strutted and swaggered like a character in a Chinese opera. . . . But he was shrewd and energetic. Even in a society where scruples were scarce, he was distrusted, having built his career on switching his allegiance to whichever faction promised to fulfill his limitless ambitions.[4]

On January 30, 1964, a group led by Khanh pulled off a bloodless coup against the Minh government, which it accused of "neutralist" tendencies. As with the coup against Diem, the U.S. mission was aware of Khanh's plotting but, disillusioned with Minh, did nothing to deter him. In retrospect the Khanh coup

---

conscious thoughts will be—of the Corps—and the Corps—and the Corps." Taylor observed wryly, "I wonder what Mrs. MacArthur thought about that."

would be viewed as a disaster; William Bundy, a senior State Department official, would later write that his coup "removed, for a long time to come, any chance for a true government of unity, or of all the available talents, or with any claim to the crucial element of legitimacy."[5] At the time, however, the forceful, articulate Khanh appeared to be a likely improvement over the vacillating Minh, and President Johnson directed McNamara and Taylor to undertake a visit to South Vietnam that would stress U.S. support for the new government.

A few days before the departure of the McNamara-Taylor mission, Johnson met with the Joint Chiefs. At this meeting Taylor adopted a position with regard to retaliation against North Vietnam that he would press increasingly in the year to come:

> [President Johnson] talked to the Chiefs about the trip and asked our opinion about what we should do next in South Vietnam. I replied that our military program should consist of two parts, an intensified counterinsurgency campaign in the south and selective air and naval attacks against targets in North Vietnam. The other Chiefs expressed general agreement, but, perhaps thinking of the Bay of Pigs, they added that if our government embarked on such a program, we must carry it out successfully regardless of cost.[6]

In Vietnam, McNamara and Taylor made a whirlwind tour of the provinces, posing next to Khanh with arms upraised, while onlookers chanted *"Vietnam muon nam"* (Vietnam for a thousand years). At the end of the visit, Taylor recalled, "there was no doubt that [Khanh] was the 'American boy,' at least for the time being."[7] But the trip was also disquieting. The two Americans found ample evidence that the military effort against the Viet Cong was foundering; the ARVN's desertion rate was high and increasing. Taylor sounded out Khanh about the possibility of U.S. retaliation against the North but aroused little enthusiasm. Khanh argued, rather plausibly, that his first priority should be to firm up his own political base. In retrospect, this might have been an excellent time for consideration of de Gaulle's somewhat nebulous proposals for the "neutralization" of Vietnam. But with so fragile a government in

Saigon, a negotiated solution appeared to promise little more than a gradual Communist takeover.

After attending the midyear NATO meeting in Paris, Taylor returned to Washington to find a discussion in progress about who should be named to succeed Lodge as ambassador to Saigon.† Lodge was viewed at this time as perhaps the only Republican capable of heading off Barry Goldwater for the Republican presidential nomination, and the Administration was not disposed to place obstacles in his way. A number of Johnson's most senior advisers, including Rusk, McNamara, and Bobby Kennedy, had indicated their willingness to give it a try in Saigon. McNamara had urged Taylor to allow his name to be considered as well, and the chairman returned from France to find to his dismay that he was the leading contender.

Taylor, who had turned down Kennedy's offer of the ambassadorship to Paris, had even less interest in going to Saigon. His father had died in 1962, and he was maintaining his widowed mother in an apartment in the Washington suburbs. He was still undecided about staying on as chairman of the JCS; he remarked to me in April 1964 that the President and McNamara would probably ask him to stay on after the elections, but that if he did, it would be for only one more year. The reasons why he ended up as Johnson's choice for Saigon remain unclear. Taylor himself thought that his main asset was expendability. But Johnson knew he would be sending a first-rate manager to a post badly in need of organization, and there may have been some thought—however misguided—that the Vietnamese generals would be comfortable dealing with a fellow soldier. One can only speculate as to what might have happened if Johnson had chosen instead to neutralize Bobby Kennedy by making him ambassador to South Vietnam.

---

† En route to Paris, Taylor was able to attend ceremonies in Normandy commemorating D-day twenty years earlier. In the church at Ste. Mère Église, the first town liberated by American paratroops, Taylor listened quietly as General Ridgway told a predominantly French audience, in English, that it had been an honor to command the division that had liberated their town. Taylor then rose and, speaking in French, said that he had known and admired General Ridgway for many years. General Ridgway was a brave soldier and a truthful person and full credence should be given anything he said—except as concerned which American division had liberated Ste. Mère Église.

In the end Taylor accepted the Saigon appointment, but with a
proviso that it be for only one year. On July 2 he met with the
Chiefs for the last time as chairman. He spoke briefly of what they
had accomplished and what remained. In wishing them luck—his
successor would be the Army's Earle Wheeler—he took the occasion to remind them of Kennedy's directive, revalidated by
Johnson, that he wanted the Chiefs to consider all aspects of a
situation, to be "more than military men." Then it was off to Hyannis Port for a farewell call on Jackie Kennedy. The gesture was
much appreciated, as the former first lady wrote in August:

> How could you be so thoughtful—and write to me from Sai-
> gon—when I am sure that every second you have been there has
> been so filled with work and with worry.
>
> For you to have come all the way to Hyannis the day you were
> leaving was just one more evidence of the devotion you always
> showed to Jack. . . .
>
> I think you more than anyone else made greatness possible
> for him once he was in the White House—made the second
> Cuba a triumph—because of all the work you did after the First
> Cuba—and stayed on when you could have left. . . .
>
> I am so proud to have known you.[8]

Taylor arrived in Vietnam on July 7, 1964. For all his previous
visits, his knowledge of the country and its culture was limited. He
was aware of its ethnic and geographic rivalries, of its factional-
ized armed forces and apathetic peasantry. But he may have
drawn an erroneous parallel between Vietnam in the 1960s and
Korea in the 1950s. In Korea, the war had brought with it an anti-
Communist consensus among the people that tended to submerge
other differences for as long as the fighting continued. In Vietnam,
such a consensus was as elusive as the Viet Cong themselves, and
Ho Chi Minh had been remarkably successful in maintaining his
credibility as a nationalist as well as a Communist.

Saigon in 1964 did not yet have an overwhelming American
presence. Its tree-lined boulevards were still evocative of Paris,
and visitors were drawn to the sight of slim Vietnamese girls clad
in graceful *ao dais* guiding their motorbikes through the down-

town traffic. As for the American ambassador, his office and his residence afforded considerable contrast. The U.S. embassy occupied an undistinguished commercial office building in downtown Saigon; it was crowded and vulnerable to terrorist attack. The ambassador's white stucco residence, however, was on a quiet residential street, behind a barrier manned by Vietnamese guards. The ambassador's car, a modified Lincoln Continental, was heavily armored on the floor and sides. Both of Taylor's two predecessors had been the targets of apparent assassination attempts, and he himself would have one close call.

Shortly after he arrived in Saigon, Taylor held a staff meeting in which he set forth the Administration's assessment of the importance of Vietnam in terms of U.S. objectives in the region. It reflected Washington's continued sensitivity to Chinese expansionism and its reluctance to acknowledge the magnitude of the split between Moscow and Peking. He characterized the Communist world as watching the course of events in Vietnam to see whether subversive insurgency was in fact the "wave of the future." In an unusual evocation of Eisenhower's domino theory—for Taylor did not believe in inexorable "laws"—the new ambassador warned that a U.S. failure in Southeast Asia "would be the prelude to the loss or neutralization of all of Southeast Asia and the absorption of that area into the Chinese empire."[9]

As he had at the Pentagon, Taylor brought some of "his people" with him. Not wishing to become bogged down in State Department administration, he had asked for the services of an old friend from his Japan days, Alexis Johnson, as deputy ambassador. Johnson was one of the department's senior officials and was fully qualified to head a mission of his own, but like Taylor he was prepared to make a one-year commitment to Saigon. The new head of MAC/V was William Westmoreland, a Taylor protégé. For his domestic staff—his wife accompanied him to Saigon—Taylor brought with him three longtime associates, sergeants Bob Blackwell, Hurley Cargill, and William Holder.

Taylor arrived with a letter from President Johnson that he, Taylor, had drafted. It probably accorded him as much authority as any American envoy has enjoyed in recent times:

As you take charge of the American effort in South Vietnam, I want you to have this formal expression not only of my confidence, but of my desire that you have and exercise full responsibility for the effort of the United States Government in Vietnam. In general terms this authority is parallel to that set forth in President Kennedy's letter of May 29, 1961, to all American ambassadors; specifically, I wish it clearly understood that this overall responsibility includes the whole military effort in South Vietnam and authorizes the degree of command and control that you consider appropriate.[10]‡

In theory, this authority might have been a source of friction with Westmoreland and his superiors in Hawaii. In practice, it was rarely a problem. Taylor's entire philosophy was based on finding qualified people and then letting them do their job. So it was with "Westy." MAC/V was expected to clear all policy cables with the embassy, but the ambassador had no intention of trying to run the war. At the same time, Taylor ran a tight ship with other elements of the U.S. mission. He and Johnson modified the "country team" structure that they had inherited from Lodge into a mission council in which the ambassador's ruling was final.

Taylor had scarcely unpacked his bags when the Administration's course in Vietnam received what he perceived as a ringing endorsement. In the first week of August, one and perhaps two U.S. destroyers in the Tonkin Gulf appeared to have come under fire from North Vietnamese patrol boats, which probably associated the U.S. vessels with raids along the east coast by South Vietnamese forces. Whether or not there was an element of provocation to the Tonkin Gulf incidents, President Johnson used the occasion to gain Congress's endorsement for U.S. actions in Vietnam. The Tonkin resolution as finally approved permitted the President to "take all necessary measures to repel armed attack against the forces of the United States." It stated further that the United States was prepared "to take all necessary steps, including

‡ In forwarding this letter to the President for signature, McGeorge Bundy observed that it "is worth reading aloud before you sign it. What it does is to give Max full control over everything in South Vietnam. This is something the military never let the Ambassador have before, and now that we have a man whom the military cannot refuse, it is time to establish the principle."[11]

the use of armed force, to assist any member of protocol state of the Southeast Asia Collective Defense Treaty requesting assistance in defense of its freedom."[12]

Taylor, in Saigon, had enough on his plate that he had not yet considered the merits of a formal declaration of war as opposed to the authority embodied in the Tonkin resolution. To his well-ordered mind, the latter represented an explicit commitment on the part of the American people:

> Sitting as ambassador in Saigon, reading the clear English of the Tonkin Gulf Resolution, [I saw] a mandate from the American people for Ambassador Taylor to try harder, to fight harder, and to stick with it because the people were all behind him. Read the prose of the Resolution again and see how it would affect a man on the other side of the world getting this word from the American Congress with near unanimity—only two dissenting votes. I was just amazed when I came home in 1965 and found the turning tide of opinion.[13]

Meanwhile, the situation in Vietnam itself was worsening. On the military front the Viet Cong were belatedly seeking to capitalize on the overthrow of Diem and the resulting political turmoil; infiltration from the North was on the rise, as were desertions from the South Vietnamese Army. The political situation continued to deteriorate. Khanh was making little progress in achieving the blend of nation building and economic reform that his country required to survive, and pessimism was widespread. Restrictive laws introduced by Khanh led to student protests, and the students were soon joined by the militant Buddhists, whose political ambitions had only been whetted by Diem's overthrow. Khanh, unable to gain approval for a new constitution, resigned in late August. He was briefly replaced by an interim Premier, but, once antigovernment demonstrations had eased, he reappeared and resumed the premiership, insisting that his leadership was essential to political stability. The only positive note was that the Communists still appeared to have limited appeal to political groups in the South. Taylor reported to Washington, "We need two or three months to get any sort of government going that has any chance of maintaining order."[14]

Rusk instructed the embassy to make it clear that the public squabbling in Saigon was trying the Administration's patience. For a time, coincidentally, affairs quieted down. In late September, Khanh announced formation of a High National Council apportioned among the country's religious and ethnic groups. Its first tasks were to draft a provisional constitution and to appoint a ceremonial President. The council deliberated through much of October, came up with a constitution, and appointed an aged but respected figure, Phan Khac Suu, as chief of state. Suu, in turn, appointed Tran Van Huong, the "stubborn and honest" mayor of Saigon, as Premier. Khanh, however, remained commander in chief of the armed forces, and no government could succeed without the Army's support.

The prospect of some degree of political stability allowed the U.S. mission to look again at a program that had long tempted Taylor: the bombing of selected targets of the military aggressor, North Vietnam. There was considerable support within the Administration for such action, assuming that the timing was right. But such a step was politically impossible in the weeks immediately preceding the U.S. presidential election, for Johnson was basing much of his campaign on the alleged impulsiveness of the Republican candidate, Barry Goldwater. Not even an attack on a major U.S. base could be permitted to threaten the Johnson landslide. Taylor wrote home on November 2:

> Sunday turned out to be a very long day, starting at 3:00 a.m. when General Westmoreland called me to report the mortar attack on the airfield at Bien Hoa. This is an important field largely filled with American aircraft to include the B-57s which we brought in for possible use against North Vietnam and China in case of an extension of the war. These planes have taken no part in the Viet Cong campaign. The deliberate attack on them is a clear indication that Hanoi had passed the word to the Viet Cong.
>
> At least six planes have been completely destroyed at $1,250,000 a copy. Four soldiers were killed by mortar rounds and about twenty others were wounded. I am giving Washington

a bad Saturday night by the cabled recommendations which I am sending in.[15]

Taylor waited until after the President's overwhelming election victory to travel to Washington to press the case for retaliation. His views were in the public domain; columnist Joseph Alsop wrote of Taylor's "reported conviction that no alternative now remains except to 'change the terms of the problem.' "[16] Meeting on November 27 with the President's top advisers, he spoke from a carefully prepared paper. He was not a bearer of glad tidings:

> After a year of changing and ineffective government, the counterinsurgency program country-wide is bogged down and will require heroic treatment to assure revival. . . . The northern provinces of South Vietnam, which a year ago were considered almost free of Viet Cong, are now in deep trouble. In the Quang Ngai-Binh Dinh area, the gains of the Viet Cong have been so serious that once more we are threatened with a partition of the country by a Viet Cong salient driven to the sea.

Even allowing for the extensive aid flowing to the South from Hanoi, and for the political disarray in South Vietnam, Taylor was at a loss to explain the growing strength of the enemy:

> The ability of the Viet Cong continuously to rebuild their units and make good their losses is one of the mysteries of the guerrilla war. We are aware of the recruiting methods by which local boys are induced or compelled to join the Viet Cong ranks and have some general appreciation of the amount of infiltration from the outside. Yet taking both of these sources into account, we still find no plausible explanation of the continued strength of the Viet Cong if our data on Viet Cong losses are even approximately correct. Not only do the Viet Cong units have the recuperative powers of the phoenix, but they have an amazing ability to maintain morale.

So what was to be done? "If, as the evidence shows, we are playing a losing game in South Vietnam . . . it is high time we change and find a better way." He proposed the initiation of gradually increasing air strikes against the North with three purposes in mind:

> First, to establish an adequate government in [South Vietnam]; second, to improve the conduct of the counterinsurgency campaign; finally, to persuade or force [North Vietnam] to stop its aid to the Viet Cong and to use its directive powers to make the Viet Cong desist from their efforts to overthrow the Government of South Vietnam.[17]

Taylor was still a "gradualist." In contrast to the Joint Chiefs, who were eager to begin an extensive bombing campaign against the North, Taylor advocated what was called "tit for tat" retaliation—bombing tied to some especially egregious attack against Americans in the South. Bombing by whatever name would not help matters much in the South, where Viet Cong strength had doubled during 1964 to around 170,000. But retaliation held out some hope of getting Hanoi to reduce the level of activity in the South and of boosting morale in Saigon. In any case, in Taylor's view there could be no real negotiations until Hanoi was "hurting."

President Johnson met with his security advisers, including Taylor, on December 1. In the meeting he made it clear that he would not consider stronger action against North Vietnam unless he was convinced that everything possible had been done to improve the situation in the South. In William Bundy's recollection:

> In effect, the President as much as put it up to Ambassador Taylor—"If you want this bombing program you have urged, you must get the Saigon political leaders into shape." It always frustrated the President especially—master pleader that he himself had always been—to try to plead through other men, and on a political terrain he did not personally know. In this case, he left no doubt that Taylor should use every possible argument, in small groups or large, whatever would do the trick.[18]

At the end of the year political stability was as elusive as ever, and President Johnson remained unwilling to extend the war to the North in the absence of a more viable regime in the South. Taylor's contention that attacks directed against Americans called for retaliation fell on deaf ears. On Christmas Eve, during a visit by Bob Hope and his troupe, the Viet Cong exploded a bomb in an officers' hotel in Saigon, killing two Americans and injuring more than fifty. The blast rattled crockery in the ambassador's residence, and there was talk of canceling the party for Hope that evening. (It was held nevertheless, with the unflappable Hope and a scaled-down guest list.) Taylor again urged retaliatory bombing, and again Johnson demurred.

Meanwhile, South Vietnam's military forces continued to decline, as a result of setbacks in the field, eroding morale, and severely strained resources. In the first week of January the government suffered a stinging military setback just forty miles from Saigon when two of its better battalions were ambushed by a small Viet Cong force. ("We never could get the Vietnamese to put out patrols," Taylor later remarked.) The ambassador, who never attempted to minimize the problems his country faced in Vietnam, sent President Johnson his most pessimistic assessment to date. Citing "continued political turmoil, irresponsibility and division within the armed forces, lethargy within the pacification program, some anti-U.S. feeling that could grow, signs of mounting terrorism by VC directly at US personnel, and deepening discouragement and loss of morale," he warned that if these trends were not reversed, "we are likely soon to face a number of unpleasant developments ranging from anti-American demonstrations . . . to the ultimate installation of a hostile government which will ask us to leave while it seeks accommodation with the National Liberation Front and Hanoi."[19]

The ambassador had his hands full as a result of Khanh's political maneuverings. He met with some of the senior Vietnamese generals at a dinner at Westmoreland's on December 8 and reiterated that the continued political instability in Saigon was undermining their cause in Washington. The generals, who claimed also to speak for Khanh, assured the Americans that the army was behind Huong. Within two weeks, however, Khanh was at the center of renewed plotting, this time focused on pressuring Huong to dismiss General Minh, whom the Khanh faction continued to view as a political threat. When Huong refused, Khanh dissolved the High National Council and placed Minh under house arrest. Taylor, furious, called a meeting at the embassy with the junta. Khanh declined to attend, but four senior officers, including generals Nguyen Van Thieu and Nguyen Chanh Thi, duly put in an appearance.

Taylor consulted with Alex Johnson over what line to take with their visitors, and Johnson agreed that the time for kid gloves was past. A partial transcript suggests the tone of the meeting:

> AMBASSADOR TAYLOR: Do all of you understand English? [Vietnamese officers indicated they did, although the understanding of General Thi was known to be weak.] I told you all clearly at General Westmoreland's dinner we Americans were tired of coups. Apparently I wasted my words. . . . I made it clear that all the military plans which I know you would like to carry out are dependent on governmental stability. Now you have made a real mess. We cannot carry you forever if you do things like this.

General Nguyen Chanh Thi took on the unenviable task of rationalizing the coup. The High National Council, he said, had in fact been plotting against the military. "You cannot have stability," he said, "until you have unity."

> GENERAL KY: It looks as though the HNC does not want unity. It does not want to fight the Communists. . . . Yesterday we met, twenty of us, from 1430 to 2030. We reached agreement that we must take some action. . . . We did what we thought was good for the country. . . .
>
> AMBASSADOR TAYLOR: I respect the sincerity of you gentlemen. Now I would like to talk to you about the consequences of what you have done. But first, would any of the other officers wish to speak?
>
> ADMIRAL CANG: It seems that we are being treated as though we were guilty. What we did was good and we did it only for the good of the country.
>
> AMBASSADOR TAYLOR: Now let me tell you how I feel about it, what I think the consequences are: first of all, this is a military coup that has destroyed the government-making process that, to the admiration of the whole world, was set up last fall largely through the statesman-like acts of the Armed Forces. You mili-

tary cannot go back to your units, General Ky. You military are now back in power. You are up to your necks in politics.[20]

Taylor's handling of this meeting would come in for a fair amount of criticism. According to Stanley Karnow, the ambassador committed a cardinal sin in his remarks to the generals. "By humiliating the young officers, he had made them 'lose face'—the most demeaning of experiences for an Asian."[21] Actually, Taylor had not lived in the East for more than six years without learning about "face." He had, over the years, negotiated sensitive issues with Japanese, Koreans, and Vietnamese. But he and Johnson felt that the Vietnamese generals needed a jolt, and that is what they gave them. American casualties in Vietnam, although far below what they would become, were increasing. Were Americans to die on behalf of some mindless junta?

Considering what was at stake for him personally, Khanh might have been expected to move rapidly to improve his relations with the U.S. mission. But this was Vietnam, and exactly the opposite happened. Khanh told Western journalists of the meeting, characterizing it as an insult to Vietnam's sovereignty. There were rumors that the American ambassador was to be declared persona non grata. Taylor called a press conference of his own to put forth his side of the story. "The fighting is going on in four fronts," he remarked ruefully. "The government vs. the Buddhists, the Buddhists vs. the government, the generals vs. the ambassador and, I hope, the generals vs. the Viet Cong."[22] To add insult to injury, Khanh began cooperating with the Buddhist militants in sponsoring anti-Huong and anti-American demonstrations to bolster his position. The new year, however, brought an armed truce. President Suu and Huong reached a compromise with the generals over the future of the High National Council, and Taylor and Khanh were photographed shaking hands at a tea party at Gia Long palace.

The political turmoil had by no means ended; the military intervened again in late January and forced the dissolution of Huong's government. But the army was losing patience with Khanh too, partly because he seemed preoccupied with personal power and partly because he showed signs of a willingness to cut a deal with the Viet Cong. On February 19 the generals decided to oust Khanh but, as a face-saving device, to appoint him an ambassador-at-large. "Khanh was a great disappointment to most of us who knew him well," Taylor would write, "because, with some character and integrity added to his undeniable ability, he might have been the George Washington of his country."[23] South Vietnamese diplomat Bui Diem would add: "In retrospect, the regime of Nguyen Khanh put an end to the idea of bringing alive in South Vietnam a democracy vital enough to ward off the political and military challenges of the Vietnamese Communist party."[24]

Taylor saw Khanh off at the airport with undisguised relief. Soon after he wrote from Saigon:

> The early part of last week was spent in holding our breath to see whether "Stinker No. 1" was really leaving town or not. Early he made noises about shooting it out with his disloyal colleagues but, when it became clear he had nobody with him, he decided to listen to the call of duty and accept the Ambassadorship-at-Large. He was put into orbit Thursday after an elaborate military ceremony followed by many *abrazos* at the airport.[25]

By the end of the year Taylor was clearly numbered among those in Johnson's confidence who were prepared to "stick it out" in Vietnam at almost any price. He acknowledged the desirability of a stronger political base in Saigon, but only reluctantly accepted political stability as a precondition for military retaliation against the North. He was convinced that the root of South Vietnam's military problems lay in the North and that the United States should take the war to its source. He was closer than he realized to winning over the one person whom he had to convince, Lyndon B. Johnson.

Chapter 23

NEVER CALL RETREAT

At Taylor's suggestion, National Security adviser McGeorge Bundy made his first visit to Vietnam in early February. It was not a happy time; just two weeks before, the Armed Forces Council had pulled the rug out from under the Huong government, in effect returning power to Khanh. His briefings completed, Bundy was packing for his return when word arrived of a Viet Cong attack on an American airfield at the market town of Pleiku in the central highlands. A mortar attack in the small hours of February 7 killed eight Americans, wounded more than a hundred, and destroyed ten aircraft. Joined by Bundy, the three senior Americans in Saigon—Taylor, Johnson, and Westmoreland—considered this latest turn of events and agreed that retaliation was called for. Bundy telephoned Washington from Westmoreland's headquarters and urged that bombing of the North begin forthwith. Deputy Secretary of Defense Cyrus Vance told Bundy that a decision to retaliate had already been made.[1]

Retaliation for Pleiku was almost instantaneous. On February 15 my father wrote me, "This has been a very busy week, beginning with our air strikes last Sunday and Monday. . . . We finally seem to have turned a corner and adopted a more realistic policy to the conduct of the war. I have been working and waiting for a year and a half to get to this point."[2] Once the initial decision to retaliate was made, bombing advocates had little difficulty in gaining presidential support for a continuation. On March 2 the retaliatory bombing urged by Taylor expanded into a more systematic campaign, one bearing the pretentious code name Rolling Thunder. Initially, the program consisted of one or two strikes a week and was limited to targets such as roads and bridges near the nineteenth parallel. Whichever side may be said to have escalated the war, the U.S. bombing, and the possibilities it afforded for Communist retaliation, moved the war into a new and more dangerous phase.

Over the years Taylor would often be charged with seeking a "military solution" in Vietnam, with his advocacy of bombing cited as evidence. Actually, neither Taylor nor McNamara had unrealistic expectations for the bombing; their intention was to inflict a level of pain on Hanoi that would bring about negotiations in which the United States would not be dealing from a position of weakness on the battlefield. They had a secondary motive as well. In Alexis Johnson's words, "We in the embassy had this one other hope for Operation Rolling Thunder: that it would quiet the growing push from Washington for the commitment of American ground forces."[3] Even after bombing began, Taylor was a gradualist; he sought not to return North Vietnam to the Stone Age but to bend the will of Hanoi's leaders. If too much destruction were visited upon the North, he felt, its cities would cease to be hostages to the U.S. Air Force and Hanoi's leaders would lose any incentive to retrench.

Taylor generally met twice a week with South Vietnam's new Premier, Phan Huy Quat, to consult on the bombing. As recalled by Quat's chief of staff, Bui Diem, Taylor and Alexis Johnson would call at the Prime Minister's office with a roll of maps "to let us know which targets were being bombed."[4] Taylor had his own recollection of these targeting sessions. According to him, Quat would examine the maps and then make a remark like, "Well, that's interesting. That's only about thirty-five miles from my uncle's farm."[5] But the Saigon Government welcomed the bombing.

Meanwhile, somewhat overshadowed by Rolling Thunder, a far more portentous development took place—the introduction of U.S. ground combat forces into South Vietnam. The ineffectiveness of much of the South Vietnamese Army, and the need to protect U.S. airfields against another Pleiku, had generated a wide consensus in Washington and MAC/V in favor of introducing U.S. troops. Although the South Vietnamese were benefiting from the mobility provided by U.S. helicopters, their weaponry was matched by the flow of Chinese weapons from North Vietnam to the Viet Cong. Moreover, U.S. authorities believed that as many as four regiments of North Vietnamese regulars were operating in the South. Westmoreland maintained that to guarantee security around all U.S. facilities would require about 75,000 soldiers, but he was prepared to settle for what he could get.

Taylor's first reaction was negative. He saw the proposed introduction of two battalions of Marines as the first step toward the commitment of U.S. ground forces in "an essentially hostile foreign country," and he added in a cable that once deployment began "it will be increasingly difficult to hold the line." He doubted whether American soldiers could do much better than the French had done in Asian forests and jungles; moreover there was the "ever present question" of how American soldiers were to distinguish "between a Viet Cong and a friendly Vietnamese farmer."[6] Taylor underwent a partial change of heart with regard to the two Marine battalions, however, after visiting the rapidly expanding U.S. base at Danang:

> Am deeply impressed with the magnitude of the security problem [at Danang] as are General Westmoreland and his principal military colleagues. Except for chronic shortage of GVN [Government of South Vietnam] forces in I Corps area, we would be inclined to urge GVN to allocate several additional battalions to the Danang area. But we know that such forces could not be made available except at prohibitive cost to the security of other areas of SVN. For these reasons we are driven to consider a solution which we have always rejected in the past, the introduction of US ground combat forces to reinforce the defense of Danang until GVN forces become available for the purpose.[7]

On March 8 two Marine battalions landed at Danang with full media coverage. Neither the Joint Chiefs nor Westmoreland informed Taylor that the landings were imminent, and the ambassador was not pleased. In Westmoreland's recollection:

> He was visibly piqued, his upset accentuated because the marines had arrived with tanks, self-propelled artillery, and other heavy equipment he had not expected. "Do you know my terms of reference," Ambassador Taylor demanded sharply, "and that I have authority over you?" "I understand fully," I replied, "and I

appreciate it completely, Mr. Ambassador." That ended the matter.[8]

Taylor would later write: "It was curious how hard it had been to get authority for the initiation of the air attack against the North and how relatively easy to get the Marines ashore. Yet I thought the latter a much more difficult decision and concurred in it reluctantly."[9]

At the end of March, Taylor returned to Washington for consultations. If the war had been controversial in the final months of the Kennedy administration it was even more so now, and the Johnson administration was increasingly polarized. No stalemated war is ever popular, and when a war is unpopular there is a search for scapegoats. At the end of January, Taylor had received a handwritten letter from Bobby Kennedy, in which Bobby, now a senator from New York, noted that "the news from Viet Nam does not seem to be improving." He went on:

> What concerns me however is not merely that fact, but that I detect at least an effort on behalf of at least some important segments of the administration to place the blame on you. I notice it in the newspapers and I detect it in other ways. . . .
>
> And I don't think there is anyone back here who defends you or who speaks up on your behalf.[10]

It was not in Taylor's nature to seek out these anonymous critics, but Kennedy's letter was a reminder that the ambassador had no institutional base. The Joint Chiefs were no happier with Taylor as a dispenser of military advice from Saigon than they had been with him as milrep; State Department professionals were inclined to sniff at any soldier in a diplomatic role; and the CIA was on a tighter leash in Saigon than it had ever been under Lodge.

The result was a campaign of uncertain paternity to bring Taylor home. McGeorge Bundy summarized for the President a marathon evening meeting on March 5 at which he, Rusk, and McNamara considered various aspects of the situation in Vietnam. Part of Bundy's memo dealt with the leadership of the Saigon mission:

> McNamara and I, if the decision were ours to make, would bring Taylor back and put Alex Johnson in charge, with a

younger man (conceivably John McNaughton) as Chief of Staff. Rusk, McNamara, and I have all learned from separate channels that within the country team it is in fact Alexis who is looked to for leadership and for coordination. Max has been gallant, determined, and honorable to a fault, but he has also been rigid, remote and sometimes abrupt. We all recognize that Taylor has served an enormously important purpose in keeping American opinion from division and criticism, but our inclination would be to bring him back not later than the first of June for a final round of consultation and discussion, and release [him] from his duties at the end of the year for which he originally contracted.[11]*

The movement to dump Taylor is a reflection of the increasingly Byzantine atmosphere surrounding the Johnson administration, but nothing came of it for the simple reason that Taylor retained the confidence of the one person who mattered, the President of the United States.

On March 30, two days after Taylor's departure for Washington, a small sedan halted alongside the U.S. embassy, apparently with motor trouble. When the embassy's Vietnamese guards ordered the driver to move on, he and a companion across the street pulled out pistols and began firing. The car, which was filled with plastic explosives, then blew up with a roar, killing twenty-two persons— many of them in the consular section on the ground floor—and injuring nearly two hundred. It was by far the worst terrorist incident directed against Americans, but Alexis Johnson would write with pride that by noon the following day, "everyone who was not confined to a hospital had shown up for work, some bloody and disfigured but determined to carry on."[12] Although the embassy itself, rather than any single person, was the enemy target, most of

---

* Asked about this memorandum in the fall of 1987, neither Bundy nor McNamara could recall what might have prompted it. McNamara characterized Taylor's performance as ambassador as "superb at all times." Bundy commented: "My own summary opinion as I look back is that it was not the ambassador but the situation that was basically at fault. So I read my own memorandum as one more piece of tinkering with the machinery when it was the basic direction of American policy that was the problem."

the furniture in Taylor's office was lacerated by flying glass, and he might well have been injured had he not been out of town.

In Washington, meanwhile, Taylor found his wife settling into an apartment on Massachusetts Avenue; she had been evacuated from Saigon with the other American dependents in February. She was her resilient self, but the two were not without personal problems. His mother, who lived alone in an apartment in Arlington, could not understand why her only son had to spend his time halfway around the world. The entire family was concerned over the health of Mrs. Taylor's only sister, who had been diagnosed as having stomach cancer but whose religion had led her to decline medical treatment.†

In his official calls, Taylor found a tremendous impetus both for accelerated bombing of the North and for the deployment of additional U.S. ground forces. The Joint Chiefs had recommended deploying two U.S. divisions and one South Korean division for offensive operations in Vietnam. Taylor argued that there was no need for these reinforcements and that the Quat government was not eager for a large American buildup. The result was a compromise in which Taylor concurred: the United States would send in two additional Marine battalions, an air squadron, and about 20,000 support troops; but the JCS proposal for the deployment of three army divisions would be put on hold.

Taylor left for Saigon with an understanding that only the Marines were in the pipeline. Even as he was in the air, however, Westmoreland was reiterating his need for reinforcements, and the Joint Chiefs were advising the President that the Vietnamese Army was deteriorating too fast to permit any delay in the dispatch of additional forces. Two U.S. divisions were dispatched as originally contemplated, prompting a protest from Taylor. On April 14 he cabled Rusk:

Recent actions relating to the introduction of US ground forces have tended to create an impression of eagerness in some quar-

---

† A few weeks later Mary Happer would be dead, killed in a Christian Science home by a close friend who then turned the gun on herself. It fell to me to inform my father, who was back in Saigon, by telephone. Grief-stricken, he called in Bob Blackwell to give him the news, lamenting that he never seemed to be around when his wife needed him.

ters to deploy forces into SVN which I find difficult to understand. I should think that for both military and political reasons we should all be most reluctant to tie down Army/Marine units in this country and would do so only after presentation of the most convincing evidence of the necessity.[13]

Informing the President of Taylor's complaint, McGeorge Bundy told Johnson, "I am sure we can turn him around if we give him just a little time to come aboard."[14]

Taylor returned to Saigon to a spirited debate over how best to employ the Marines around Danang and the new U.S. forces in the pipeline. Should they be used in a defensive role, one that would minimize casualties, or should they be used in a mobile, offensive mode? Taylor leaned toward the former, for he was concerned about the effect on the South Vietnamese if Americans were to take over the brunt of the fighting. Not that the soldier-diplomat advocated an entirely defensive role: he favored allowing limited offensive operations in the immediate area of the American enclaves. But Taylor's views on tactics would be overruled, as would be his opposition to the Americanization of the ground war. Westmoreland's persistent requests for authority to "take the war to the enemy" soon gained approval in Washington.

At a meeting of the Administration's security advisers in Honolulu in April, a major objective was to "get Taylor on board" with respect to U.S. troop deployments. There, the ambassador insisted that what was needed was progress on four fronts: in the war on the ground, which would determine whether the economy could function or not; in the process of nation building, which was moving so haltingly; in the development of South Vietnam's economy; and, finally, in the bombing program, which held out some hope of curbing infiltration from the North.

No one appears to have challenged this analysis, but the focus was on the introduction of U.S. combat forces. Whereas Taylor sought an acceleration in the bombing campaign, the consensus was that the tempo of the bombing was "about right." The meeting revealed a strong consensus in favor of increasing U.S. forces by nine U.S. battalions, deployment of which would bring total strength in Vietnam to about 82,000. Taylor acquiesced reluc-

tantly, and on his return to Saigon found that Quat shared his
misgivings. The ambassador volunteered nothing about policy differences in the U.S. camp, but the South Vietnamese were not
fooled. In the recollection of Bui Diem, Quat's chief of staff, the
Prime Minister "knew that Taylor had been unenthusiastic about
the first deployment, and now the ambassador was presenting him
with something far more ominous."[15] But Taylor reminded Quat
of South Vietnam's continuing manpower problems and emphasized the limited nature of the proposed deployments. After consulting with his generals, Quat "requested" the nine combat battalions being offered by the United States.

The Joint Chiefs were elated, but as time went on Taylor's misgivings would be fully justified:

> [In theory] the South Vietnamese would find and fix the enemy
> and then we would come in and join them to destroy the enemy.
> Well, that . . . made all the sense in the world except that it
> didn't work. The South Vietnamese weren't up to that. . . .
> They couldn't find and fix, and very soon, without anyone mak-
> ing a definite decision, we were sending American troops out to
> find and fix and destroy virtually on their own. . . . Our
> replacements came in, our new officers full of vim and enthusi-
> asm. They didn't want to sit back there waiting in enclaves until
> the slow South Vietnamese, as they viewed the South Vietnam-
> ese, gradually, tentatively, and timidly rounded up a target for
> them to strike.[16]

Meanwhile, the Quat government appeared to be taking hold.
The Prime Minister had succeeded in persuading the Armed
Forces Council to dissolve itself, an act that made it more difficult
for the Army to bring political pressure on the government. He
sponsored municipal and provincial elections in which, despite
Communist harassment, some 70 percent of eligible voters participated. Both Taylor and Alexis Johnson viewed Quat as the ablest
of the civilian premiers with whom they dealt, and regretted the
circumstances that led to his downfall. Under some prodding
from the American embassy to get rid of two incompetent ministers, Quat triggered a confrontation with President Suu over the
right of the Premier to appoint and dismiss cabinet ministers. By

June, Quat was out. The normally quiescent Suu then surprised everyone by returning power to the military, in the form of a ten-man National Leadership Council.

The new government was headed by General Nguyen Van Thieu as President and a flamboyant Air Force officer, General Nguyen Cao Ky, as Premier. This would be the fifth and last government with which Taylor would deal as American ambassador, and his first impressions were not favorable. "I am disturbed by the selection of General Ky as Prime Minister," he cabled President Johnson. "While he is a well-motivated, courageous, and patriotic officer who has matured considerably over the past two years, he is completely without the background and experience necessary for an assignment as difficult as this one."[17]

Although Taylor wanted the United States to stay the course in Vietnam, he pulled no punches in his assessments from Saigon. On June 3, after two months of intermittent bombing of the North, Taylor concluded that no amount of bombing would, by itself, lead Hanoi to abandon its insurgency in the South:

> Such a change in DRV attitudes can probably be brought about only when, along with a sense of mounting pain from the bombings, there is also a conviction on their part that the tide has turned or soon will turn against them in the South. Obviously these two conditions have not been met and our job in the coming months will be to bring them about. This may take a long time and we should not expect quick results. . . . This does not mean that we must "win" in the South to bring about a change in DRV attitudes, but rather [that] the DRV must perceive that the tide has turned or is likely to turn.[18]

Because of his appreciation of the fragile situation in South Vietnam, Taylor took a dim view of the flurry of diplomatic activity that had followed the first bombing of the North. In his view, there was nothing in the situation in Vietnam that should bring Ho Chi Minh to the conference table for meaningful negotiations, and for the United States to pursue negotiations from a position of weakness conveyed the wrong message. To bring about a change in an enemy's conduct, he would write, "the sword must appear inexorable and inescapable."[19] Although he appreciated the domestic political concerns that prompted Johnson's diplomatic overtures and bombing pauses, he believed that they undermined the "gradualism" of which he himself was still an advocate.

Taylor returned to Washington yet again in June 1965, expecting only to discuss the transition to a successor following his eventful year in Saigon. Westmoreland, however, had cabled a picture of deterioration within the South Vietnamese army so sharp as to constitute a crisis; his estimate was that another 75,000 U.S. forces would be required by fall. The result was yet another full-dress council of war. Taylor opposed sending reinforcements on the scale requested by Westmoreland but conceded that an additional 8,000 U.S. troops should be sent immediately, with a South Korean division to follow. On returning to Saigon for the last time, however, he found the situation almost as bad as Westmoreland had indicated.

The upshot was a trip to Vietnam by McNamara. Upon his return to Washington on July 20, he confirmed that the military situation was "worse than a year ago," and the economy "deteriorating." McNamara concluded:

> We must choose among three courses of action with respect to Vietnam all of which involve different probabilities, outcomes and costs:
>
> (a) Cut our losses and withdraw under the best conditions that can be arranged—almost certainly conditions humiliating the United States and very damaging to our future effectiveness on the world scene.
>
> (b) Continue at about the present level, with the U.S. forces limited to say 75,000, holding on and playing for the breaks. . . .
>
> (c) Expand promptly and substantially the U.S. military pressure against the Viet Cong in the South and maintain the military pressure against the North Vietnamese in the North while launching a vigorous effort on the political side to lay the groundwork for a favorable outcome.[20]

McNamara, with Taylor's full support, predictably came down for option (c). The media would call it "escalation."

On July 8 Washington announced that Taylor would be re-
signing as ambassador at the end of the month, in accordance
with his understanding with President Johnson, and that his successor would be Henry Cabot Lodge.‡ Taylor was not consulted in
regard to Lodge's reappointment and was not especially pleased,
but at least he, Taylor, would be going home. After a high-level
series of meetings in Saigon about troop levels for the remainder
of the year, the ambassador packed his bags. In the final months,
his personal security had become a problem. Intelligence reports
indicated that his name was at the top of the VC assassination list,
and security measures for the ambassador were increased. For the
first time since World War II he carried a weapon, in this case a
.32 caliber pistol in his briefcase. At night he slept with a shotgun
by his bed, and his driver-bodyguard was careful to vary his route
between the residence and the embassy. Nevertheless, there was
one close call. On July 20 Taylor was attending a political rally at
the Saigon stadium when police uncovered an explosive charge
just outside the exit used by diplomats. Concealed wires led to a
detonator in some nearby shrubbery. The police made four arrests
and stated that the bomb had been intended for the American
ambassador.

Early in July, Taylor had a houseguest, his son Tom. A captain
in the ambassador's old outfit, the 101st Airborne, Tom Taylor was
an advance man for a contingent of the 101st that was on its way
to Camranh Bay by sea. For two weeks, after the paratroopers'
ancient transport broke down in the Pacific, the younger Taylor
enjoyed the good life: tennis at the Circle Sportif by day, cool
drinks at the ambassador's residence at night. But briefings on
what the arriving Americans should expect tended to be discon-
certing. General John Throckmorton warned a group of new advisers, including Tom Taylor, that their foremost mission was "to

‡ On July 4 Taylor had informed McGeorge Bundy that he agreed on the desirability of Lodge's coming out to Saigon with the McNamara party, but opposed any
extended overlap with his successor. "I would not wish to stay on for month as
'lame duck' ambassador and would like to depart Saigon shortly after departure of
visiting group." Saigon Embtel 38, July 4, 1965, National Security File, "Deployment of U.S. Forces to Vietnam," LBJ Library.

save their own asses." Those who were attached to ARNV units should be prepared to find their Vietnamese commanders "cowardly, corrupt and mendacious"; at the first premonition of disaster, U.S. advisers were to get on the radio and request evacuation.

After his fortnight in Saigon, Tom Taylor traded the ambassador's residence for a tent in the jungle, where in the year that followed he would pick up both a wound and a Silver Star. But among his memorable recollections would be the arrival of the 101st at Camranh Bay. "The troops came ashore ready to fight," he recalled, "but they were met by Vietnamese hawking Coke and other pauses that refresh. The Vietnamese knew only one denomination of U.S. currency, the 'dollah,' so that was what everything cost. Coke, straw hats, companionship—all one dollah."[21]

No assignment in Taylor's varied career would prove more controversial than his year as American ambassador in Saigon. To be sure, even his critics would concede that much of the political turbulence was beyond his or any envoy's capacity to control. But he was intimately involved with two key decisions relative to the growing American involvement in Vietnam, the initiation of U.S. bombing and the introduction of American combat troops.

By any reasonable standard, Taylor earned solid marks as head of the U.S. mission. Alexis Johnson described him as "an excellent ambassador, intelligent, savvy, and forceful both in Saigon and Washington, with a deft touch for bureaucratic maneuvering and embassy management."[22] In sharp contrast to his predecessor, Taylor worked closely with the different elements of the mission and made himself accessible to his staff. Although his confrontation with Khanh's lieutenants was hardly orthodox diplomacy, the ambassador's critics have suggested no more promising tactic for bringing the junta to its senses.

If one considers the type of government Taylor was attempting to generate for the South Vietnamese, it is interesting that, even in wartime, he was working toward something more than a facade of civilian government. He was insistent that the generals come up with a government worthy of the sacrifices being made by both their own people and the Americans. Frances FitzGerald, no admirer of U.S. policy toward Vietnam, notes that "previously [Taylor] had never cared much for GVN politics, but on becoming ambassador he was to place more importance on the creation of representative bodies and the establishment of civilian rule than either McNamara or Cabot Lodge."[23]

It is also worth recalling that Taylor, in addition to his strategic and political responsibilities, supervised the massive nonmilitary programs administered by the U.S. mission. During Taylor's brief tenure the Agency for International Development equipped a medical school and built hospitals. It helped establish a school for public administration and provided communications equipment for remote villages. It rebuilt roads, schools, and homes that had been destroyed by the Communists, and it cared for tens of thousands of Vietnamese refugees. In some economic sectors, the 1964–65 period was one of considerable progress. Inevitably, however, progress in areas such as land reform and education was overshadowed by the political vacuum in Saigon and by setbacks in the guerrilla war.

In later years family members and close friends would ask Taylor why, given the political anarchy he was obliged to deal with in Saigon, he did not recommend that the United States pack up and go home. Washington had, after all, acted in good faith to "save" a country that seemed incapable of helping itself. He addressed this question squarely in his memoirs:

> In response to this valid question, I must in honesty reply that it never occurred to me to recommend withdrawal. There were too many good reasons for not thinking about retreat. In the first place, we had not exhausted our alternatives or made inroads into our vast resources. We could still try a number of things which might supply the new ingredient we were seeking to reverse the adverse trend. There were many ways in which we might make use of American air and ground forces in North Vietnam, in South Vietnam, or in the cross-border sanctuaries. We could use our Navy to blockade the enemy coasts. . . .
>
> Furthermore, we had every reason to keep up the American will to persist in Saigon following the expression of national determination after the Tonkin Gulf affair.[24]

Few will question that in 1965 the United States still had a number of yet-untried military options. Yet Taylor's suggestion that Congress was leading the charge in America's deepening involvement in Vietnam was a bit disingenuous; passage of the Tonkin Gulf resolution had, in fact, required considerable arm twisting by the Administration. The unfortunate fact was that Taylor and his colleagues were unwilling to face the possibility of defeat by a third-rate power. By 1965 they wanted to win the war more than the South Vietnamese did.

Their logic has been held up to ridicule in some quarters, but it is by no means indefensible. As far as Taylor was concerned, much more was at stake than Vietnam itself. At issue was a new form of aggression by proxy, the "war of national liberation." The belief that such wars were the most immediate Communist threat to Western interests was not simply a manifestation of paranoia on the part of Johnson and his advisers. Khrushchev, in January 1961, had characterized such wars as "not only admissible but inevitable"; he also had cited the insurgencies in Algeria and Vietnam specifically as enjoying full Soviet support. General Giap, the commander of the North Vietnamese army, had raised the rhetorical stakes even higher, remarking that "South Vietnam is the model of the national liberation movement of our time. If the special warfare that the United States imperialists are testing in South Vietnam is overcome, then it can be defeated anywhere in the world."[25]

In terms of Washington's prosecution of the war, Taylor would summarize his position with the observation that he was a hawk on bombing but a dove on U.S. troops. He sought to make Hanoi pay a price for its infiltration of the South, and as the war continued, bombing would prove to be the one weapon in the U.S. arsenal that would command Hanoi's full attention. At the same time, he fought a rearguard action against Americanization of the war for as long as it appeared feasible to do so. When voted down, as he was on the April 1965 troop deployments, he supported the decisions that had been reached just as he had supported those arrived at during the Cuban missile crisis. But it was a handicap for Taylor to be outside the military chain of command and halfway around the world from Washington. In McGeorge Bundy's opinion, Taylor's presence in Saigon "meant that there was no senior person in Washington to tell LBJ that we don't want to turn this into a war between Americans and Vietnamese."[26]

Although Taylor pulled no punches in reporting on the political disintegration in Saigon, he could be faulted for overlooking some danger signals with regard to enemy intentions. Already there were signs that Hanoi was prepared to outwait the United States. Militarily, the North Vietnamese had shown themselves capable of compensating with their own manpower for increases in U.S. and South Vietnamese military capabilities. The United States was fighting not just the Viet Cong, but a portion of the world's fourth-largest army.

As a soldier, Taylor knew that his country as yet had employed only a fraction of the means at its disposal against North Vietnam, and he assumed that the enemy also was aware of this. He viewed the shortcomings of the U.S. military effort as transitory and correctable; this perspective tended to obscure the vast gap in motivation between the Americans and their allies on the one hand, and the determined Communists on the other. But Taylor's normally keen sense of what constituted a vital interest for his country seems somehow to have been on hold in this period. It was almost as though the global strategist had given way to an Old Testament prophet, determined to smite the wicked in a very small place. At a time when the proper word from Maxwell Taylor might have led President Johnson to review the nature of the U.S. commitment to South Vietnam, Taylor acquiesced in a war of attrition against a determined foe who did not have to concern itself with popular opinion. He was a victim of the mirror-image trap: because, had he been in North Vietnam's Politburo, he would have reached an accommodation to end the bombing, Taylor assumed that Ho Chi Minh would do so also. For Taylor the question was the same as it had been in 1961: how to change a losing game, not how to call the game off.

Part Four

THE MANDARIN

We soldiers, sailors, and airmen regard a military mind as something to be sought and developed—an indispensable professional asset which can only be acquired after years of training in reflecting and acting on military and related problems.

—*Maxwell D. Taylor, 1964*

Chapter 24

WAR ON THE HOME FRONT

Taylor returned from Saigon in early August. His immediate plans did not go beyond resuming his position on a few boards. But when President Johnson asked him to stay on as a special consultant he was far more amenable than he had been to his posting abroad. Meeting with the President, Taylor agreed to devote about half of his time to the new job, an arrangement that led him to remark later that "he got the daylight hours and I got the hours of darkness."[1] He also agreed to undertake some speaking engagements on the subject of Vietnam.

One of his first outings, while still on the State Department payroll, was to the Commonwealth Club in San Francisco, and the near-riot that attended his appearance there was something of a milestone in the antiwar movement. I was then a midlevel officer in the State Department, and because senior ambassadors were entitled to a horse-holder on excursions such as this, the choice quite naturally fell on me. We were met at the San Francisco airport on an overcast autumn day by Commonwealth Club representatives, who looked vaguely uneasy as they informed us that they had been warned by police to expect some demonstrators at the luncheon. The warning was well founded. At the fringe of many political movements one finds groups whose primary motivation is to find outlets for their own venom; our limousine had scarcely turned into the driveway at the Fairmont Hotel when we were surrounded by several hundred demonstrators, who spat, shouted obscenities, and climbed over the car, all the while waving placards that bore an unflattering likeness of America's erstwhile ambassador to Vietnam. The hotel manager, accompanied by a couple of bodyguards, managed to spirit the guest speaker through the lobby, which was also filled with jostling demonstrators, to his own mezzanine office. Taylor dismissed the demonstrators from his mind and delivered his talk in the dining room, over considerable background noise from outside. San Francisco was Taylor's first exposure to the excesses of the antiwar movement, but it would not be his last.

Back in Washington, the ex-ambassador returned to work as consultant in the same office—Room 300—in the Executive Office Building that he had occupied as milrep. His staff was considerably smaller, however, consisting as it did of two secretaries and an Army officer who rotated every year. His mandate from President Johnson was a broad one, directing first that he keep abreast of the situation in Vietnam, but asking in addition that Taylor review all government activities in the counterinsurgency area.

The counterinsurgency review cited in the President's letter was to occupy Taylor for the next six months. Taylor had returned from Saigon convinced that there was a need for more effective coordination among the many agencies with overseas responsibilities. As ambassador, he had been inundated with proposals for programs for Vietnam; yet these had never been reviewed in Washington with an eye to what was feasible for a small country facing a large number of problems. Taking as their model the ambassador's role as head of the mission council in Saigon, Taylor and Alex Johnson set about making the State Department the President's "executive agent" in directing all overseas activities. President Johnson approved the restructuring in March 1966 and implemented its provisions in a National Security Administrative Memorandum (NSAM) that read in part as follows:

> To assist the President in carrying out his responsibilities for the conduct of foreign affairs, he has assigned to the Secretary of State authority and responsibility to the full extent permitted by law for the overall direction, coordination and supervision of interdepartmental activities of the United States Government overseas.[2]

To implement the NSAM in Washington required a number of new committees, topped by a Senior Interdepartmental Group (SIG), chaired by the Under Secretary of State. All except the most cosmic policy matters were to be dealt with in this new framework.

The NSAM may have been workable, but in practice it foundered on personalities. Under Secretary of State George Ball was not interested in the new arrangement and, in any case, was about to leave the government. Heavyweights like McNamara took their problems, cosmic or otherwise, directly to the White House. Secretary of State Rusk did not seize on opportunities to exercise his new authority. In its three years of operation the SIG dealt with "such third-order problems as the size of the U.S. military-aid program to the Congo [and] the question of Export-Import Bank credits for a harbor improvement project on the island of Antigua."[3] Its performance fell short of assuring its survival into the Nixon administration, which in any case intended to transfer power to the White House to the maximum extent feasible. Taylor would write, "The leaders of the State Department had missed a great opportunity in failing to exploit the grant of authority given them by President Johnson and had vindicated those who had warned me that State would never rise to the challenge."[4]

Meanwhile, Taylor found himself in a seemingly endless round of conferences aimed at improving the conduct of the war in Vietnam. Although still a "gradualist," he thought the bombing campaign was proceeding too slowly and too fitfully. By 1966 he supported attacks on all targets of value to the enemy outside the main populated areas and so wrote to President Johnson in March:

> My own conclusion is that the time has now come to raise significantly the level of pressure on North Viet-Nam by attacking POL stocks, interdicting effectively the two railways linking Hanoi with China, and mining Haiphong and the two secondary ports in the area. In the eyes of the Hanoi leaders, the ground war in South Viet-Nam must now appear to be going rather badly and it is important that they receive an equally discouraging impression from the air war.[5]

The latter half of 1965 had seen a rapid expansion of the American presence in Vietnam, with U.S. combat forces reaching about 150,000 in late October. Nevertheless, in a Gallup Poll taken in the fall of 1965, 64 percent of the respondents supported greater

American involvement. A few months later, in early 1966, 61 percent of those polled favored escalation if the latest bombing pause failed to bring a response from Hanoi.[6] Although popular protests were still the exception—there was as yet no draft—the number of critics in Congress was growing, motivated in part by genuine concern over the situation in Southeast Asia and in part by a desire to challenge presidential primacy in the formulation of foreign policy.

Much of Taylor's time was spent on the lecture circuit. He would later estimate that he delivered more than 140 speeches, most of them paid lectures, on the subject of Vietnam. Some of his audiences were professional groups—my favorite was the American Poultry and Hatchery Association—but many of his presentations were at educational institutions, where the reception was occasionally unfriendly. In October 1965 he was scheduled to speak at Foothill College in Los Altos, California. Well before the 8 P.M. starting time the entrance was filled with picketers, and other protesters had been admitted to the hall without tickets. The latter sought to drown out Taylor's opening remarks, whereupon the moderator, a Professor Roth, turned the rostrum over to the protesters, one of whom denounced the speaker and was in turn heckled by the audience. The result was a melee; an Associated Press photograph showed Taylor being escorted from the hall after having been splattered with red paint. The acting president of Foothill wrote an apology, noting helpfully that the paint had been judged to be water soluble but offering reimbursement for any damages. Taylor replied graciously, "I am sure that the action of the intruders was more embarrassing to you than to me."[7]

Early in 1966 U.S. strategy in Vietnam came in for criticism from the political center, criticism that reflected a growing dissatisfaction with the pace of visible progress. General Jim Gavin, Taylor's onetime colleague, argued in *Harper's* in favor of a strategy for Vietnam that would limit U.S. involvement to the protection of a few key bases such as Camranh Bay and Danang. "If we should maintain enclaves on the coast," Gavin wrote, "desist in our bombing attacks in North Vietnam, and seek to find a solution through the United Nations or a conference in Geneva, we could very likely do so with the forces now available."[8]

Under different circumstances Taylor himself had once been associated with an "enclave" strategy. When the first U.S. ground forces had arrived in Vietnam, he had sought to limit their combat to a fifty-mile radius, lest the ground war be totally Americanized. But his assumption then was that the South Vietnamese would be carrying out offensive operations on the ground and that U.S. bombing would bring the war to the North Vietnamese. Gavin, in contrast, was advocating a defensive strategy reminiscent of that once favored by the French. Johnson asked Taylor to respond to Gavin, which he did in a speech in New York City:

> Several critics of our current strategy in South Vietnam have come out in support of a "holding strategy," calling for a permanent cessation of the bombing of targets in North Vietnam, a halt to further U.S. reinforcements, a withdrawal of U.S. ground forces to enclaves along the coast, and a renewal of efforts to find a peaceful solution in the United Nations or at Geneva.

Taylor went on to note that advocates of such a strategy believed that it would allow the United States to reduce its exposure in Vietnam and that it would reduce the danger of an expanded war involving China. Taylor believed that the danger of Chinese involvement was slight and that the consequences of an enclave strategy would be serious:

> Among other things, [such a strategy] would result in the abandonment of many of the Vietnamese people whom we have promised to defend, except those lucky enough to live within the range of the guns of our coastal enclaves. The effect of such a retreat on the morale of our proud United States forces . . . and on the attitude of our South Vietnamese allies . . . would be disastrous. Whether any Vietnamese government could survive such conduct by its American ally or, if it survived, whether it would resist the urge to seek an accommodation with the Viet Cong while time remained, is hard to predict.[9]

Even today, there appears to have been no clear winner in this exchange. One suspects that U.S. forces would have adapted readily to a more limited military mission, and it is likely that the resulting reduction of U.S. casualties would have slowed the growth of the antiwar movement in the United States. Whether the time thus gained would have been put to good use by the South Vietnamese is a very different matter.

While in Saigon, Taylor had been a rather remote figure to most of the American public. He was perceived only vaguely as one of the Kennedy set who had stayed on with Johnson and who supported the war in Vietnam. He was shortly to gain considerably more visibility, not through any of his lectures but as a result of growing hostility in the Senate to the American involvement in Vietnam. William Fulbright, the chairman of the Senate Foreign Relations Committee, had broken with the Administration on the Vietnam issue, and in February 1966 he launched a series of televised hearings to publicize his case.

Taylor was one of the principal administration witnesses, and his testimony occupied most of the day on February 17. He had prepared his testimony with care, clearing his prepared statement with the President. He began with an assessment of Communist objectives ("The purpose of the Hanoi camp is perfectly clear and has been since 1954. It is to absorb the 15 million people of South Vietnam into a single Communist state.") He saw the primary American purpose as equally clear, quoting from the President's speech of April 7, 1965, at Johns Hopkins University: "Our objective is the independence of South Vietnam and its freedom from attack."

But Taylor conceded that the United States, like its adversaries, had secondary objectives as well, noting that "we intend to show that the 'war of liberation,' far from being cheap, safe and disavowable, is costly, dangerous and doomed to failure." He went on to discuss, and then to summarize, the four-point program that the United States was pursuing in Vietnam:

In summary then, our four-point strategy consists of a complex but coherent package of measures designed to improve the effectiveness of our forces on the ground in South Vietnam, to exploit our air superiority by attacking military targets in North

Vietnam, to stabilize the political, social and economic systems in South Vietnam and to seek an honorable negotiated settlement of the conflict. It is limited as to objective, as to geographical scope, as to weapons and forces employed, and as to targets attacked. All parts of it are interrelated; all parts are indispensable; we must be successful on all fronts.[10]*

The Foreign Relations Committee contained a disproportionate number of critics of the war, including Wayne Morse of Oregon, Frank Church of Idaho, and Eugene McCarthy of Minnesota, in addition to Fulbright himself, and the grilling that Taylor received on February 17 was as thorough as any that he would experience. It began innocuously with a question from a moderate, Senator John Sparkman of Alabama. Would the general care to address the charge that we were interfering in what was essentially a civil war in Vietnam? Taylor responded that there was an internationally recognized demarcation line in Vietnam: the two halves of the country had been administered as separate entities since 1954. His next questioner was the acerbic Morse:

> MORSE: You know we are engaged in historic debate in this country, where there are honest differences of opinion. I happen to hold to the point of view that it isn't going to be long before the American people as a people will repudiate our war in Southeast Asia.
>
> TAYLOR: That, of course, is good news to Hanoi, Senator.
>
> MORSE: I know that that is the smear that you militarists give to those of us who have honest differences of opinion with you, but I don't intend to get down in the gutter with you and engage in that kind of debate. . . . All I am asking is, if the people decide that this war should be stopped . . . are you going to take the position that that is weakness on the home front in a democracy?
>
> TAYLOR: I would feel that our people were badly misguided and did not understand the consequences of such a disaster.
>
> MORSE: Well, we agree on one thing, that they can be badly

---

* The full text of this major exposition of Taylor's views is included as Appendix C.

misguided, and you and the President, in my judgment, have been misguiding them for a long time in this war.[11]

One line of questioning not limited to dovish senators concerned the possibility that the war in Vietnam might lead to war with China. Taylor emphasized that the limited U.S. objectives relative to Vietnam should not appear threatening to China; but he emphasized that for the United States to allow itself to be intimidated by China would require "complete supineness on the part of our foreign policy in the Far East."[12] Morse, however, preferred to believe that the Administration was courting war with both the Soviet Union and China:

MORSE: Do you think there are a considerable number of Russians in Hanoi?

TAYLOR: I doubt there are any great number. Undoubtedly there are some technicians there in connection with the surface-to-air missiles.

MORSE: Do you think if we should mine or blockade or bomb the harbor outside of Hanoi, we would increase the danger of Russia coming into the war?

TAYLOR: No, sir.

MORSE: . . . I judge from your statements that you are not very much concerned about either Russia or China coming into this war.

TAYLOR: Under the present circumstances, that is correct.[13]

Taylor had anticipated severe questioning about the revolving-door governments he had dealt with in Saigon, and he was not disappointed. Church raised the key issue of popular support for the Saigon Government:

CHURCH: Do you think the Ky regime enjoys widespread support from the people in the countryside?

TAYLOR: No, sir.

CHURCH: You think he does not.

TAYLOR: Let me qualify [my reply] because that sounds, perhaps, misleading. I made the statement this morning, the government in Saigon is rarely known to the peasantry; there have been so many Saigon governments since the fall of Diem, I am quite sure that many of the peasants have never heard of the present leaders in Saigon. On the other hand, they are . . . completely committed to anti-Communism, and they know that government forces, whether they know the leaders or not, represent safety and security. In that sense they are committed to the government.[14]

As the day drew near its close, Fulbright himself sought to portray the American military role in Vietnam as one of indiscriminate targeting of civilians, and U.S. methods as virtually indistinguishable from those of the enemy.

> FULBRIGHT: I don't see any great distinction between using the weapons that we happen to have and others don't, to kill innocent people, to burn them slowly, whether they be babies or brothers or fathers or uncles, and disemboweling with a knife because a knife is all you have got. . . .
>
> TAYLOR: But we are not deliberately attacking civilian populations in South Vietnam. On the contrary, we are making every effort to avoid their loss. . . .
>
> FULBRIGHT: It is not by accident that we are [employing weapons such as napalm]. . . . People use what they have at their command.
>
> TAYLOR: I would just say that the observation does not apply to what we are trying to do in South Vietnam because this is not an unlimited war. This is, as I have often said, a limited war, with a limited objective, one of the objectives being to try to protect the civilian population which we are trying to rescue and not destroy.[15]

Taylor's final tiff with the chairman concerned the role of public opinion in a democracy.

> FULBRIGHT: [In your prepared statement] you say, "They have not forgotten that the Vietminh won more in Paris than in Dien Bien Phu and believe that the Viet Cong may be as fortunate in Washington." What did they win more in Paris than in Dien Bien Phu?
>
> TAYLOR: It was the weakening will to continue the conflict which had been growing over the months and years and the fact

that the home front and political front had reached the conclusion that the struggle was hopeless, and hence they must end it very rapidly.

FULBRIGHT: You don't consider Dien Bien Phu a decisive battle?

TAYLOR: It was in a sense; it tilted the scale of decision, but actually the French had strong military forces which were not involved at Dien Bien Phu at all and could have continued the conflict.[16]

For one who recognized, as he did, the necessity for national unity on the subject of Vietnam, Taylor found his day on Capitol Hill an ordeal. That evening, even as the phone rang with messages of congratulations on his testimony, an angry Taylor was characterizing the Fulbright committee as "the worst" on the Hill. He viewed its chairman as "close to treason" for using his position to send a message of comfort to the very leaders in Hanoi whose behavior the United States sought to change. He had no special insight into what motivated the senator from Arkansas, but speculated that Fulbright was frustrated over Johnson's failure to give him Rusk's job at State.

A few days later Taylor mentioned that he, Rusk, and McGeorge Bundy had spent some three hours with the President discussing Vietnam. He quoted Johnson as philosophizing on the fact that the troublemakers in the Senate—persons such as Frank Church and George McGovern—tended to be from the Midwest, where the tradition of political mavericks like George Norris and Robert La Follette ran deep. Morse, Johnson had said, doubtless considered himself in this tradition.

One of the little coincidences of Washington living was that the Taylors' apartment at 4000 Massachusetts Avenue was on the same hall as that of Senator Morse. From time to time each would open his door to pick up the morning paper, find his neighbor similarly engaged, nod briskly, and retreat into his own domain.

The early months of 1966 were busy ones for Taylor. His appearance before the Fulbright committee had generated an immense amount of correspondence at a time when he was getting ready for yet another move. From New York City, Richard Nixon wrote to congratulate Taylor for his handling of "the barbs of Wayne Morse and his colleagues."[17] From the White House came an effusive note from Bill Moyers, "The President was very proud of you, and less importantly, so were all of us who believe we must carry forward the pursuit of our policy in Southeast Asia."[18]

Somehow the Taylors found time to move from their apartment to an attractive corner town house in Chevy Chase near Connecticut Avenue. The fact that it was on two floors eventually became a liability, for Taylor had developed some arthritis in his knees. But it was convenient to downtown, and the quiet neighborhood offered scope for the general's daily walks. His neighbors commented knowingly that the Taylors' elaborate TV antenna permitted the general to communicate directly with Saigon.

In June 1966 Taylor took on another part-time job. The Institute for Defense Analysis (IDA) was a Defense Department think tank that had been established in 1956. It was one of seven federally funded defense research organizations, but unlike most of the others it was not tied to a single service but to the Joint Chiefs. It was technically oriented, employing consultants from leading universities to evaluate proposed weapons and other high-tech systems. Taylor pointed out that he had a continuing commitment to the White House, but the IDA trustees offered him the presidency on a part-time basis. He eventually served as president of IDA for about three years.

While administration hawks defended LBJ's Vietnam policy, the Thieu-Ky government in Saigon lurched along, faring somewhat better against the Viet Cong but coming under political pressure from the same Buddhist activists who had played so large a role in the overthrow of Diem and Huong. The Buddhist Institute, whose popular support was a barometer of war weariness in the South, sponsored demonstrations, hunger strikes, and even immolations in urban areas, sometimes tipping off Western media representatives in advance. The U.S. bombing continued. According to Pentagon statistics, during 1966 the United States mounted 7,000 missions against roads, 5,000 against vehicles, and more than 1,000 against railroad yards, hitting some targets several times.[19] Although the North Vietnamese would later acknowledge their fear of U.S. air power, it was difficult to demonstrate at the time that it had any real impact on the level of infiltration. Meanwhile, U.S. ground strength rose to about 385,000.

In June, Taylor was present at an NSC meeting at which the Joint Chiefs urged bombing attacks on oil installations in North Vietnam. Notes taken at the meeting reflect the frustration generated by a policy that "ought" to be producing results but was not, and they show a weary, dispirited President:

> THE PRESIDENT: Suppose your dreams are fulfilled. What are the results?
>
> GENERAL WHEELER: Over the next 60 to 90 days, this [bombing] will start to affect the total infiltration effort. . . .
>
> THE PRESIDENT: People tell me what not to do, what I do wrong. I don't get any alternatives. What might I be asked next? Destroy industry, disregard human life? Suppose I say no, what else would you recommend?
>
> GENERAL WHEELER: Mining Haiphong.
>
> THE PRESIDENT: Do you think this will involve the Chinese Communists and the Soviets?
>
> GENERAL WHEELER: No, sir.
>
> THE PRESIDENT: Are you more sure than MacArthur was?
>
> GENERAL WHEELER: This is different. We had ground forces moving to the Yalu. . . .
>
> THE PRESIDENT: Would General Taylor give me his views.
>
> GENERAL TAYLOR: I am optimistic. I think we have to press hard on all fronts—economic, political, military and diplomatic. I see a movement upward all the way. Personally, I would bomb Haiphong at the same time and get the political flak over with.[20]

Taylor continued to participate in the President's Tuesday lunches, a status symbol in the capital but a chore that Taylor, with his hearing impairment, found onerous. Because he believed that the Administration's existing programs, if vigorously implemented, would create a climate for negotiations, he was wary of Johnson's constant search for diplomatic approaches. In March 1967 he accompanied the President to a meeting on Guam with Thieu and Ky, who used the occasion to present Johnson with a copy of South Vietnam's new constitution. Taylor found the trip for the most part unproductive:

I got back to Washington just in time to pack my bags for the whirlwind trip to Guam. You have read in the newspapers, no doubt, about its accomplishments or lack thereof. Personally, I thought it was an awfully long ride to take to see old associates repeating the same stories I had heard either in Washington or in Saigon.

In any event, it was an interesting exercise in U.S. press attitudes. The press had in pre-conference speculation inflated this meeting into something extraordinary in spite of the fact that all officials were saying that it was just a routine get-together. When, in fact, it turned out to be just that, the press compared the obvious lack of corresponding results with their own inflated version of what they expected to happen. Hence, in their books the conference was a complete flop.[21]

In April, in a move probably aimed at dealing with dissent on the home front, Johnson brought Westmoreland home from Vietnam for a series of public appearances. Johnson was by then concerned not only with doves on the Hill but also with reappraisals within his own official family. McNamara was urging that the air war against the North be "stabilized," contending that larger raids would not deter the enemy but would pose the risk "of drawing us into open war with China." He suggested limiting U.S. troop commitments to fewer than five hundred thousand and urged that tough measures be undertaken to get the Saigon Government to improve its performance. Finally, he was considering offering the Communists a total bombing halt in return for negotiations. His thinking was far different from that of Taylor, who had serious doubts about the message conveyed by bombing pauses and who feared that the Communists would capitalize on any easing of the military pressure. He had remarked to me in 1966 that the worst thing that could happen would be for the Communists to agree to peace talks and then to immobilize the United States in Korea-style negotiations while they consolidated their hold on the South Vietnamese countryside.

Taylor may have had little insight into McNamara's misgivings or into the continuing erosion of popular support for the war. In April he wrote:

This has been an active week in official Washington, primarily because of Westy's visit to the "old country." I am sure that the President must be happy over the results. Westy handled himself very well on all public occasions and said the right things at the right times. . . . I saw Bobby today on the tennis court at Hickory Hill and observed that it was a hell of a note when it is necessary to bring a general half way around the world to make a reasonably good talk on Vietnam before Congress. I had a feeling that this observation did not go over well.[22]

In July 1967 Johnson asked Taylor and presidential adviser Clark Clifford to undertake a trip to Southeast Asia to attempt to bolster third-country support for the effort in Vietnam. At that time more than a dozen countries had some form of contingent in Vietnam, but most of these were militarily insignificant. Ultimately, Taylor and Clifford visited four capitals—Seoul, Bangkok, Canberra, and Wellington—in addition to a stop for briefings in Saigon. The trip was not a resounding success. A scheduled stop in the Philippines had to be omitted when President Marcos declined to receive the Americans.

On the sensitive subject of troop contributions, each country had reasons why more should not be expected of it. The South Koreans were worried about the North Koreans; the Thais were ostensibly concerned about their own Communist guerrillas. The Australians and New Zealanders noted that their own defense arrangements were complicated by the planned withdrawal of British forces from Malaysia and Singapore. Taylor, however, had embarked on the trip with modest expectations; in his memoirs he would note that he and Clifford probably contributed to an eventual increase in third-country contributions to about seventy thousand. He discounted the lack of enthusiasm in the region for a greater role in the Vietnam conflict, writing in August:

By and large, I think that we did as much as could be expected. We were not charged with recruiting in the direct sense that the press reported, but rather with a discussion of the conduct of the war. . . . Naturally, such a discussion included a consideration of troop requirements which we were not hesitant to present in specific terms.[23]

Clifford's reaction appears to have been quite different. Having been brought up on the domino theory, he was puzzled that Thailand, with its long border along the Mekong, had sent only 2,500 men to Vietnam. "It was strikingly apparent to me," he would write, "that the other troop-contributing countries no longer shared our degree of concern about the war in South Vietnam. General Taylor and I urged them to increase their participation. In the main, our plea fell on deaf ears."[24] If Vietnamese communism was not a threat to the region, how much of an American effort there was justified?

By autumn Robert McNamara was becoming increasingly outspoken concerning the course of the war. At one of the President's Tuesday luncheons in October, he told the President bluntly that his course of action in Vietnam was failing and proposed an alternative. In a memorandum to the President he recommended an end to the U.S. ground buildup and a bombing halt at the end of the year. According to McNamara, the bombing halt would have dual objectives:

> We would hope for a response from Hanoi, by some parallel reduction in its offensive activity, by a movement toward talks, or both. At a minimum, the lack of any response from Hanoi would demonstrate that it is North Vietnam and not the United States that is blocking a peaceful settlement.[25]

Johnson directed that McNamara's memo be circulated anonymously among certain of his advisers, and Taylor was one of those chosen to comment. In his rebuttal Taylor noted that the United States continued to face four basic alternatives in Vietnam, which he characterized as All-out, Stick-it-out, Pull-back, and Pull-out. He viewed the McNamara proposal as a variant of the pull-back alternative, and did not think much of it.

> While this course of action might tend to allay the fears of those who are concerned over an expansion of the conflict, it would provide fresh ammunition for the numerically larger number of critics who say that we are embarked on an endless and hopeless struggle or that we are really not trying to win. . . . Like

other variations of the Pull-back alternative, it would probably degenerate into an eventual pull-out.

Taylor went on to note that a bombing halt would discourage the South and to some degree would reduce the protection afforded U.S. ground forces in Vietnam. But in recommending "strongly" against McNamara's proposed course of action, Taylor's main concern was the effect it would have in Hanoi:

> Probably the most serious objection of all to this Pull-back alternative would be the effect on the enemy. Any such retreat will be interpreted as weakness and will add to the difficulty of getting any kind of eventual solution compatible with our overall objective of an independent South Vietnam free from the threat of subversive aggression.[26]

Three days later, in another memorandum for the President, Taylor elaborated on the policy options open to the opposing sides in Vietnam. In considering enemy options, he speculated on the possibility of a Communist diversion outside Vietnam, citing among several possible areas Thailand, Korea, and Berlin. But the paper is of greatest interest because in it Taylor acknowledged for perhaps the first time that the stick-it-out policy that he advocated for the United States might prove politically impractical:

> On the negative side, it is not clear that the U.S. public has the moral resources to support indefinitely this slow, seemingly indecisive strategy of gradualism which runs counter to the impatient, impetuous American temperament. This evident disinclination for a long, drawn-out test of will in concert with the noisy demonstrations of the radical minorities encourages Ho Chi Minh and his advisers to hang on . . . or to escalate.[27]

Chapter 25

1968:
THE CLIMACTIC YEAR

Late in 1967 Taylor became closely involved with an episode in the Vietnam War that continues controversial to this day, the siege of Khesanh. Khesanh was a highway town just south of the DMZ near the Laotian border, one that Westmoreland saw as having considerable military potential. He wanted a U.S. force there to harass the Ho Chi Minh Trail and eventually to launch forays against Communist sanctuaries in Laos. In the final months of 1967 Westmoreland expanded the airstrip and garrisoned the town with some six thousand U.S. Marines and a battalion of Vietnamese.

With the new year, the enemy moved in strength against Khesanh. At least two North Vietnamese divisions were identified in the vicinity, a fact that did not bother Westmoreland, who was eager to meet the enemy in remote areas where he could employ his weaponry to good advantage. The trouble was that, at least superficially, Khesanh was all too reminiscent of Dien Bien Phu, where the loss of a beleaguered French outpost had signaled the end of the First Indochina War.

Westmoreland had provided the Marines with massive fire-power, and he was confident of his ability to keep the garrison supplied indefinitely. But he had a very nervous President looking over his shoulder in Washington. In January 1968, as television news emphasized the isolation of the Marine garrison, Johnson directed the Joint Chiefs to provide him with a written statement of their confidence that Khesanh would not fall. At the same time, he asked Taylor to supervise the installation of a scale model of the Khesanh area in the White House situation room. In Stanley

Karnow's words: "Johnson, dressed in a bathrobe, would prowl around the chamber during the night—reading the latest teletype messages from the field, peering at aerial photos, requesting casualty figures."[1]

The Khesanh episode is one more example of the politico-military confusion that led to the ultimate Vietnam debacle. Taylor was not happy about Khesanh, primarily because he could not see that the Marines were accomplishing much in such a remote corner of the country. The town "looked like the last place you would want to have a large garrison, a garrison allegedly for the purpose of limiting infiltration . . . particularly when the Marines really dug themselves in."[2] Taylor's strategic priorities were far different from those of the JCS and the commander in the field. Whereas Westmoreland sought to bring the enemy's main force into battle away from populated areas, Taylor looked for progress in nation building and the protection of important populated areas. President Johnson was still prowling the White House situation room when the war reached a turning point: the Tet offensive.

In the early hours of January 30, 1968, the Vietnamese Communists launched a series of coordinated attacks against major population centers in South Vietnam. In the two days that followed, thirty-nine of South Vietnam's forty-four provincial capitals and at least seventy-one other towns came under attack by a total of 70,000 Communist troops. Violating a truce that they themselves had pledged to observe during Tet, the Vietnamese New Year, the Communists carried the war to more than a hundred urban areas that heretofore had been insulated from the fighting in the countryside.

In many locales the Communist attacks, carried out by both Viet Cong and North Vietnamese Army units, were repelled with heavy losses. The South Vietnamese fought well, and the Communists were often uncomfortable carrying out frontal attacks rather than their more usual hit-and-run raids. Both sides fought savagely, but the Communists "displayed unprecedented brutality, slaughtering minor government functionaries and other innocuous figures as well as harmless foreign doctors, schoolteachers, and missionaries."[3] Tet was a radical departure from the Communists' strategic reliance on prolonged war, a departure based on a mistaken belief that countrywide attacks would trigger a popular uprising against the Saigon Government. In fact, there were no known instances in which the Communists were welcomed by the population, and few desertions by government forces.

On the public relations front, however, it was a different story. The Communists mounted their boldest stroke against Saigon itself, employing about 4,000 men. A landmark in the city was the new U.S. embassy, constructed with a special view to security after the 1965 embassy bombing. The Communists made it a priority target nonetheless, and in the early hours of January 31 a commando group blasted its way through the outside wall. American television viewers in their living rooms were treated to the sight of dead Viet Cong in the smoke-filled embassy compound, while American soldiers dodged among the rubble as they sought to flush out the remaining enemy.

Two months earlier Westmoreland had spoken at the National Press Club in Washington, where he had exuded confidence. In answer to one question, he had stated that it might be possible to phase down U.S. troop levels in Vietnam in about two years. Now, in the wake of Tet, he was reduced to telling Western reporters that the Communists had acted "very deceitfully" in taking advantage of the Tet truce "to create maximum consternation."[4] Under the circumstances, it is hardly surprising that most of the American public gave little credence to administration statements that Tet had represented a major setback for the Communists.

Meanwhile, Khesanh had taken on a new urgency. Given the Communists' reckless expenditure of manpower in urban areas, might they not overrun Khesanh as they had Hue? On February 3 Taylor participated in a gloomy White House session devoted to what to do about Khesanh. In Taylor's words, "While no one suggested that we should not be there, it was quite apparent that most of us wished that we were not."[5] Taylor himself did not improve the mood with a remark that Khesanh was, after all, only an outpost, and outposts were not meant to be held indefinitely. All recognized that the United States had built up the importance of Khesanh in the public mind, and that it would be very difficult to rationalize any withdrawal.

As the weeks went on, Khesanh took a heavy toll of the Communists; B-52 strikes added to the casualties inflicted by the Marines' heavy artillery. After the war, estimates of Communist dead would exceed ten thousand, while the Marines suffered fewer than five hundred killed in action.[6] Taylor, however, was never enthusiastic about the operation, and on February 14 he addressed a memorandum to the President:

> My review of Westy's cables does not convince me of the military importance of maintaining Khe Sanh at the present time if it is still feasible to withdraw. Whatever the past value of the position, it is a positive liability now. We are allowing the enemy to arrange at his leisure a set-piece attack on ground and in weather favorable to him and under conditions which will allow us little opportunity to punish him except by our air power.[7]

In the end, however, it was the Communists who broke off the fighting. They began withdrawing in March, and the following month the area was cleared by U.S. forces.

When Taylor had returned from his year in Saigon, he had asked President Johnson for appointment to the Foreign Intelligence Advisory Board. The board, which dated back to the Eisenhower administration, was a rather toothless group of elder statesmen whose oversight function was created in part to deflect more vigorous congressional review of intelligence matters. In the wake of Tet, however, the board took on a new importance. Johnson not only appointed Taylor as requested, but told Taylor that he wanted him to succeed Clark Clifford as chairman, because Clifford was about to be named Secretary of Defense. He directed that the board investigate the charges that U.S. forces had been surprised at Tet.

The board sent a working group to Saigon, where it concluded that "the intensity, coordination, and timing of the enemy attack were not fully anticipated."[8] Later, Westmoreland himself would concede as much. The board's report to Johnson concluded very narrowly that there was no evidence that a lack of intelligence had prevented any U.S. unit from carrying out its mission. This narrow focus on the positive aspect of a major intelligence failure was in sharp contrast to Taylor's searching investigation into the Bay of Pigs.

Meanwhile, conflicting interpretations of the meaning of the Tet offensive were turning it into a critical juncture in the war. By mid-February, Westmoreland was impressed with the losses inflicted on the enemy and was considering whether he should resume the offensive. In this he was encouraged by the Joint Chiefs, who remained the most hawkish group in Washington. The chairman, General Wheeler, arrived in Saigon on February 23 to work out with MAC/V a request for reinforcements. There, the American military worked out plans for an increase in U.S. troops by a total of 206,000 in three increments, with the first reinforcement of 25,000 to be sent immediately. Taylor's oft-articulated hope that the Chiefs would consider the political impact of their recommendations was forgotten as they sought to expand the U.S. commitment to a cause that the American public was increasingly viewing as lost.

When Wheeler returned on February 28, he presented a summary of his recommendations to the President. McNamara, at his last cabinet meeting, expressed his disagreement; he favored disengagement and suggested that an additional 200,000 men would probably not prove decisive. Johnson, after hearing Wheeler's recommendations, directed Clark Clifford to head a task force to consider Wheeler's report and come up with its own recommendations. If the 206,000-man increase were approved, the total number of U.S. troops in Vietnam would approach 700,000. Johnson told Clifford, "Give me the lesser of evils."[9]

What began as an examination of Wheeler's troop increase request evolved into a major reexamination of U.S. policy in Vietnam. Clifford had come to the Pentagon with the reputation of a hawk, but there were several varieties of this bird. In his own words, he had supported the Kennedy-Johnson policies in Vietnam "as long as they appeared to be succeeding."[10] In the wake of his trip to Asia with Taylor in 1967, he had begun to have doubts as to their ultimate success.

On February 28 he chaired the first meeting of what came to be known as the Clifford Task Force. Those present included Secretary of State Rusk; outgoing Secretary of Defense McNamara; Secretary of the Treasury Fowler; and senior representatives from the White House, CIA, and Defense, including Taylor. Under Clifford's guidance, the members divided into small groups, each of which was to look into one of the issues that the President should take into account in dealing with Wheeler's requests. Gradually, a subtle evolution took place. The question came to be not merely one of reinforcements but of policy: Should the United States continue on the same track in Vietnam?

Taylor was quick to detect the new drift. "As the drafts were prepared and submitted to the committee of the whole for review," he wrote, "it became clear to me that some of the civilians in the Department of Defense were taking a new tack which caught me by surprise. . . . Rather than regarding [Tet] as a net victory which should be exploited if the resources could be made available, they appeared to feel that Tet had proved that success in Vietnam could never be attained by military means."[11]

Clifford would offer a more complex explanation for this metamorphosis. He found in his review no disposition to remove the restrictions under which the United States was operating in Vietnam: no invasion of the North, lest it trigger Chinese intervention; no mining of Haiphong, lest a Soviet ship be sunk; no pursuit into Laos or Cambodia, lest the war become open-ended. Clifford later wrote:

"Given these circumstances, how can we win?" We would, I was told, continue to evidence our superiority over the enemy; we would continue to attack in the belief that he would reach the stage where he would find it inadvisable to go on with the war. He could not afford the attrition we were inflicting on him. And we were improving our posture all the time.

I then asked, "What is the best estimate as to how long this course of action will take? Six months? One year? Two years?" There was no agreement on an answer. Not only was there no agreement, I could find no one willing to express any confidence in his guesses. Certainly, none of us was willing to assert that he could see "light at the end of the tunnel" or that American troops would be coming home by the end of the year.[12]

Taylor agreed with many of Clifford's findings, but he interpreted them very differently. In his view, the United States was
involved in a contest of wills that went far beyond the immediate
results in Vietnam. We still had four basic options: to expand the
war, to continue on the present course, to reduce the U.S. exposure, or to withdraw forthwith. He favored the second course and
applied it to the specific questions before the Clifford Task Force:

> I had no difficulty in deciding my own position. I favored giving
> Westmoreland at once the 25,000 men requested, but merely
> noting his contingency figure of 206,000 as illustrative of what
> might be needed under one rather extreme set of circumstances.
> . . . I strongly supported General Wheeler in urging a call-up of
> reserves to add a three-division balanced force to our strategic
> reserve at home. Not only was such a call-up justified by mili-
> tary considerations, but it would have a useful value in demon-
> strating to our friends and enemies alike that we meant business
> and did not consider turning back.[13]

In his memorandum for the task force, Taylor endorsed these
views and addressed the issue of Westmoreland's strategy. He had
long had misgivings about the "very broad interpretation" that
Westmoreland had put on his mission, one that allowed him to
operate throughout South Vietnam, including its remote, un-
derpopulated areas. Characteristically, Taylor had been reluctant
to criticize the commander on the ground. Now, however, he recommended that Westmoreland be given guidance "which would
assist him in establishing the priorities for his efforts necessary to
bring his mission within capabilities of those forces allotted him."
This new guidance "should make it clear that Westmoreland's mission was primarily the suppression of attacks on the cities, the
restoration of order in the areas attacked at Tet, and the creation
of a mobile reserve ready to pass to a vigorous offensive with the
resumption of favorable weather in the spring."[14]

The Clifford Task Force eventually came up with recommendations not far from what Taylor advocated. It recommended that
Westmoreland be sent 23,000 additional men but reserved judgment on any additional increase. It supported a reserve call-up of
245,000 men. But it was divided on the question of further bomb-

ing, and its overall tone was far more pessimistic than anything presented to the President before.

A full-dress reappraisal of Vietnam policy was under way, and Taylor sought to assist the President in dealing with a blizzard of paper. On March 9 he summarized for the President a diverse group of internal memoranda and newspaper editorials growing out of Tet. He found a polarization of views, with View A holding that the enemy lost in Tet and that the United States should exploit its advantage, and View B holding that the enemy had won and that the United States should hedge its losses.

> As you might expect, I hold more to View A than to View B, but I must admit that the returns are not all in. . . . Left unanswered is the primary concern of the holders of View B that Vietnam is a sponge with an inexhaustible capacity for absorbing U.S. resources and, hence, at some point we must call a halt. There is no positive answer to this fear which is a real one, other than to point to a few countervailing considerations.
>
> a. North Vietnam has many constraints on increases of its military strength in the south such as finite quantities of trained leadership, difficulties in local recruiting in the south, the manpower requirements in the north resulting from our bombing campaign, and concern over denuding the homeland of combat-ready units.
>
> b. Logistical factors place some limit (though hard to define) on the number of troops and/or the tempo of operations which Hanoi can sustain in South Vietnam. . . .
>
> c. This is the fourteenth year of war for North Vietnam just as it is for South Vietnam and it is hard to believe that Hanoi is enjoying the conflict or can hold out indefinitely as the pessimists believe.[15]

The Korean War had been in some respects as controversial as the war in Vietnam, but its effect on the American political fabric had been far less traumatic. Dissent then was limited largely to conservative elements opposed to the restraints imposed on U.S.

military power. The Vietnam War, in contrast, coincided with what was widely perceived as a breakdown in traditional shared values in the United States. The most visible manifestations were to be seen in the drug culture and the New Left: long hair, hippie communes, and rejection of all manifestations of authority. Often associated with these symptoms, however, was a quality for which Americans had long been criticized, a desire for immediate wish gratification. Most Americans supported administration policy in Vietnam, but they insisted that the conflict be resolved quickly.

Interwoven with these cultural indicators were signs of a more profound change: an erosion in America's sense of nationality. Those who burned flags and destroyed draft cards were one manifestation; but even among people who did not think of themselves as radical there was a growing tendency to think in terms smaller than the nation. Blacks focused on black issues, Jews sought special benefits for Israel, and other groups found binding ties that seemed more relevant than common citizenship. In Canada, a group of American deserters issued a manifesto that expressed support "with the National Liberation Front of South Vietnam and the black liberation struggle at home."[16]

Most members of the Establishment—the heavyweights of Wall Street and academe who set the agendas for both political parties—had supported the decisions made in the Kennedy years to come to the aid of South Vietnam. The initiation of the bombing campaign had tended to split the intelligentsia, however, and by 1968 academics and others routinely denounced the war not merely as mistaken but as immoral. For many, it was not even a subject for rational discussion; on New England college campuses, a person who supported the Administration on Vietnam was scarcely to be considered a member of the same species. Encouraged by Johnson's sagging polls, antiwar elements became increasingly willing to challenge the Administration. All they needed was the right candidate.

In the period following Taylor's return from Saigon, Bobby Kennedy had become increasingly critical of the conduct of the war, especially the bombing. His attitude grew out of a combination of factors, including his visceral loathing for Lyndon Johnson, a turn to the Left among many of the Kennedy brothers' former associates, and Bobby's own increasing identification with America's youth. He and Taylor were still close; as recently as 1965 Bobby had named one of his children for the general. Taylor still went out to Hickory Hill for tennis, but by mutual consent he and Bobby stayed away from the subject of Vietnam. Whereas Bobby hectored Bob McNamara on the subject of the war throughout 1967, he made no comparable effort with Taylor.

On March 16, 1968, after antiwar Democrat Eugene McCarthy had demonstrated Johnson's political vulnerability, Bobby declared for the presidency and embarked on a whirlwind tour of the important primary states in which he demonstrated a charisma that quickly eclipsed McCarthy. He attacked the Vietnam War as immoral and was enthusiastically applauded when he told college crowds that Saigon should start drafting its own eighteen- and nineteen-year-olds—overlooking the fact that the Thieu government had belatedly begun doing just that. Taylor wrote in March:

> We are certainly having our share of national troubles these days, not the least of which is Bobby's candidacy. He is being so careless with the facts in support of his arguments that he is creating endless future problems for himself and also for me when I am asked what I think of them.
>
> As for Bobby's chances, no one seems to be giving him much encouragement except the public polls which show him leading the President at the moment. . . . The most obvious possibility is that the combination of Kennedy and McCarthy will succeed in splitting the Democratic vote to the point that Tricky Dick will walk into the White House without a hand being placed upon him.[17]

At this busy time Taylor was a member not only of the Clifford Task Force but of a somewhat overlapping group known as the Wise Men, a group of elder statesmen whom Johnson had first called together in November 1967 as one more source of counsel on Vietnam. The group included diplomats Dean Acheson, Robert Murphy, and George Ball; former administration stalwarts McGeorge Bundy and Henry Cabot Lodge; and Johnson intimates Clark Clifford and Abe Fortas. At their first meeting on November

2, the consensus among the Wise Men had been that the conduct of the war was satisfactory; Taylor could recall only one member, whom he did not identify, as favoring a cutback in the bombing. "The theme that dominated the session," he recalled, "was the public information problem—how to get a better understanding of the issues and of the situation on the part of the general public and of special groups such as the media and the universities."[18]

On March 25, in the wake of Tet, Johnson once again summoned the Wise Men, and this time he received a jolt. The meeting opened with briefings by the CIA, the Joint Chiefs of Staff, and State, briefings that in Taylor's recollection differed only slightly from those of the previous November. The reaction, however, was very different. After a day of sharp debate, the Wise Men met with the President and gave him a largely negative assessment. McGeorge Bundy, in a summary memorandum for the President, called attention to "a very significant shift in our position." He quoted Dean Acheson as saying that "we can no longer do the job we set out to do in the time we have left," and said that his view was supported by five members, himself included. Only three of the group—Murphy, Fortas, and Taylor—favored a continuation of the war essentially as it was being prosecuted.

Because the Wise Men represented one group on whose support Johnson had come to rely, their shift in sentiment was important. The shift came as a surprise to Taylor; he would later attribute the pessimism among his colleagues to the biased media coverage of Tet, but this explanation does not of itself explain a major shift on the part of a knowledgeable and sophisticated group. Other factors that influenced the Wise Men almost certainly included the degree of surprise achieved by the Communists at Tet—hardly a sign of popular support for the government—and the seemingly endless demand for additional increments in U.S. forces. In any case, their shift in attitude, orchestrated in part by Clark Clifford, was a turning point in the war. In Taylor's view, "This dramatic and unexpected reversal of position on the part of so many respected friends made a deep impression on the President."[19]

The next bombshell came from the White House. It is now known that President Johnson had dropped a number of hints that he might not run in 1968. For instance, in the fall of 1967, according to Walt Rostow, he had warned a group of intimates not to plan on his being a candidate the following year.[20] Nevertheless, as his staff worked on drafts of a major speech on Vietnam, to include an offer of unconditional negotiations with Hanoi, there was no suggestion that LBJ would append to it the declaration of his noncandidacy that he had contemplated delivering on several previous occasions.

On March 31 a somber President spoke to the nation on television. After a brief review of his administration's efforts to find a basis for peace talks, he announced a unilateral reduction of hostilities ("Tonight I have ordered our aircraft and our naval vessels to make no attacks on North Viet-Nam, except in the area north of the demilitarized zone where the continuing enemy buildup directly threatens Allied forward positions."). He called on Ho Chi Minh to respond positively to "this new step toward peace." He then spoke directly to a nation divided over Vietnam, in which college students routinely burned their draft cards, spelled America with a *k*, and charged their President with war crimes.

> What we won when all of our people [were united] must not now be lost in suspicion, distrust, selfishness, and politics among any of our people.
>
> Believing this as I do, I have concluded that I should not permit the Presidency to become involved in the partisan divisions that are developing in this political year. . . .
>
> Accordingly, I shall not seek, and I will not accept, the nomination of my party for another term as your President.[21]

No one watching the President that evening was more surprised than Taylor. He had reviewed an early version of the speech, offering some suggestions for its military sections. Sunday evening, a few hours before delivery, Rostow had called to say that there had been some last-minute changes, but he had given no hint of what was to come. Mrs. Taylor wrote, "We were really floored at the announcement, which was quite poignant from this guy who had relished politics for most of his life."[22]

Washington was still reverberating from the aftershock of the Johnson speech when the assassination of Martin Luther King, Jr., triggered rioting and looting in many cities, including Washington. To the extent that labels are applicable, Taylor was a true moderate in matters of race. As commander of the Eighth Army, he had implemented the final desegregation of the U.S. forces under his command, a step that he had regarded as long overdue. Later, as chief of staff, he had resigned from one Washington club that, without being avowedly segregationist, had never admitted a black member. As a presidential adviser, however, he was sufficiently preoccupied with security problems that he had little time for domestic issues, and he refused to weigh in on subjects on which he had not done his homework. He wrote following the King assassination:

> The repercussions of that event are not yet over. As you have read, we have had extensive rioting and burning in Washington, although the loss of life has been much lower than might have been anticipated in the circumstances. I am afraid, however, [that] this is only the first round of violence and that the King murder will be used as an excuse for black extremism which will probably generate an equal extremism among irresponsible white elements.[23]

Meanwhile, what of LBJ's withdrawal from the presidential race? Taylor's first reaction to Johnson's withdrawal speech was to ask how it might be used to restore a degree of national unity on the subject of Vietnam. In a memo to the President on April 1, he pursued this thought:

> The avowed Presidential candidates and other prominent politicians are praising your action and saying the right things about the need to eliminate divisions among our people. Might it not be possible to assemble several leading members of both parties at the White House and get them to issue a joint statement endorsing the peace overture contained in your speech last night and offering continued support to our war efforts if Hanoi rejects your proposition? I have in mind such men as Eisenhower, Goldwater and Nixon on the Republican side and Truman, R. Kennedy and McCarthy for the Democrats.[24]

Nothing came of this proposal, which may have been naïve, given the determination of Kennedy and McCarthy to base their campaigns on opposition to the war. Unity on the key issue of Vietnam would have deprived both Democrats of their excuse for running, while the endorsement of Establishment Republicans would have carried little weight with the radical elements that were in the forefront of anti-Vietnam activism.

As the reaction to King's assassination subsided, attention turned to the forthcoming negotiations in Paris relative to Vietnam. Taylor was extremely pessimistic concerning these talks, and his pessimism was amply justified. Only months before, the New York *Times* had featured prominently a series of articles from Hanoi by Harrison Salisbury in which he included without attribution long quotations from Communist propaganda handouts and endorsed Hanoi's contention that the American bombing had inflicted heavy civilian damage. The North Vietnamese, who were fully aware of public opinion in the United States, announced at the outset of the Paris talks that they would discuss only "the unconditional cessation of bombing and all other war acts by the United States against the Democratic Republic of Vietnam."[25] After an initial period of euphoria, the talks quickly reached an impasse. The U.S. delegation, headed by Averell Harriman, called for the withdrawal of North Vietnamese forces from South Vietnam, whereas Hanoi's delegation demanded that the Saigon Government be broadened to include representatives of the Viet Cong. It was all part of Hanoi's avowed strategy of "Fight fight, talk talk," and Washington's eagerness for a negotiated solution played into the Communists' hands.

Although Taylor was dismayed by the increasingly antiwar tone of the Kennedy presidential campaign, he walked a fine line, as reflected in one letter in the spring of 1968:

This afternoon I went out to Hickory Hill for tennis for the first time since the recent series of political shockers. I find that Bobby is looking for a general to endorse his position on Vietnam, but I failed to volunteer for the task. I did suggest Jim Gavin or [former Marine commandant] Dave Shoup after making derogatory comments about both. However, in the emergency I felt that Bobby and his advisors should take on any general from any service—including the Salvation Army—if he could be persuaded to say the right thing.[26]

Two months later the nation was stunned by its second political assassination in one year, the killing of Bobby Kennedy by a Palestinian militant. When Ethel Kennedy returned from California, the Taylors were among the close friends who were asked to come out to Hickory Hill. A few days later, Taylor marched for the second time as an honorary pallbearer for a member of the Kennedy family. Later in the summer, he wrote a tribute in which he reflected on his friendship with the younger Kennedy:

> During these years, I sometimes reproached him for having uprooted Diddy and me from our quiet life with the Performing Arts in New York and [for] having brought us back to the Washington stage where it is hard to perform long without getting more boos than cheers. But it was a complaint in jest, and I hope and believe that Bob recognized it as such. The fact is that I shall always be indebted to him for changing the course of events in a way which allowed me to play a small part in the historical drama of John F. Kennedy, to know Ethel, Jackie, and the others of his extraordinary family and to have my life enriched by the friendship of Bobby Kennedy.[27]

In the summer my return on home leave from the American embassy in Singapore was the occasion for some long conversations within the family. My father commented that, as the Johnson administration moved toward its close, there were few hawks to be found. He listed in this category the President, Secretary Rusk, Walt Rostow, and himself. He spoke disparagingly of the latest bombing halt, not because he was opposed to deescalation as such but because of the continuing immunity accorded key cities like Hanoi and Haiphong. His policy would have been to scale down the number of bombing missions from time to time, but with a clear understanding that these would be resumed, with no areas sacrosanct, if violence increased in the South.

He characterized Johnson as fully committed to obtaining an honorable settlement of the war. He described how LBJ had been "furious" over one cable from the American delegation in Paris, which discussed several possible U.S. moves in terms of their likely effect on the American presidential campaign. According to Taylor, Johnson had said he "didn't give a damn" about their effect on the election. He said that Cyrus Vance had been sent to Paris as Harriman's deputy because he, Taylor, along with Clifford, had doubts about Harriman's commitment on the Vietnam issue. He had no doubt that Harriman would carry out his instructions, but he believed that the man who had helped bring down Diem was basically uninterested in the terms of an agreement on Vietnam and sought only to remove Vietnam as an issue in U.S.-Soviet relations.

With his penchant for looking to the future, Taylor was thinking beyond the Paris negotiations for the long-term implications of an unsatisfactory outcome in Vietnam. An invitation to deliver the principal address at the annual George C. Marshall dinner provided him with an opportunity to reflect on some of these. He spoke openly of the influence of television on foreign policy—a problem with which General Marshall had never had to deal. "Television," he said, "has brought the battlefield into our living rooms with a vividness most disturbing to those who have never known war, somehow conveying the impression that it is we Americans who almost alone have been responsible for the cruelties and brutalities of the war as pictured on the screen." He went on to consider the entire concept of "strategic gradualism" in fighting a war:

> Military operations anywhere in the world are to some extent a threat to world peace. . . . It is this concern which has been the primary cause for the slow, cautious use of our air arm which has characterized our air operations in North Viet-Nam. But whatever justification this prudence has had, it has been branded by the critics as timidity and has contributed greatly to the unpopularity of the war and to the difficulty of explaining it to the satisfaction of many of our citizens.

To Taylor, the Vietnam experience raised fundamental questions as to whether a democracy like the United States, with a volatile electorate, could successfully engage in a limited war for limited objectives. He found the implications disturbing:

> What happens to the Truman Doctrine and the worldwide system of alliances which commit us contingently to over 40 nations? . . . The Communist leaders have stated very clearly that they have their own solution to the problem of expansion by force in a world fearful of World War III. They see the same dangers as we and have concluded that both nuclear war and limited war are to be avoided because of their unpredictable consequences. On the other hand, they find in the "War of Liberation" a form of force which is relatively cheap, not too dangerous, and which has the advantage of being disavowable. . . . We of the Free World are left with the question of how to resist this kind of aggression if, indeed, democracies are not capable of using force in distant places because their people can not understand the need.[28]

Chapter 26

THE LAST HAWK

For most of his life Taylor was a nominal Democrat, although the Army's nonpartisan traditions had led him to downplay his personal preferences. In 1968, however, there was a change. Although he liked and admired Hubert Humphrey, the Democratic standard-bearer that year, Taylor changed his registration to Independent, out of recognition that the party of Harry Truman and "Scoop" Jackson had largely been taken over by the antiwar movement. Although he shared with much of the nation a visceral dislike for Richard Nixon, he viewed the narrow Republican victory in 1968 as the lesser of evils.

"The LBJ administration is moving at a snail's pace toward its end," Taylor wrote in December 1968. "While I continue to write soul-stirring notes to the President on the subject of South VietNam, I am afraid that I'm talking to the wind."[1] One of many memorandums he sent forward during this period addressed the frequent charge that Vietnam was somehow an unjust or immoral war. In a section designed as a speech insert, Taylor called attention to the tight restraints that had been imposed on U.S. forces: "Our commanders are operating under the strictest orders ever imposed upon military forces in time of war to use every means to minimize civilian casualties." He cited the massive economic aid being provided the Vietnamese and asked the rhetorical question: What if the United States had not intervened on behalf of South Vietnam?

There is little doubt that, by now, Ho Chi Minh would have achieved his life-long objective of imposing a Communist regime on South Viet-Nam in spite of the resistance of the large majority of its inhabitants. In so doing, it may be expected that he would have used the same kind of harsh, repressive measures as he did in North Vietnam during 1954–55. In that period, it is conservatively estimated that over 50,000 North Vietnamese were executed by Ho's firing squads and many more were put in concentration camps—and these cruelties were carried out in a stronghold of Communist sympathizers.[2]*

Views like this did not make for great popularity on the contemporary lecture circuit. In May 1969 Taylor was scheduled to address an open meeting of faculty and students at the University of Rochester, only to be advised by security personnel shortly before the meeting that the hall had been preempted by members of the radical Students for a Democratic Society (SDS) and that trouble was expected. In Taylor's words, "President Wallis and I sat in the university garden smelling the flowers while two deans attempted to shame the students into becoming a respectful audience, but they didn't shame. After about half an hour . . . we adjourned to the President's house where I gave my talk to a handful of students and faculty [and] was recorded by the university radio station."[3]

Taylor was angered by recurring charges that American troops had performed badly in Vietnam and that drug use and "fraggings"—assaults by soldiers against their own officers—were commonplace. So pervasive was the negative impression of U.S. troop behavior, an impression assiduously fostered by much of the media, that Taylor proposed that President Johnson consider a speech insert such as the following:

The combat performance of United States forces and their allies is [a] cause for pride. Our fighting men in 1966–67 frustrated the enemy strategy of the so-called "prolonged conflict" and obliged Hanoi to pass to a hazardous general offensive in 1968. This venture has cost the enemy at least a quarter of a million fatali-

---

* At that time, liberals generally scoffed at charges that a Communist victory in Vietnam would bring about a "bloodbath." When the Communists united the country in 1975, most antiwar critics ignored the execution of an estimated ten thousand South Vietnamese and the incarceration of thousands more. The exodus of the boat people over the years, however, would serve as a reminder of the type of regime that had been imposed by kindly Uncle Ho.

ties this year and the outcome convinced the Communist leaders that they must accept our long-standing offer to negotiate.[4]

As for the President's handling of Vietnam, Taylor respected his demonstrated willingness to court unpopularity over the war issue, but did not feel that it was an issue that lent itself to Johnson's constant search for consensus. Quite apart from this, he was never quite so comfortable with the LBJ style as he had been with Kennedy's, a point that came through in one interview:

TAYLOR: Certainly from the national defense point of view [Johnson] was an ideal president, as I saw it. But I never felt that we were warm friends, perhaps because I knew he had one strong thing against me. I had a Robert Kennedy son named after me.

INTERVIEWER: Do you really think that was a handicap?

TAYLOR: I know it did [sic]. I don't think . . . he really distrusted me, but every now and then he'd say, "How is that Kennedy boy named after you?" I wasn't sure he was joking. The Kennedy-Johnson animosity was very real and very deep, [although] it seemed to me [that LBJ] tried everything under the sun to be friendly with the Kennedys and bury the feud.[5]†

The inauguration of Richard Nixon brought an end to Taylor's period as a presidential consultant. His only continuing governmental position was as a member of the Foreign Intelligence Advisory Board; Taylor stood down as chairman but was retained by Nixon as a member during his first year in office. Taylor continued for the time being as the part-time president of the Institute for Defense Analysis but resigned in 1969 in order to devote full time to the writing of his memoirs.

In June 1971 came the controversial affair of the Pentagon Papers. In mid-1967 Secretary McNamara had commissioned a classified study of the record of U.S. involvement, one that would con-

---

† Taylor may have underestimated the regard in which he was held by President Johnson, who, after all, had taken no action on the Bundy memorandum recommending that he be brought home from Saigon. According to Walt Rostow, Johnson once remarked to him that he was aware of Taylor's continued close association with the Bobby Kennedys, but had no doubt of Taylor's loyalty to the Johnson administration and its objectives.

sider material as far back as the Truman administration. The massive study, comprising some 3,000 pages of narrative and 4,000 pages of additional documentation, was passed to the New York *Times* by antiwar Pentagon bureaucrats. By any normal standard the leaking of the Pentagon Papers was a case of simple theft, but the Nixon administration's inept handling of its legal aspects brought repeated rebuffs in the courts. A team of *Times* writers edited the documents and published them both in the newspaper and as a paperback.

Taylor was largely undamaged by these revelations, which, as published, underscored his initial opposition to the deployment of U.S. combat forces to Vietnam. But he was furious at the journalistic irresponsibility represented by the publication of sensitive government documents, many of them highly revealing concerning policy differences in an ongoing conflict. The *Times* sought to defend its action on the grounds of the people's "right to know," and ran an op-ed article by James Reston in which Reston suggested that critics of the *Times* were close "to the Marxist view of the press—that it should be the servant of the government."

Taylor's commentary appeared the same day. He charged that the newspaper's action in selectively publishing the Pentagon Papers reflected "the right of the *Times* to determine" what the public learns. "There has been an arrogance in the way the *Times* has thrown down the gauntlet in challenging the Government's right to identify and protect its secret[s]." He continued:

> There should be ways for reasonable men to reconcile the needs of a free press and of national security without resort to exaggerated classification of documents by the Government or resort to the role of "fence" on the part of the press. . . . The press should be able to fulfill its secular role of exposing rascals and mistakes in Government without making common cause with the enemies of Government.[6]

Over the years Taylor's family and friends had periodically urged him to write an autobiography. He had not been idle since *The Uncertain Trumpet,* having published in 1967 a volume of essays on security affairs under the title *Responsibility and Response.*

But with the passing of the Johnson administration he decided that the time was ripe for a full memoir. He solicited advice on what form it might take, and I recall directing his attention to William Allen White's autobiography and to George Kennan's memoirs as formats that he might wish to emulate. The final version was very much his own, however, and very much a book about Vietnam.

Indeed, Taylor had planned a book exclusively about Vietnam until his editor at W. W. Norton, Evan Thomas, joined in urging a somewhat broader work. Nevertheless, the allocation of space tells a great deal about his priorities. He devoted seven pages to his secret trip to Rome in 1943 and six pages to D-day in Normandy. His four difficult years as Army chief of staff were treated in one of the thirty-five chapters. In contrast, no fewer than fourteen chapters dealt wholly or in part with Vietnam. He wrote in the Foreword, "My book makes no claim to being finished history. . . . Rather, it recounts my personal involvement in a series of historic episodes and records my own impressions of what took place."[7] Beyond testifying to the author's admiration and affection for the Kennedy family, the book dealt with issues rather than personalities and was never a threat to the best-seller list. And as Taylor had never learned to type, the draft manuscript was a mountain of carefully penned legal pages.

As Taylor neared the end of his book, his editors at Norton discovered that the general was strangely unrepentant about his decisions relating to Vietnam—indeed, that he was prone to defend them, given the information available to him and his colleagues at the time they were made. The result was a remarkable attempt on the part of the senior Norton staff to educate the general on the error of his ways. A slightly sheepish Evan Thomas forwarded to Taylor an anonymous memorandum from a "senior colleague" who Taylor believed was the president of the company:

I have now read all of this MS from the Bay of Pigs to the end, and I strongly doubt whether it would be a service to anyone to publish it in its present form. Our own reputation (to dispose of the least important element first) would not suffer much, because anyone can see we publish all sorts of books, and no one can remember a publisher's name, anyhow. But General Taylor's reputation, and that of the cause he served, would be damaged beyond repair.

The writer then went on to consider the sources of opposition to the Vietnam War, which, in his view, were insufficiently dealt with in *Swords and Plowshares*. Antiwar sentiment was based in part on the wisdom of the American people in rejecting Asia. ("It is, after all, not worth forty-five thousand American lives to guarantee a life free from oppression to illiterate peasants on the other side of the world.") He then took the general to task for suggesting that media reporting had contributed to popular disillusionment with the war. "In sweeping our crimes and follies under the rug, the general renounces an opportunity to examine the real lessons of the war."[8]

Taylor was angered by this communication, particularly since he had dealt at length with the errors of omission and commission relative to Vietnam. In fact, although *Swords and Plowshares* was written in 1971, at a time when an independent South Vietnam still seemed a possibility, much that he said remains pertinent today. For one thing, the book reflected Taylor's final break with "gradualism":

There was a certain logic in this gradualism if not carried to excess. The purpose of rational war is to break the will of the adversary and cause him to adjust his behavior to our purposes, not to destroy him. . . . While this carefully controlled violence may have had some justification at the start, it ended by defeating its own purposes. . . . The restrained use of our air power suggested to the enemy a lack of decisiveness.

If gradualism worked against the political purpose of inducing the enemy to seek an accommodation, it also violated the military principles of surprise and mass as means to gain prompt success. . . . This was a misguided attempt to translate the principle of gradualism and limited violence from the strategic to the tactical realm—a fallacy which ignored the fact that for the soldier or pilot in the presence of an armed enemy any war is total since his survival is at stake.[9]

Quite apart from the problems associated with gradualism, Taylor was bothered by the inability of the Johnson administration to take advantage at the bargaining table of the weakened military position in which the Communists found themselves after Tet. Notwithstanding Johnson's oft-expressed resolve never to "pay" for the privilege of sitting down with the Communists, in the end his administration did exactly that, by limiting the bombing. Moreover, once the U.S. delegation reached Paris, talks had promptly bogged down over Communist demands for a complete cessation of bombing, to which Washington ultimately acceded. "In exchange for this major blue chip," Taylor lamented, "we got the so-called understandings that the enemy would not attack urban centers in South Vietnam, would not violate the DMZ, would permit aerial reconnaissance of North Vietnam, and would enter at once into productive negotiations. The enemy never complied with these understandings, and soon were claiming that they never existed."[10]

Swords and Plowshares appeared in 1972 to mixed reviews. Marvin Kalb of CBS News called it "the first really honest account of the Vietnam War written from the inside. . . . An excellent book." Herbert Cheshire, writing in *Business Week*, commented that Taylor tells his story "with modesty, with more than passable literary skill, and with deep feeling for the sweep of history." Taylor's own mail was predictably dominated by congratulatory letters from old military associates, but here, too, there were surprises. Economist John Kenneth Galbraith, a critic on the war, wrote that he had read *Swords and Plowshares* with "much interest and admiration."

With most of the liberal intelligentsia, however, it was a different story. Like the armchair strategists at Norton, antiwar extremists were furious that the author did not come groveling and beg forgiveness. New York writer David Halberstam complained that *Swords and Plowshares* contained "no sense of remorse," while Neil Sheehan, one of the "editors" of the Pentagon Papers, dismissed it as "bad history." In fact, there was ample remorse in Taylor's memoir, but there was also a conviction that the U.S. policy in Vietnam, flawed though it was, could have been carried through to a satisfactory conclusion by a country that had not been misled by the media. In Manhattan, this was not a popular view.

His memoir completed, Taylor followed the tortuous course of the Paris peace negotiations with intense interest. After Henry Kissinger went on television to announce the provisions of a cease-fire, he asked for Taylor's comments and got them, in a three-page letter. The general saw the Paris terms as providing for the return of U.S. prisoners in return for placing the Saigon Government at considerable peril, a peril not limited to the withdrawal of U.S. forces. He cited a number of likely problem areas:

> The North Vietnamese forces, estimated at about 150,000, will remain in South Vietnam ready to make exorbitant claims to territorial control. The Hanoi text makes no reference to their presence, an omission which suggests that the terms of the agreement do not apply to them. . . .
>
> In Korea it took about two years to work out a cease-fire agreement and nine months to carry out its provisions. Yet the situation in Korea was much more favorable for a cease-fire than that in Vietnam. To announce a cease-fire before international advisory personnel are in place . . . is likely to invite immediate violations.[11]

The Vietnam cease-fire agreement was signed in Paris on January 27, 1973. There were two months of national euphoria as the surviving U.S. prisoners were returned and the remaining U.S. forces were withdrawn from South Vietnam. An angry President Thieu denounced the agreements that had left more than 150,000 soldiers of the Vietnamese People's Army on his territory, but the American public wanted to hear no more about Vietnam. President Nixon had been triumphantly reelected in November 1972, but already revelations about the Watergate break-in were titillating the American public and weakening the Nixon administration.

Could South Vietnam succeed on its own? In March 1973 Taylor characterized both sides as "tired—terribly tired," but he was still hopeful of an acceptable outcome. He endorsed Nixon's "Christmas bombing" of December 1972, which had brought the North Vietnamese back to the negotiating table and led to the peace accords, but he was concerned that Nixon's weakened presidency would limit Washington's freedom of action in the future. The Cooper-Church amendment of 1970 had already prohibited the introduction of U.S. ground troops or advisers into Cambodia. Then, in 1973, an amendment to an appropriations act effectively denied the use of U.S. funds for military purposes anywhere in Indochina, including Vietnam. "With it," wrote Henry Kissinger, "vanished any Communist fear of a penalty for violating the [Vietnam cease-fire] agreement."[12]

South Vietnam did not fall right away. Indeed, for much of 1973–74 it appeared that it might not fall at all. But the impact of the cutback in U.S. aid was quickly felt; the South Vietnamese soldier who once carried six grenades soon carried only two. In December 1974 eight thousand North Vietnamese regulars seized Phuoc Long province north of Saigon, capturing a provincial capital for the first time in three years. When there was no U.S. response, Hanoi resumed its offensive.

In March 1975 a South Vietnamese defeat at Ban Me Thuot turned into a rout. A willingness to fight to the last man is not part of the Sino-Vietnamese ethic; soon the rout turned into a panic. On April 29, 1975, with the Communists shelling the Saigon airport, the United States initiated the largest helicopter evacuation on record. For millions of Americans, TV pictures of the wave of helicopters evacuating Americans and a few fortunate Vietnamese from the roof of the American embassy would symbolize the end of the ill-advised Vietnam venture.

Taylor made no effort to find a silver lining in the defeat. Speaking to one reporter about the collapse of South Vietnam he remarked, "We all have a share in it, and none of it is good. There are no heroes, just bums. I include myself in that."[13] Asked after one presentation whether America's involvement in Vietnam was "correct after all," he was equally succinct. "We failed, so I guess you could say it wasn't correct."[14] His dismay went beyond the fact of defeat to the way in which defeat had come about. He believed that although Nixon's earlier use of air power had made it possible for the United States to enforce the terms of the cease-fire, a combination of congressional disillusionment with the war and a presidency weakened by Watergate had tied the government's hands.

He might have said with Lord Melbourne, "What all the wise men promised has not happened, and what all the damned fools said would happen has come to pass."

Over the years, Taylor would analyze at length the errors that had been made concerning Vietnam. High on his list would be the Kennedy administration's complicity in the overthrow of Diem, the lack of conviction with which we carried out the bombing of North Vietnam, the absence of a formal declaration of war with which to unite the American people, and the failure of U.S. negotiators in Paris to translate gains made on the battlefield into an enforceable cease-fire. Curiously, given his own record, he tended to downplay as one of our errors the Americanization of the ground war, a development that did much to increase American casualties and to undercut support for the war in the United States.

Swords and Plowshares, written three years before Saigon fell, was almost prescient in anticipating Hanoi's ability to exploit political weakness in Washington to achieve its objective. In it, Taylor characterized his country as being in a period of "declining power," its armed forces of little use in the absence of the political will to employ them when needed. He continued to downplay the threat of a nuclear war—the one form of aggression to which the United States was still prepared to respond. But he foresaw a period of diminished U.S. credibility, in which its allies, uncertain of Washington's ability to deliver on its commitments, would be increasingly vulnerable to Communist pressure. "This concern over the ability of a democracy to resort to arms for reasons other than survival may be offensive to readers who will view it as the desire of a militarist to keep war alive," he wrote. "The fact is that, without the limited war option and the forces that go with it, we have little of substance with which to defend our interests."[15]

Taylor, in retirement, spoke freely and without hesitation on issues related to Vietnam, though his interviews rarely produced insights beyond those set forth in *Swords and Plowshares*. Because he found the role of a prophet of gloom distasteful, he did not dwell upon his belief that the United States had entered a period of decline as a world power, a decline that was perhaps irreversible. Privately, however, he had grave doubts as to whether a country preoccupied with material well-being could long bear the burdens that were the lot of any great power. In his copy of C. E. M. Joad's *Decadence: A Philosophical Inquiry,* purchased in 1969, he marked a passage that he clearly related to the America of the 1960s:

It follows that a society whose members aim at wealth, power, fame and social position is a society whose values are inconsistent with stability and contentment, since where men value as ends in themselves goods which are limited and dividing, the possessors will be few and the deprived many, with the result that many will be restless and disappointed. Now, restless and disappointed citizens are a source of weakness and instability, as the history of European States immediately prior to the rise of Fascism abundantly testifies.[16]

Chapter 27

PRECARIOUS SECURITY

In 1971 the Taylors made the last of their many moves, from the town house in Chevy Chase to a cooperative apartment at 2500 Massachusetts Avenue. Their first-floor apartment was immediately next to the Japanese embassy where, on Pearl Harbor day, passing motorists had stopped to watch the plume of smoke from documents being destroyed in the embassy courtyard. A visitor entered the Taylor apartment by a foyer dominated by a stand of flags. The Stars and Stripes were flanked by banners representing two of the general's commands, the 101st Airbone Division and the Eighth Army. The flags of the Army chief of staff and the chairman of the Joint Chiefs of Staff completed the ensemble.

In their new location the Taylors combined the advantages of a downtown location with living quarters all on the first level. Their neighbors were congenial, and they continued to have the assistance of their outstanding cook-housekeeper, retired sergeant Hurley Cargill. Although my father's tennis days were drawing to a close, he exercised with barbells and took long walks. His daily constitutionals made him a familiar figure to the Special Police who watched over the embassies in his neighborhood.

Since 1966 Taylor had been a member of the Alibi Club, a congenial group of overachievers who met each Friday in the club's venerable town house on I Street. Alibi members saw a far mellower Taylor than had the Joint Staff at the Pentagon or the U.S. mission in Saigon. So, too, did visitors to 2500 Massachusetts Avenue. An Army colleague, Bruce Palmer, would write that although Taylor had once struck many as cold and unbending, in retirement he was "a genial host, and a witty conversationalist with a well-developed sense of humor."[1]

Now fully retired from government, Taylor was active on the

boards of several institutions, including the Institute for Defense Analysis, the Bullock Funds, and William Draper's Population Crisis Committee. He was also in demand as a speaker, although most of the invitations now were from the armed forces schools. His reduced schedule suited him fine; he viewed this period primarily as one for writing about the security matters with which he had dealt for most of his career.

He spent little time bemoaning the result in Vietnam. Rather, he addressed himself to the implications of the defeat there and to the internal weaknesses in American society, as he perceived them, that had contributed to the final debacle. In numerous articles in the late 1970s, Taylor sought to assess anew his country's security priorities. As one who believed in defining any problem he attacked, Taylor started by deciding that the traditional definition of "national security" in terms of freedom from military attack was too narrow. In the wake of the OPEC oil crisis of 1973 he told one interviewer that "the economic factor is certain to be a preponderant one in our relations with other powers. As the oil crisis reminds us, we are entering an era of scarcities, which will be felt worldwide."[2]

In 1974 he addressed this subject at greater length in *Foreign Affairs* and, characteristically, came up with an organizational solution. He proposed to expand the National Security Council to deal with "all forms of security threats, military and nonmilitary." In his judgment, such a move required no additional legislation:

> With an appropriate expansion of membership to give representation to the domestic and environmental sectors and perhaps with a modification of title (I would prefer "National Policy Council"), the [NSC] could be held to a more exacting compliance with its 1947 mandate. In this expanded form, the body could design a comprehensive national security program meeting criteria of rationality and legitimacy such as I have proposed for the military component.[3]

Far from sharing the euphoria of those who felt that the U.S. pullout from Vietnam had ended a period of military overextension, Taylor saw increasing external challenges in a period when the country was looking inward. He saw the most likely threats as falling into three categories: the continuing Soviet threat; the growing dependence of the U.S. economy on imports; and instability in the Third World, "where most of the markets essential to our economy are found." He told one interviewer in 1980:

Our [military] forces must continue to deter strategic nuclear war and be able to prevent or defeat a major attack on NATO. In addition, many new tasks may arise from the need to maintain access to raw-material markets overseas. For the moment our principal concern is over Middle East oil, but we are developing increasing needs for mineral imports. Thus a new mission for the armed forces is taking shape: The protection of essential markets and their access routes.[4]

Meanwhile, Taylor was dismayed at the implications of the War Powers Act of 1973, which sharply limited the President's ability to respond to a military emergency. Over the years, a succession of presidents would find ways of circumventing the act, which remains of dubious constitutional validity. Taylor, however—a firm champion of the executive branch—viewed the measure with apprehension, pointing out that had it been in effect in 1950 there might have been no response to the invasion of South Korea. He applauded President Ford's 1975 action in sending a military force to reclaim the *Mayaguez*, an American freighter that had been seized by the Cambodian Communists, as a demonstration of a President's refusal to be intimidated by legislative interference in the conduct of foreign affairs.

The administration of Jimmy Carter saw the flowering of the all-volunteer Army, continued reductions in U.S. military strength, and—a real calamity—legislation that opened the service academies to women. Taylor had no objection whatever to women in the armed services, but he thought it ridiculous that West Point, with its commitment to providing combat leaders, should turn away some future Grant or Lee in favor of a woman who would not be allowed near a battlefield. Elsewhere, he opposed Carter's decision to grant blanket amnesty to draft evaders of the Vietnam era. "I have no vindictive feelings toward these people," he told an interviewer, "they shouldn't be blamed for eternity." But he believed that a general amnesty would constitute a precedent "which could be most dangerous the next time we are faced with a national emergency."[5]

One of Taylor's principal concerns during the Carter years was the all-volunteer Army. Since his period as superintendent at West Point he had favored some form of national service, and he viewed the volunteer army on which his country had chosen to rely instead as a dangerous political expedient. In a letter to Justice Lewis Powell he wrote, "While it is a serious defect of the present system that it turns over our defense in [peacetime] to the poor and the colored, it is much more serious that such a system cannot defend us successfully in war."[6] Why not? He characterized the volunteer Army as working "at exorbitant cost while there is no shooting war," but as one that "will not produce the manpower necessary to replace heavy combat losses in wartime."[7] He expanded on this subject in an article for the Washington *Post*:

> We are paying a considerable price today for the [all-volunteer force] because of its limited contribution to the deterrent function in time of peace. There is little that is impressive about a military force with the visible manpower deficiencies that plague ours. . . . If attacked by a formidable enemy, [NATO] would have to fight with no assurance of prompt reinforcement from the United States either in units or in loss replacements. In such a case, their plight would resemble that of the small British Army, rushed to France at the outbreak of World War I and destroyed there in a gallant attempt to stem the German invasion. The British also did not believe in conscription.[8]

In 1976 Taylor published his fourth and last book, a slim volume of security essays titled *Precarious Security*. In many respects it picked up where the final chapters of his memoirs had left off, for he was still examining the causes and consequences of his country's losing effort in Vietnam. In this final book, however, he took a global view of security, which he had not done either in *The Uncertain Trumpet*, with its focus on Eisenhower's budgetary priorities, or in *Swords and Plowshares*, with its emphasis on Vietnam.

As he contemplated the future, he was less inclined to view Communist military expansion as the main security challenge to the United States. Long before *glasnost,* he felt that the Soviet leadership was sufficiently conservative, and sufficiently preoccupied with problems at home, to abstain from ventures that might provoke the West. Indeed, he came to view world population growth as the most likely cause of political instability, quoting estimates that the world's population was expected to double by the year 2000, with the greatest growth in the Third World countries least equipped to handle it. Translating this trend into terms meaningful to one U.S. ally, he noted that "some 3 million Israelis are today circled by 70 million hostile Arab neighbors who will double in number by the year 2000, while Israel adds perhaps 2 million."[9]

Closer to home, Taylor took off after Congress, deploring congressional meddling in foreign affairs as typified by the War Powers Act. He characterized Congress as having "botched" the 1975 trade bill by injecting an extraneous issue, that of Jewish emigration from the Soviet Union. He charged that "a large majority of the Senate, by public espousal of the Israeli cause, seriously impaired the American position as a fair-handed mediator in the Mideast conflict."[10] Recalling the *Mayaguez* incident, he noted that President Ford may have violated two laws—the War Powers Act and the statute barring U.S. military activity in Indochina after August 1973—in the course of freeing an American ship from the Cambodians.

As for the defense establishment, Taylor reiterated a familiar complaint: the fact that the Defense Department could never be certain of its spending authority from one year to the next. He urged an arrangement whereby the country would commit a fixed percentage of its gross national product for defense, and tentatively suggested a figure in the area of 8 percent. But he also gave vent to his growing impatience with defense management, writing:

> In their own interest, the armed forces will be obliged to control the skyrocketing prices of new equipment which result from a combination of inflation and the increasing complexity of modern weapons and equipment. It takes only a few billiondollar carriers and *Trident* submarines, multimillion-dollar air-

craft, and million-dollar tanks to absorb all the new equipment funds that the services are likely to receive.[11]

At a time when patriotism and calls for national unity were out of fashion, the author took on the special interest groups, writing of the danger from "frustrated, alienated, misguided, or revolutionary people who, finding no good in American leaders, institutions, motives, or accomplishments, see no hope for improvement without radical change." Such groups, he wrote, "appear dedicated to the downfall of America by undermining its strength and reinforcing self-destructive tendencies already at work within our society."[12]

As with much of Taylor's writing, the book's virtue or lack thereof was very much in the eye of the beholder. The New York Times dismissed Precarious Security with a review titled "A Sermon by the General." One Laurence Radway, writing in Orbis, characterized the author as the ultimate pessimist. "For him the trumpet is always uncertain, security forever precarious." Other reviews tended to be cautiously favorable, citing the author's professional credentials without endorsing his recommendations. Andrew J. Pierre, writing in Foreign Affairs, commented that "General Taylor's reputation for clear thought, lucid analysis, and the ability to separate the central issues from the chaff which surrounds them, is once again demonstrated in this pithy book."[13]

In 1978 the Carter administration succeeded in recruiting Taylor as a supporter of the controversial series of treaties that would return the Panama Canal to Panama. The issue was one to which Taylor devoted considerable thought, and he did not reach his final judgment lightly. He testified before the Senate Armed Services Committee that the primary threat to the Canal was not an overt act of war, but sabotage either with or without foreign instigation. His support for the treaties, he testified, grew out of his belief that they offered "the best prospect for the efficient and unimpeded operation of the canal." Should Panama fail to protect it, he noted, the treaties gave the United States "the continuing right to take whatever steps it deems necessary, to include military action . . . to restore order."[14]

As yet another presidential election year beckoned, Taylor focused on a curious phenomenon: the tendency of the election process to act as a spur to the arms race. In an article for the Washington *Post,* he noted that "regardless of who wins the [1980] election, the new president will feel obliged . . . to support a military program purporting to seek either military parity with or superiority over the Soviet Union." He went on to deplore the numbers race with respect to intercontinental missiles which, in his view, ignored critical factors such as reliability, survivability, and destruction potential:

> By giving top priority to strategic weapons and thereby to preparations to forestall the least probable of all our major military threats, [a missile race] will lead us to expend much of our resources on the wrong things or in the wrong order of priority. It will confirm us in the neglect of our conventional forces. . . . Yet these are the forces we need right now to discourage any further Soviet advance toward Middle East oil fields, the control of which would give Moscow irresistible political and economic leverage over the NATO nations and Japan. They are also the forces that guarantee the security of our home base in the Western Hemisphere, ensure an ability to reinforce our overseas deployments in Europe and Asia and prevent the interruption of our trade with important overseas markets.[15]

In a letter to Justice Powell, Taylor added that the U.S. objective should be "not to match Soviet numbers, but to meet [the] mission requirements of U.S. forces. Such a procedure does not ignore the very real Soviet threat which would generate many of the tasks for which we must make provision."[16]

The period in which Taylor wrote had seen a questioning by some military writers as to whether deterrence, or mutually assured destruction, should still be the cornerstone of U.S. strategy. Soviet doctrine, some said, made no distinction between nuclear and conventional war, and this fact, combined with the Soviets' demonstrated willingness to accept heavy losses in war, sharply reduced the deterrent effect of the U.S. nuclear arsenal. Taylor was unimpressed by this argument. He saw the Soviets' superiority in conventional forces as giving them no reason to instigate a nuclear war. He also believed that not even the Soviets would willingly lead their country into a nuclear exchange that would make the devastation of World War II pale by comparison. "The past record of the Kremlin leaders," he wrote, "indicates an extreme reluctance to run unnecessary risks, particularly if there is a safer way to gain the desired end." The Soviets, in his view, were content to await the collapse of capitalism from its internal weaknesses and contradictions.[17]

As Army chief of staff and later as chairman of the JCS, Taylor had shared the traditional military preoccupation with enemy "capabilities"—which dictated that the United States be capable of meeting virtually every threat worldwide. In retirement, he was far more attuned to intentions as opposed to capabilities. In a letter to Justice Powell, Taylor elaborated on what he perceived would be the form of future threats from the Soviet Union:

> For our leaders in Washington today, the Soviet capabilities most feared appear to be three: a surprise strategic attack upon vital U.S. targets; a major conventional attack on NATO; and a miscellany of possible . . . measures—political, subversive, military and terrorist—for obtaining direct or indirect control of Mideast oil. When I measure each one by its probability and damage potential, the first two get such low marks in probability that, despite their potential destructiveness, I am obliged to give them second and third priority respectively behind the Mideast threat.[18]

This focus on intentions as opposed to capabilities placed Taylor among those opposed to one of the Pentagon's pet projects, the MX missile. In May 1980, in a letter to Congressman Paul Simon, Taylor had reiterated his belief that nuclear war was an unlikely contingency, and added that he was not convinced that the MX was the right missile even if a need could be demonstrated. The following year, at the outset of the Reagan administration, he elaborated on his opposition to the MX in a letter to Senator Alan Cranston:

> A surprise attack on our silo ICBMs could be very damaging but its probability of occurrence is very low. I can conceive of no national purpose or vital interest that might induce the cautious

old men in the Kremlin to run the risks inherent in such an action. . . .

Even if convinced of the need [for] an MX, I would prefer any feasible mode that kept its launching off U.S. soil.[19]

"If you think I'm a dove, you're wrong," Taylor told a group of reporters at a breakfast. "All I am is a hawk who's afraid we're going to spend our money foolishly."[20] He was as disparaging about the Army's new main battle tank, the M-1, as about the MX missile. Why, he asked, did the Army need a tank that can go fifty miles per hour while firing in three directions? "Personally," he wrote Justice Powell, "I would not be too unhappy if the economic situation obliged the [Reagan] administration to slow down its military program, provided it used the available resources to assure the task readiness of existing conventional forces."[21]

As the Reagan administration took office, one subject of speculation was the fate of the incumbent chairman of the Joint Chiefs, General David Jones of the Air Force. Until his final year in office Carter had paid little attention to defense, and the victory of Islamic extremism in Iran had underscored the eroding Western position in the Middle East. The abortive attempt to rescue American hostages in Iran, which collapsed as a result of malfunctioning helicopters, seemed to epitomize the country's defense shortcomings. The Reagan entourage, capitalizing on popular dismay over the hostage debacle, had promised a rebuilding of the country's defenses and a new broom in the Pentagon. First to go, it was said, would be General Jones.

Taylor was no fan of Jones, whom he believed to have been an ineffective chairman. But he was as opposed to any politicization of the Joint Chiefs in 1981 as he had been as Army chief of staff, and he tended to blame the shortsightedness of the Carter years on the President and on Defense Secretary Harold Brown rather than on Jones. In an article in the Washington *Post* he discoursed on the qualities of a good chairman, among which he listed some degree of sympathy with the objectives of the incumbent Administration. However, recalling the wholesale sacking of the Truman Chiefs by Eisenhower, Taylor came to Jones's defense. Reagan would be unjustified in taking action against him, Taylor wrote, unless he had reason to believe that the general had participated actively in party politics, had harbored views on important military matters antithetical to his own, or had displayed in office personal qualities that disqualified him for continuation. For whatever reason, General Jones served out his term.

In his lectures at the various military schools, Taylor found himself dealing regularly with questions growing out of the first pop history of the Vietnam period, David Halberstam's *The Best and the Brightest.* Halberstam, whose reporting from Saigon had upset first the Kennedy White House and eventually even his employers at the New York *Times,* reflects a well-known truth of American journalism: that no writer who attributes unworthy motives to persons in power will ever die broke.

Reaching back to Taylor's first year with the Kennedy administration, Halberstam dismissed his report on the Bay of Pigs as "not very astute politically." Halberstam characterized his personal whipping boy, General Harkins, as "a puppet controlled by Taylor" and implied that back-channel communications between Taylor and Harkins—a medium employed by virtually every component of a U.S. mission abroad—were somehow disreputable. Remarkably, Halberstam stated that Taylor "disagreed with nothing" in the controversial cable of August 24, 1963, that led to Diem's overthrow, a statement that would come as a surprise to those present at the angry meeting in Kennedy's office the following Monday. In one mind-boggling display of ignorance, Halberstam explained that "since [Taylor] was too proud to wear a hearing aid, he was denied a political career of his own."[22]

Taylor dealt with Halberstam's charges as they arose in questions. No, he had never attempted to muzzle Colonel John Paul Vann, one of Harkins's critics. No, President Kennedy had never taken him to task concerning his back-channel communications with Harkins. Asked about Halberstam in an interview, Taylor dismissed him with the remark, "This lad must have *villains.*"[23]*

---

* Halberstam's polemic has long since been overshadowed by objective studies of the Vietnam period, but it is a sobering thought that this form of journalism not only enriches the author but can gain him a Pulitzer Prize. Halberstam claimed to have conducted some five hundred interviews for his book, but did not list them because "the relationship of reporter to source is very much under attack." One of those he never quite got around to interviewing was Maxwell Taylor.

Chapter 28

CARRYING ON

With the arrival of the 1980s, Maxwell Taylor finally showed signs of slowing down. He was bothered by arthritis, especially in his knees, and could get around only by employing two walking sticks, and soon, only with a walker. His problems of locomotion caused him to cut down drastically on his activities outside Washington and to resign from several boards that required travel to New York City. The arthritis tended to mask a far more insidious illness, amyotrophic lateral sclerosis, which his doctors later speculated he may have contracted as early as 1975. ALS, often called Lou Gehrig's disease, attacks the nervous system, most often of men in their twenties and thirties. In older victims the progress of the disease tends to be slow, and Taylor would live with ALS for more than a decade.

In his Massachusetts Avenue apartment, his routine was as regular as it had ever been at the Pentagon. Still an early riser, he would have a light breakfast, read the newspaper, and then move to his desk in the small, sun-filled study at the back of the apartment. He was always writing—sometimes an article for a professional magazine or the Washington *Post*, often simply the memos, notes, and outlines through which he worked out his thoughts on some issue that might, at a future date, find its way into print. Any quote that struck his fancy went into his loose-leaf book of quotations. His own aphorisms and vignettes were penned into notebooks variously titled Philosophy, Economy, Power, Government Policy, and so forth. One entire book was devoted to definitions ("Boredom: An unhappy or restless state of mind resulting from a lack of interest in one's thoughts, surroundings, events or activities"). His desk drawers were filled with longhand notes with captions like "Why no use of nukes since Nagasaki?," "Important tasks that A[rmed] F[orces] can't do," "MX—Pro and Con." As he worked away, the family parakeet would occasionally perch on his shoulder, accompanying his thoughts with high-pitched exhortations to "Beat Navy!"

Lunch was followed by a short nap and then, occasionally, by an interview. Taylor was very accessible to scholars, particularly those concerned with Vietnam, but he scrutinized query letters with an eye to the respondent's seriousness of purpose. Those who showed signs of not having done their homework in *Swords and Plowshares* were so informed. Other than the evening news and occasional weekend sports, Taylor watched almost no television. But he went to lunch at least once a month at the Alibi Club for as long as he was physically able.

Among the last substantive issues to which Taylor addressed himself in retirement were the need for a more rational allocation of defense resources—a favorite subject for the general—and the sensitive subject of JCS reform. It is a commentary on the entrenched support for the status quo in many defense matters that the views of the country's most prominent soldier carried little weight in either instance.

In 1983 Taylor returned to his "how much is enough" theme, urging the Reagan administration to define its missile requirements not in terms of the numbers ascribed to the Soviets but in terms of what was required to deter a Soviet attack. It was not the number of U.S. weapons that would deter an adversary, he pointed out, but their destructive potential. Taylor never put a number to the quantity of strategic missiles that would be required for deterrence, but he clearly envisaged a number that was but a fraction of the existing U.S. nuclear arsenal. In another article, he suggested that the Soviets have no intention of attacking the United States, because they have no national objective sufficiently important to justify such a risk. He took on the triad doctrine, the theory that, as a hedge against the failure of any single system, the U.S. nuclear arsenal must include weapons deliverable by land, sea, and air:

Over the years, the requirements imposed by Triad have seriously constrained the development of our strategic policy. Its dogma has been used to justify retaining highly vulnerable [intercontinental missiles] based on U.S. soil and to defend the essentiality of the MX missile despite all its obvious liabilities.[1]

A second issue to which Taylor addressed himself was the perennial one of JCS reform. The general, in retirement, was no more satisfied with the functioning of the Joint Chiefs than he had been first as Army chief of staff and subsequently as chairman. In testimony before a subcommittee of the House Armed Services Committee in 1982, Taylor criticized the functioning of the Chiefs in three capacities: as advisers to the President and Secretary of Defense, as a link in the chain of command leading to the unified commands, and as providers of staff support to the Secretary of Defense.

Taylor was most concerned about what he perceived as the inability or unwillingness of the Chiefs to be useful military advisers. He told the subcommittee that the Chiefs "have rarely, if ever, performed an advisory role of any importance at the level of national policy." He faulted both the Chiefs and their civilian superiors for this situation, but tended to come down hardest on the JCS. "The fact is," he testified, "that the Chiefs have traditionally been loath to volunteer advice to higher authority, particularly if its substance would impinge seriously upon service interests. In my day, the slogan in the JCS was 'just answer the mail.' "[2]

Taylor proposed radical surgery: dissolving the JCS and allowing the service chiefs to "give their undivided attention" to the management of their respective services. The Secretary of Defense's need for military staff support would be met by transferring the rest of the Joint Staff to the Secretary of Defense, to be used to meet his own requirements. For long-term strategic advice, Taylor advocated a new entity, a National Military Council. He envisaged a council of perhaps five persons, "respected multistar officers, retired or about to retire," but he did not rule out civilian members as well. It would be to this group, rather than to the double-hatted, service-oriented JCS, that the White House would look for long-term strategic guidance.

Taylor had periodically attempted to reorganize elements of the national security bureaucracy with proposals that were designed to improve governmental performance. He did not feel it his responsibility to judge the political feasibility of his proposals, and as a result his record was mixed. The Kennedy administration had buried his proposal for a cold war strategy committee, and little had come of his later attempt to increase the State Department's role in program administration. At least two of his initiatives deserved a better fate: his 1974 proposal for an enlarged role for the National Security Council and now, on very familiar turf, his proposals for JCS reform. Even here, however, the time was not ripe. The Reagan administration was not interested in a major restructuring of the Chiefs, only in tinkering. Caspar Weinberger, in particular, showed no interest in changes that would increase the military as opposed to the civilian component in the planning process. On Capitol Hill, no one of prominence was prepared to lead where the Reagan administration would not follow.

Taylor watched with interest as the Reagan administration restored a new activism to foreign affairs, but when it came to specific policies he often found himself reserving judgment. He applauded the Administration's decision to intervene in Grenada, but viewed the operation itself as confirmation of command weaknesses in the Pentagon. He had mixed feelings about the 1982 Israeli invasion of Lebanon but hoped that it might lead to a withdrawal of all foreign troops. He wrote in 1982 that "any withdrawal should certainly include any Marines [that] we have been foolish enough to commit to this international cauldron."[3] Slightly more than a year later, 241 Marines would be dead, killed by a terrorist bomb in Beirut.

Another development that Taylor followed closely was General Westmoreland's libel suit against CBS. In a "documentary" aired in 1982, TV journalist Mike Wallace had charged that Westmoreland, in Vietnam, had suppressed intelligence data that pointed toward increasing Communist strength—information that, had it been accepted in Washington, might have changed decisions relative to the war. In attempting to impute political motives to Westmoreland, CBS coached witnesses, edited testimony, and ignored the fact that there had long been differences over how to "count" part-time Viet Cong sympathizers who spent comparatively little time in the field. In an article for the Washington *Post*, Taylor characterized the Wallace program as "a hatchet job" and the charges against Westmoreland as "groundless."[4]*

As 1984 turned into 1985, Taylor's health deteriorated. His voice—the first area attacked by his disease—was almost gone; on "bad" days even family members could not understand him. Curiously, he felt that he was articulating well, and for a time was puzzled that those around him had so much difficulty understanding him. Walking was equally difficult; he could barely negotiate his apartment on a walker. Because his physician at Walter Reed, Dr. Larry Mohr, had emphasized the importance of remaining active as long as possible, Taylor fought his disease with the same dogged persistence that he had brought to the battlefield. He resisted a wheelchair up to his final year, and as a result suffered frequent falls. Normally, the devoted Sergeant Cargill could get the general back on his feet. On weekends, however, Mrs. Taylor was sometimes reduced to calling around the building for assistance.

The articles for the *Post* ended, and with them Taylor's plans for an anecdotal volume along the lines of Eisenhower's *At Ease*. But he was determined to keep his mind active. He would test his memory by attempting to write out verses from Shakespeare and the Greek philosophers. He translated poems from English into French and biblical verses from English into Spanish. In one notebook he laboriously penned lines from Edward Dyer:

> My mind to me a kingdom is;
> Such present joys therein I find
> That it excels all other bliss
> That Earth affords or grows by kind.

He was sustained in his final years by a small, very personal library, and the volumes in his bedside bookcase told much about

---

* Although Taylor contributed to Westmoreland's legal fund, he had doubts from the outset about the $120 million libel suit, believing as he did that no citizen could win a case against such a corporate giant. Taking comfort from what the case had revealed of CBS's shoddy standards, Taylor wrote to Westmoreland after the case was settled that "after having taken on too big an opponent, CBS, on the wrong battlefield, the courthouse, you have achieved important effects that will make for a worthy victory over the enemy."

their owner. Many concerned philosophy. Bertrand Russell's *Human Society in Ethics and Politics* was flanked by A. E. Taylor's biography of Plato and Jowett's translation of the dialogues of Plato. Other volumes in philosophy included Josiah Royce's *The Religious Aspect of Philosophy* and Joad's *Guide to the Philosophy of Morals and Politics.*

Over the years he gave away many books on military subjects. Among those he retained to the end were Clausewitz's *On War*, in German, Forrest Pogue's multivolume biography of George Marshall, Antonia Fraser's *Cromwell: The Lord Protector*, and the German-language memoirs of a onetime antagonist, Heinz Guderian (inscribed, "In memory of the day of my captivity in Berchtesgaden"). The largest number of books reflected Taylor's lifelong interest in languages. In addition to a variety of dictionaries—French-German, for example—there were *Don Quixote* in Spanish, Balzac and Molière in French, and several well-worn Bibles in French, German, and Japanese.

On Christmas Eve in 1985 Taylor collapsed in his bedroom and was admitted to Walter Reed yet again. At that time Dr. Mohr estimated his prospects for survival at no more than even, but the patient began a partial recovery, a pattern that was typical of his illness. Shortly after the new year he was back in his apartment, wasted but insistent on carrying on. When not translating poetry, he turned to his own doggerel, often on the subject of age:

> It's a sign of age you can't ignore
> Though your hair is not yet gray,
> When things fall more to the floor
> And the floor gets farther away.

In January 1986 he wrote to Justice Powell,

> As to my health, I can't complain for a man of 84 who has been very lucky up to now. What I complain about most is a combination of weak legs and an unclear voice. Even Diddy has trouble with the latter and often must transmit my words by telephone. I get some comfort from the old jingle:
>> A wise old owl lived in an oak,
>> The more he saw, the less he spoke.

The less he spoke the more he heard.
Why can't I be like that bird?

Well, now I have to resemble the bird whether I want to or not.[5]

Taylor never berated the fate that had condemned him to one of the most debilitating of diseases, one that prevented him even from conversing with his bride of six decades. But here, too, he would not give in. On their joint birthday in 1986 he passed her a note, "Merry birthday to my beloved one. MDT."

In the last year of his life, as he sought to keep a grip on his mind, he asked his editor daughter-in-law, Priscilla, who shared his interest in linguistic curiosities, to bring him a book of English synonyms. She promptly delivered the latest *Webster's New World Thesaurus* ("More than 300,000 synonyms and antonyms"), which had just crossed her desk. When she next dropped by, however, he handed her a note with a smile, "I'm returning the excellent Thesaurus. It's a book of great value but I want a book for only synonyms and antonyms." It was some days before she recognized this as a request for a more detailed explanation of the etymology of words and dusted off her 1945 version of *Crabb's English Synonyms Explained.* He kept the book close by for the rest of his life, studying the evolution of the English language and its finer shades of meaning.

On a wintry night in January 1987 Taylor was attempting to mount his walker when he fell, striking his head and breaking his collarbone. A District of Columbia ambulance refused to take him to Walter Reed and went instead to Georgetown Hospital, where doctors in the emergency room knew nothing of the underlying disease of their unconscious patient. When transferred to Walter Reed the following day, Taylor was diagnosed as having pneumonia in addition to his broken collarbone. After several days he regained consciousness for a time, but he never again left the hospital. In mid-March he lapsed into a coma, and on Easter Sunday, April 19, the life that had begun in a crossroads Missouri town came to a peaceful close.

The tributes poured in. President Reagan called the general "one of the outstanding figures of our time . . . a soldier's soldier and a statesman's statesman." King Baudouin of Belgium penned a two-page tribute, recalling a meeting with the general at West Point decades before and concluding, "My countrymen will never forget the significant role he played in the liberation of Europe and the Battle of the Bulge." Jacqueline Kennedy Onassis wrote to Mrs. Taylor:

> I always felt so lucky to have known him. . . . His intelligence, the optimism and gaiety of his charm—this soldier, scholar, statesman, linguist, author—one found all these qualities in one man in the early days of this country, not in the twentieth century.[6]

There were two eulogies at the services, one from Ambassador Philip Bonsal, who had been one of a faithful group of visitors to 2500 Massachusetts Avenue right up to the end, the other from my brother Tom. There were few dry eyes in the overflow congregation when my brother, in turn, quoted a tribute from my daughter Alice, living in England:

> He was as tall, straight and full-sapped as a young oak tree. He had eyes resonant with laughter, eyes that crinkled like my father's eyes, eyes that could warm a room. He was agelessly handsome, well-knit to the bone, and he radiated that kind of inner certainty that many people seek and some are born with.

At the graveside, a short distance from the Tomb of the Unknown Soldier, there were nineteen guns, followed by taps. A score of aging veterans of the 101st Airborne Division delivered a final salute, standing ramrod stiff with, according to the New York *Times*, "the cocky air of elite troops."

The reader who has lasted this far will have recognized in Maxwell Taylor a talented, inner-directed person who probably would have risen to the top of any of a number of professions, including business, the law, or education. It was the nation's good fortune that a generation of able soldiers accommodated themselves to two decades of peacetime service in an Army where promotion was almost nonexistent and professional opportunities few. But Taylor viewed the Army of his day as a challenging succession of graduate schools in his chosen profession. The system served him well, for it gave him the skills to command a division in war after having commanded nothing larger than an artillery battalion in peacetime.

Even as a junior officer, Taylor's personal outlook served him well. Like the stonecutter who thought himself a builder of cathedrals, Taylor never lost sight of the fact that he was engaged in the worthy cause, the defense of his country. In the Army's structured society, he developed the orderly, disciplined work habits that stood him in good stead for most of his life. However, the "military mind" in which Taylor set such store was not without its perils. A lifetime spent among those who believed, as he did, in "Duty, Honor, Country" was hardly preparation for dealing with the America of the 1960s.

World War II brought challenges and opportunities, and Taylor made the most of them. In Normandy, Holland, and the Ardennes he was able to satisfy himself that he possessed the elusive quality of military leadership; by some combination of competence and chemistry, when he spoke, people obeyed. It is curious that, having demonstrated his professionalism under fire, Taylor rarely looked back. Far from being the stereotypical old soldier reliving the last war, he neither rejoiced over past success nor brooded over failure. Rather, he looked ahead to what the future was likely to bring.

What distinguished Taylor among some very able military contemporaries was that he carried his strategic analysis beyond the problem at hand and sought to view it from every possible dimension. His main concern during the Cuban missile crisis, for example, was that the Soviets might take advantage with Washington's preoccupation with Cuba to make an aggressive move against Berlin. It was this quality of "geopolitical wisdom"—Robert McNamara's term—that made Taylor indispensable to two presidents. He looked at every issue from the perspective of its impact on his country's vital interests, and he could conceive of no role for his country other than as leader of the free world.

Two tours of duty in the 1950s had an important bearing on Taylor's thinking. The first was his year in Berlin, where he came to admire a people who refused to be intimidated by the Communists. There, too, he became convinced that as long as the United

States possessed nuclear weapons, Communist expansion was likely to be carried out by proxies, not by the Red Army. A second influential period was that spent in Korea and Japan in the early 1950s. In Korea he saw Americans turn a military rabble into an effective army and turn military disaster into a truce that permitted South Korea to survive and prosper. If this acceptable result could be achieved in Korea, where was it not possible?

In the area of strategic doctrine, it is somewhat ironic that Taylor is best remembered as the critic of massive retaliation who coined the term *flexible response*. The defects of Eisenhower's defense policies were obvious, and Taylor was not the first to call attention to them. His most innovative thinking, ironically, related to Vietnam. The policy of gradualism that he long espoused flew in the face of the conventional wisdom, which, with Clausewitz, called for a quick, climactic battle. Taylor, influenced by the Korean experience, espoused a limited war, one aimed at altering Hanoi's behavior by means short of total war. Because the Johnson administration miscalculated the temper of both its own people and North Vietnam's leadership, gradualism failed. The impact of this failure cannot be fully assessed at this time, but it is likely to place sharp limits on the military options available to the United States in any future crisis short of all-out war.

I once had occasion to ask him if he dreamed at night. His reply was that he did not often dream but that when he did the theme was the same: he was trying to reach a goal, but there was some obstacle between him and his objective. The determination with which he approached any challenging problem was part of his undoing with respect to Vietnam. He was loath to give up any fight when the means for success were at hand. Although he fully appreciated the political dimensions of the Vietnam War, both nationally and internationally, he was slow to recognize the growth of special interest groups in his own country, and the difficulty of achieving unity behind anything as abstract as the containment of communism. He freely acknowledged that much was flawed in the Kennedy-Johnson policies in Vietnam, but he believed that even imperfect policies should command the loyalty of good citizens.

Considering the controversial actions with which he was associated, Taylor appears to have had remarkably few personal enemies. Except for a few writers of the New Left, even critics conceded that Max Taylor was working for what he perceived to be his country's best interest. He, in turn, had no venom for his critics; there were no dark corners to his personality. Even in the most informal family gatherings, he rarely questioned the character or motives of those with whom he disagreed.

His working style, however, did not make for close confidants. His practice was to employ whatever staff was available to him to marshal all the facts bearing on a problem, but then to work it out for himself. This method was in contrast to the preference of many people to thrash out a problem in discussion; it also tended to inhibit compromise. Perhaps because of this style, Taylor had his share of bureaucratic setbacks. He had little success in gaining support for his policies from the Eisenhower administration. Similarly, he was outflanked in 1968 when Clark Clifford and perhaps others made post-Tet conversions among the Wise Men on the subject of Vietnam.

For all his pragmatism, Taylor was also an idealist. He was impatient with special interests and even with partisan politics. His ideal was government by the wise and virtuous, working in the national interest. It was because of this that some of his recommendations had an ivory tower quality, especially those involving government reorganizations. For all his political acumen, he was not always a match for his colleagues in bureaucratic infighting.

America tends to remember its artists and sports heroes for their triumphs; it is far less generous with its politicians and soldiers. Nevertheless, Maxwell Taylor deserves to be remembered, and to be remembered for more than being a valiant soldier and a valued presidential counselor. For his was a voice that held—when such views seemed hopelessly out of fashion—that the United States is more than a collection of interest groups; that it has enduring security requirements that it must deal with rationally; and that citizenship in twentieth-century America carries with it obligations as well as privileges.

Appendix A

"Leading the American Soldier"

by Major General Maxwell D. Taylor

I have set for myself a difficult task today in undertaking to discuss the leading of the American soldier with this much-lectured class. It is a subject which any officer should undertake with the greatest humility, as no experience is broad enough, no wisdom is deep enough, to provide the final word on such a subject. It is a subject particularly difficult to treat without falling into abstractions which are meaningless without the illumination of some past experience. Like so many other elements in our schooling, it is possible to appreciate fully the principles of leadership only after having bungled some of our early efforts in that field.

I think the proper start for a discussion of leading the American soldier is to consider what sort of fellow we have to deal with, to determine what are the characteristics which condition his use in war. At the outset, I should like to make it clear that in my opinion we must distinguish between the two types of American soldiers, even at the risk of overstating the contrast. The first type is the Regular Army volunteer whom we met in the peacetime Army between World War I and World War II. He is the type which has always been present in our volunteer peacetime Army. The second type is the one of primary concern to us today, the drafted citizen soldier who came to arms, sometimes willingly, sometimes unwillingly, to meet the national emergency of war. Now, I am not sure whether the peacetime Regular Army will ever exist again as my contemporaries knew it. However, it is well to point out what sort of soldiers composed it. They were generally of two sorts—first,

---

This talk was first delivered before the First Class, U.S. Military Academy, on May 27, 1946.

the old-time noncommissioned officer who was as much a professional soldier as the Regular officers themselves. The typical NCO was a man of great simplicity of character, devoted to his officers and to the outfit in which he was spending his life. Such men were the guides and counsellors of the young lieutenants reporting to their first assignments. They watched over the professional development of their young officers whose subsequent careers they followed with interest and pride. They were extremely competent in the details of the military profession. They knew company administration, stable management, and Army regulations better than most officers. They relieved the unit commanders of the administrative burdens of their command and the routine problems of housekeeping. However, when war came they contributed comparatively little. In general, they were too old for field service so that most of them stayed in the Zone of the Interior as temporary officers in the military police or in one of the supply services. Their age and lack of physical condition required their elimination from combat units.

As for the enlisted men of this peacetime Army, those who did not become NCOs were usually not of a very high type. Without either the ability or the desire to become noncommissioned officers, they seldom spent more than one or two enlistments in the Army. The fact that they were willing to serve for little pay and with no promotion was ordinarily proof of lack of ambition and energy. Such soldiers added very little to the national military potential, as they did little more than keep the lawns and hedges well trimmed on our Regular Army garrisons. From the point of view of leadership, these soldiers were docile and presented no particular difficulty beyond the need for occasional disciplinary action against those who got drunk or went AWOL. The service they rendered was unimaginative and unenthusiastic.

Such Regular Army peacetime soldiers were in marked contrast to the type we received when the war permitted the Army to draw on the entire nation for military manpower. While the strong words of the Duke of Wellington are not directly applicable, I might quote his comments on the relative character of the French conscript and the British Regular Army volunteers as suggesting the difference between our peacetime Regular volunteers and our wartime conscript. Wellington said in 1831, "The French system of conscription brings together a fair sample of all classes. Ours is composed of the scum of the earth—mere scum of the earth. It is always wonderful that we should be able to make so much of them afterwards. The English soldiers are fellows who have all enlisted for drink."

These words could not be applied without offense to the personnel of our peacetime Regular Army, but they do emphasize the difference which conscription makes in bringing to the Army a cross section of the entire nation. The best and the worst, the intelligent and the stupid, the loyal and the subversive, all find their way into the Army uniform and eventually stand before the officers of the Army as a challenge to their ability to produce effective leadership for the nation in arms.

Let us now consider the traits of these men who find themselves suddenly transplanted from civil life into the military service. In the first place, they are generally completely ignorant of the Army and are pretty sure that they will not like its ways. Many have grown up in areas traditionally hostile to the armed services; many come from families with pacifistic tendencies where they have been taught to view the Army, and Army officers in particular, with deep suspicion. Almost to a man, they will bring the national characteristic of resentment to discipline and authority which, in my opinion, presents the greatest obstacle we have to face in the creation of good troops from the American selectee.

One has only to read the daily papers or listen to the talk which goes on around him or in the halls of Congress to realize that Americans as a nation are innately critical of constituted authority. The average citizen is accustomed to freedom of speech and exercises it to the limit. He is accustomed to attacking his political leaders and sees no reason why the same methods should not be carried over to criticism of military leaders. Our pioneer forefathers were deeply individualistic and resisted restraint even to the point of lawlessness. This tradition of disregard for law is visible today in mass picketing, mob violence, and, less dramatically but nonetheless typically, in the shower of pop bottles that falls around the unfortunate umpire at a baseball game.

Few of our public or private enterprises escape this American attitude, this love of giving the Bronx cheer. Certainly, the Army cannot expect or claim any immunity. As officers, we must recognize and expect this attitude in our wartime soldiers. It is a phenomenon we cannot and probably should not want to change because, as I shall show you later, it is a necessary concomitant of the vigorous martial virtues which are also inherent in most of our citizens.

While their insubordinate impulses create difficulties for their officers, our conscript soldiers have compensating qualities of initiative, enthusiasm, and dash which more than make up for the headaches which result from their less desirable traits. But the critical tendency puts officers to the test; they cannot expect a blind and uncritical obedience of the German or the Jap; they cannot expect to receive a respectful hearing by reading military gospel from a book. No institution is sacrosanct to your American soldiers; they will criticize all, and it behooves their officers to be on sound ground and to "know their stuff" if they expect to carry conviction. They must show the soldiers the "why" of things if they expect them to display the enthusiasm and the eagerness to learn of which they are capable. Remember the words which Von Steuben wrote back to Europe: "The genius of this American nation is not in the least to be compared with that of the Prussians, Austrians or French. You say to your soldier, 'Do this' and he doeth it. But I am obliged to say, 'This is the reason why you ought to do that' and then he does it."

This, then, is a rough picture of the kind of soldier whom you will be required to lead in war. I will now try to point out some of the qualities which I believe an officer must develop if he is to lead such men successfully. I will say in advance that there is no unanimity as to what characteristics are most important in the formation of leaders. The classification which I shall use is my own and is susceptible to criticism. Nevertheless, I suggest that all the great leaders of the past and the present have been conspicuous for the following three qualities. First, they have been devoted to the welfare of their troops. Secondly, they have been richly endowed with human understanding. And finally, they have stood out by their professional competence and ability. Now let me expand briefly on each of these characteristics.

The citizen soldier in war finds himself in a strange environment. He is torn from his family and his friends and thrown among strangers. Surrounded by strange institutions and customs, he feels vaguely threatened by the unfamiliar present and, even more, by the uncertain future. His conception of war and battle has been distorted by false literature, abetted by Hollywood, which has given him a "What Price Glory" idea of military life. He suffers from the absence of a standard of values to guide him in this new world in which he finds himself. At such a time, the soldier needs to look to someone in whom he has confidence, someone who will build up in him the feeling that he is a protected human entity. That someone must be his commanding officer.

We find in G.I. gripes the recurring note that certain officers did not look after their men; they thought of themselves first and placed the requirements of their troops in the background. In the great wartime officer corps of over 800,000, in which Regular officers were in significant minority, there were many who failed in their responsibility to their men. Such officers are responsible for the regrettable state of our officer-soldier relations following the war. They are the antithesis of what you gentlemen should want to be. If you read the pages of history with reflection, you find that no man ever rose to military greatness who did not succeed in convincing his troops that he put them first, above all else.

Few leaders in all history have had the whole-hearted support of their men to the extent that the Army of Northern Virginia was devoted to its commander, Robert E. Lee. While much of this support can be attributed to the professional qualities of General Lee, a large measure of his success was due to the fact that the Army of Northern Virginia knew that General Lee did his best to provide for their welfare. He was loyal to them, and they were loyal to him. When he ordered them to dig entrenchments, a work which they always hated, they knew that the work was necessary and was done to protect their lives. They knew when he ordered them into battle that he had wisely planned so that they could succeed with minimum losses. Soldiers were not cannon fodder to General Lee; they were comrades associated in the common enterprise of defeating the enemy and serving a cause to which they were all devoted. Furthermore, his soldiers saw that this comradeship was no mere lip service, for General Lee lived as simply as they did; his table was no better than theirs, and often worse. When friends sent him chickens, eggs, and other delicacies, General Lee would send them to the hospital, feeling that the wounded, more than he and his staff, deserved these small luxuries.

Washington was like Lee in his devotion to his men. He, the aristocrat accustomed to a life of relative luxury, set a personal example in bearing the vicissitudes of fortune at Valley Forge, an example which produced around him a loyal group that was the nucleus of the force that made the gallant fight at Trenton and changed the whole war in our favor. His constant effort to better the condition of his troops was known to them and was an important factor in developing the Army into a potent military weapon.

The work of impressing upon the soldier the fact that his officers are interested in his welfare should start from the first day when he joins his unit and be continuous thereafter. The recruit is particularly susceptible to the right sort of treatment. He usually arrives through the replacement system after a very unhappy period of weeks or months. He has been exposed to all manner of inconvenience and annoyances; he has been shoved about with no one to whom he can look for sympathy. He has come from what the soldiers contemptuously call the "repple depples" where he has often been commanded by officers assigned to the replacement service because of lack of ability to command in combat. By the time he reaches his first regiment, he is likely to be disgruntled by this treatment which he has received along the line. That is the moment which the alert commander will seize to convince the recruit that all this has been changed, that he now has a home which is the unit which he has just joined. He must be taught the history of that unit and be shown that it is one with a distinguished record of service. The note should be, "You are joining a proven outfit that is glad to have you. It will look after you, but you must look after the reputation of the outfit. Its past history has been paid for by the blood of the killed and the wounded; it is up to you to live up to the record which these men have made at such a price."

But this talk will not be convincing unless, when the recruit reaches his company or battery, he finds that it really is a happy organization. The old soldiers will be quick to tell him whether the commander looks after his men or not. What you should hope that your recruits will hear is that the "Old Man" is always on the job, that he sees that the rations come up on time, that the mail is never delayed, that he is always looking for a new rest center where the men can be relieved of some of the tedium of life in a theater of war. If your recruit learns this from the old-timers, you will have no trouble in filling the vacancies in your ranks with loyal and effective replacements.

One aspect of caring for troops is to see that they are not exposed to unnecessary hardships. The successful leader, by intelligent planning, will avoid the march which must be followed by a counter-march. By his skill, he will choose dispositions which will spare his men hardships and losses. Sherman convinced his men of his concern for their welfare by the thoroughness with which he trained them and by the consideration which he showed for them in campaign. The men soon learned that the extreme marches he required really saved them needless casualties. They noted how he marched his troops at night to spare them the burning sun of day. He himself rode in the fields beside the marching columns to avoid crowding the men off the road. This is the reverse of the picture which I saw all too frequently overseas where thoughtless officers raced their jeeps past marching troops and splattered them with mud. The deep cursing which such officers caused in the ranks was a fitting commentary on this display of negative leadership.

No leader worth his salt will fail to feel and show his sincere sorrow for the dead and his sympathy for the wounded. Julius Caesar, after one military disaster where he had lost heavily, allowed his beard and hair to grow and vowed he would not cut them until his soldiers had avenged their comrades' death. Stonewall Jackson was always seen in his field hospitals, visiting the sick and wounded. Soldiers cannot be allowed to think that they are scratched off the list and forgotten when the fortunes of battle lay them low.

All that I have been saying about devotion to the troops adds up to this. The badge of rank which an officer wears on his coat is really a symbol of servitude—servitude to his men. The privileges which he receives from his rank—the fact that an orderly pitches his tent, that a soldier digs his foxhole, that someone prepares and serves his food—all of these privileges go to the officer, not for any intrinsic personal merit but because the officer is entitled to more time and leisure for thought and preparation in serving his troops. If his behavior shows that in all things the enlisted man comes first, he will receive loyal, uncomplaining service from his men, without the grumbling and "bitching" which are the merited lot of the selfish officer.

I would mention as a second attribute of the successful leader the gift of human understanding, the ability to treat men as individuals and not as Army serial numbers. American troops in particular resent any suggestion that they are without individuality, that they are ciphers and not people. They want to be known for themselves and will resist any effort to mold them into an anonymous pattern. All great soldiers have succeeded in convincing their men that they know and respect them as individuals. To accomplish this they go among their men freely, mingling with them and giving the soldiers a chance to look them over and size them up. The officer who barricades himself behind his rank is properly suspected of having weaknesses to conceal—probably more than he really has. The successful commander claims no infallibility, and is not afraid to expose himself to close view. Instead, he is often seen among his men; he learns their surnames and calls them by name at every opportunity. It is said of Caesar that he never lacked a pleasant word for his soldiers. He remembered the face of anyone who had done a gallant deed, and when not in the presence of the enemy encouraged amusements in which he frequently joined. Such little human acts as these inspired his legionaries with a devotion which went far to account for his success.

Another subtle approach to the affection of your men is an interest in their families. Ask your soldier about his wife and children—he will be delighted to tell you his life story and will be flattered by the interest which his commander shows. If you write an occasional letter to a member of his family—to his father, for example, describing the good work which the son is doing—your act will reverberate throughout the entire command and you will have made a life-long friend of the soldier in question.

An officer shows understanding of the type we are discussing if he goes out of his way to explain the basis of his orders and the reason for the actions required of his men. During the last war, most successful generals went to great pains in explaining their detailed plans before asking troops to execute them. You recall that General Montgomery, in the battle of El Alamain, ordered that every man in the Eighth Army be told the plan of attack. In our American landings in North Africa, in Sicily, at Salerno, and in Normandy, commanders were most careful to brief their men on what to expect and why. This explaining of "why" to the troops goes beyond the need to explain individual battles or campaigns; it should cover the entire question of why we are fighting. Nothing keeps a man going in war like a strong belief in his cause. We need only recall the fervor which sustained the Southern states in our Civil War. It was the Confederate soldier's love of his cause that kept him going for four long years when he was poorly equipped, badly fed, and nearly always fighting against odds. It was only when a similar spirit became common among the armies of the North that the tide of victory swung to their side.

I think that this discussion of the need for human understanding can be summed up by saying that it is the exercise of common sense in human relations. There are times to be stern; there are times to be lenient. There are times to be exacting; there are times to be tolerant. This feeling for the right course of action to be taken with men is instinctive in some officers and often lacking in others, but it can be cultivated and developed by all. I recommend that you observe the behavior of senior officers whom you respect and who are obviously successful with soldiers. Model yourself upon them as you, too, will some day be a model to those who follow you.

The last of the three virtues of the successful leader is professional competence. The leader must know his business, and the men must know that he knows. War is a terribly serious business, and our citizen soldiers want their lives protected by experts. They may tend to belittle the Regular Army in times of peace, but, when war comes, our citizens want to feel that their lives and fortunes are in the hands of professionals. It becomes your duty as Regular officers to devote your lives to providing this professional leader-

ship. The members of every generation of graduates from West
Point have at least once in their career known the crisis of war. As
future officers, you gentlemen must have with you constantly the
feeling of preparing to run a great race where the stakes will be
the lives of your men, your personal fortunes, and even the future
of your nation. If you make your peacetime career one of constant
self-improvement, you will of necessity impress your soldiers with
your professional competence. The training of your troops will be
realistic, the plans which you draw will be sound, and it will be
clear to all that you know your job.

Professional competence is more than a display of book knowledge or of the results of daily schooling. It requires the display of
qualities of character which reflect inner strength and justify confidence in one's self. To give an impression of strength an officer
must consider his personal appearance, his physical condition, his
tone of voice, his style of life—all of which give an impression of
his character. This does not mean the development of an artificial
personality. All of us have certain traits that were given to us at
birth. We all have a core of personality that cannot be reversed but
can be constantly developed. A facade of sham will not serve. If
you would have your troops believe that you are strong, you must
be strong. If you would teach them to be rugged, you must avoid a
soft life yourself. If you would have your men be brave, you must
yourself be an example of valor.

To bring the full force of his character to bear effectively on his
men, an officer must resort to every device of personal leadership.
I know that some military thinkers say that the day is past in
modern war when the leader can place himself in front of his men
and inspire them in action in the tradition of Civil War brigadiers
who charged on foot at the head of their men. I do not believe this
for one moment. Personal leadership is still possible within limits,
and it should be supplied by every commander. General Doolittle
electrified a discouraged Allied world by his personal leadership
when he flew his B-25 off the flight deck of the *Hornet*. General
Patton was a model to his subordinate officers and men by his
personal intervention on the battlefield. There was no point of the
front where he, an army commander, did not go and show himself
to his troops. He condemned with passionate fierceness the type of

commander who stays in his command post and does not visit the troops. For such commanders he was terror incarnate; they would flee at word of his approach to avoid the blistering criticism that would fall upon them if they were caught behind their front line.

One particularly delightful story about General Patton was told to me by one of his most energetic corps commanders. After the crossing of the Rhine, the Third Army was driving deep into southern Germany, and this particular corps had gone well in advance of the rest of the army. General Patton came up, by the one road that was intermittently open, to visit the corps commander. The latter by this time was getting a bit jittery at his exposed position. He pointed out that, by Patton's own G-2, there were 60,000 Germans on one flank and 80,000 or more on another. "And here," said the corps commander, pointing it out to General Patton, "here is my advance guard, two days' march in front of the Army." General Patton looked at the big red circles marking the German concentrations on either flank of the corps and said, "Just ignore those bastards. Go ahead." His presence at the critical point provided the needed impetus to keep the momentum of the Army rolling forward.

The vastness of General Eisenhower's responsibilities in Europe did not prevent his giving personal leadership to his troops. Although the size of his command made his visits infrequent at any given point, when he did come around he knew how to get among the troops, and chat with the individual men, so that they had the feeling of knowing General Eisenhower personally. They received a vivid impression of the solidness, the professional efficiency, and the high character which are his outstanding attributes. As a result, they went cheerfully and willingly into the dangers which his campaigns entailed.

I have now discussed at some length the three qualities which all successful leaders have had: devotion to the troops, human understanding, and professional competence. What are the rewards which fall to the officer who combines felicitously these three attributes?

First and foremost, he can expect to get the best out of his troops, and American troops at their best are without equal. No foreign army can compare with ours when the latter is properly led. American soldiers have courage, physical vigor, initiative, and dash—all of these are rich talents which they bring and place in the hands of the commander who knows how to unify them with the catalyst of true discipline. By true discipline, I mean that willing and cheerful subordination of the individual to the success of the team which is the Army. Do not confuse this kind of discipline with the external manifestations of traditional discipline: the salute, the knock on the orderly room door, the formulae of deference to superiors—in short, military courtesy as it is rigidly prescribed in our field manuals. The latter all have their place, particularly in the peacetime Army, but they are not indices of the discipline which really counts. The Army of Northern Virginia would have rated very low in military discipline in the restricted sense. It would never have won "first line" at a West Point parade, but by its spirit it has won a place among the great fighting units of all time—alongside Xenophon's Ten Thousand, Caesar's Tenth Legion, and Napoleon's Old Guard. American troops with their natural qualities plus discipline are irresistible.

Having achieved true discipline among his men, the successful commander will be victorious in battle. Victory feeds upon itself and soon creates the feeling of invincibility and pride of organization which, together, magnify the intrinsic strength of the command manyfold. Your troubles are at an end when the threat of dismissing a man from your company or regiment becomes a punishment more dreaded than court-martial. You need feel no concern when your soldiers brawl in the taverns to prove that they "belong to the best damned outfit in the Army." Such a spirit may cause you some headaches with the Military Police, but you need have no fear for your military reputation with such men on your side. The great divisions of all of our wars have had this spirit which accounted in a large measure for their success.

I know of no finer example than that of the 1st Division in World War I. That division suffered 7,000 casualties between the 4th and 11th of October, 1918. They came out of the line expecting a month's rest, but instead were ordered quickly back into the Meuse-Argonne battle. On the 29th of October, the division commander delivered the following message:

Memorandum for Members of the 1st Division: It will be well for us to bear in mind at all times, especially on the eve of active operations, (1) That we were the first assault division of the AEF; (2) That we have on four battlefields always taken all objectives assigned us; (3) That we have gone through the best German Divisions for a total of 30 kilometers and have never abandoned an inch of ground to the enemy; (4) That for every prisoner, we have taken over a hundred Germans; (5) That the above record has been due to the pride and spirit of each individual member of the Division.

In the course of this talk, I wonder whether I have painted too dark a picture of the life of the professional officers, as though his career were only one of vexatious responsibilities. Must we expect only recriminations and no reward? If I have painted such a picture, I have been wrong. As for all duty well done, the rewards that come to the successful commander are rich, indeed. American troops, led in the spirit which I have described to you, will bring fame and honor to the officer who has known how to use their talents; they will put stars on his shoulders and ribbons on his chest and make his name live in the pages of history. And beyond these material rewards, to have commanded troops who have rendered such conspicuous services to the nation will bring to the officer an abiding sense of accomplishment, in having brought to the bloody business of war its redeeming virtues of human loyalty and the fraternal devotion which bind fighting men together—officers and men alike—in mutual respect.

Appendix B

"The American Soldier"

by General Maxwell D. Taylor

At a meeting of the Phi Beta Kappa Society in 1837, Ralph Waldo Emerson delivered a famous oration entitled "The American Scholar." In it he proclaimed to the academic world the emancipation of American scholarship from dependence upon the European influence from which it had drawn its inspiration since colonial days. "Our day of dependence, our long apprenticeship to the learning of other lands, draws to a close," said Emerson. . . . We have listened too long to the courtly muses of Europe." This pronouncement came to be regarded as the Declaration of Independence of American scholarship, recording the dawn of a new intellectual era for the maturing republic.

I have often felt that a West Point graduation should sometime have been the occasion for a similar address dedicated to the American Soldier—and I use that term broadly this morning to mean the American man-at-arms, be he soldier, sailor, airman, or marine. Like other forms of American scholarship, American military thought was also once in European bondage but likewise has become emancipated. Our Civil War marked the turning point in this trend. Drawing confidence from the experience acquired in that war, American military leadership became more and more independent of the European tradition which once controlled its thinking and limited the soar of its initiative. Since World War I, the American Soldier has generated his own military doctrine, devised his own strategy, produced his own weapons, and developed his own relationship to civil authority, largely without benefit of

This commencement address was delivered at the U.S. Military Academy, June 5, 1963.

the theories of the Napoleons or the Schlieffens of the Old World. The American military doctrine which proved itself in World War II was essentially the product of our native school system wherein student officers in the years of peace meditated on the requirements of future war. The soundness of their judgments is the more surprising since they were reached by men who had never had the benefit of experience in the command of large units, for large units in our armed forces in that period were woefully few. Officers like General Eisenhower and General Mark Clark were fortunate if they obtained in time of peace the command of a battalion before receiving in time of war the command of an army or a theater of war. In spite of a monotonous life and the absence of challenge which is often conducive to stagnation of thought, such men learned to think in broad terms unrelated to their routine tasks and prepared themselves on the company drill field for an international role.

The American Soldier, working in close association with the American Scientist and Engineer, was responsible for effecting the greatest change in weapons since the invention of gunpowder— the introduction of nuclear arms and their missile delivery systems. Thus he contributed to giving America preeminence in this awe-inspiring category of weapons and at the same time in the sobering responsibility for their use in a world beset with fears and tensions. As the military adviser of civilian leadership, the American Soldier acquired the task of fitting these weapons into a strategy of flexibility adapted to the shifting requirements of national defense. With an understanding of the effects of nuclear weapons, he has come to realize that these are not all-purpose weapons—on the contrary, they must be supplemented by non-nuclear means of use in limited wars and in guerrilla insurgencies of the kind we have known in Korea and Vietnam. Thus, the American voice is now heard in allied councils urging greater balance of effort without undue reliance on immediate resort to nuclear weapons to arrest the initial phases of aggression. This is the so-called "new" American strategy which some of our European friends have misunderstood—it is not really a "new" strategy at all but merely the logical readjustment of former concepts to the changing requirements of the defense of the West. The American

Soldier has learned that there is no single, unchanging formula for preserving the peace.

Yet, as I said at the outset, no orator has thus far seen fit to memorialize the deeds of the American Soldier and of American arms. Even if an Emerson were here today with this purpose—and all too clearly one is not—any oration in praise of the independence of the American Soldier would be largely postlude to the present fact of the ascendent role of America in military affairs.

Abroad, this ascendency of American arms and American military concepts is accepted as a matter of course—it is imperfectly or reluctantly recognized at home. Abroad, the successes of our armed forces in World War II and Korea and the visible deterrent power of our arms today, as shown in the Cuban crisis, have enforced this appreciation of American primacy—for in the military field as in other fields of endeavor, it is success that brings conviction.

Abroad, the success of the American military effort has led to an inquiry into its causes, into the form of its concepts, and the nature of its tactics and technique. Hence, allied and neutral powers send their representatives to our military schools in vast numbers; last year, approximately 17,000 students came to the United States to learn the American way of waging war and of keeping the peace. These same countries draw heavily on our military literature to guide their own studies. A few decades ago we in the United States learned from foreign military textbooks. In the Superintendent's quarters here at West Point some of you have no doubt seen the desk of Sylvanus Thayer, the great superintendent whom we know as the Father of the Military Academy. There you have noted some of the military texts to which he turned for counsel in administering West Point at about the same time that Emerson was delivering his oration in Cambridge. Most of these books are in French, a few in the English of the mother country. Today, the library of the head of any foreign military academy is apt to be filled with books written in the English of the military centers of the United States. Last month, I stood on a hilltop in Iran and with the military representatives of the CENTO Alliance watched with the Shah a military demonstration presented by the Iranian Army and Air Force. The explanation to the assembled international audience was made in English by Iranian officers in uniforms similar to the U.S. field uniform and the briefing bore the unmistakable mark of Fort Benning or Fort Sill. One sensed the influence of the American Soldier in his role as teacher of the armies of freedom.

If recognized and respected abroad, at home the achievements of the American Soldier are often ignored or perhaps taken for granted. We are not an immoderately modest people. We like to boast of our wealth, our size, our scenery, and our climate. We laud the American Scholar, the American Businessman, the American Scientist, the Yankee Trader—but it rarely occurs to us to boast of the American Soldier. It is true that our generals and admirals have led vast forces to victory in some of the greatest campaigns of history—the invasions of Normandy, the conquest of Japan, the liberation of Italy, the defeat of Communist aggression in Korea. The lands, seas, and air spaces which they have conquered and the prisoners which they have taken dwarf the deeds of the great conquerors which provided the familiar faces in the history books of our childhood. But still no orations are devoted at home to the ascendency of the American Soldier.

Why is this so? One incomplete answer would be that we Americans are made uneasy by the responsibilities of military leadership. As a nation we are still prone to clichés about men on horseback and the dangers of the military to democracy. We still have trouble distinguishing between what is military and what is militaristic; between what is peaceful and what is pacifistic. We must perhaps progress further before there will be wholehearted acceptance at home of the continuing need for a large and respected military profession in the United States in the same way that there is a need for a class of businessmen, professional men, scientists, clergymen, and scholars. Uncle Sam has become a world renowned soldier in spite of himself.

Why am I raising these matters with the West Point class of 1963? Because you are about to become an American Soldier, one of the band who, having emancipated themselves from foreign authority, now set the dominant tone in matters of national defense, strategy, tactics, and advanced weaponry.

If you are to be a useful member of this honorable company, you must bring to it the qualities which have made the American Soldier the figure he is today. Let me remind you of a few of these qualities. First, he has the professional competence without which he has no right to command his fellows or advise his superiors. West Point has given you the basic ingredients of academic knowledge to provide a solid foundation for your future professional development. Awaiting you as officers in the service is a very complete military school system which will offer you advanced levels of instruction in phase with the advancing levels of your responsibilities. Following each return from school, you will receive assignments in command and staff where you will have daily occasion to apply the instruction received in the graduate school system. With diligence, I have no doubt that you can and will acquire the professional competence necessary to join the ranks of the American Soldier.

Beside and above professional attainments, the American Soldier has always carried the stamp of character, integrity, and reliability—all virtues which have been set before you as precepts of conduct during your four years at West Point. If you have heeded and respected the teachings of our Alma Mater, I have no doubt that in this category also you will qualify for fellowship in the profession of arms.

However, there is a final and more difficult test to pass, the need for the kind of wisdom which expresses itself in breadth of human understanding—understanding of your men, of your associates, and of your superiors. This is the quality which is the indispensable attribute of leadership. To understand people requires an understanding of their problems and interests. Since the American Soldier walks and talks with the leaders of his own and foreign governments, to be effective in these contacts he must be familiar with the principles of government and politics. He must have a just appreciation of our national objectives and of the role of military power in attaining them. He must understand the proper relation of the military in support of civil policy, and comport himself in accord with the code which has always guided the American Soldier in the past—loyal support of the Commander-in-Chief and the civil authority which he represents.

Let me close with a few words about the responsibility of the military to advise and support civil authority. Military men who have spent their lives in the uniform of their country acquire a unique expertise in preparing for war and in waging it. No theoretical studies, no intellectual attainments on the part of the layman can be a substitute for the experience of having lived and delivered under the stress of war. Hence, the voice of the American Soldier is entitled to a serious hearing in our national councils—and I am happy to report that he today receives that hearing. If his views on subjects within his competence do not always carry the day, it is not because our civilian leaders do not seek his advice and listen to his arguments.

When he fails to persuade it may be that he has been misunderstood or that his view has been only a partial one, outweighed by other and higher considerations of national policy. Or it may be that he has not been sufficiently persuasive—that he has talked the jargon of the Pentagon without using the lay language which can always be found, if sought hard enough, to make any technical military matter understandable to the attentive civilian leader. If the American Soldier is to be true to the principle of civilian control of the military—and his past record makes impossible any question of the sincerity of that commitment—he must be willing to have his judgments challenged and expect to be called upon for the proof of their rightness. Hence, he must be a skillful and effective advocate, able to carry conviction before judges who are unimpressed by service stripes and who are immune to appeals to the military scriptures of the past. If he is such an advocate he will have no need to fear the IBM machines or the cost-effectiveness charts of the research analysts—these men and their methods also have a place in modern defense planning—in fact, he will learn to use their techniques as a part of his own professional equipment.

Thus armed, the American Soldier is prepared to play his part at the national council table, there to present the military case logically and persuasively, seeking with all his might to obtain the decision which he believes is right. But when civil authority makes the decision, it then becomes his own decision—thereafter to support loyally and to execute faithfully in the tradition of the American Soldier.

Gentlemen, I congratulate you on your graduation day and welcome you to the fraternity of arms, to comradeship with the American Soldier.

Appendix C

Statement by General Maxwell D. Taylor (Ret.)

Before the Fulbright Committee,

February 17, 1966

Mr. Chairman, Gentlemen:

I want to thank you, Mr. Chairman, and the members of the committee for your willingness to hear my views on the situation in South Viet-Nam. I am afraid that they will not be new to many of you since you have often heard me express them in the days when I was an official of the Government. I agree thoroughly with the motivating purpose of these hearings, namely, to analyze the reasons why we are involved in South Viet-Nam, the importance of this involvement and the effectiveness with which we are dealing with the resultant problems. If my personal views can assist in clarifying these points, I am most happy to present them.

For the purpose of providing a basis for our subsequent discussion, with your permission I would like to make a continuous statement which will undertake to answer three basic questions. First, what are we doing in South Viet-Nam? Secondly, how are we doing it? Finally, can we improve upon what we are doing?

A simple statement of what we are doing in South Viet-Nam is to say that we are engaged in a clash of purpose and interest with the militant wing of the Communist movement represented by Hanoi, the Viet Cong, and Peking. Opposing these Communist forces, in the front rank stand the government and people of South Viet-Nam supported primarily by the United States but assisted in varying degree by some thirty other nations.

The purpose of the Hanoi camp is perfectly clear and has been since 1954. It is to absorb the 15,000,000 people of South Viet-Nam into a single Communist state under the leadership of Ho Chi Minh and his associates in Hanoi. In the course of accomplishing this basic purpose, the Communist leaders expect to undermine the position of the United States in Asia and to demonstrate the efficacy of the so-called "War of Liberation" as a cheap, safe, and disavowable technique for the future expansion of militant Communism.

Our purpose is equally clear and easily defined. In his Baltimore speech of April 7, 1965, President Johnson did so in the following terms: "Our objective is the independence of South Viet-Nam and its freedom from attack. We want nothing for ourselves—only that the people of South Viet-Nam be allowed to guide their own country in their own way." This has been our basic objective since 1954. It has been pursued by three successive administrations and remains our basic objective today.

Like the Communists, we have secondary objectives derived from the basic one. We intend to show that the "War of Liberation," far from being cheap, safe, and disavowable, is costly, dangerous, and doomed to failure. We must destroy the myth of its invincibility in order to protect the independence of many weak nations which are vulnerable targets for subversive aggression—to use the proper term for the "War of Liberation." We cannot leave while force and violence threaten them.

The question has been raised as to whether this clash of interests is really important to us. An easy and incomplete answer would be that it must be important to us since it is considered so important by the other side. Their leadership has made it quite clear that they regard South Viet-Nam as the testing ground for the "War of Liberation" and that after its anticipated success there, it will be used widely about the world. Kosygin told Mr. Reston in his interview of last December: "We believe that national liberation wars are just wars and they will continue as long as there is national oppression by imperialist powers." Before him, Khrushchev, in January 1961, had the following to say: "Now a word about national liberation wars. The armed struggle by the Vietnamese people or the war of the Algerian people serve as the latest example of such wars. These are revolutionary wars. Such wars are not only admissible but inevitable. Can such wars flare up in the future? They can. The Communists fully support such just wars and march in the front rank with peoples waging liberation struggles." General

Giap, the Commander-in-Chief of the North Vietnamese forces, has made the following comment: "South Viet-Nam is the model of the national liberation movement of our time. If the special warfare that the United States imperialists are testing in South Viet-Nam is overcome, then it can be defeated anywhere in the world." The Minister of Defense of Communist China, Marshal Lin Piao, in a long statement of policy in September 1965, described in detail how Mao Tse-tung expects to utilize the "War of Liberation" to expand Communism in Latin America, Africa, and Asia.

These testimonials show that, apart from the goal of imposing Communism on 15,000,000 South Vietnamese, the success of the "War of Liberation" is in itself an important objective of the Communist leadership. On our side, we can understand the grave consequences of such a success for us. President Eisenhower, in 1959, stressed the military importance of defending Southeast Asia in the following terms. He said: "Strategically, South Viet-Nam's capture by the Communists would bring their power several hundred miles into a hitherto free region. The remaining countries of Southeast Asia would be menaced by a great flanking movement. The loss of South Viet-Nam would set in motion a crumbling process which could as it progresses have grave consequences for the forces of freedom." This view has often been referred to as the "domino theory." I personally do not believe in such a theory if it means belief in a law of nature which requires the collapse of each neighboring state in an inevitable sequence, following a Communist victory in South Viet-Nam. However, I am deeply impressed with the probable effects world-wide, not necessarily in areas contiguous to South Viet-Nam, if the "War of Liberation" scores a significant victory there. President Kennedy commented on this danger with moving eloquence: "The great battleground for the defense and expansion of freedom today is the southern half of the globe—Asia, Latin America, Africa, and the Middle East—the lands of the people who harbor the greatest hopes. The enemies of freedom think they can destroy the hopes of the newer nations and they aim to do it before the end of this decade. This is a struggle of will and determination as much as one of force and violence. It is a battle for the conquest of the minds and souls as much as for the conquest of lives and territory. In such a struggle, we can not fail to take sides." Gentlemen, I think a simple answer to the question, what are we doing in South Viet-Nam, is to say that for more than a decade we have been taking sides in a cause in which we have a vital stake.

My second question was: How are we doing in the pursuit of our objectives in South Viet-Nam? Both sides in the struggle have over the years developed the current strategies which are now in confrontation. During 1964 and 1965, the Hanoi leadership attempted to exploit the political turbulence which followed the fall of President Diem in November 1963. Greatly encouraged by the disorder which marked the political scene in Saigon, the Communist leadership made a massive effort to press on to victory. To meet the growing needs in military manpower, they began the infiltration of personnel of the North Vietnamese Army, first as individual replacements, later as formed tactical units. Utilizing this new strength, they intended to make the monsoon offensive of 1965 a major drive for significant military victories. Concurrently, they increased the sabotage directed at the land communication system in South Viet-Nam for the purpose of hampering the distribution of commodities and thus adding to the economic stresses in the South. Terrorism was stepped up and directed with added frequency at United States personnel and installations. They apparently hoped to be able to seize and hold politically important localities, such as district and provincial capitals, to demoralize the Vietnamese people and government and to demonstrate to the United States that we were backing a cause which must inevitably fail.

Faced with this growing threat, the Vietnamese Government and our American officials were obliged to develop a counter strategy to blunt and defeat the intensified efforts of our adversaries. It evolved out of the experience of the preceding months and years and assumed its full form with the critical decisions in 1965 to introduce United States ground forces and to initiate the bombing campaign against military targets in the North. Both of these courses of action had been under consideration at least since November 1961, when I presented my report to President Kennedy following a visit to Saigon to appraise the growing criticality of the situation there. We did not take either action at that time but my report contained the following comment with regard to the possible necessity of using air power against the source of the Viet Cong support in North Viet-Nam: "While we feel that the program recommended represents those measures which should be taken now, I would not suggest that it is the final word. If the Hanoi decision is to continue the irregular war declared on South Viet-Nam in 1959 with continued infiltration and covert support of guerrilla bands in the territory of our ally, we will then have to decide whether to accept as legitimate the continued guidance, training, and support of a guerrilla war across an international boundary. Can we admit the establishment of the common law that the party attacked and his friends are denied the right to strike the source of the aggression after the fact that external aggression is clearly established?" By February 1965, it became clear that we could no longer tolerate this clandestine support from the immune sanctuary in North Viet-Nam which served as the external base for the Viet Cong insurgency.

In brief, the strategy which we have been and are pursuing consists of four components. The first includes the many activities directed at increasing the effectiveness of our ground combat against the Viet Cong and North Vietnamese units in South Viet-Nam. For this purpose, we have made the utmost efforts to increase the indigenous forces of South Viet-Nam, always mindful that this is a Vietnamese war in which we should do only those things which the Vietnamese cannot do for themselves or cannot do in time to avert defeat. From July 1954 to July 1955, the armed forces and police of South Viet-Nam were increased by some 140,000 trained men, a very creditable effort on the part of this small country where military leadership and administrative experience are inevitably in short supply. As of today, the overall military strength in South Viet-Nam is approaching 700,000, the largest military force in being among all of our allies.

Encouraging though the results have been in increasing the Vietnamese strength, during the year cited, our intelligence authorities believed that the Viet Cong increased their total strength by some 60,000. In other words, we were advancing at a rate only a little better than two to one in our favor. Since history has shown that the government forces successfully opposing a guerrilla insurgency in the past have required a much greater preponderance of strength—ten to one or twelve to one, for example—it was quite clear that the Vietnamese could not raise forces fast enough to keep pace with the growing threat of the Viet Cong in time. It was this sobering conclusion that led to the decision to introduce American ground forces with their unique mobility and massive fire power to compensate for the deficiency in Vietnamese strength. With such forces available, it was felt that the ratios of required strength cited above would lose much of their validity.

I am thoroughly aware of the concern of this committee over the growing requirement for American troops in South Viet-Nam. Is this an endless requirement in an open-ended war? I do not believe that anyone can give a completely satisfactory reply to this question but I can suggest the consideration of certain limiting factors which have a bearing on the matter.

First, on our side, we are not setting as an objective for our ground forces the occupation of all South Viet-Nam or the hunting down of the last armed guerrilla. We are in Viet-Nam to safeguard the people who are the real target of the enemy. Terrain has little meaning except insofar as it supports people. Thus the extent of control and protection of population is the true measure of progress rather than control of territory. By the former indicator we are not doing too badly. Senator Mansfield estimates in his recent report that the government controls about 60 percent of the population, the Viet Cong about 22 percent, leaving 18 percent contested. When I left Saigon last July, those figures were 53 percent, 25 percent, 22 percent.

The point I wish to make is that when one expresses our military objective in terms of securing a high proportion of the population, the troop requirement loses some of its impression of open-endedness. Under this concept, the prime target of our United States forces becomes the main-line enemy units which constitute the greatest threat to population—not the entire guerrilla force wherever found.

Another limiting factor is the logistic difficulty of the Viet Cong in supporting increased numbers of troops in combat. The combination of air attacks on their lines of supply and of increasing ground attacks on their units which must then consume supplies at an increased rate places some kind of ceiling on the forces they can maintain in South Viet-Nam. I wish I knew exactly where that ceiling is but our basic data on Viet Cong logistics are too uncertain to permit precision. But the point is that there are factors which tend to keep our troop requirement finite and limit the capability of Hanoi to support large numbers of additional forces in the South.

The second component of our strategy relates to the use of air power against military targets in North Viet-Nam. It is well to remind ourselves of the reasons which impelled us to this decision. There were three which we recognized perfectly at the time of the decision and which remain valid today. The first was to give the people of South Viet-Nam the assurance for the first time of imposing a direct penalty on the source of the aggression. For eleven years they had suffered the depredations of the Viet Cong without exacting any price from the country which provided the direction and support. The morale of the people and that of the armed forces in Viet-Nam received an unestimable lift from the decision to use the air forces of both our countries against military targets in the homeland of the enemy—a lift which has certainly contributed to sustaining their will to continue the fight.

The second reason for the decision was to use air power, insofar as it could be effective, to limit and render more difficult the infiltration of men and supplies from North Viet-Nam to South Viet-Nam. It was perfectly clear from the start as it is clear today that air power would not be able to stop infiltration. We were quite sure, however, that it could impose a ceiling on the forces which could be sustained in combat in South Viet-Nam. I do not believe that anyone who has reflected on the effect of the destruction of bridges, ports, railyards and similar facilities, and on the effect of the limitation of daylight movement on the roads throughout a large part of North Viet-Nam can avoid the conclusion that the air campaign has had an important effect in slowing down infiltration and in raising its price. A testimonial to its effectiveness was the feverish activity in North Viet-Nam during the bombing pause to repair bomb damage and to move transport in daylight.

The third reason for the decision to use our air power was to provide a sobering reminder to the leaders in Hanoi that progressively they must pay a mounting price for the continuation of their support of the Viet Cong insurgency. In spite of their defiant statements of determination to endure these attacks forever, I for one know from experience that no one derives any enjoyment from receiving incoming shells and bombs day after day and I have no doubt that the warning message is getting through to the leadership of Hanoi. In a very real sense, the objective of our air campaign is to change the will of the enemy leadership. We hope that, in due course, the combination of the Viet Cong failure to win victory on the ground in South Viet-Nam and the effect of continued air attacks will present to the Hanoi leadership a situation so disadvantageous that they will decide that it is in their interest to halt their aggression, redefine their aims, and join with us in discussing ways and means of improving the lot of all Viet-Nam.

The third component of our current strategy includes all of those nonmilitary activities which are so important but which receive too little public attention. It is not that our leaders have been unaware of the importance of better government, better living conditions, and the promise of a better future for the people of this country. Unfortunately, lack of security and governmental instability were for a long time factors limiting the effectiveness of the many programs for development and reconstruction. But now, with the growing military effectiveness of our forces on the ground and the slowly developing maturity of the civil leadership in Saigon and in the provinces, I hope that conditions will permit much greater progress than in the past in bringing the benefits of a comparatively normal life to this war-weary people. As you know, the recent Honolulu Conference devoted most of its time to a consideration of these nonmilitary activities. If we are to leave a viable country after the end of the Viet Cong insurgency, it is essential that we make progress even under the conditions of war in stabilizing the government, the society, and the economy.

The fourth component of our strategy is that which relates to our political and diplomatic efforts to initiate the discussion of a peaceful settlement of this conflict. The so-called "peace offensive" is so well known as to require no discussion at this time, as is also the discouraging lack of response from the other side. I am obliged to feel that the Hanoi leadership is not yet convinced that it must mend its ways. Perhaps they still hope for some kind of military victory in the South. Certainly, they are not convinced that in some way the United States cannot be detached from the support of South Viet-Nam. They hope against hope that through international or domestic pressures our government can be forced off course. They have not forgotten that the Viet Minh won more in Paris than in Dien Bien Phu and believe that the Viet Cong may be as fortunate in Washington. They doubt the will of the American public to continue the conflict indefinitely. In a contest of patience, they expect to win even though North Viet-Nam like the South has been constantly at war for over twenty years. Until it becomes perfectly clear to them that we are going to stay on course regardless of anything they can do, I am afraid we are not likely to see them at a conference table. Or if they come unconvinced of the inevitability of the failure of their present course, we can expect them to stall, delay, and maneuver just as they did at Panmunjom in Korea for over two years.

In summary then, our four-point strategy consists of a complex but coherent package of measures designed to improve the effectiveness of our forces on the ground in South Viet-Nam, to exploit our air superiority by attacking military targets in North Viet-Nam, to stabilize the political, social, and economic systems in South Viet-Nam, and to seek an honorable negotiated settlement of the conflict. It is limited as to objective, as to geographical scope, as to weapons and forces employed, and as to targets attacked. All parts of it are inter-related; all parts are indispensable; we must be successful on all fronts. The key, I believe, is inexorable pressure at all points, directed at the will, the ability, and the means of the Communist aggressors.

It is a fair question to ask whether this is the best strategy to attain our basic objective. I am the first to concede that we can and must do better in all four categories of our efforts but, unhappily, progress toward peaceful negotiations is a bilateral affair which can progress only with some cooperation from Hanoi. As you know, thus far that cooperation has been withheld.

Having conceded the need and possibility for improvement within the components of our current strategy, I must add in hon-

esty that I know of no new strategic proposal which would serve
as a better alternative to the one which I have described—that is,
provided we do not sacrifice our basic objective. There are, of
course, the two old alternatives which we have always rejected
and I hope will continue to reject—to withdraw and give up our
basic objective or to widen the war with massive air attacks on the
North Vietnamese or even on Chinese targets. These two courses
of action appear so to contravene our national and international
interests that I shall not take the time of the committee to discuss
them here.

The only new proposal of which I am aware is the so-called
"Holding Strategy" which, in its least extreme form, calls for a
cessation of United States reinforcements and a limitation of military operations to those necessary for the security of our forces
and for the maintenance of our military presence. On several occasions, I have expressed myself in opposition to such a course of
action. To button up our troops in defensive positions and thus to
the sacrifice of their unique attributes of mobility and firepower
would constitute the abandonment of our allies on the battlefield
and would assign a most inglorious mission to our troops who, for
the present, have high morale and complete confidence in their
ability to cope with the Viet Cong in the field. The effect of such
behavior on our Vietnamese allies could be disastrous. At a minimum, it would destroy all confidence in Viet-Nam in ultimate success and would encourage the timid and the wavering to turn to
the Viet Cong for protection and to the Liberation Front for political accommodation. Another serious result of such passivity
would be the impossibility of obtaining honorable terms at any
peace table. The Communists are tough enough to deal with when
one has the upper hand. They would never give us acceptable
terms if the military situation reflected weakness on our part and
a readiness to withdraw. Our only alternative would be to accept
dishonorable terms or to continue to sit out the war indefinitely
on a supine defensive. I can hardly see the American public or this
Congress long supporting such a course of action. Thus, I am
obliged to conclude that the so-called "Holding Strategy" is really
not an alternative way of reaching our objective of an independent
South Viet-Nam free from attack. We could never reach it on such

a course. Rather than being a true alternative, it amounts to the modification and erosion of our basic objective and hence appears to me to be unacceptable.

In conclusion, I feel that our present strategy is the best that has been suggested and that it is important that we adhere to it, always striving to improve our performance within the confines of its general concept. Certainly, it is not without risks—but little of value in this world is accomplished without risk. It seems to me that the risks entailed are warranted by the importance of our stake in Southeast Asia. Congress recognized this importance in the wording of the Joint Resolution of August 1964: "The United States regards as vital to its national interest and to world peace the maintenance of international peace and security in Southeast Asia." I subscribe to those words and believe that we should live by them and by the words of President Johnson when he said in regard to our commitment in South Viet-Nam: "We will not be defeated. We will not grow tired. We will not withdraw either openly or under the cloak of a meaningless agreement." Thank you, gentlemen.

Notes

Prologue The White House Calling
1. William Manchester, *The Glory and the Dream* (Boston: Little, Brown and Co., 1974), p. 1095.
2. Haynes Johnson, *The Bay of Pigs* (New York: W. W. Norton and Co., 1964), p. 167.
3. Maxwell D. Taylor, *Swords and Plowshares* (New York: W. W. Norton and Co., 1972), p. 180.
4. Ibid., p. 184.
5. John F. Kennedy to Evan Thomas, December 17, 1959, author's collection.
6. John F. Kennedy to Taylor, April 9, 1960, author's collection.

Chapter 1 Misplacing the Strait of Malacca
1. Omar N. Bradley, *A General's Life* (New York: Simon and Schuster, 1983), p. 17.
2. Maxwell D. Taylor, *Swords and Plowshares* (New York: W. W. Norton and Co., 1972), pp. 22–23.
3. Taylor to Nellie Craig Toombs, December 20, 1954, Taylor Papers.
4. Taylor, "Robert E. Lee," author's collection.
5. U.S. Army, *Senior Officers Debriefing Program,* Carlisle Barracks, Pa., sec. I, p. 8.
6. Ward Just, *Military Men* (New York: Alfred A. Knopf, 1970), p. 15.
7. Thomas J. Fleming, *West Point* (New York: William Morrow and Co., 1969), p. 305.
8. Taylor, *Swords and Plowshares,* p. 26.
9. Cadet Record, U.S. Military Academy.

Chapter 2 The Old Army
1. U.S. Army, *Senior Officers Debriefing Program,* sec. I, p. 9 (hereafter SODP).
2. Maxwell D. Taylor, *Swords and Plowshares* (New York: W. W. Norton and Co., 1972), p. 33.
3. Ibid., p. 35.
4. SODP, sec. I, p. 36.
5. Taylor, "Tactical Doctrine of the Japanese Army," April 1, 1939, author's collection.
6. Leonard Mosley, *Marshall: Hero for Our Times* (New York: Hearst Books, 1982), p. 127.

Chapter 3   General Marshall

1. Taylor, untitled remarks, July 24, 1986, Taylor Papers.
2. Clay Blair, *Ridgway's Paratroopers* (New York: Dial Press, 1983), p. 11.
3. U.S. Army, *Senior Officers Debriefing Program,* sec. I, pp. 21–22.
4. Maxwell D. Taylor, *Swords and Plowshares* (New York: W. W. Norton and Co., 1972), p. 37.
5. Ibid., p. 41.
6. Eric Larrabee, *Comander in Chief: Franklin Delano Roosevelt, His Lieutenants, and Their War* (New York: Harper & Row, 1987), pp. 101–2.
7. Blair, *Ridgway's Paratroopers,* p. 4.
8. Leonard Rapport and Arthur Norwood, Jr., *Rendezvous with Destiny* (Greenville, Tex.: 101st Airborne Division Association, 1965), p. 12.
9. James Gavin, *On to Berlin* (New York: Viking Press, 1978), pp. 2–3.
10. Napier Crookenden, *Dropzone Normandy* (New York: Charles Scribner's Sons, 1976), p. 23.
11. Blair, *Ridgway's Paratroopers,* p. 36.
12. Taylor, *Swords and Plowshares,* p. 45.
13. Blair, *Ridgway's Paratroopers,* p. 36.

Chapter 4   Sicily

1. Donald R. Burgett, *Currahee!* (Boston: Houghton Mifflin Co., 1967), pp. 13–14.
2. Thomas White, personal communication to the author, November 13, 1987.
3. Matthew B. Ridgway, *Soldier* (New York: Harper & Brothers, 1956), p. 65.
4. Thomas White, personal communication to the author, November 13, 1987.
5. Taylor, speech at Elizabeth, N.J., September 20, 1947, Taylor Papers.
6. Albert N. Garland and Howard M. Smyth, *Sicily and the Surrender of Italy* (Washington, D.C.: Office of the Chief of Military History, 1965), p. 184.
7. Maxwell D. Taylor, *Swords and Plowshares* (New York: W. W. Norton and Co., 1972), p. 50.
8. Ridgway, *Soldier,* pp. 74–75.
9. Taylor, *Swords and Plowshares,* p. 52.
10. John Toland, *Adolf Hitler* (Garden City, N.Y.: Doubleday & Company, Inc., 1976), p. 748.
11. Taylor, *Swords and Plowshares,* p. 53.

Chapter 5   "Situation Innocuous"

1. Albert N. Garland and Howard M. Smyth, *Sicily and the Surrender of Italy* (Washington, D.C.: Office of the Chief of Military History, 1965), p. 490.
2. Harold Macmillan, *War Diaries: The Mediterranean 1943–1945* (New York: St. Martin's Press, 1984), p. 220.
3. W. T. Gardiner, log of Taylor-Gardiner mission to Rome, September 1943, Taylor Papers.
4. Taylor, memorandum, "Mission to Rome," September 9, 1943, Taylor Papers.
5. Ibid.
6. Ibid.
7. Ibid.
8. Stephen E. Ambrose, *Eisenhower*, Vol. 1 (New York: Simon and Schuster, 1983), p. 260.
9. Maxwell D. Taylor, *Swords and Plowshares* (New York: W. W. Norton and Company, Inc., 1972), p. 63.
10. Nigel Hamilton, *Master of the Battlefield: Monty's War Years* (New York: McGraw-Hill, 1983), pp. 399–402.
11. Robert Murphy, *Diplomat Among Warriors* (Garden City, N.Y.: Doubleday & Company, Inc., 1964), p. 195.
12. Samuel Morison, *History of U.S. Naval Operations in World War II* (Boston: Little, Brown and Co., 1954), pt. IX, pp. 241–42.
13. Taylor, *Swords and Plowshares*, p. 64.
14. Ibid., p. 65.
15. Macmillan, *War Diaries*, p. 215.

Chapter 6   Normandy

1. Leonard Rapport and Arthur Norwood, Jr., *Rendezvous with Destiny* (Greenville, Tex.: 101st Airborne Division Association, 1965), p. 41.
2. Marshall Foundation National Archives Project, Item 2900, Reel 120.
3. Gerald Higgins to the author, March 29, 1987.
4. S. H. Matheson to the author, June 14, 1987.
5. Marshall Foundation, "101st Airborne Jumpmaster Reports," 1944.
6. Maxwell D. Taylor, *Swords and Plowshares* (New York: W. W. Norton and Co., 1972), p. 72.
7. New York *Times*, April 24, 1987.
8. George E. Koskimaki, *D-Day with the Screaming Eagles* (New York: Vantage Press, 1970), pp. 33–34.
9. Clay Blair, *Ridgway's Paratroopers* (New York: Dial Press, 1983), p. 219.
10. Taylor, "Airborne D-Day, Normandy," Telecast June 7, 1946, Taylor Papers.

11. Koskimaki, *D-Day with the Screaming Eagles*, p. 72.
12. Taylor, *Swords and Plowshares*, p. 79.
13. Donald R. Burgett, *Currahee!* (Boston: Houghton Mifflin Co., 1967), p. 85.
14. Taylor, untitled speech to First Class at West Point, December 12, 1945, author's collection.
15. David Howarth, *D-Day: The Sixth of June* (New York: McGraw-Hill, 1959), pp. 85–86.
16. S. L. A. Marshall, *Night Drop* (Boston: Little, Brown and Co., 1962), p. 270.
17. Koskimaki, *D-Day with the Screaming Eagles*, p. 169.
18. Blair, *Ridgway's Paratroopers*, p. 220.
19. Napier Crookenden, *Dropzone Normandy* (New York: Charles Scribner's Sons, 1976), p. 108.
20. Blair, *Ridgway's Paratroopers*, p. 222.
21. Gerald Higgins to the author, March 29, 1987.

Chapter 7   Carentan
1. Max Hastings, *Overlord: D-Day and the Battle for Normandy* (New York: Simon and Schuster, 1984), p. 166.
2. Maxwell D. Taylor, *Swords and Plowshares* (New York: W. W. Norton and Co., 1972), p. 83.
3. Clay Blair, *A General's Life* (New York: Simon and Schuster, 1983), p. 260.
4. Leonard Rapport and Arthur Norwood, Jr., *Rendezvous with Destiny* (Greenville, Tex.: 101st Airborne Division Association, 1965), p. 239.
5. Harry Kinnard, interview with the author, June 3, 1987.
6. George Koskimaki to the author, March 20, 1987.
7. Gerald Higgins to the author, March 29, 1987.
8. Rapport and Norwood, *Rendezvous with Destiny*, p. 249.
9. Taylor, "Airborne Operation NEPTUNE: 101st Airborne Division," July 19, 1944, Taylor Papers.
10. Los Angeles *Times*, June 3, 1974.
11. Ned Moore, interview with the author, March 5, 1987.

Chapter 8   The Bridge Too Far
1. Gerald Higgins to the author, March 29, 1987.
2. Taylor diary, September 1–3, 1944, Taylor Papers.
3. Michael Carver, interview with the author, September 23, 1988.
4. Stephen E. Ambrose, *Eisenhower*, vol. 1 (New York: Simon and Schuster, 1983), p. 348.
5. Charles B. MacDonald, *The Siegfried Line Campaign* (Washington, D.C.: Office of the Chief of Military History, 1963), p. 121.
6. Ibid., p. 122.

7. Ryan, *A Bridge Too Far*, p. 89.
8. Matthew Ridgway to Taylor, August 14, 1944, Ridgway Papers.
9. MacDonald, *The Siegfried Line Campaign*, p. 140.
10. Ryan, *A Bridge Too Far*, p. 211.
11. Maxwell D. Taylor, *Swords and Plowshares* (New York: W. W. Norton and Co., 1972), p. 88.
12. Ibid., p. 90.
13. M. C. Dempsey to Taylor, September 18, 1944, author's collection.
14. Taylor diary, September 19, 1944, Taylor Papers.

Chapter 9   The Island
1. Lewis Brereton, *The Brereton Diaries* (New York: William Morrow and Co., 1946), pp. 367–68.
2. Maxwell D. Taylor, *Swords and Plowshares* (New York: W. W. Norton and Co., 1972), p. 91.
3. Leonard Rapport and Arthur Norwood, Jr., *Rendezous with Destiny* (Greenville, Tex.: 101st Airborne Division Association, 1965), pp. 407–13.
4. Taylor to Ridgway, November 7, 1944, Ridgway Papers.
5. Steve Karabinos to the author, April 4, 1987.
6. Taylor, "General Comments on Participation of 101st Airborne Division in Holland Campaign," 1944, Taylor Papers.
7. Freeport *News*, September 13, 1974.
8. U.S. Army, *Senior Officers Debriefing Program*, Carlisle Barracks, Pa., sec. III, pp. 1–3.
9. John Toland, *Adolf Hitler* (Garden City, N.Y.: Doubleday & Company, Inc., 1976), p. 824.

Chapter 10   Four Thousand Miles to Bastogne
1. Taylor, untitled report, c. January 1945, Ridgway Papers.
2. Charles B. MacDonald, *The Mighty Endeavor* (New York: Oxford University Press, 1969), p. 364.
3. Julian Ewell, interview with the author, August 9, 1987.
4. David Gold, interview with the author, October 28, 1988.
5. James L. McDonough and Richard S. Gardner, *Sky Riders* (Nashville, Tenn.: Battery Press, 1980), pp. 106–7.
6. Ibid., p. 100.
7. Charles B. MacDonald, *A Time for Trumpets* (New York: William Morrow and Co., 1985), p. 522.
8. Leonard Rapport and Arthur Norwood, Jr., *Rendezvous with Destiny* (Greenville, Tex.: 101st Airborne Division Association, 1965), p. 593.
9. McDonough and Gardner, *Sky Riders*, p. 107.
10. MacDonald, *A Time for Trumpets*, p. 525.
11. Ibid., p. 532.

12. Thomas White, personal communication to the author, November 13, 1987.
13. Taylor, "3,000 Miles to Bastogne," Washington *Post,* December 15, 1984.
14. Rapport and Norwood, *Rendezvous with Destiny,* p. 590.
15. Ibid., p. 591.

Chapter 11   Bastogne to Berchtesgaden
1. Maxwell D. Taylor, *Swords and Plowshares* (New York: W. W. Norton and Co., 1972), pp. 103–4.
2. Taylor diary, January 10, 1945, Taylor Papers.
3. Ridgway Papers.
4. Taylor, comments on *Rendezvous with Destiny,* February 1947, author's collection.
5. Taylor, "To the Reinforcement Joining the 101st Airborne Division," 1945, Taylor Papers.
6. Clay Blair, *Ridgway's Paratroopers* (New York: Dial Press, 1983), p. 223.
7. Taylor, "Message from the Division Commander," May 9, 1945, Taylor Papers.
8. Taylor to Lewis Powell, May 24, 1985.
9. Taylor diary, May 10, 1945.
10. Gerald Higgins to the author, March 29, 1987.
11. Taylor, *Swords and Plowshares,* p. 111.
12. Carl Kohls to the author, April 5, 1987.
13. Bradley McKennan to the author, April 6, 1987.
14. Steve Karabinos to the author, April 4, 1987.

Chapter 12   The Superintendent
1. Larry Legere, personal communication to the author, April 28, 1987.
2. Maxwell D. Taylor, *Swords and Plowshares* (New York: W. W. Norton and Co., 1972), p. 26.
3. Eisenhower to Taylor, January 2, 1946, Superintendent's Correspondence, U.S. Military Academy Library.
4. Taylor, "Talk to Incoming Class of New Cadets," July 1, 1948, Taylor Papers.
5. Stephen E. Ambrose, *Duty, Honor, Country: A History of West Point* (Baltimore: Johns Hopkins University Press, 1966), p. 299.
6. Gerald Higgins to the author, May 24, 1987.
7. Larry Legere, personal communication to the author, April 28, 1987.
8. Quoted by Gerald Higgins to the author, March 29, 1987.
9. U.S. Military Academy, Annual Report of the Superintendent, 1946–49.

10. Taylor to Charles A. Plumley, August 20, 1946, Superintendent's Correspondence, U.S. Military Academy Library.
11. Unsigned memorandum, 1946, Superintendent's Papers, U.S. Military Academy Library.
12. Taylor to Eisenhower, October 21, 1946, Superintendent's Correspondence, U.S. Military Academy Library.
13. Taylor, *Swords and Plowshares*, p. 116.
14. Taylor, "Postwar Trends in American Strategy," August 2, 1948, Taylor Papers.
15. Taylor, "The Army as a Career," December 21, 1948, Taylor Papers.
16. Taylor, Armistice Day address, Kansas City, November 11, 1947, Taylor Papers.
17. Dwight D. Eisenhower, *Crusade in Europe* (Garden City, N.Y.: Doubleday & Company, Inc., 1948), p. 184.
18. Eisenhower to Taylor, November 19, 1948, Eisenhower Library.

Chapter 13   Berlin to Panmunjom
1. Taylor to Eisenhower, June 17, 1949, Eisenhower Library.
2. Maxwell D. Taylor, *Swords and Plowshares* (New York: W. W. Norton and Co., 1972), p. 125.
3. Taylor, speech to officers of tactical units, May 22, 1950, Taylor Papers.
4. Taylor, statement to the press, May 29, 1950, Taylor Papers.
5. Taylor, briefing for Admiral Sherman, March 27, 1950, Taylor Papers.
6. Matthew Ridgway, oral history interview, 1984, Ridgway Papers.
7. J. Lawton Collins, *War in Peacetime* (Boston: Houghton Mifflin Co., 1969), p. 147.
8. Taylor, U.S. Army, *Senior Officers Debriefing Program*, Carlisle Barracks, Pa., sec. III, p. 24.
9. Ibid., pp. 23–24.
10. Russell F. Weigley, *History of the United States Army* (Bloomington, Ind.: Indiana University Press, 1984), p. 521.
11. Taylor, *Swords and Plowshares*, p. 132.
12. S. H. Matheson to the author, June 14, 1987.
13. Taylor to Herbert L. Johnson, August 16, 1951, Taylor Papers.
14. Tom Taylor, interview with the author, November 12, 1987.

Chapter 14   Korea
1. Maxwell D. Taylor, *Swords and Plowshares* (New York: W. W. Norton and Co., 1972), p. 139.
2. Ibid., p. 138.
3. New York *Times*, March 13, 1953.
4. U.S. Army, *Senior Officers Debriefing Program*, Carlisle Barracks, Pa., sec. III, p. 27.

5. Taylor, *Swords and Plowshares,* p. 143.
6. Mark W. Clark, *From the Danube to the Yalu* (New York: Harper and Brothers, 1954), pp. 257–58.
7. Ellis O. Briggs, "Proud Servant," unpublished autobiography, 1975.
8. Joseph C. Goulden, *Korea: The Untold Story of the War* (New York: McGraw-Hill, 1982), p. 636.
9. Ned Moore, interview with the author, May 13, 1987.
10. Briggs, "Proud Servant."
11. Larry Legere, personal communication to the author, April 28, 1987.
12. Taylor, *Swords and Plowshares,* p. 147.
13. Ibid., pp. 147–48.
14. Gerald Ford to the author, June 12, 1987.
15. Taylor to Earl D. Compton, January 24, 1954, Taylor Papers.
16. Taylor, *Swords And Plowshares,* p. 152.
17. Taylor to Matthew Ridgway, March 12, 1954, Taylor Papers.

Chapter 15   Chief of Staff
1. Matthew Ridgway to Taylor, April 19, 1954, Taylor Papers.
2. Taylor to Matthew Ridgway, May 2, 1954, Taylor Papers.
3. New York *Times,* May 15, 1955.
4. Matthew Ridgway, interview with Dr. Maurice Matloff, 1984, Ridgway Papers.
5. James Gavin, *War and Peace in the Space Age* (New York: Harper and Brothers, 1958), p. 173.
6. Ibid., p. 155.
7. Charles Wilson to Robert Stevens, May 26, 1955, Taylor Papers.
8. Maxwell D. Taylor, *The Uncertain Trumpet* (New York: Harper and Co., 1960), p. 110.
9. U.S. Army, *Senior Officers Debriefing Program* (hereafter SODP), General Williston Palmer, 1972, U.S. Army History Research Collection.
10. Taylor, "Memorandum for the Vice Chief of Staff," July 25, 1955, Taylor Papers.
11. Donald A. Seibert, "The Regulars," unpublished manuscript, Army War College.
12. Baltimore *Sun,* March 25, 1956.
13. SODP, General Clyde Eddleman, 1975, U.S. Army Military Historical Series.
14. Bernard W. Rogers, interview with the author, October 25, 1987.
15. William Westmoreland, interview with the author, December 14, 1987.
16. John Service to the author, August 17, 1987.
17. DeWitt Smith, interview with the author, July 6, 1987.

Chapter 16 The Valley of Indecision

1. Dwight D. Eisenhower, *Mandate for Change* (Garden City, N.Y.: Doubleday & Company, Inc., 1963), pp. 446–47.
2. A. J. Bacevich, *The Pentomic Era* (Washington, D.C.: National Defense University Press, 1986), p. 13.
3. Maxwell D. Taylor, *The Uncertain Trumpet* (New York: Harper and Co., 1960), p. 37.
4. Bacevich, *The Pentomic Era*, pp. 99–100.
5. Ibid., p. 99.
6. Carter Magruder to the author, May 14, 1987.
7. George Forsythe to the author, September 2, 1987.
8. Bacevich, *The Pentomic Era*, pp. 45–46.
9. Washington *Star*, June 5, 1956.
10. George Forsythe to the author, September 2, 1987.
11. Taylor, *The Uncertain Trumpet*, pp. 40–41.
12. U.S. Army, *Senior Officers Debriefing Program* (hereafter SODP), General Clyde Eddleman, 1975, U.S. Army Military History Research Collection.
13. Clyde Eddleman, interview with the author, July 21, 1987.
14. Quoted in Taylor, *The Uncertain Trumpet*, p. 26.
15. Henry Kissinger, *Nuclear Weapons and Foreign Policy* (New York: Harper and Brothers, 1957), p. 132.
16. Bacevich, *The Pentomic Era*, pp. 93–94.
17. SODP, sec. IV, p. 7.
18. Andrew J. Goodpaster, Oral History Interview, January 16, 1978, Eisenhower Library.
19. Taylor, *Swords and Plowshares*, p. 170.
20. Al Wedemeyer to Taylor, June 3, 1959, author's collection.
21. Andrew Goodpaster, interview with the author, June 17, 1987.

Chapter 17 "A Frightening and Timely Book"

1. "Meet the Press" transcript, July 12, 1959.
2. Taylor to Douglas MacArthur, June 30, 1959, author's collection.
3. Douglas MacArthur to Taylor, July 7, 1959, author's collection.
4. New York *Times*, April 9, 1964.
5. Taylor, untitled remarks, March 14, 1960, author's collection.
6. Maxwell D. Taylor, *The Uncertain Trumpet* (New York: Harper and Co., 1960), pp. 175–76.
7. Taylor to Wilbur Brucker, October 22, 1959, author's collection.
8. Wilbur Brucker to Taylor, January 25, 1960, author's collection.
9. New York *Herald Tribune Book Review*, January 3, 1960.
10. New York *Times*, January 3, 1960.
11. Taylor to Gerald Templer, August 23, 1960, author's collection.

12. New York *Times*, February 5, 1960.
13. Dean Acheson to Taylor, February 8, 1960, author's collection.
14. Taylor to George Decker, August 23, 1960, author's collection.
15. Taylor to G. L. Cross, May 9, 1960, author's collection.
16. Taylor to the author, August 1, 1960.
17. Edgar B. Young, *Lincoln Center: The Building of an Institution* (New York: New York University Press, 1980), p. 109.
18. New York *Times*, November 2, 1960.

Chapter 18 The New Frontier

1. Taylor, oral history interview, 1964, I-6, John F. Kennedy Library.
2. Haynes Johnson, *The Bay of Pigs* (New York: W. W. Norton and Co., 1964), p. 225.
3. Cuba Study Group Report, June 13, 1961, Memorandum No. 3, Taylor Papers.
4. Peter Wyden, *The Bay of Pigs* (New York: Simon and Schuster, 1979), p. 319.
5. Ibid., p. 138.
6. Ibid., p. 142.
7. Cuba Study Group Report, June 13, 1961, Memorandum No. 3, Taylor Papers.
8. John F. Kennedy to Taylor, April 22, 1961, author's collection.
9. Taylor, "Bobby Kennedy," September 3, 1968, Taylor Papers. Similar language appears in *Swords and Plowshares* (New York: W. W. Norton and Co.), p. 185.
10. Taylor, oral history interview, 1964, II-10, John F. Kennedy Library.
11. Julian Ewell, interview with the author, August 9, 1987.
12. New York *Times*, June 27, 1961.
13. Taylor, oral history interview, 1964, II-12, John F. Kennedy Library.
14. McGeorge Bundy, interview with the author, November 10, 1987.
15. Theodore Sorensen, *Kennedy* (New York: Harper and Row, 1965), pp. 586–87.
16. Tom Taylor, interview with the author, July 1961.
17. Sorensen, *Kennedy*, p. 591.
18. Taylor, oral history interview, 1964, II-16, John F. Kennedy Library.
19. Sorensen, *Kennedy*, p. 594.
20. Taylor to Tom Taylor, July 8, 1962.
21. Ethel Kennedy to Mrs. Maxwell Taylor, July 23, 1963, author's collection.
22. Taylor, oral history interview, 1964, II-9, John F. Kennedy Library.
23. Ibid., II-31.
24. Peter Collier and David Horowitz, *The Kennedys* (New York: Summit Books, 1984), p. 291.

25. Ernest Volkman, *Warriors of the Night* (New York: William Morrow and Co., 1985), p. 79.

Chapter 19 Vietnam: Changing a Losing Game

1. Clark Clifford, "A Viet-Nam Reappraisal," *Foreign Affairs*, July 1969.
2. William P. Bundy, unpublished manuscript, chap. 3, p. 31.
3. Taylor to Tom Taylor, May 13, 1962.
4. Theodore Sorensen, *Kennedy* (New York: Harper and Row, 1965), p. 644.
5. Peter Collier and David Horowitz, *The Kennedys* (New York: Summit Books, 1984), p. 274.
6. Stanley Karnow, *Vietnam: A History* (New York: Penguin Books, 1984), pp. 213–14.
7. Walt Rostow, *The Diffusion of Power* (New York: Macmillan Company, 1972), p. 270.
8. Maxwell D. Taylor, *Swords and Plowshares* (New York: W. W. Norton and Co., 1972), p. 226.
9. Marvin Kalb and Elie Abel, *Roots of Involvement* (New York: W. W. Norton and Co., 1971), p. 129.
10. Taylor, *Swords and Plowshares*, pp. 229–30.
11. Ibid., p. 238.
12. Cablegram from Taylor to John F. Kennedy, November 1, 1961, Pentagon Papers.
13. Ibid.
14. Karnow, *Vietnam: A History*, p. 252.
15. Rostow, *The Diffusion of Power*, p. 278.
16. George McT. Kahin, *Intervention* (New York: Alfred A. Knopf, 1986), p. 136.
17. U.S. Army, *Senior Officers Debriefing Program*, sec. V, p. 37.
18. Rostow, *The Diffusion of Power*, p. 279.
19. Taylor, oral history interview, 1964, John F. Kennedy Library.
20. New York *Times*, July 22, 1962.
21. St. Louis *Post-Dispatch*, July 22, 1962.
22. Senate Armed Services Committee Hearing, August 9, 1962.
23. Ibid.
24. Taylor to Tom Taylor, October 14, 1962.
25. Joseph Alsop, "Musical Chairs," New York *Herald Tribune*, 1962.

Chapter 20 Confrontation in Cuba

1. Theodore Sorensen, *Kennedy* (New York: Harper and Row, 1965), p. 719.
2. Robert F. Kennedy, *Thirteen Days* (New York: W. W. Norton and Co., 1969), p. 23.

3. Arthur M. Schlesinger, Jr., *A Thousand Days* (Boston: Houghton Mifflin Co., 1965), p. 841.
4. Taylor, oral history interview, 1964, John F. Kennedy Library.
5. Sorensen, *Kennedy*, p. 675.
6. Taylor, "Reflections on a Grim October," Washington *Post*, October 5, 1982.
7. Papers of John F. Kennedy, Presidential Recordings, Cuban Missile Crisis Meetings, October 16, 1962, John F. Kennedy Library.
8. Thomas M. Coffey, *Iron Eagle* (New York: Crown Publishers, 1986), pp. 391–92.
9. Kennedy, *Thirteen Days*, p. 38.
10. Maxwell D. Taylor, *Swords and Plowshares* (New York: W. W. Norton and Co., 1972), p. 268.
11. Paul Nitze, interview with the author, September 30, 1987.
12. Taylor, oral history interview, 1964, John F. Kennedy Library.
13. David L. Larson, ed., *The Cuban Crisis of 1962* (Boston: Houghton Mifflin Co., 1963), p. 43.
14. Taylor, *Swords and Plowshares*, p. 274.
15. *Department of State Bulletin*, November 19, 1973.
16. Kennedy, *Thirteen Days*, p. 98.
17. Papers of John F. Kennedy, Presidential Recordings, Cuban Missile Crisis Meetings, October 27, 1962, pp. 38–39, John F. Kennedy Library.
18. Ibid., pp. 40–41.
19. Kennedy, *Thirteen Days*, p. 109.
20. Lt. Gen. F. T. Unger to the author, August 23, 1987.
21. Edwin D. Guthman and Jeffrey Shulman, eds., *Robert Kennedy in His Own Words* (New York: Bantam Books, 1988), p. 14.
22. Taylor to the author, October 28, 1962.
23. Taylor to the author, November 11, 1962.
24. Taylor to Tom Taylor, December 2, 1962.
25. Taylor, interview with Richard Neustadt, 1983, Alfred P. Sloan Foundation.
26. Ibid.
27. Taylor, oral history interview, 1964, John F. Kennedy Library.
28. Herbert S. Dinerstein, *The Making of a Missile Crisis* (Baltimore: Johns Hopkins University Press, 1976), p. 237.

Chapter 21   Chairman of the JCS
1. Taylor to Tom Taylor, October 7, 1962.
2. Robert McNamara, interview with the author, November 24, 1987.
3. Thomas M. Coffey, *Iron Eagle* (New York: Crown Publishers, 1986), pp. 422–23.
4. Taylor to the author, October 28, 1962.

5. Bruce Palmer, Jr., *The Twenty-five Year War* (New York: Simon and Schuster, 1984), p. 20.

6. Jack Raymond, *Power at the Pentagon* (New York: Harper and Row, 1964), p. 290.

7. William P. Bundy, unpublished manuscript, chap. 8, p. 21.

8. George McT. Kahin, *Intervention* (New York: Alfred A. Knopf, 1986), p. 141.

9. Palmer, *The Twenty-five Year War*, p. 11.

10. William Westmoreland, *A Soldier Reports* (Garden City, N.Y.: Doubleday & Company, Inc., 1976), p. 67.

11. Special National Intelligence Estimate, "The Situation in South Vietnam," July 10, 1963, Pentagon Papers.

12. Stanley Karnow, *Vietnam: A History* (New York: Penguin Books, 1984), p. 286.

13. Taylor, interview for the Robert F. Kennedy oral history project, 1969, John F. Kennedy Library.

14. State Department to Lodge, August 24, 1963, Pentagon Papers.

15. Roswell Gilpatric to Taylor, March 30, 1970, author's collection.

16. Karnow, *Vietnam: A History*, p. 288.

17. Paul Harkins to Taylor, August 31, 1963, Pentagon Papers.

18. New York *Times*, September 15, 1963.

19. Maxwell D. Taylor, *Swords and Plowshares* (New York: W. W. Norton and Co., 1972), p. 297.

20. "Report of McNamara-Taylor Mission to South Vietnam," October 2, 1963, Pentagon Papers.

21. Ibid.

22. Taylor, *Swords and Plowshares*, p. 299.

23. Ibid., p. 301.

24. Theodore Sorensen, *Kennedy* (New York: Harper and Row, 1965), p. 736.

25. Washington *Post*, August 16, 1963.

26. Ibid.

27. Taylor, oral history interview, 1964, John F. Kennedy Library.

28. Elspeth Rostow, interview with the author, November 20, 1987.

Chapter 22 Saigon

1. New York *Times*, February 5, 1964.

2. Taylor, manuscript notes, April 5, 1964, author's collection.

3. Bui Diem and David Charnoff, *In the Jaws of History* (Boston: Houghton Mifflin Co., 1987), p. 108.

4. Stanley Karnow, *Vietnam: A History* (New York: Penguin Books, 1984), p. 335.

5. William P. Bundy, unpublished manuscript, chap. 12, p. 15.

6. Maxwell D. Taylor, *Swords and Plowshares* (New York: W. W. Norton and Co., 1972), p. 309.
7. Ibid., p. 310.
8. Jacqueline Kennedy to Taylor, August 2, 1964, author's collection.
9. Douglas Kinnard, *The War Managers* (Hanover, N.H.: University Press of New England, 1977), p. 19.
10. Johnson to Taylor, July 2, 1964, author's collection.
11. McGeorge Bundy, memorandum for the President, June 24, 1964, National Security File, "Deployment of U.S. Forces to Vietnam," LBJ Library.
12. Lyndon B. Johnson, *The Vantage Point* (New York: Holt, Rinehart and Winston, 1971), p. 118.
13. Taylor, oral history interview, 1972, University of Virginia Library, Taylor Papers.
14. Karnow, *Vietnam: A History,* p. 380.
15. Taylor to the author, November 2, 1964.
16. Washington *Post,* November 5, 1964.
17. Taylor, "The Current Situation in South Vietnam," November 27, 1964, Pentagon Papers.
18. Bundy, unpublished manuscript, chap. 19, p. 14.
19. George McT. Kahin, *Intervention* (New York: Alfred A. Knopf, 1986), p. 262.
20. Embassy Saigon airgram to the State Department, December 24, 1964, Pentagon Papers.
21. Karnow, *Vietnam: A History,* p. 382.
22. Richard Critchfield, *The Long Charade* (New York: Harcourt, Brace and World, 1968), p. 96.
23. Taylor, *Swords and Plowshares,* p. 337.
24. Bui Diem and Charnoff, *In the Jaws of History,* p. 110.
25. Taylor to the author, February 28, 1965.

Chapter 23 Never Call Retreat

1. McGeorge Bundy, interview with the author, November 10, 1987.
2. Taylor to the author, February 15, 1965.
3. U. Alexis Johnson, *The Right Hand of Power* (Englewood Cliffs, N.J.: Prentice-Hall, 1984), p. 427.
4. Bui Diem and David Charnoff, *In the Jaws of History* (Boston: Houghton Mifflin Co., 1987), p. 130.
5. Taylor, interview with Dorothy Pierce, January 9, 1969, Taylor Papers.
6. Stanley Karnow, *Vietnam: A History* (New York: Penguin Books, 1984), pp. 415–16.
7. George McT. Kahin, *Intervention* (New York: Alfred A. Knopf, 1986), p. 315.

8. William Westmoreland, *A Soldier Reports* (Garden City, N.Y.: Double-day & Co., Inc., 1976), p. 125.
9. Maxwell D. Taylor, *Swords and Plowshares* (New York: W. W. Norton and Co., 1972), p. 338.
10. Kennedy to Taylor, n.d. [January 1965], author's collection.
11. McGeorge Bundy, memorandum to the President, March 6, 1965, National Security File, "Deployment of U.S. Forces to Vietnam," LBJ Library.
12. Johnson, *The Right Hand of Power*, p. 434.
13. Saigon Embtel 3384, April 14, 1965, National Security File, "Deployment of U.S. Forces to Vietnam," LBJ Library.
14. Kahin, *Intervention*, p. 318.
15. Bui Diem and Charnoff, *In the Jaws of History*, p. 135.
16. Taylor, U.S. Army, *Senior Officers Debriefing Program*, Carlisle Barracks, Pa., sec. V, p. 10.
17. Taylor to President Johnson, June 17, 1965, quoted in Larry Berman, *Planning a Tragedy* (New York: W. W. Norton and Co., 1982), p. 70.
18. Berman, *Planning a Tragedy*, pp. 64–65.
19. Taylor, *Swords and Plowshares*, p. 352.
20. Quoted in Lyndon B. Johnson, *The Vantage Point* (New York: Holt, Rinehart and Winston, 1971), p. 145.
21. Tom Taylor, personal communication to the author, December 10, 1987.
22. Johnson, *The Right Hand of Power*, p. 431.
23. Frances FitzGerald, *Fire in the Lake* (New York: Vintage Books, 1972), p. 338.
24. Taylor, *Swords and Plowshares*, p. 327.
25. Giap, quoted by Taylor, statement before the Fulbright Committee, February 17, 1966.
26. McGeorge Bundy, interview with the author, November 10, 1987.

Chapter 24   War on the Home Front

1. U.S. Army, *Senior Officer Debriefing Program*, Carlisle Barracks, Pa., sec. VI, p. 2.
2. U. Alexis Johnson, *The Right Hand of Power* (Englewood Cliffs, N.J.: Prentice-Hall, 1984), p. 399.
3. John F. Campbell, *The Foreign Affairs Fudge Factory* (New York: Basic Books, 1971), p. 88.
4. Maxwell D. Taylor, *Swords and Plowshares* (New York: W. W. Norton and Co., 1972), p. 362.
5. Taylor, memorandum to the President, March 29, 1966, author's collection.
6. Norman Podhoretz, *Why We Were in Vietnam* (New York: Simon and Schuster, 1982), p. 87.

7. Taylor to H. H. Semans, October 11, 1965, Taylor Papers.
8. James Gavin, "A Communication on Vietnam," *Harper's*, February 1966.
9. Taylor, address to the Rotary Club of New York, February 3, 1966, Taylor Papers.
10. Taylor, statement before the Fulbright Committee, February 17, 1966, Taylor Papers.
11. J. William Fulbright, ed., *The Vietnam Hearings* (New York: Vintage Books, 1966), pp. 187–88.
12. Ibid., p. 207.
13. Ibid., pp. 208–9.
14. Ibid., pp. 217–18.
15. Ibid., pp. 222–23.
16. New York *Times*, February 18, 1966.
17. Richard Nixon to Taylor, March 3, 1966, author's collection.
18. Bill Moyers to Taylor, n.d., Taylor Papers.
19. Stanley Karnow, *Vietnam: A History* (New York: Penguin Books, 1984), p. 454.
20. NSC meeting notes, June 22, 1966, National Security File, LBJ Library.
21. Taylor to the author, March 26, 1967.
22. Taylor to the author, April 30, 1967.
23. Taylor to the author, August 7, 1967.
24. Clark Clifford, "A Viet-Nam Reappraisal," *Foreign Affairs*, July 1969.
25. Lyndon B. Johnson, *The Vantage Point* (New York: Holt, Rinehart and Winston, 1971), p. 372.
26. Taylor, memorandum to the President, November 3, 1967, National Security File, "Country File, Vietnam," LBJ Library.
27. Taylor, memorandum to the President, November 6, 1967, National Security File, LBJ Library.

Chapter 25   1968: The Climactic Year

1. Stanley Karnow, *Vietnam: A History* (New York: Penguin Books, 1984), p. 541.
2. U.S. Army, *Senior Officers Debriefing Program*, Carlisle Barracks, Pa., sec. V, pp. 26–27.
3. Karnow, *Vietnam: A History*, p. 525.
4. Ibid., p. 526.
5. Herbert Y. Schandler, *The Unmaking of a President* (Princeton, N.J.: Princeton University Press, 1977), p. 91.
6. Karnow, *Vietnam: A History*, p. 540.
7. Taylor to the President, February 14, 1968, White House Meeting File, LBJ Library.
8. Schandler, *The Unmaking of a President*, p. 76.

9. Lyndon B. Johnson, *The Vantage Point* (New York: Holt, Rinehart and Winston, 1971), p. 393.
10. Clark Clifford, interview with the author, July 2, 1987.
11. Maxwell D. Taylor, *Swords and Plowshares* (New York: W. W. Norton and Co., 1972), pp. 387–88.
12. Clark Clifford, "A Viet-Nam Reappraisal," *Foreign Affairs*, July 1969.
13. Taylor, *Swords and Plowshares*, p. 388.
14. Taylor, undated memorandum, "Vietnam Alternatives," quoted in Schandler, *The Unmaking of a President*, p. 163.
15. Taylor, memorandum to the President, March 9, 1968, "March 31st Speech," National Security File, LBJ Library.
16. Marvin E. Gettleman et al., eds., *Vietnam and America: A Documented History* (New York: Grove Press, 1985), p. 316.
17. Taylor to the author, March 25, 1968.
18. Taylor, *Swords and Plowshares*, p. 378.
19. Ibid., p. 391.
20. Walt Rostow, *The Diffusion of Power* (New York: Macmillan Company, 1972), p. 521.
21. Johnson, "A New Step Toward Peace," Department of State, 1968.
22. Mrs. Maxwell Taylor to the author, April 7, 1968.
23. Taylor to the author, April 7, 1968.
24. Taylor, memorandum to the President, April 1, 1968, Taylor Papers.
25. Taylor, *Swords and Plowshares*, p. 394.
26. Taylor to the author, April 15, 1968.
27. Taylor, "Bobby Kennedy," September 3, 1968, Taylor Papers.
28. Taylor, George Catlett Marshall banquet address, October 30, 1968, Taylor Papers.

Chapter 26 The Last Hawk

1. Taylor to the author, December 15, 1968.
2. Taylor, memorandum to the President, March 23, 1968, Taylor Papers.
3. Taylor to the author, May 18, 1969.
4. Taylor, memorandum to the President, December 31, 1968, Taylor Papers.
5. Taylor, oral history interview, June 1981, LBJ Library.
6. Taylor, "Misleading Documents," New York *Times*, June 23, 1971.
7. Maxwell D. Taylor, *Swords and Plowshares* (New York: W. W. Norton and Co., 1972), p. 16.
8. Unsigned memorandum with letter, Evan Thomas to Taylor, July 7, 1971.
9. Taylor, *Swords and Plowshares*, pp. 403–4.
10. Ibid., pp. 406–7.
11. Taylor to Kissinger, October 30, 1972.

12. Henry Kissinger, *Years of Upheaval* (Boston: Little, Brown and Company, 1982), p. 338.
13. Taylor, UPI interview, May 1975.
14. Washington *Post,* May 16, 1975.
15. Taylor, *Swords and Plowshares,* pp. 418–19.
16. C. E. M. Joad, *Decadence: A Philosophical Inquiry* (London: Faber and Faber, 1948), pp. 328–29.

Chapter 27   Precarious Security
1. Bruce Palmer, Jr., *The Twenty-five-Year War* (New York: Simon and Schuster, 1984), p. 20.
2. Los Angeles *Times,* December 19, 1973.
3. Taylor, "The Legitimate Claims of National Security," *Foreign Affairs,* April 1974.
4. *U.S. News and World Report,* June 23, 1980.
5. "A Talk with Gen. Maxwell D. Taylor," *Army,* April 1977.
6. Taylor to Lewis F. Powell, Jr., April 25, 1981.
7. Maxwell D. Taylor, *Precarious Security* (New York: W. W. Norton and Co., 1976), p. 62.
8. Taylor, "Volunteer Army: Long Enough," Washington *Post,* June 16, 1981.
9. Taylor, *Precarious Security,* p. 6.
10. Ibid., p. 47.
11. Ibid., p. 61.
12. Ibid., pp. 134–35.
13. *Foreign Affairs,* October 1976.
14. Taylor, statement before the Senate Armed Services Committee, January 1, 1978, author's collection.
15. Taylor, "Arms—but No Arms Race," Washington *Post,* September 12, 1980.
16. Taylor to Lewis F. Powell, Jr., August 23, 1980.
17. Taylor, "Can We Depend on Deterrence?" Washington *Post,* June 30, 1981.
18. Taylor to Lewis F. Powell, Jr., July 22, 1981.
19. Taylor to Senator Alan Cranston, August 11, 1981, author's collection.
20. Chicago *Sun-Times,* September 4, 1981.
21. Taylor to Lewis F. Powell, Jr., December 7, 1981.
22. David Halberstam, *The Best and the Brightest* (Greenwich, Conn.: Fawcett Crest Books, 1973), p. 572.
23. U.S. Army, *Senior Officers Debriefing Program,* Carlisle Barracks, Pa., sec. IV, p. 43.

Chapter 28   Carrying On

1. Taylor, "Strategic Forces: What to Do," Washington *Post*, March 6, 1983.
2. Taylor, testimony before the Investigations Subcommittee of the House Armed Services Committee, July 14, 1982.
3. Taylor to Lewis F. Powell, Jr., July 11, 1982.
4. Taylor, "The Hatchet Job on Westmoreland," Washington *Post*, February 5, 1982.
5. Taylor to Lewis F. Powell, Jr., January 21, 1986.
6. Jacqueline Kennedy Onassis to Mrs. Maxwell Taylor, May 2, 1987.

Acknowledgments

Grateful acknowledgment is made to the following persons for permission to reprint passages from unpublished material: Mrs. Ellis O. Briggs, McGeorge Bundy, William B. Bundy, Field Marshall Lord Michael Carver, General M. C. Dempsey, General Clyde Eddleman, General Julian Ewell, President Gerald Ford, General George I. Forsythe, Roswell Gilpatric, Dr. David Gold, General Gerald J. Higgins, Steve Karabinos, Mrs. Ethel Kennedy, Carl W. Kohls, Laurence J. Legere, Bradley McKennan, Robert McNamara, General Carter Magruder, General S. H. Matheson, General Ned Moore, Paul Nitze, Mrs. Jacqueline Kennedy Onassis, General Bernard W. Rogers, Mrs. Elspeth Rostow, Colonel Donald A. Seibert, John S. Service, General DeWitt C. Smith, General F. T. Unger, General William C. Westmoreland, Thomas J. White, and the estates of Dean Acheson, Wilbur Brucker, President John F. Kennedy, and General Douglas MacArthur.

Index

JOHN M. TAYLOR, a veteran of several government agencies, has written extensively on American and other historical topics. His books include two other biographies, *Garfield of Ohio* and *Korea's Syngman Rhee*. A revised edition of his book on U.S. presidential letters, *From the White House Inkwell*, appeared in April 1989. He has also been a frequent contributor to magazines such as *American Heritage, American History Illustrated,* and *Yankee*.

Born in West Point, New York, Taylor spent several years in Japan as a youth. The family returned to the United States in 1939. Taylor graduated with honors in history from Williams College in 1952 and subsequently earned a master's degree in history from the George Washington University.

The author and his wife, Priscilla, have two daughters and a son and live in McLean, Virginia.